DOOMSDAY CLOCK
PART 2

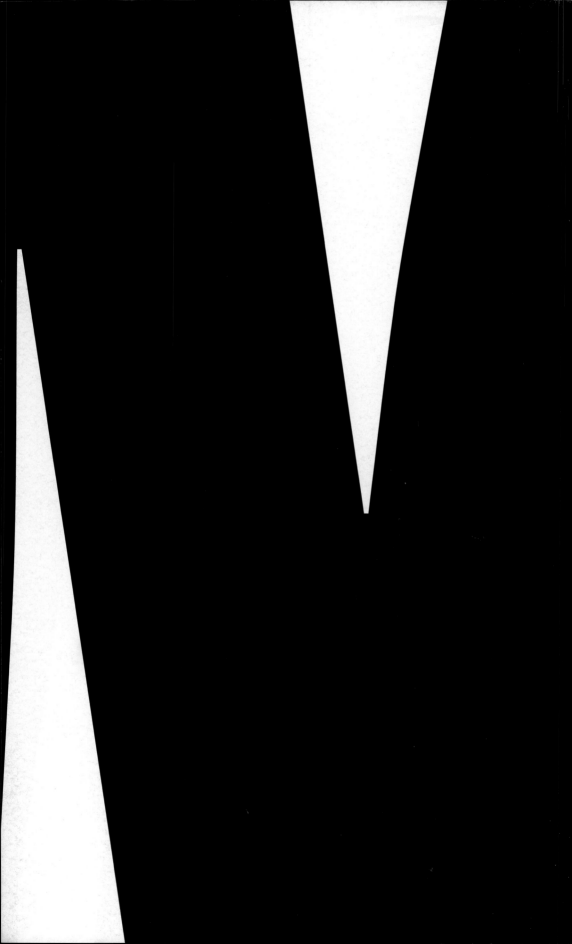

DOOMSDAY CLOCK
PART 2

GEOFF JOHNS
writer

GARY FRANK
illustrator

BRAD ANDERSON
colorist

ROB LEIGH
letterer

AMIE BROCKWAY-METCALF
original issue back matter design

**GARY FRANK and
BRAD ANDERSON**
collection cover artists

Watchmen created by
Alan Moore and Dave Gibbons.

Superman created by
Jerry Siegel and Joe Shuster.
Supergirl based on characters
created by Jerry Siegel and Joe Shuster.
By special arrangement
with the Jerry Siegel family.

Publisher's Note: The doomsday clock is a symbol created in 1947 by the Science and Security Board of the academic journal *Bulletin of the Atomic Scientists*, in response to the world's growing geopolitical insecurities and rising fear of nuclear war. The time on the clock—the proximity to midnight—indicates the view of the Science and Security Board regarding the likelihood of a global catastrophe. Initially, the clock was set to 11:53 p.m., but in 1953, with both the U.S. and the Soviet Union testing thermonuclear devices, the clock reached 11:58 p.m., its most ominous reading since its inception. By 1968 the situation had improved with the signing of the first Strategic Arms Limitation Treaty (SALT I) by the U.S. and the Soviet Union, and the clock eased back to 11:48. However, the two countries' jockeying for power and the apparent failure of a second round of SALT negotiations in 1984 pushed the clock forward to three minutes before midnight, where it remained for the duration of *Watchmen's* initial publication. In 1991 the clock was set at 11:43 p.m., the farthest from midnight that it had ever reached up to that point, in recognition of the signing of the SALT II accords by the U.S. and the Soviet Union. In 2007, however, the Science and Security Board decided that the clock should also reflect the risk of climate change and life science technological issues. The clock returned to three minutes to midnight in January 2015 due to "[un]checked climate change, global nuclear weapons modernizations, and outsized nuclear weapons arsenals." The doomsday clock moved to two and a half minutes until midnight in 2017, to two minutes until midnight in 2018, and most recently to 100 seconds to midnight in 2020.

BRIAN CUNNINGHAM Editor – Original Series
AMEDEO TURTURRO Associate Editor – Original Series
JEB WOODARD Group Editor – Collected Editions
ROBIN WILDMAN Editor – Collected Edition
STEVE COOK Design Director – Books
AMIE BROCKWAY-METCALF Publication Design
KATE DURRÉ Publication Production

BOB HARRAS Senior VP – Editor-in-Chief, DC Comics

DAN DiDIO Publisher
JIM LEE Publisher & Chief Creative Officer
BOBBIE CHASE VP – New Publishing Initiatives
DON FALLETTI VP – Manufacturing Operations & Workflow Management
LAWRENCE GANEM VP – Talent Services
ALISON GILL Senior VP – Manufacturing & Operations
HANK KANALZ Senior VP – Publishing Strategy & Support Services
DAN MIRON VP – Publishing Operations
NICK J. NAPOLITANO VP – Manufacturing Administration & Design
NANCY SPEARS VP – Sales
JONAH WEILAND VP – Marketing & Creative Services
MICHELE R. WELLS VP & Executive Editor, Young Reader

DOOMSDAY CLOCK PART 2

Published by DC Comics. Compilation, cover, and all new material
Copyright © 2020 DC Comics. All Rights Reserved. Originally published in
single magazine form in *Doomsday Clock* 7-12. Copyright © 2018, 2019 DC Comics.
All Rights Reserved. All characters, their distinctive likenesses, and related elements
featured in this publication are trademarks of DC Comics. The stories, characters,
and incidents featured in this publication are entirely fictional. DC Comics does not read or
accept unsolicited submissions of ideas, stories, or artwork. DC – a WarnerMedia Company.

DC Comics, 2900 West Alameda Ave., Burbank, CA 91505
Printed by LSC Communications, Kendallville, IN, USA. 4/3/20. First Printing.
ISBN: 978-1-77950-118-9

Library of Congress Cataloging-in-Publication Data is available.

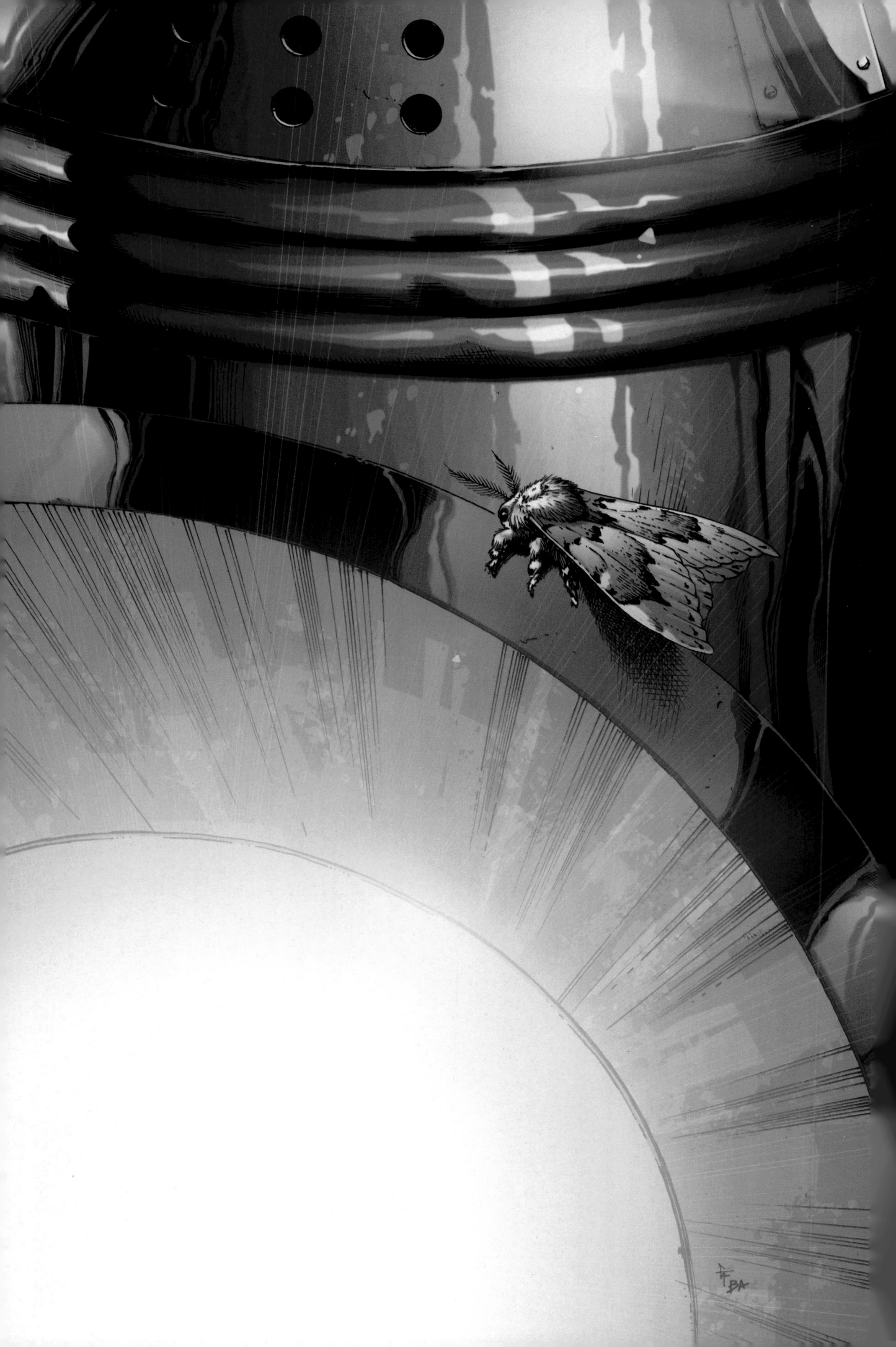

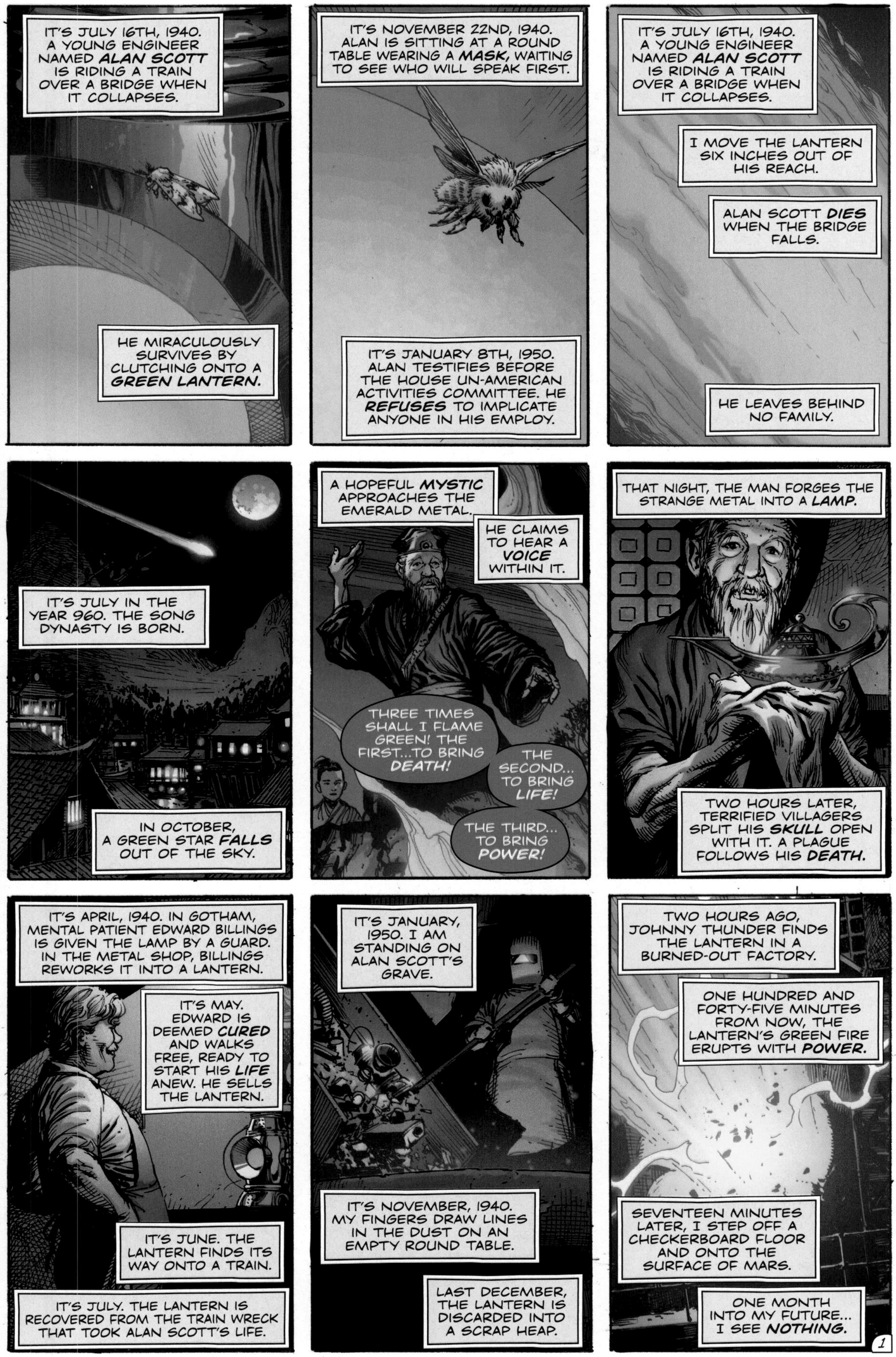
IT'S JULY 16TH, 1940. A YOUNG ENGINEER NAMED ALAN SCOTT IS RIDING A TRAIN OVER A BRIDGE WHEN IT COLLAPSES.
HE MIRACULOUSLY SURVIVES BY CLUTCHING ONTO A GREEN LANTERN.
IT'S NOVEMBER 22ND, 1940. ALAN IS SITTING AT A ROUND TABLE WEARING A MASK, WAITING TO SEE WHO WILL SPEAK FIRST.
IT'S JANUARY 8TH, 1950. ALAN TESTIFIES BEFORE THE HOUSE UN-AMERICAN ACTIVITIES COMMITTEE. HE REFUSES TO IMPLICATE ANYONE IN HIS EMPLOY.
IT'S JULY 16TH, 1940. A YOUNG ENGINEER NAMED ALAN SCOTT IS RIDING A TRAIN OVER A BRIDGE WHEN IT COLLAPSES.
I MOVE THE LANTERN SIX INCHES OUT OF HIS REACH.
ALAN SCOTT DIES WHEN THE BRIDGE FALLS.
HE LEAVES BEHIND NO FAMILY.
IT'S JULY IN THE YEAR 960. THE SONG DYNASTY IS BORN.
IN OCTOBER, A GREEN STAR FALLS OUT OF THE SKY.
A HOPEFUL MYSTIC APPROACHES THE EMERALD METAL.
HE CLAIMS TO HEAR A VOICE WITHIN IT.
THREE TIMES SHALL I FLAME GREEN! THE FIRST...TO BRING DEATH!
THE SECOND... TO BRING LIFE!
THE THIRD... TO BRING POWER!
THAT NIGHT, THE MAN FORGES THE STRANGE METAL INTO A LAMP.
TWO HOURS LATER, TERRIFIED VILLAGERS SPLIT HIS SKULL OPEN WITH IT. A PLAGUE FOLLOWS HIS DEATH.
IT'S APRIL, 1940. IN GOTHAM, MENTAL PATIENT EDWARD BILLINGS IS GIVEN THE LAMP BY A GUARD. IN THE METAL SHOP, BILLINGS REWORKS IT INTO A LANTERN.
IT'S MAY. EDWARD IS DEEMED CURED AND WALKS FREE, READY TO START HIS LIFE ANEW. HE SELLS THE LANTERN.
IT'S JUNE. THE LANTERN FINDS ITS WAY ONTO A TRAIN.
IT'S JULY. THE LANTERN IS RECOVERED FROM THE TRAIN WRECK THAT TOOK ALAN SCOTT'S LIFE.
IT'S JANUARY, 1950. I AM STANDING ON ALAN SCOTT'S GRAVE.
IT'S NOVEMBER, 1940. MY FINGERS DRAW LINES IN THE DUST ON AN EMPTY ROUND TABLE.
LAST DECEMBER, THE LANTERN IS DISCARDED INTO A SCRAP HEAP.
TWO HOURS AGO, JOHNNY THUNDER FINDS THE LANTERN IN A BURNED-OUT FACTORY.
ONE HUNDRED AND FORTY-FIVE MINUTES FROM NOW, THE LANTERN'S GREEN FIRE ERUPTS WITH POWER.
SEVENTEEN MINUTES LATER, I STEP OFF A CHECKERBOARD FLOOR AND ONTO THE SURFACE OF MARS.
ONE MONTH INTO MY FUTURE... I SEE NOTHING.

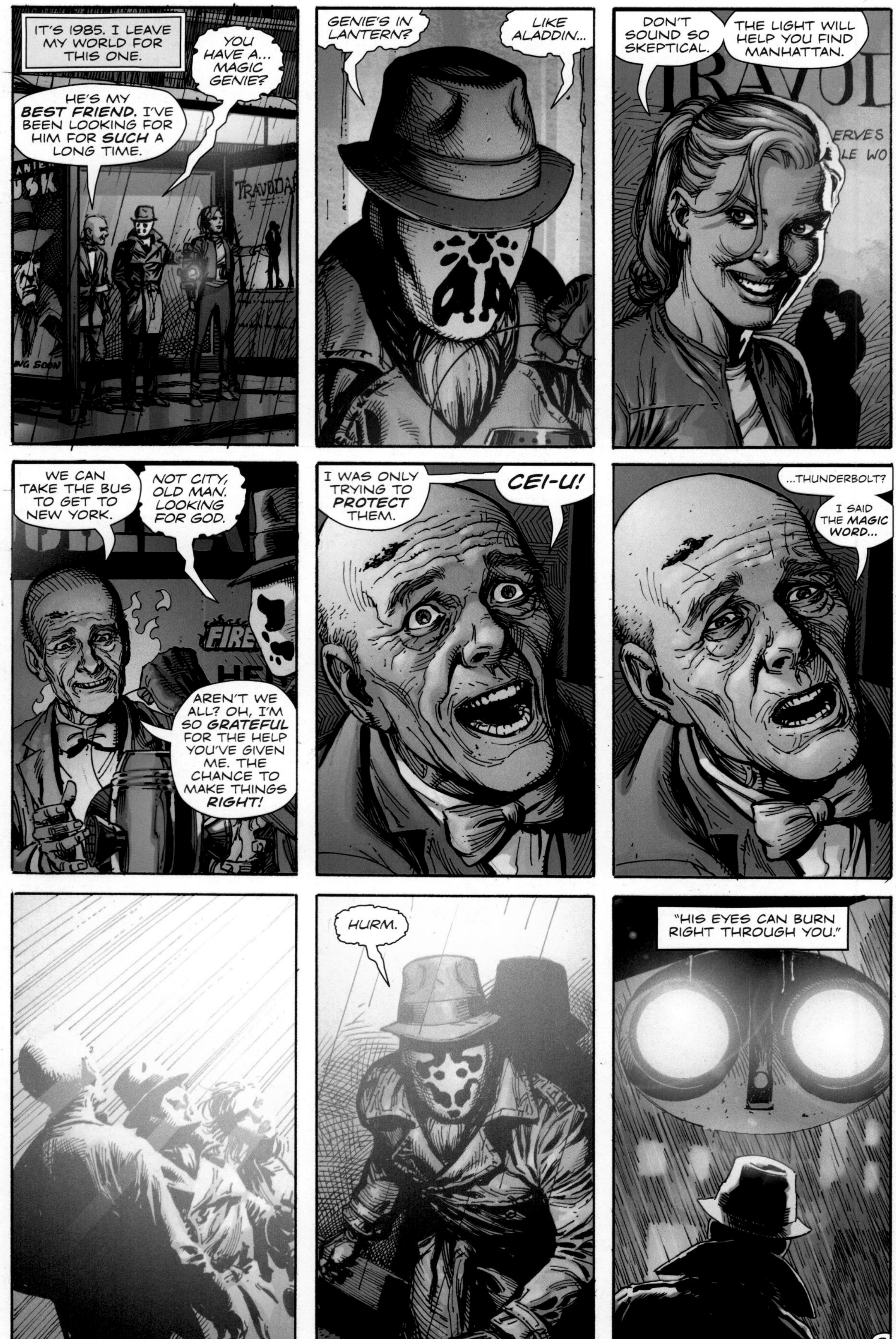
IT'S 1985. I LEAVE MY WORLD FOR THIS ONE.
YOU HAVE A... MAGIC GENIE?
HE'S MY BEST FRIEND. I'VE BEEN LOOKING FOR HIM FOR SUCH A LONG TIME.
TRAVODAR
GENIE'S IN LANTERN?
LIKE ALADDIN...
DON'T SOUND SO SKEPTICAL.
THE LIGHT WILL HELP YOU FIND MANHATTAN.
TRAVOI
ERVES
LE WO
WE CAN TAKE THE BUS TO GET TO NEW YORK.
NOT CITY, OLD MAN. LOOKING FOR GOD.
FIRE
AREN'T WE ALL? OH, I'M SO GRATEFUL FOR THE HELP YOU'VE GIVEN ME. THE CHANCE TO MAKE THINGS RIGHT!
I WAS ONLY TRYING TO PROTECT THEM.
CEI-U!
...THUNDERBOLT?
I SAID THE MAGIC WORD...
HURM.
"HIS EYES CAN BURN RIGHT THROUGH YOU."
2

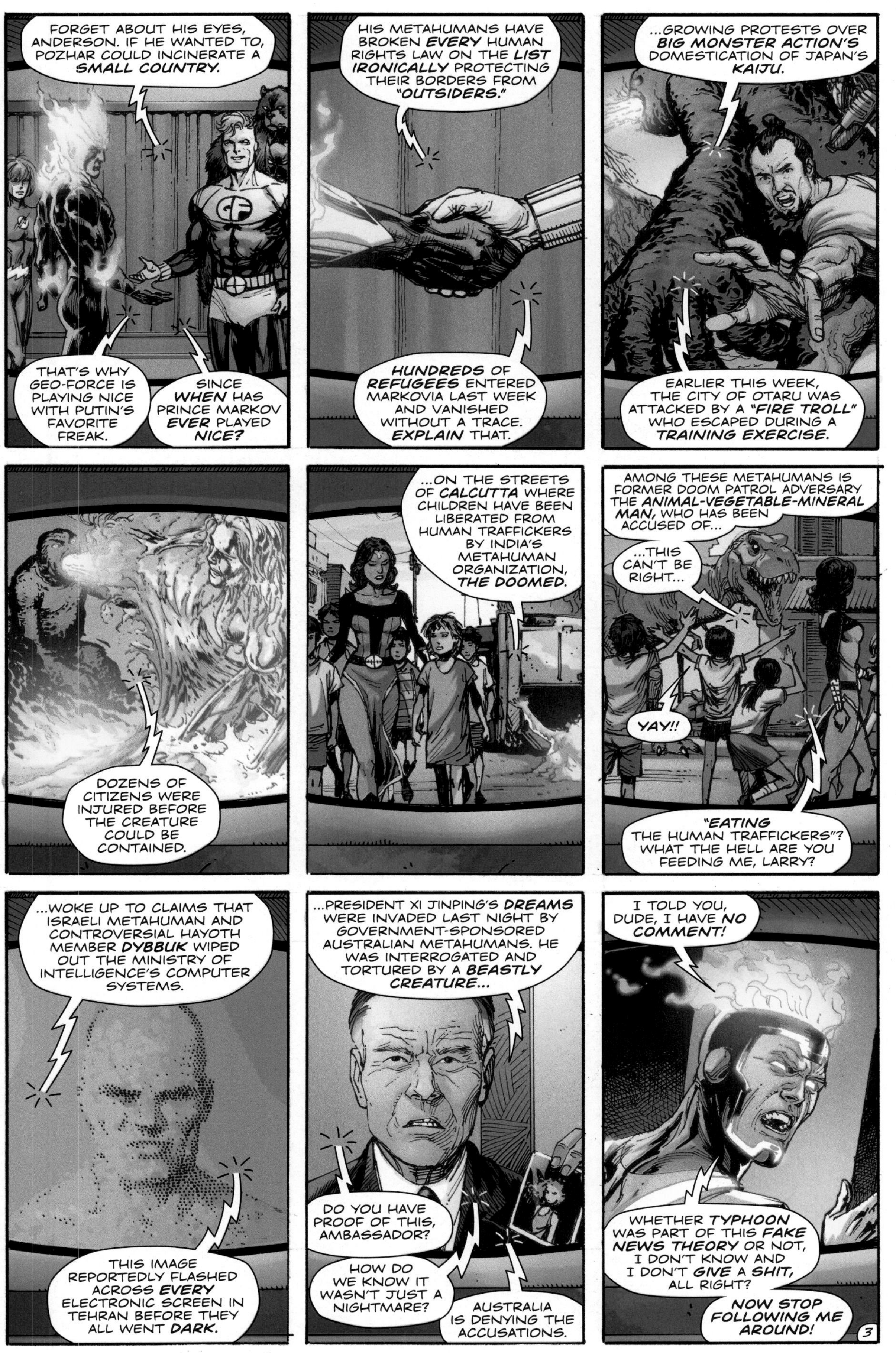
FORGET ABOUT HIS EYES, ANDERSON. IF HE WANTED TO, POZHAR COULD INCINERATE A SMALL COUNTRY.
THAT'S WHY GEO-FORCE IS PLAYING NICE WITH PUTIN'S FAVORITE FREAK.
SINCE WHEN HAS PRINCE MARKOV EVER PLAYED NICE?
HIS METAHUMANS HAVE BROKEN EVERY HUMAN RIGHTS LAW ON THE LIST IRONICALLY PROTECTING THEIR BORDERS FROM "OUTSIDERS."
HUNDREDS OF REFUGEES ENTERED MARKOVIA LAST WEEK AND VANISHED WITHOUT A TRACE. EXPLAIN THAT.
...GROWING PROTESTS OVER BIG MONSTER ACTION'S DOMESTICATION OF JAPAN'S KAIJU.
EARLIER THIS WEEK, THE CITY OF OTARU WAS ATTACKED BY A "FIRE TROLL" WHO ESCAPED DURING A TRAINING EXERCISE.
DOZENS OF CITIZENS WERE INJURED BEFORE THE CREATURE COULD BE CONTAINED.
...ON THE STREETS OF CALCUTTA WHERE CHILDREN HAVE BEEN LIBERATED FROM HUMAN TRAFFICKERS BY INDIA'S METAHUMAN ORGANIZATION, THE DOOMED.
AMONG THESE METAHUMANS IS FORMER DOOM PATROL ADVERSARY THE ANIMAL-VEGETABLE-MINERAL MAN, WHO HAS BEEN ACCUSED OF...
...THIS CAN'T BE RIGHT...
YAY!!
"EATING THE HUMAN TRAFFICKERS"? WHAT THE HELL ARE YOU FEEDING ME, LARRY?
...WOKE UP TO CLAIMS THAT ISRAELI METAHUMAN AND CONTROVERSIAL HAYOTH MEMBER DYBBUK WIPED OUT THE MINISTRY OF INTELLIGENCE'S COMPUTER SYSTEMS.
THIS IMAGE REPORTEDLY FLASHED ACROSS EVERY ELECTRONIC SCREEN IN TEHRAN BEFORE THEY ALL WENT DARK.
...PRESIDENT XI JINPING'S DREAMS WERE INVADED LAST NIGHT BY GOVERNMENT-SPONSORED AUSTRALIAN METAHUMANS. HE WAS INTERROGATED AND TORTURED BY A BEASTLY CREATURE...
DO YOU HAVE PROOF OF THIS, AMBASSADOR?
HOW DO WE KNOW IT WASN'T JUST A NIGHTMARE?
AUSTRALIA IS DENYING THE ACCUSATIONS.
I TOLD YOU, DUDE, I HAVE NO COMMENT!
WHETHER TYPHOON WAS PART OF THIS FAKE NEWS THEORY OR NOT, I DON'T KNOW AND I DON'T GIVE A SHIT, ALL RIGHT?
NOW STOP FOLLOWING ME AROUND!

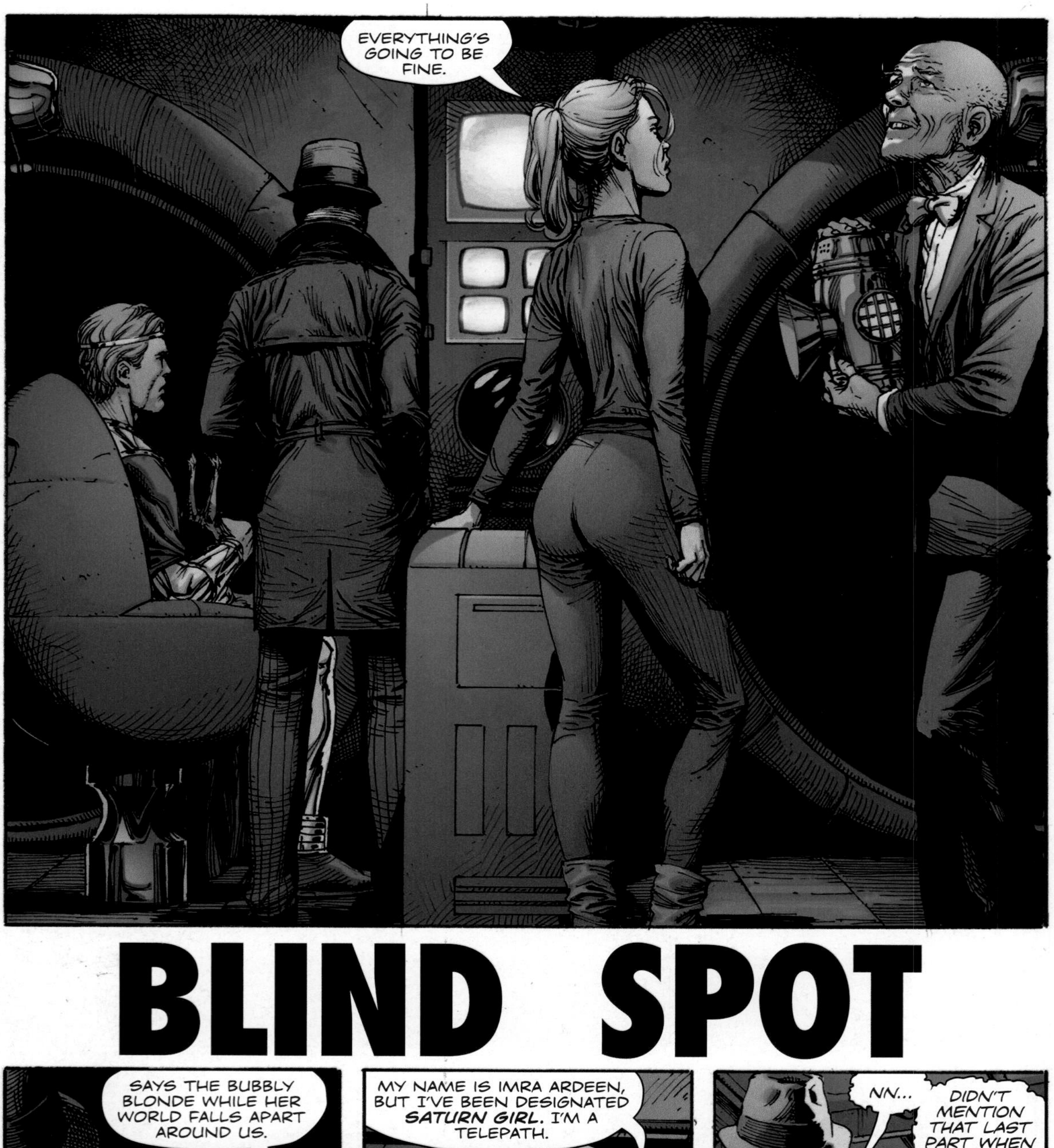
EVERYTHING'S GOING TO BE FINE.

BLIND SPOT

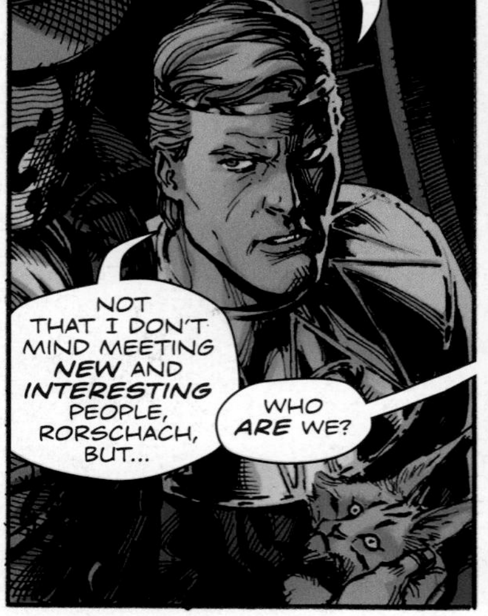
SAYS THE BUBBLY BLONDE WHILE HER WORLD FALLS APART AROUND US.
NOT THAT I DON'T MIND MEETING ***NEW*** AND ***INTERESTING*** PEOPLE, RORSCHACH, BUT...
WHO ***ARE*** WE?

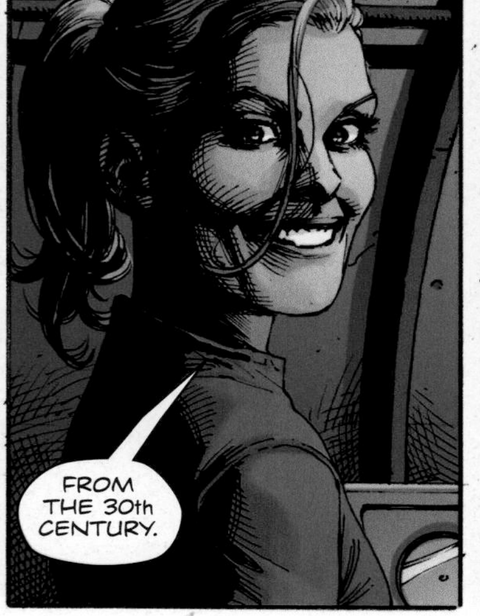
MY NAME IS IMRA ARDEEN, BUT I'VE BEEN DESIGNATED ***SATURN GIRL.*** I'M A TELEPATH.
FROM THE 30th CENTURY.

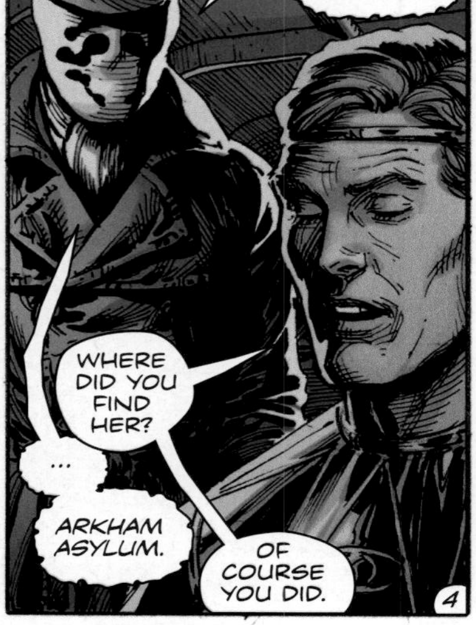
NN...
DIDN'T MENTION THAT LAST PART WHEN WE MET.
WHERE DID YOU FIND HER?
...
ARKHAM ASYLUM.
OF COURSE YOU DID.

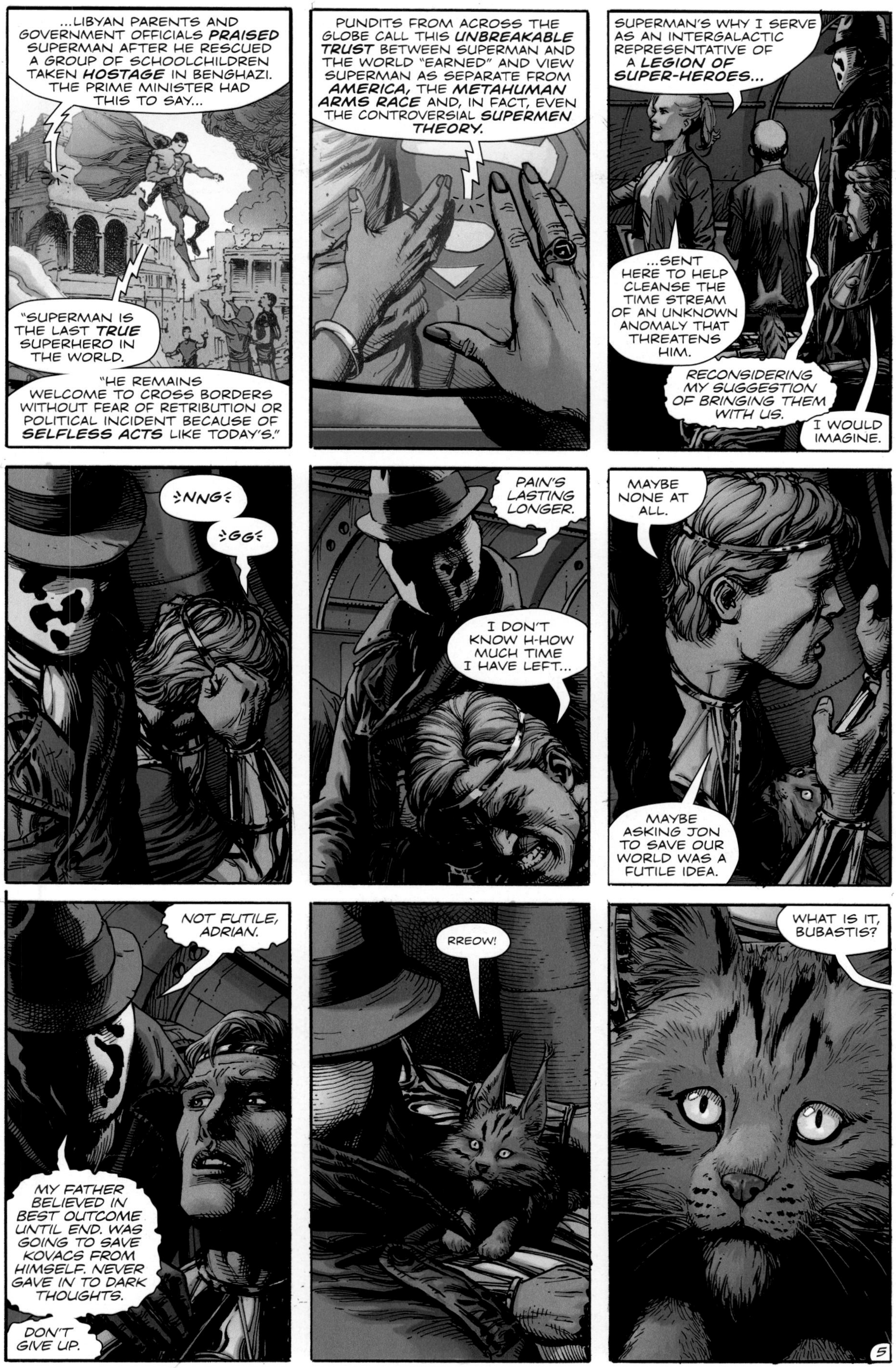
...LIBYAN PARENTS AND GOVERNMENT OFFICIALS PRAISED SUPERMAN AFTER HE RESCUED A GROUP OF SCHOOLCHILDREN TAKEN HOSTAGE IN BENGHAZI. THE PRIME MINISTER HAD THIS TO SAY...
"SUPERMAN IS THE LAST TRUE SUPERHERO IN THE WORLD.
"HE REMAINS WELCOME TO CROSS BORDERS WITHOUT FEAR OF RETRIBUTION OR POLITICAL INCIDENT BECAUSE OF SELFLESS ACTS LIKE TODAY'S."
PUNDITS FROM ACROSS THE GLOBE CALL THIS UNBREAKABLE TRUST BETWEEN SUPERMAN AND THE WORLD "EARNED" AND VIEW SUPERMAN AS SEPARATE FROM AMERICA, THE METAHUMAN ARMS RACE AND, IN FACT, EVEN THE CONTROVERSIAL SUPERMEN THEORY.
SUPERMAN'S WHY I SERVE AS AN INTERGALACTIC REPRESENTATIVE OF A LEGION OF SUPER-HEROES...
...SENT HERE TO HELP CLEANSE THE TIME STREAM OF AN UNKNOWN ANOMALY THAT THREATENS HIM.
RECONSIDERING MY SUGGESTION OF BRINGING THEM WITH US.
I WOULD IMAGINE.
NNG
GG
PAIN'S LASTING LONGER.
I DON'T KNOW H-HOW MUCH TIME I HAVE LEFT...
MAYBE NONE AT ALL.
MAYBE ASKING JON TO SAVE OUR WORLD WAS A FUTILE IDEA.
NOT FUTILE, ADRIAN.
MY FATHER BELIEVED IN BEST OUTCOME UNTIL END. WAS GOING TO SAVE KOVACS FROM HIMSELF. NEVER GAVE IN TO DARK THOUGHTS.
DON'T GIVE UP.
RREOW!
WHAT IS IT, BUBASTIS?

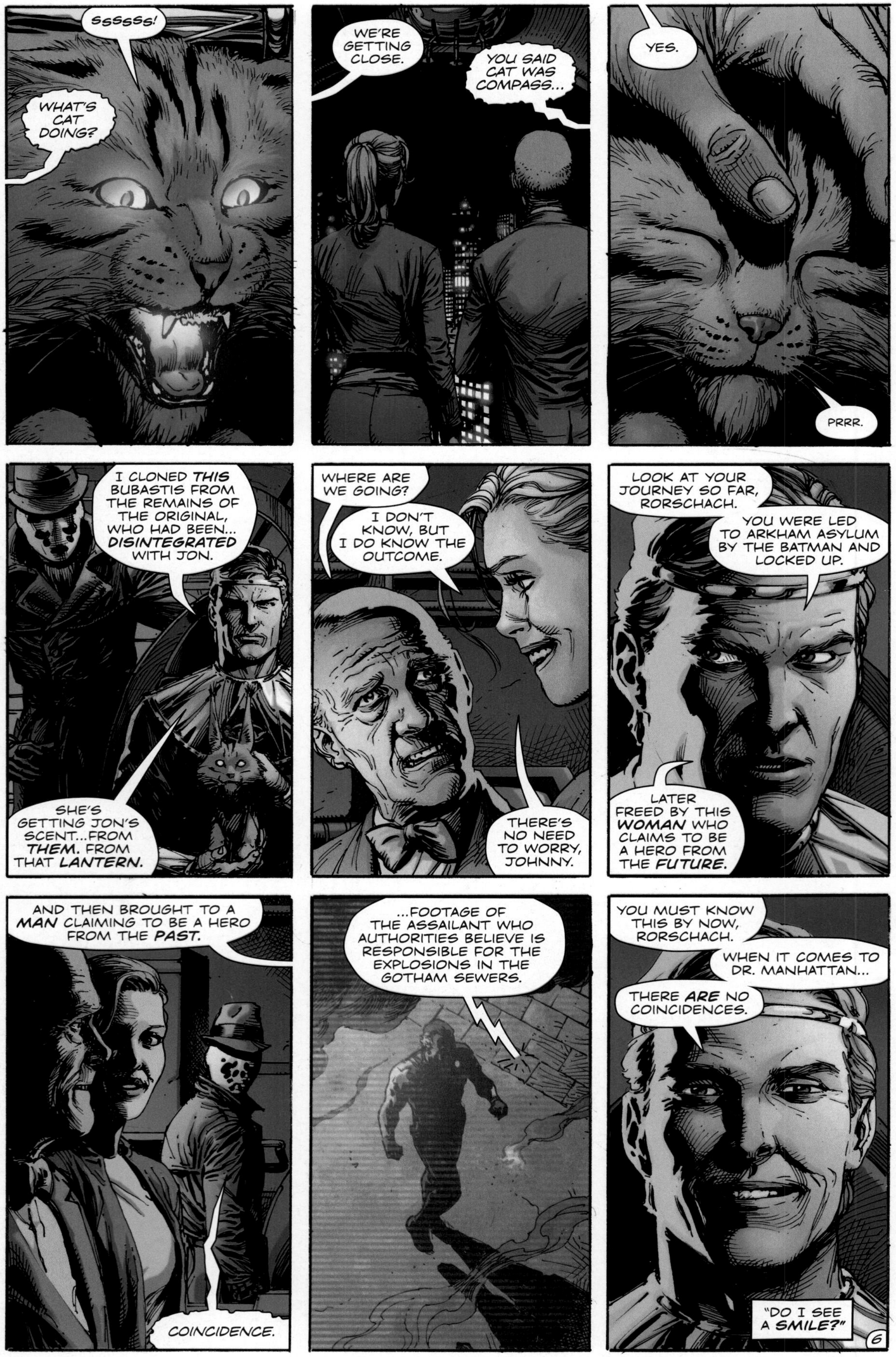

SSSSSS!
WHAT'S CAT DOING?
WE'RE GETTING CLOSE.
YOU SAID CAT WAS COMPASS...
YES.
PRRR.
I CLONED **THIS** BUBASTIS FROM THE REMAINS OF THE ORIGINAL, WHO HAD BEEN... **DISINTEGRATED** WITH JON.
SHE'S GETTING JON'S SCENT...FROM **THEM.** FROM THAT **LANTERN.**
WHERE ARE WE GOING?
I DON'T KNOW, BUT I DO KNOW THE OUTCOME.
THERE'S NO NEED TO WORRY, JOHNNY.
LOOK AT YOUR JOURNEY SO FAR, RORSCHACH.
YOU WERE LED TO ARKHAM ASYLUM BY THE BATMAN AND LOCKED UP.
LATER FREED BY THIS **WOMAN** WHO CLAIMS TO BE A HERO FROM THE **FUTURE.**
AND THEN BROUGHT TO A **MAN** CLAIMING TO BE A HERO FROM THE **PAST.**
COINCIDENCE.
...FOOTAGE OF THE ASSAILANT WHO AUTHORITIES BELIEVE IS RESPONSIBLE FOR THE EXPLOSIONS IN THE GOTHAM SEWERS.
YOU MUST KNOW THIS BY NOW, RORSCHACH.
WHEN IT COMES TO DR. MANHATTAN...
THERE **ARE** NO COINCIDENCES.
"DO I SEE A **SMILE?"**

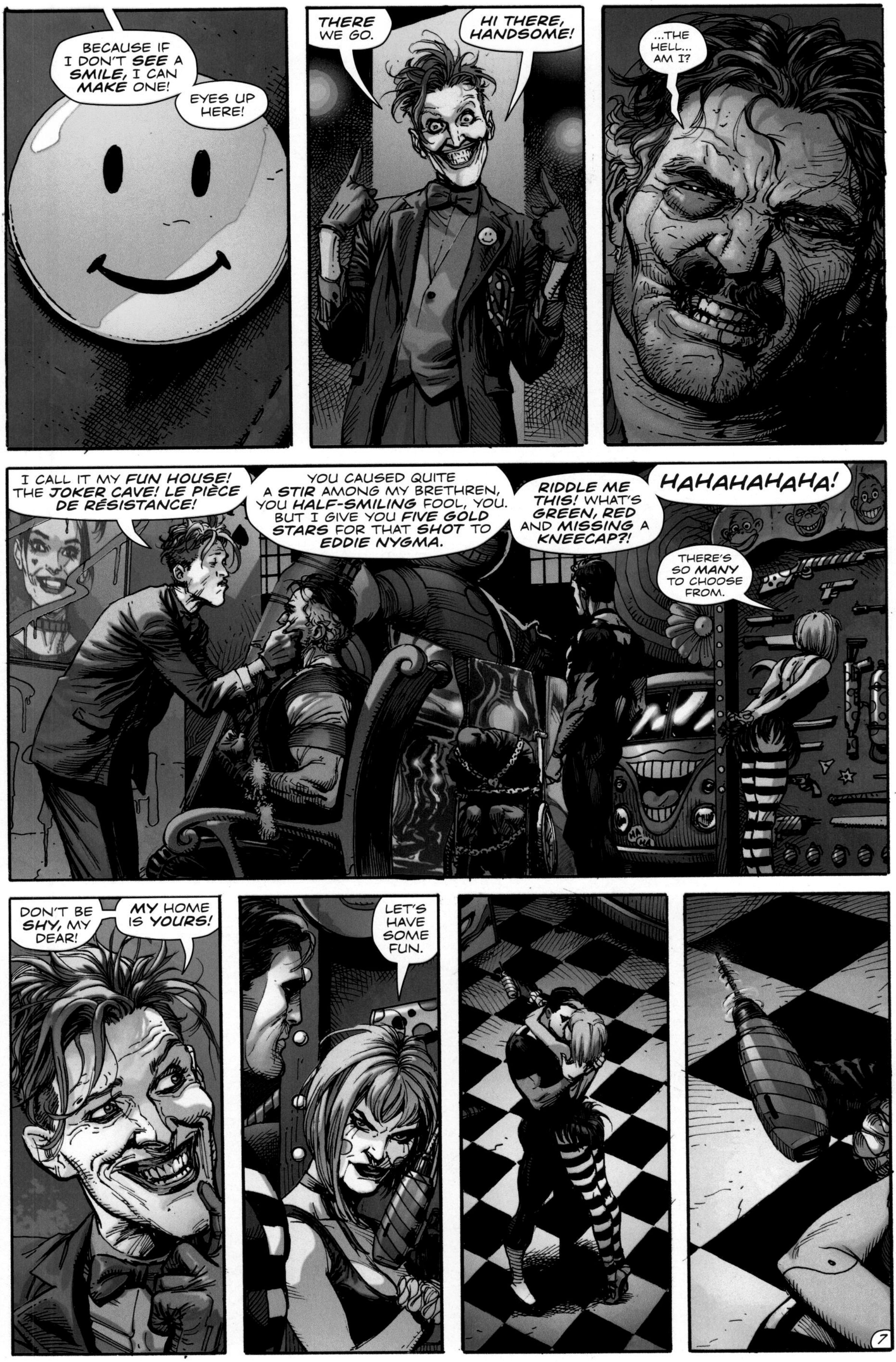
BECAUSE IF I DON'T SEE A SMILE, I CAN MAKE ONE!
EYES UP HERE!
THERE WE GO.
HI THERE, HANDSOME!
...THE HELL... AM I?
I CALL IT MY FUN HOUSE! THE JOKER CAVE! LE PIÈCE DE RÉSISTANCE!
YOU CAUSED QUITE A STIR AMONG MY BRETHREN, YOU HALF-SMILING FOOL, YOU. BUT I GIVE YOU FIVE GOLD STARS FOR THAT SHOT TO EDDIE NYGMA.
RIDDLE ME THIS! WHAT'S GREEN, RED AND MISSING A KNEECAP?!
HAHAHAHAHA!
THERE'S SO MANY TO CHOOSE FROM.
DON'T BE SHY, MY DEAR!
MY HOME IS YOURS!
LET'S HAVE SOME FUN.

UGH! GET A *ROOM*, YOU TWO! YOUR *SINCERITY* IS *SICKENING*.

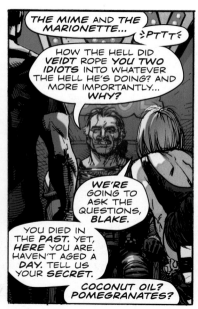

THE *MIME* AND *THE MARIONETTE*... ≶PTTT≶

HOW THE HELL DID *VEIDT* ROPE *YOU TWO IDIOTS* INTO WHATEVER THE HELL HE'S DOING? AND MORE IMPORTANTLY... *WHY?*

WE'RE GOING TO ASK THE *QUESTIONS*, *BLAKE*.

YOU DIED IN THE *PAST*. YET, *HERE* YOU ARE. HAVEN'T AGED A *DAY*. TELL US YOUR *SECRET*.

COCONUT OIL? POMEGRANATES?

A *NAKED BLUE MAN?*

WHY DON'T YA UNCUFF ME AND I'LL *SHOW* YOU, SWEETHEART.

NNNNNYYAAₐ!

OH, HONEY, THAT'S THE *EASY* PAIN.

TELL US WHERE DR. MANHATTAN IS AND I'LL ONLY DRILL INTO YOUR ARMS.

WHO KNOWS *WHERE* OR *WHEN* THAT ASSHOLE IS?

LISTEN, ALL DOC ASKED ME TO DO WAS TAKE OUT VEIDT'S *CAT*, OKAY? SO I WAS HAVIN' A LITTLE BIT OF *FUN* WITH YOU. THAT'S ALL.

I'LL SHOW YOU FUN...

WHAT, BABY?

WHAT IS IT?

8

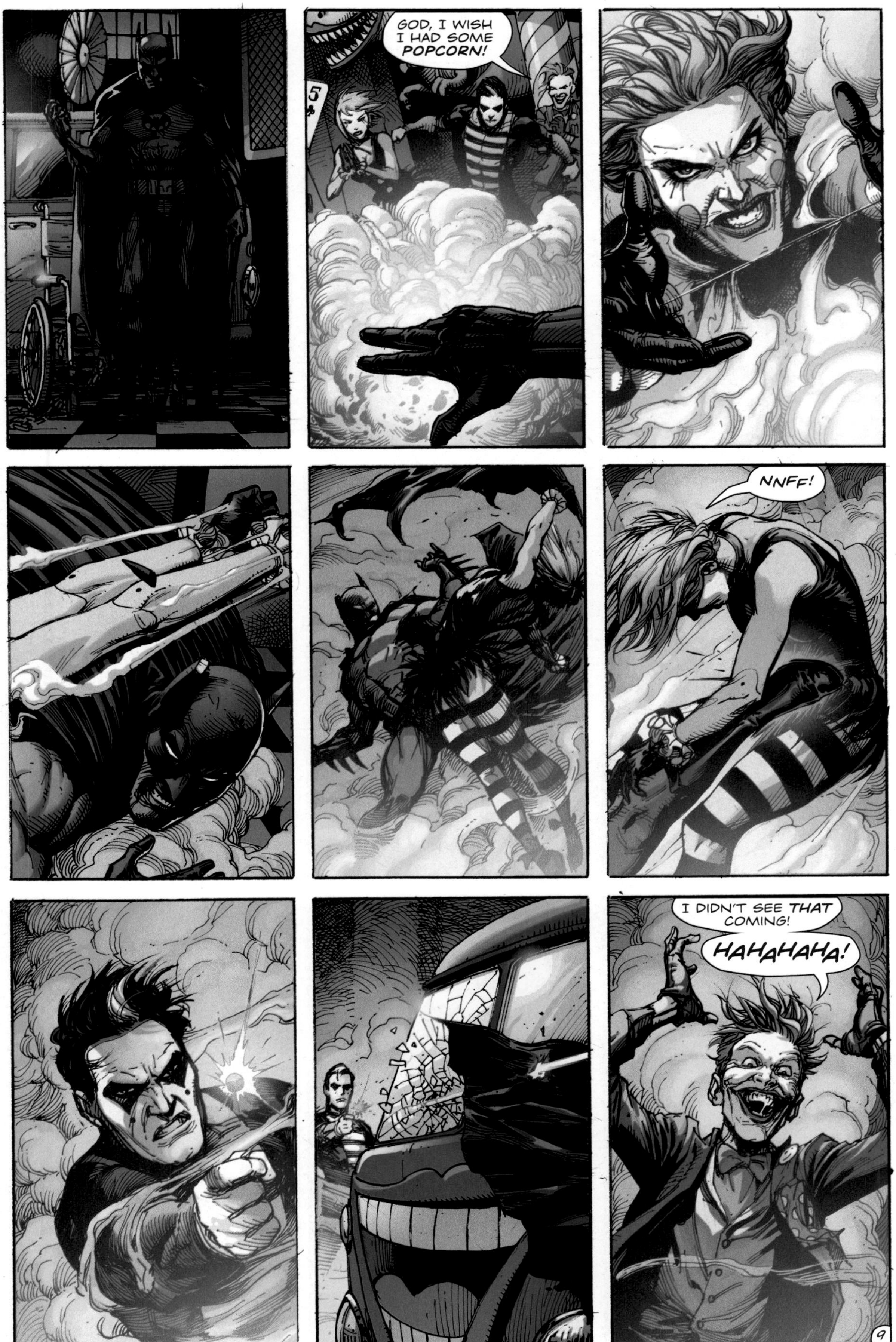
GOD, I WISH I HAD SOME POPCORN!
NNFF!
I DIDN'T SEE THAT COMING!
HAHAHAHA!

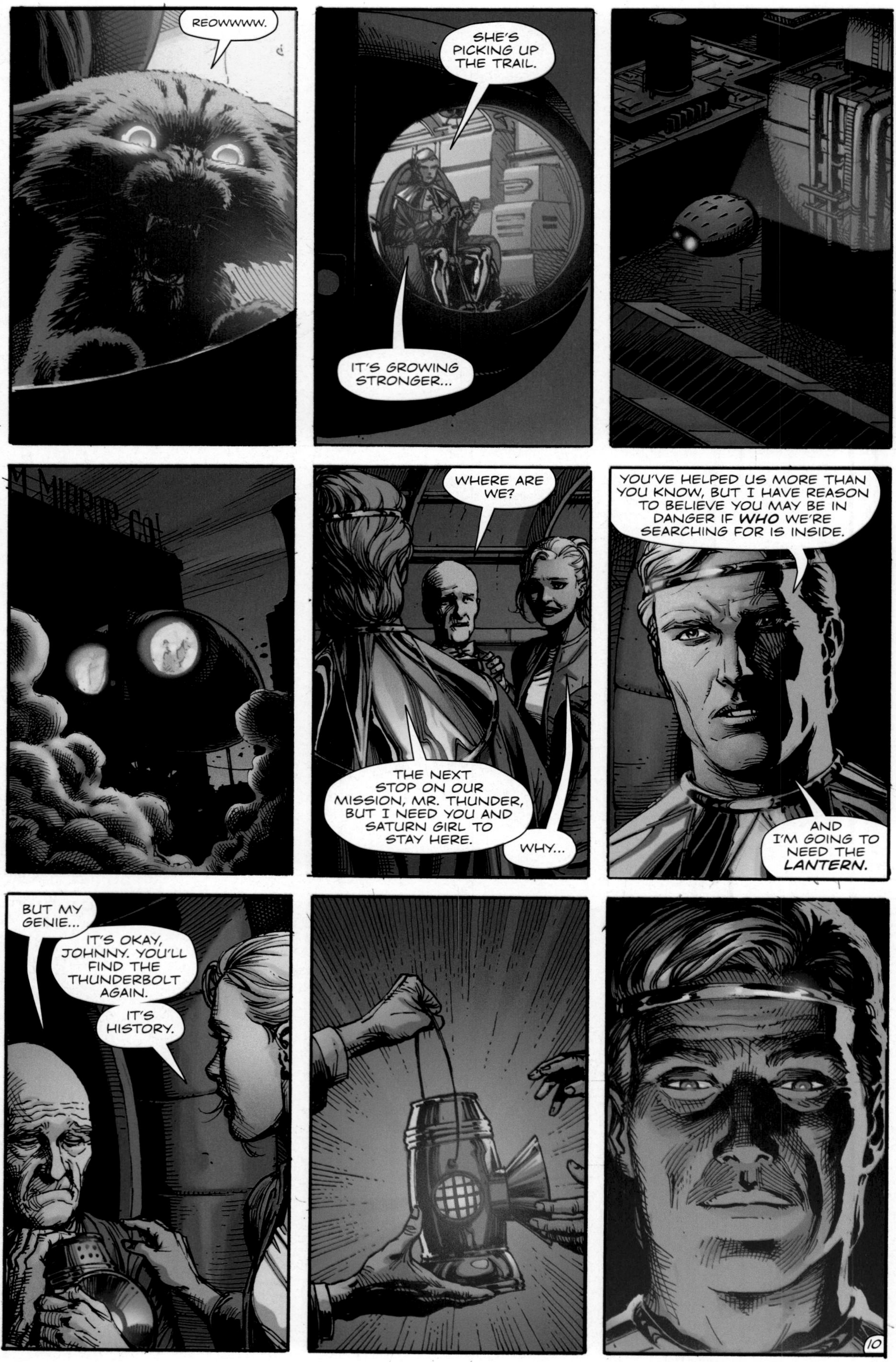
REOWWWW.
SHE'S PICKING UP THE TRAIL.
IT'S GROWING STRONGER...
WHERE ARE WE?
THE NEXT STOP ON OUR MISSION, MR. THUNDER, BUT I NEED YOU AND SATURN GIRL TO STAY HERE.
WHY...
YOU'VE HELPED US MORE THAN YOU KNOW, BUT I HAVE REASON TO BELIEVE YOU MAY BE IN DANGER IF ***WHO*** WE'RE SEARCHING FOR IS INSIDE.
AND I'M GOING TO NEED THE ***LANTERN.***
BUT MY GENIE...
IT'S OKAY, JOHNNY. YOU'LL FIND THE THUNDERBOLT AGAIN.
IT'S HISTORY.

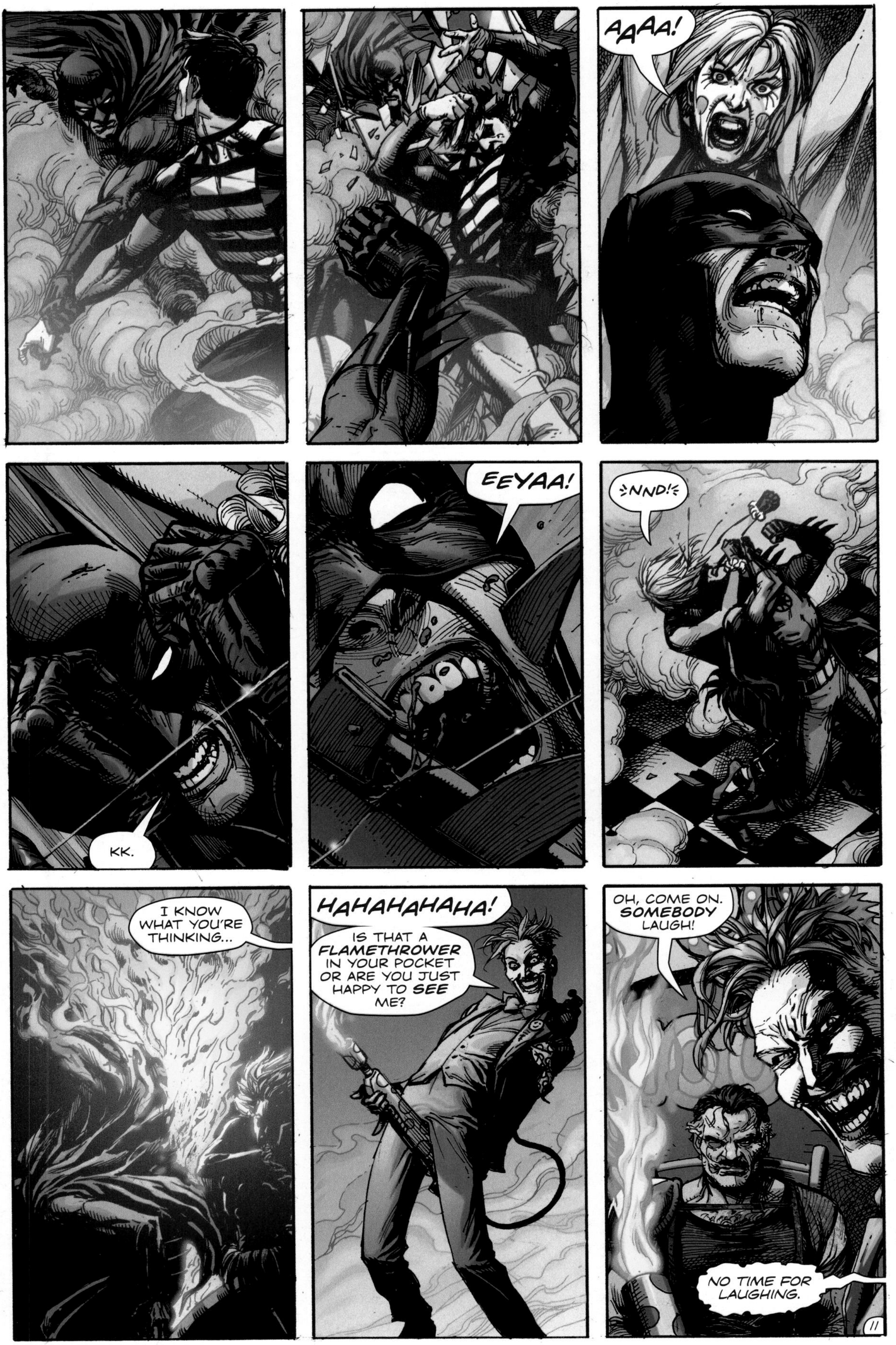
AAAA!
KK.
EEYAA!
NND!
I KNOW WHAT YOU'RE THINKING...
HAHAHAHAHA!
IS THAT A FLAMETHROWER IN YOUR POCKET OR ARE YOU JUST HAPPY TO SEE ME?
OH, COME ON. SOMEBODY LAUGH!
NO TIME FOR LAUGHING.
11

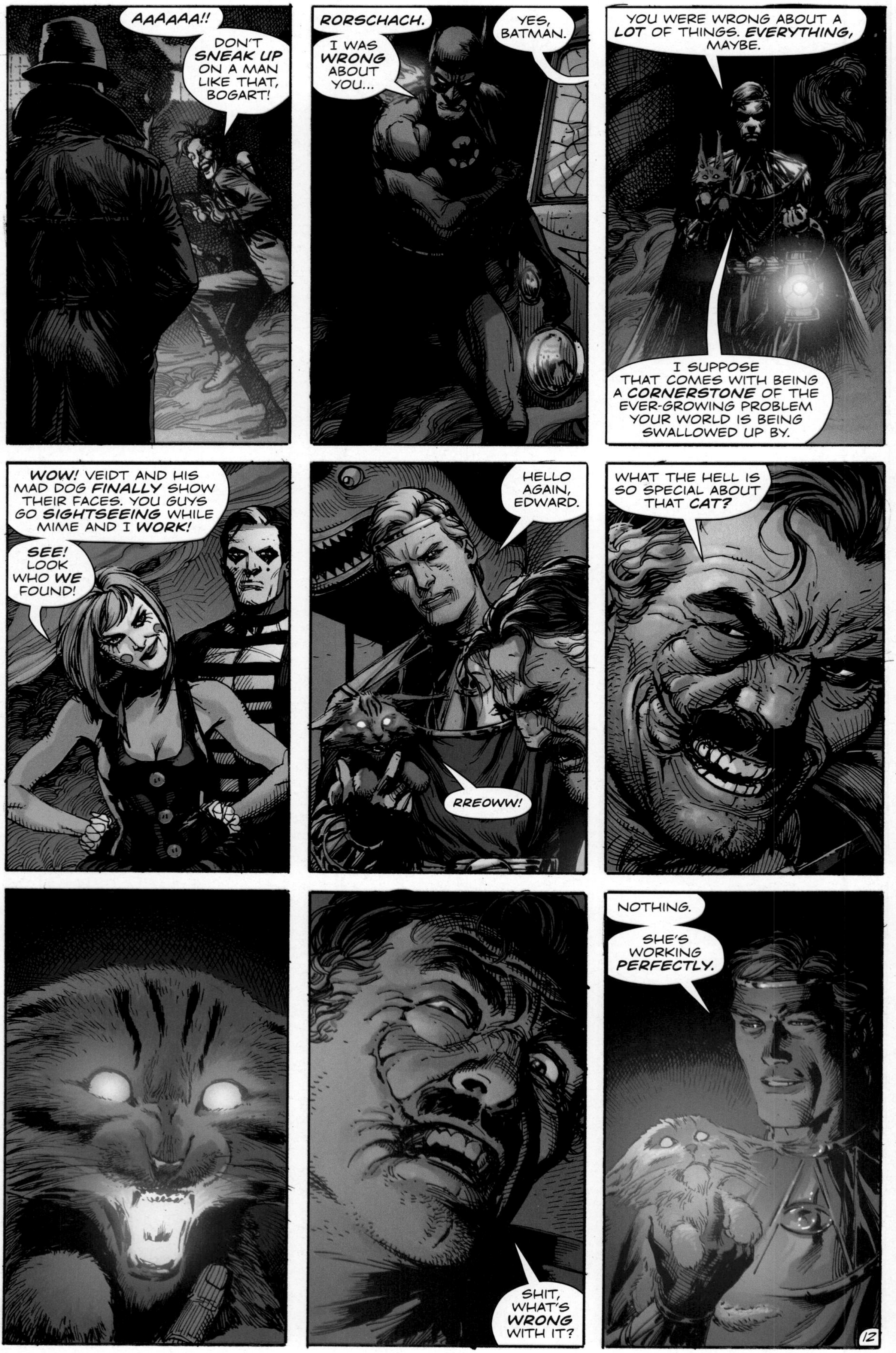
AAAAAA!!
DON'T SNEAK UP ON A MAN LIKE THAT, BOGART!
RORSCHACH.
I WAS WRONG ABOUT YOU...
YES, BATMAN.
YOU WERE WRONG ABOUT A LOT OF THINGS. EVERYTHING, MAYBE.
I SUPPOSE THAT COMES WITH BEING A CORNERSTONE OF THE EVER-GROWING PROBLEM YOUR WORLD IS BEING SWALLOWED UP BY.
WOW! VEIDT AND HIS MAD DOG FINALLY SHOW THEIR FACES. YOU GUYS GO SIGHTSEEING WHILE MIME AND I WORK!
SEE! LOOK WHO WE FOUND!
HELLO AGAIN, EDWARD.
RREOWW!
WHAT THE HELL IS SO SPECIAL ABOUT THAT CAT?
SHIT, WHAT'S WRONG WITH IT?
NOTHING.
SHE'S WORKING PERFECTLY.
12

BUBASTIS SEES JON'S TEMPORAL FINGERPRINTS.

ON THIS LANTERN.

AND ON YOU, EDWARD.

AS SHE FEEDS, JON SHOULD FEEL A STRONG PULL TO HER. NOT UNLIKE A MAGNET.

AND TO DENY IT WILL PROVE PAINFUL.

EVEN FOR HIM.

WHERE ARE YOU, JON?

SHOW YOURSELF!

I CAN MAKE THIS HURT MORE THAN IT DOES!

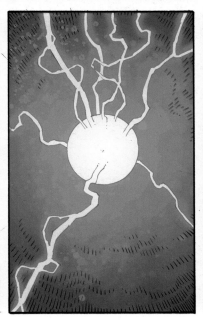

13

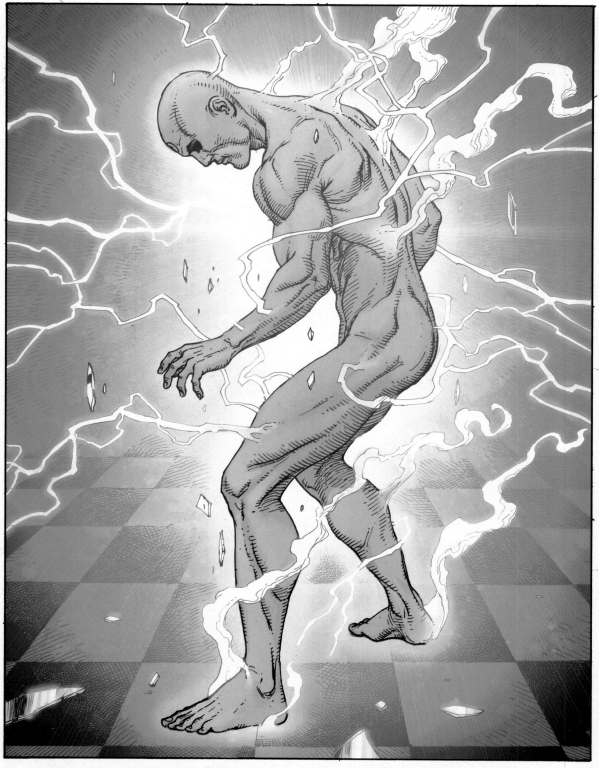

HELLO, JON.

14

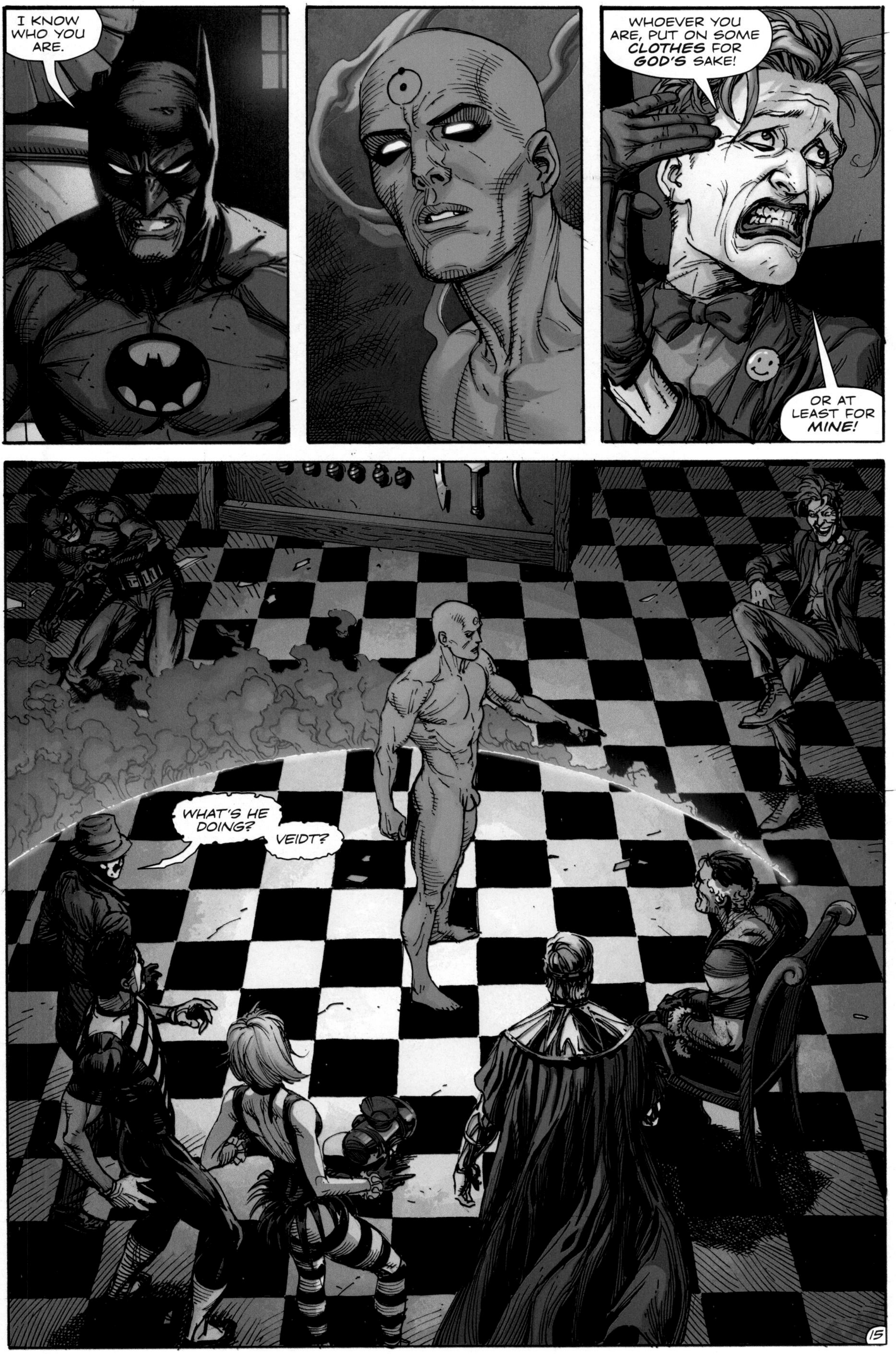
I KNOW WHO YOU ARE.
WHOEVER YOU ARE, PUT ON SOME CLOTHES FOR GOD'S SAKE!
OR AT LEAST FOR MINE!
WHAT'S HE DOING?
VEIDT?

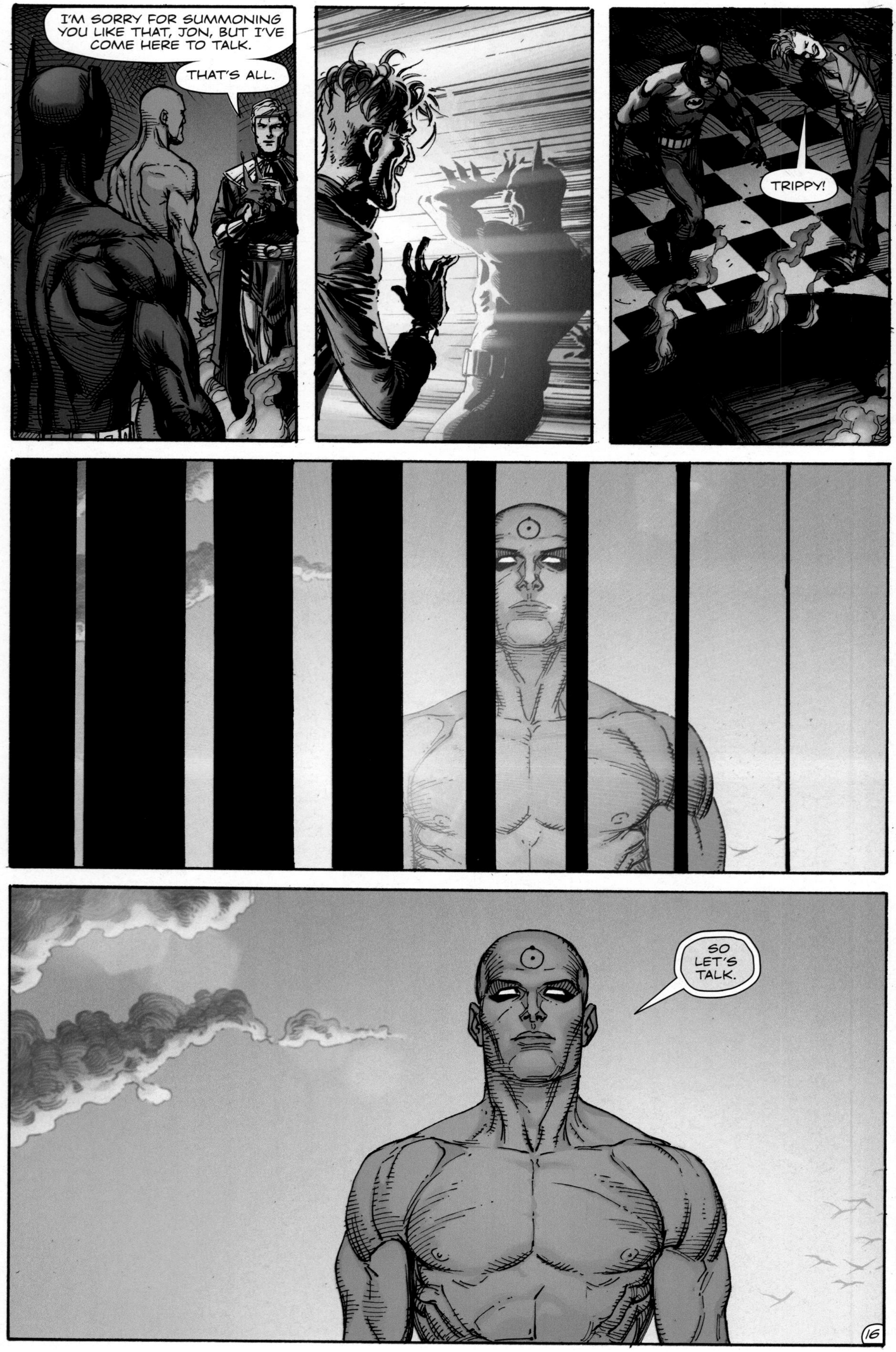
I'M SORRY FOR SUMMONING YOU LIKE THAT, JON, BUT I'VE COME HERE TO TALK.
THAT'S ALL.
TRIPPY!
SO LET'S TALK.

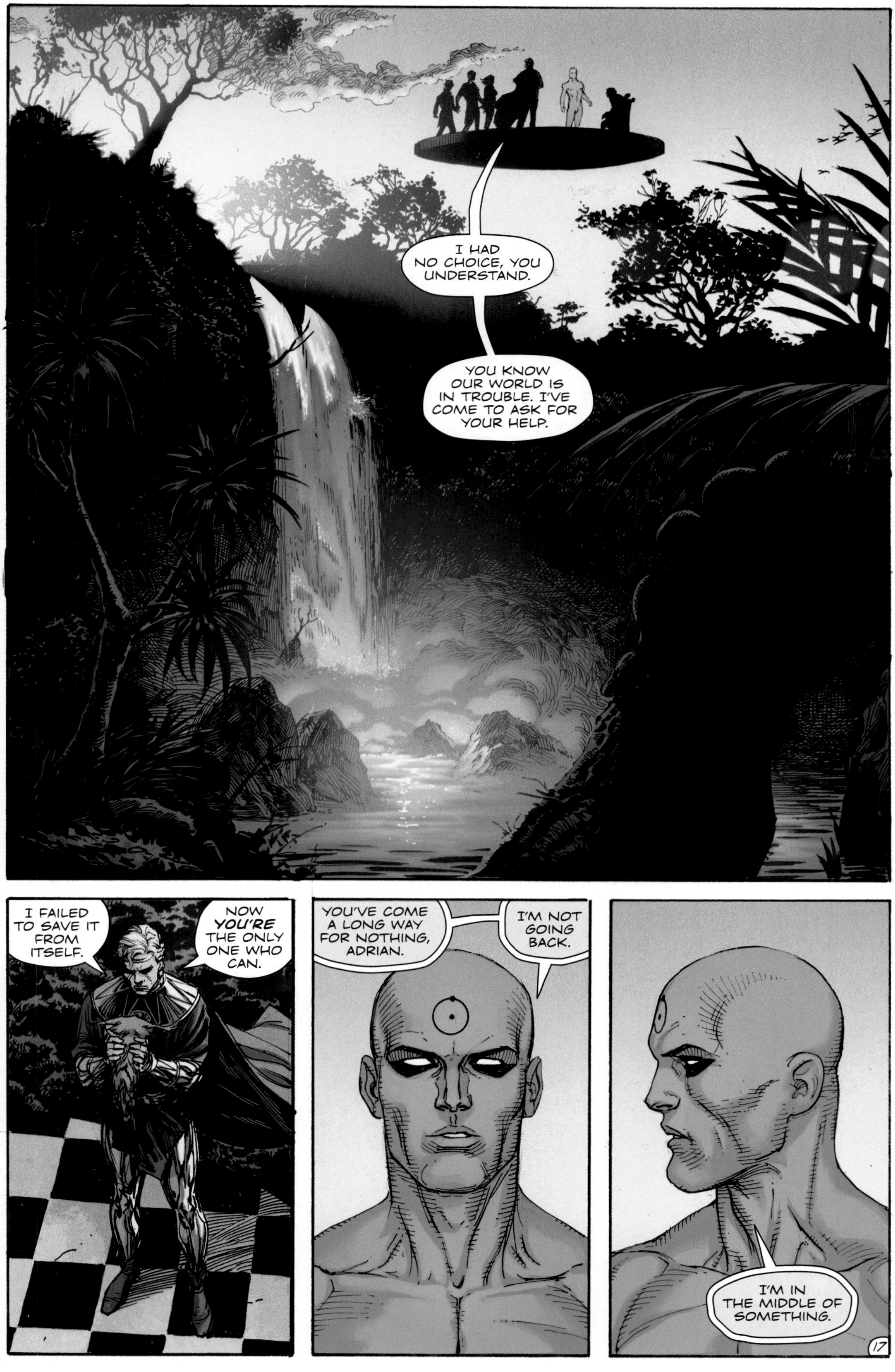
I HAD NO CHOICE, YOU UNDERSTAND.
YOU KNOW OUR WORLD IS IN TROUBLE. I'VE COME TO ASK FOR YOUR HELP.
I FAILED TO SAVE IT FROM ITSELF.
NOW *YOU'RE* THE ONLY ONE WHO CAN.
YOU'VE COME A LONG WAY FOR NOTHING, ADRIAN.
I'M NOT GOING BACK.
I'M IN THE MIDDLE OF SOMETHING.

YOU'RE THINKING I'VE ONCE AGAIN TURNED MY BACK ON HUMANITY.

THAT'S WHY YOU ASKED LAURIE TO COME WITH YOU. TO REMIND ME. SHE REFUSED.

BUT SHE LED YOU TO *THEM.*

ERIKA MANSON AND MARCOS MAEZ.

I'M AT ROCKEFELLER WITH LAURIE, LISTENING TO HER COMPLAIN ABOUT THE SECURITY CAMERAS INSTALLED IN OUR LIVING QUARTERS.

AS I REMOVE THEM, I'M TOLD THERE'S A BANK ROBBERY IN PROGRESS ONE MILE AWAY.

I ARRIVE TO DISPATCH THE CRIMINALS.

YOU BELIEVE I AM HESITANT TO USE EXTREME FORCE WHEN I LEARN ERIKA MANSON IS PREGNANT.

BUT I DID NOT SPARE YOU BECAUSE YOU WERE PREGNANT, ERIKA MANSON.

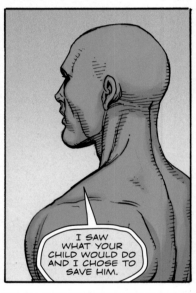

I SAW WHAT YOUR CHILD WOULD DO AND I CHOSE TO SAVE HIM.

WHAT ARE YOU TALKING ABOUT? WHAT DID MY CHILD DO?

WHICH CHILD?

WHAT DO YOU MEAN *WHICH* CHILD?

AH, YES. SOMETIMES I FORGET WHAT'S BEEN AND WHAT WILL BE.

YOU'RE PREGNANT AGAIN.

WHAT?

18

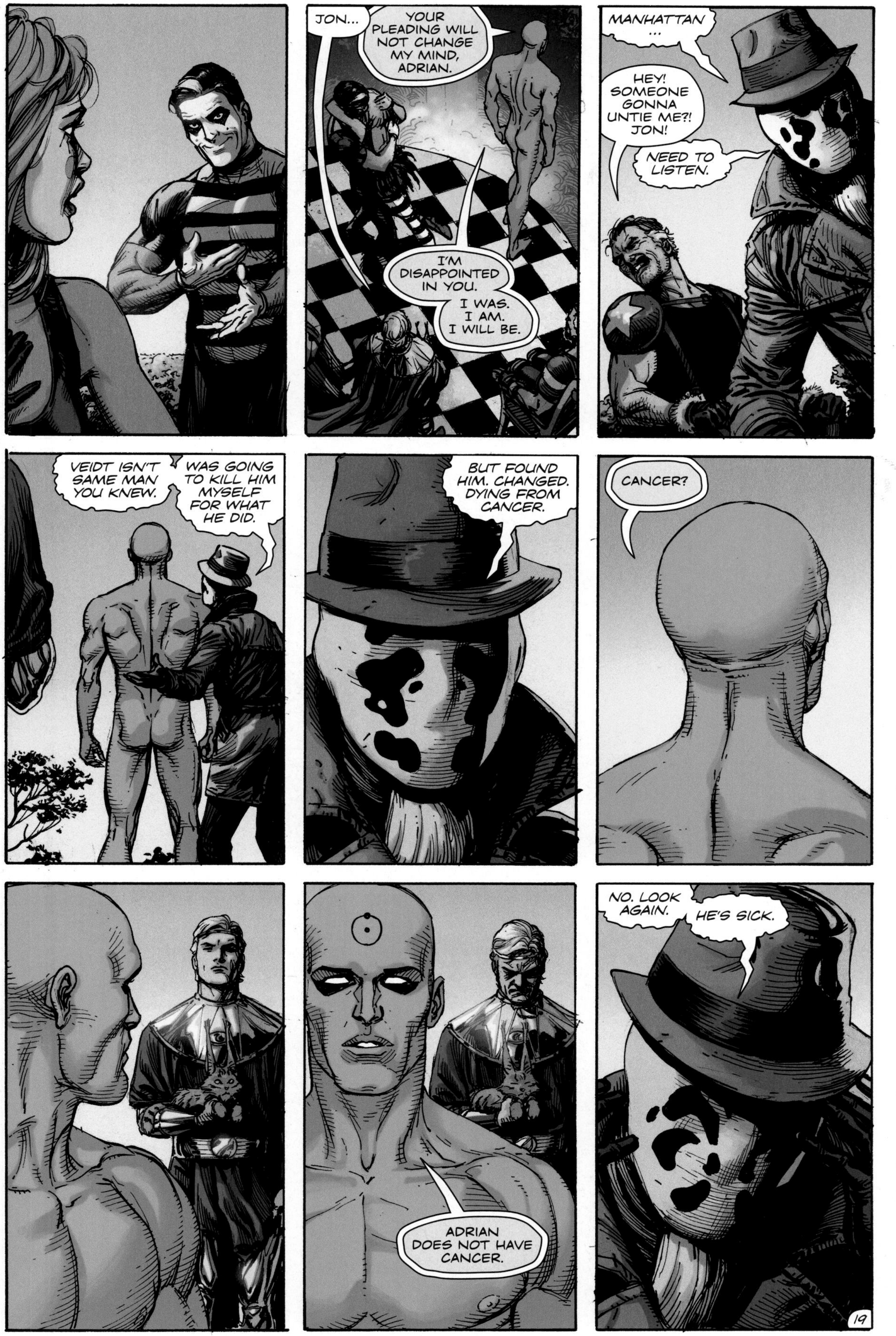
JON...
YOUR PLEADING WILL NOT CHANGE MY MIND, ADRIAN.
I'M DISAPPOINTED IN YOU.
I WAS. I AM. I WILL BE.
MANHATTAN ...
HEY! SOMEONE GONNA UNTIE ME?! JON!
NEED TO LISTEN.
VEIDT ISN'T SAME MAN YOU KNEW.
WAS GOING TO KILL HIM MYSELF FOR WHAT HE DID.
BUT FOUND HIM. CHANGED. DYING FROM CANCER.
CANCER?
ADRIAN DOES NOT HAVE CANCER.
NO. LOOK AGAIN.
HE'S SICK.

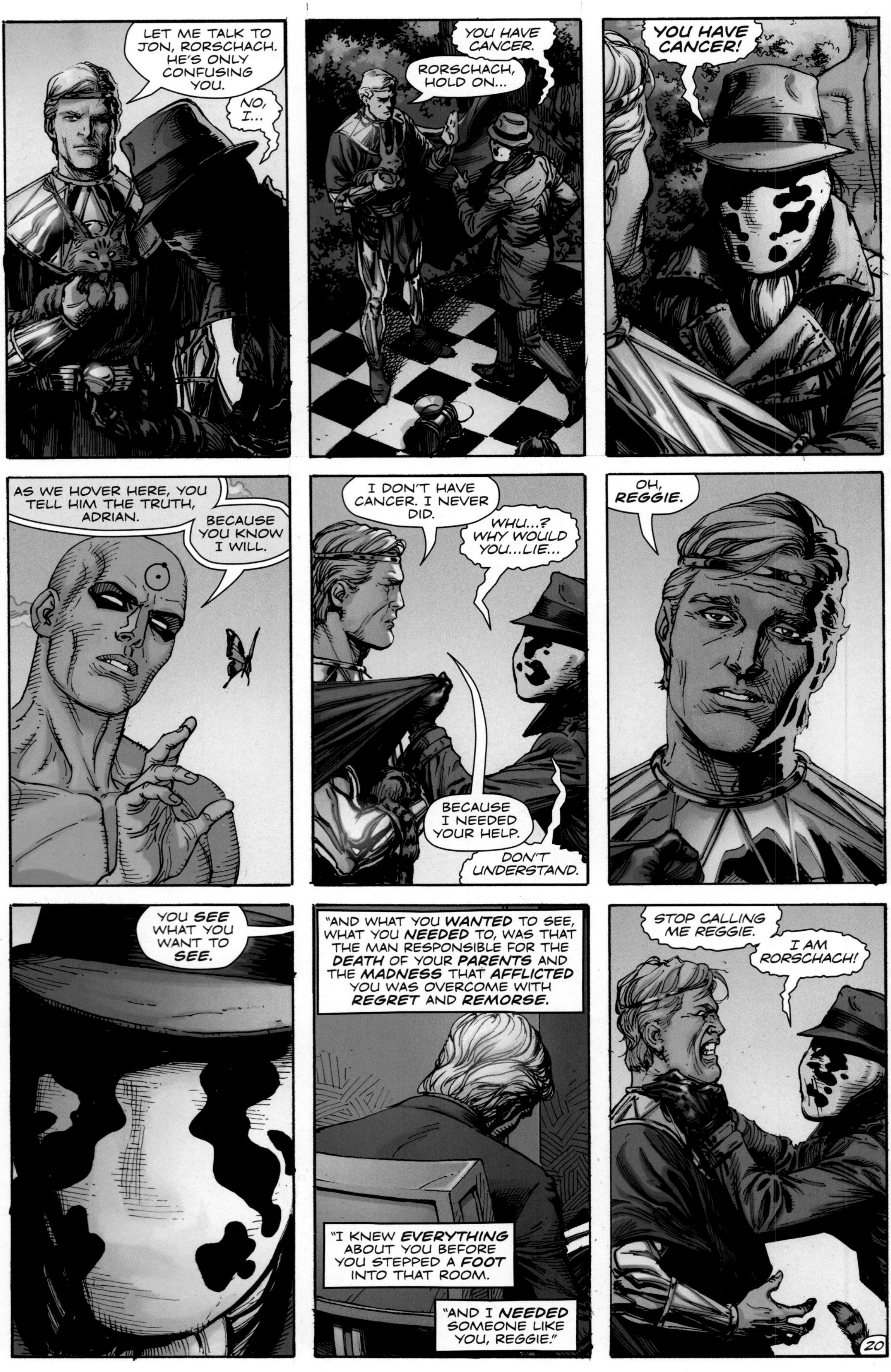
LET ME TALK TO JON, RORSCHACH. HE'S ONLY CONFUSING YOU.
NO, I...
YOU HAVE CANCER.
RORSCHACH, HOLD ON...
YOU HAVE CANCER!
AS WE HOVER HERE, YOU TELL HIM THE TRUTH, ADRIAN.
BECAUSE YOU KNOW I WILL.
I DON'T HAVE CANCER. I NEVER DID.
WHU...? WHY WOULD YOU...LIE...
BECAUSE I NEEDED YOUR HELP.
DON'T UNDERSTAND.
OH, REGGIE.
YOU SEE WHAT YOU WANT TO SEE.
"AND WHAT YOU WANTED TO SEE, WHAT YOU NEEDED TO, WAS THAT THE MAN RESPONSIBLE FOR THE DEATH OF YOUR PARENTS AND THE MADNESS THAT AFFLICTED YOU WAS OVERCOME WITH REGRET AND REMORSE.
"I KNEW EVERYTHING ABOUT YOU BEFORE YOU STEPPED A FOOT INTO THAT ROOM.
"AND I NEEDED SOMEONE LIKE YOU, REGGIE."
STOP CALLING ME REGGIE.
I AM RORSCHACH!
20

RORSCHACH? **PLEASE.**

YOU SAW WHAT YOU WANTED TO SEE WITH **RORSCHACH,** TOO.

YOU BELIEVED YOU WERE TAKING UP THE MASK OF A **FRIEND** OF YOUR FATHER'S.

"BUT **WALTER KOVACS** WAS **NEVER** YOUR FATHER'S **FRIEND.**

"IF **BYRON LEWIS** HADN'T KEPT MOST OF YOUR FATHER'S NOTES FROM YOU, YOU WOULD'VE SEEN THAT.

"BYRON WAS TRYING TO **PROTECT** YOU FROM THE TRUTH: THAT RORSCHACH BROKE DOWN YOUR FATHER'S **UNDYING POSITIVITY** AND LEFT HIM A **SHELL** OF THE MAN HE WAS.

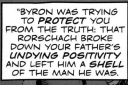

"HIS RELATIONSHIP WITH YOUR MOTHER DETERIORATED INTO **NOTHINGNESS.**

"SHE **LEFT** HIM, REGGIE.

YOUR MOTHER AND FATHER DID NOT DIE IN A **LOVING EMBRACE.**

THEY DIED **DESPISING** ONE ANOTHER.

ALONE.

NO.

NO.

IS IT **TRUE?**

IS IT?

21

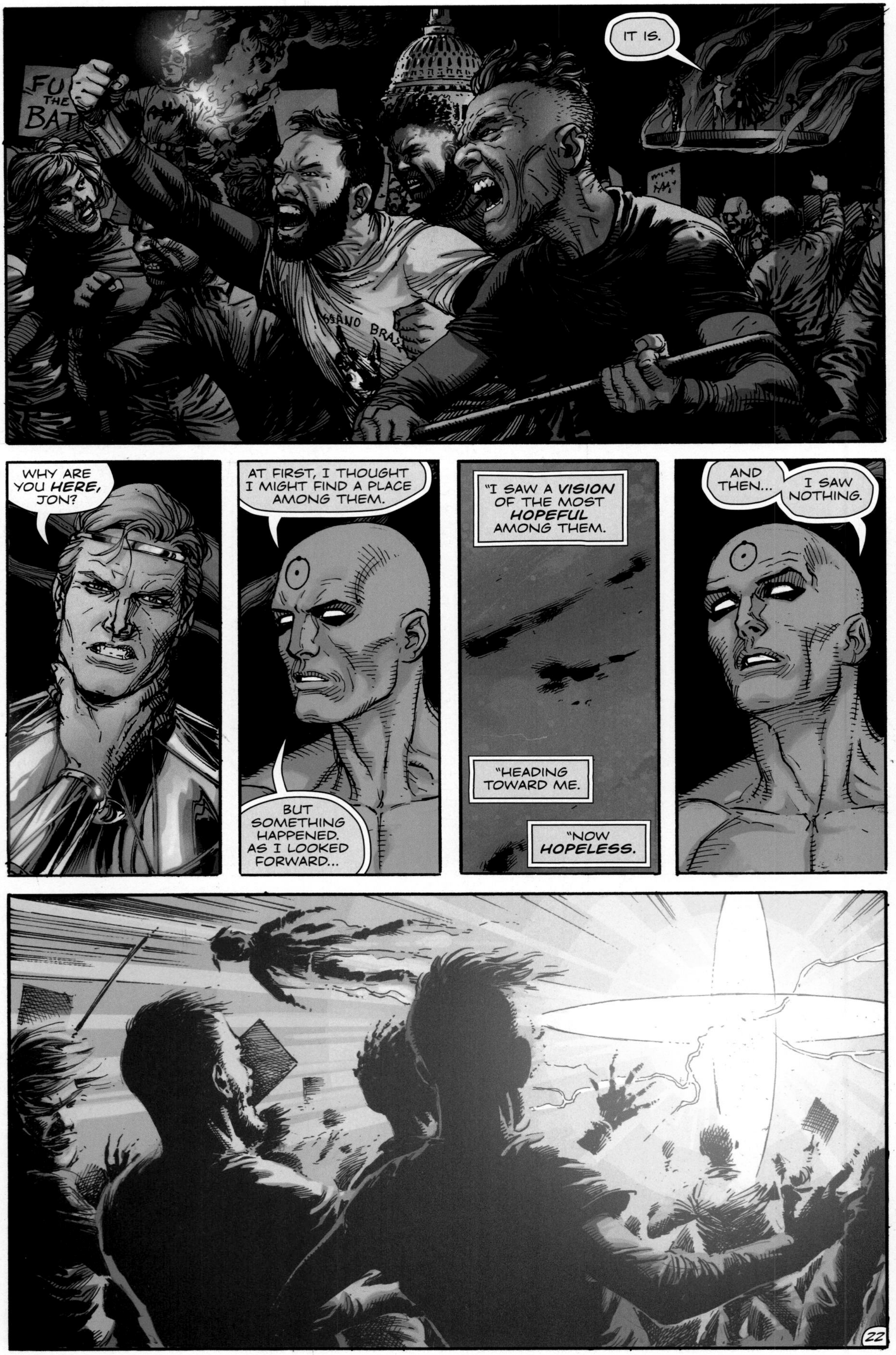
FU THE BAT
IT IS.
WHY ARE YOU **HERE,** JON?
AT FIRST, I THOUGHT I MIGHT FIND A PLACE AMONG THEM.
BUT SOMETHING HAPPENED. AS I LOOKED FORWARD...
"I SAW A **VISION** OF THE MOST **HOPEFUL** AMONG THEM.
"HEADING TOWARD ME.
"NOW ***HOPELESS.***
AND THEN...
I SAW NOTHING.

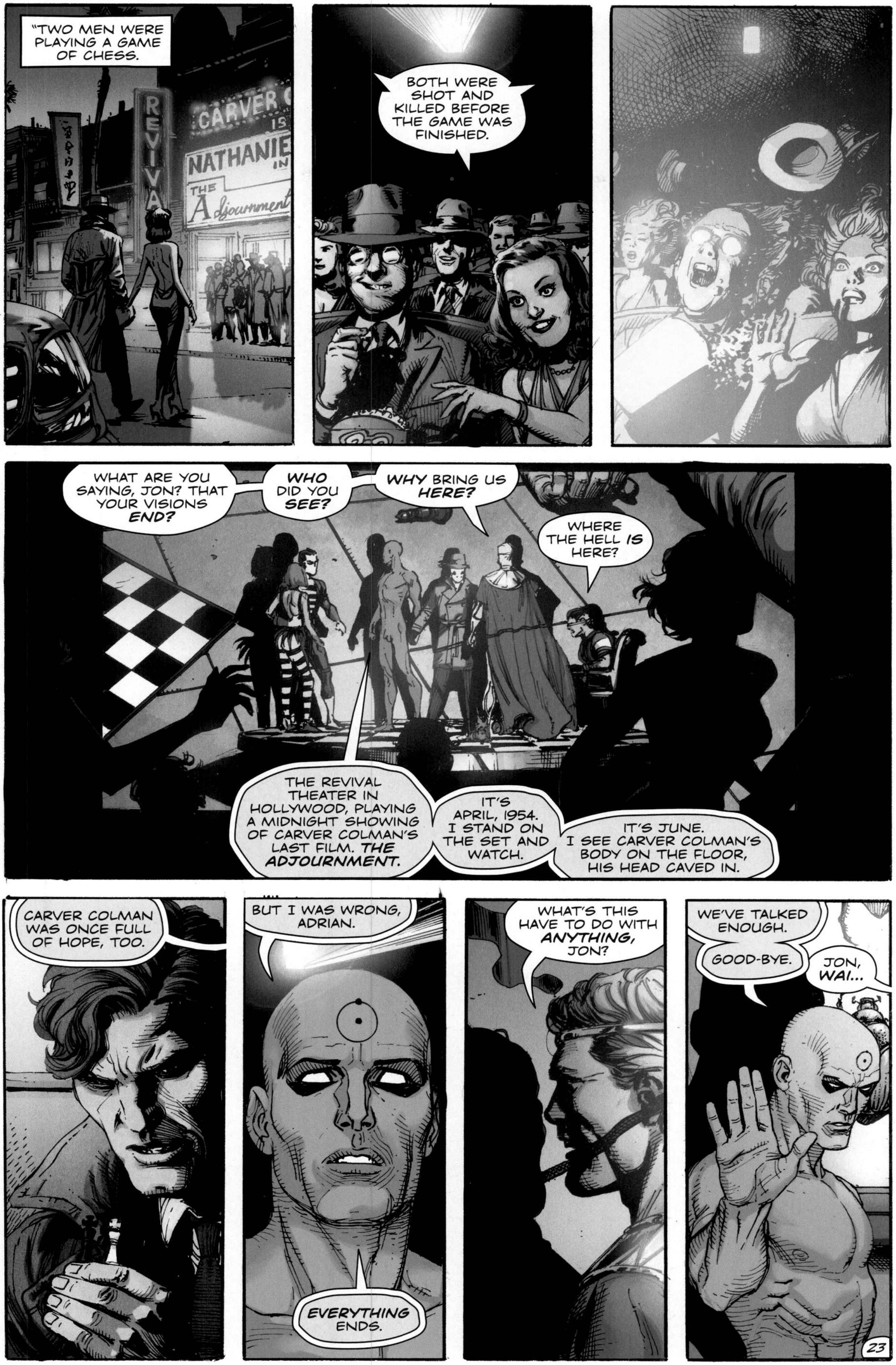
"TWO MEN WERE PLAYING A GAME OF CHESS.
REVIVAL
CARVER C
IS
NATHANIE
IN
THE Adjournment
BOTH WERE SHOT AND KILLED BEFORE THE GAME WAS FINISHED.
WHAT ARE YOU SAYING, JON? THAT YOUR VISIONS END?
WHO DID YOU SEE?
WHY BRING US HERE?
WHERE THE HELL IS HERE?
THE REVIVAL THEATER IN HOLLYWOOD, PLAYING A MIDNIGHT SHOWING OF CARVER COLMAN'S LAST FILM. THE ADJOURNMENT.
IT'S APRIL, 1954. I STAND ON THE SET AND WATCH.
IT'S JUNE. I SEE CARVER COLMAN'S BODY ON THE FLOOR, HIS HEAD CAVED IN.
CARVER COLMAN WAS ONCE FULL OF HOPE, TOO.
BUT I WAS WRONG, ADRIAN.
EVERYTHING ENDS.
WHAT'S THIS HAVE TO DO WITH ANYTHING, JON?
WE'VE TALKED ENOUGH.
GOOD-BYE.
JON, WAI...
23

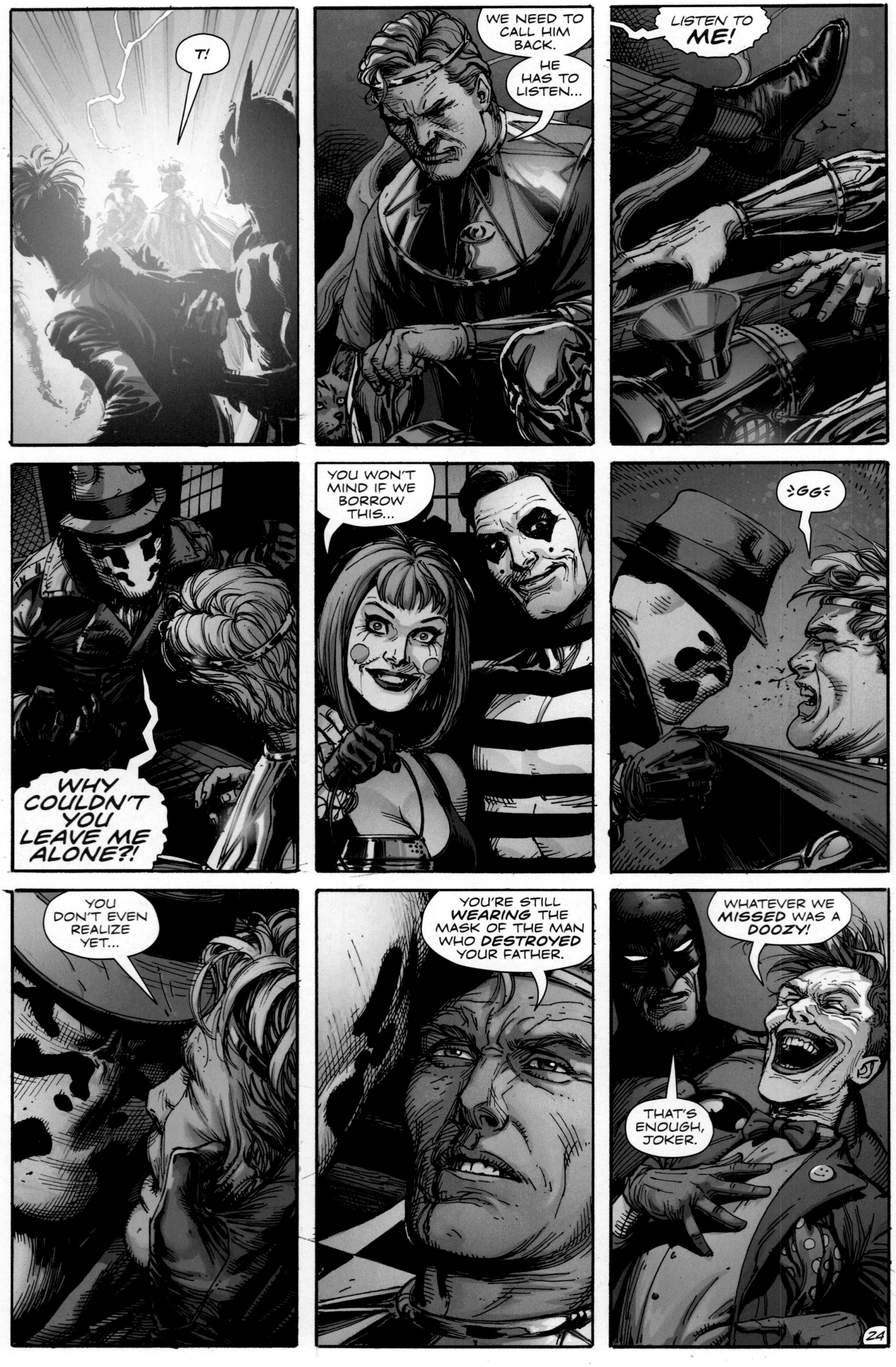
T!
WE NEED TO CALL HIM BACK.
HE HAS TO LISTEN...
LISTEN TO **ME!**
WHY COULDN'T YOU LEAVE ME ALONE?!
YOU WON'T MIND IF WE BORROW THIS...
GG
YOU DON'T EVEN REALIZE YET...
YOU'RE STILL **WEARING** THE MASK OF THE MAN WHO **DESTROYED** YOUR FATHER.
WHATEVER WE **MISSED** WAS A **DOOZY!**
THAT'S ENOUGH, JOKER.
24

HUSH NOW. DADDY'S SPEAKING!

I SHOULD HAVE DONE THIS MONTHS AGO.

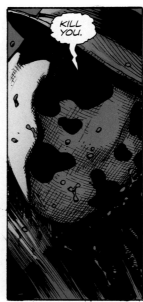

KILL YOU.

A LITTLE CONSTRUCTIVE CRITICISM, IF I MAY...

TOUCH...

DON'T TOUCH ME!

GET THE FREAK!

FORGET THE LANTERN, WE GOT BLAKE.

LET'S GO CELEBRATE, LOVER.

WE'RE HAVING A BABY.

HEH... HA HO... HEH...

DID YOU ENJOY IT AS MUH-MUCH AS I DUH-DID?

DEAD.

RORSCHACH IS DEAD.

25

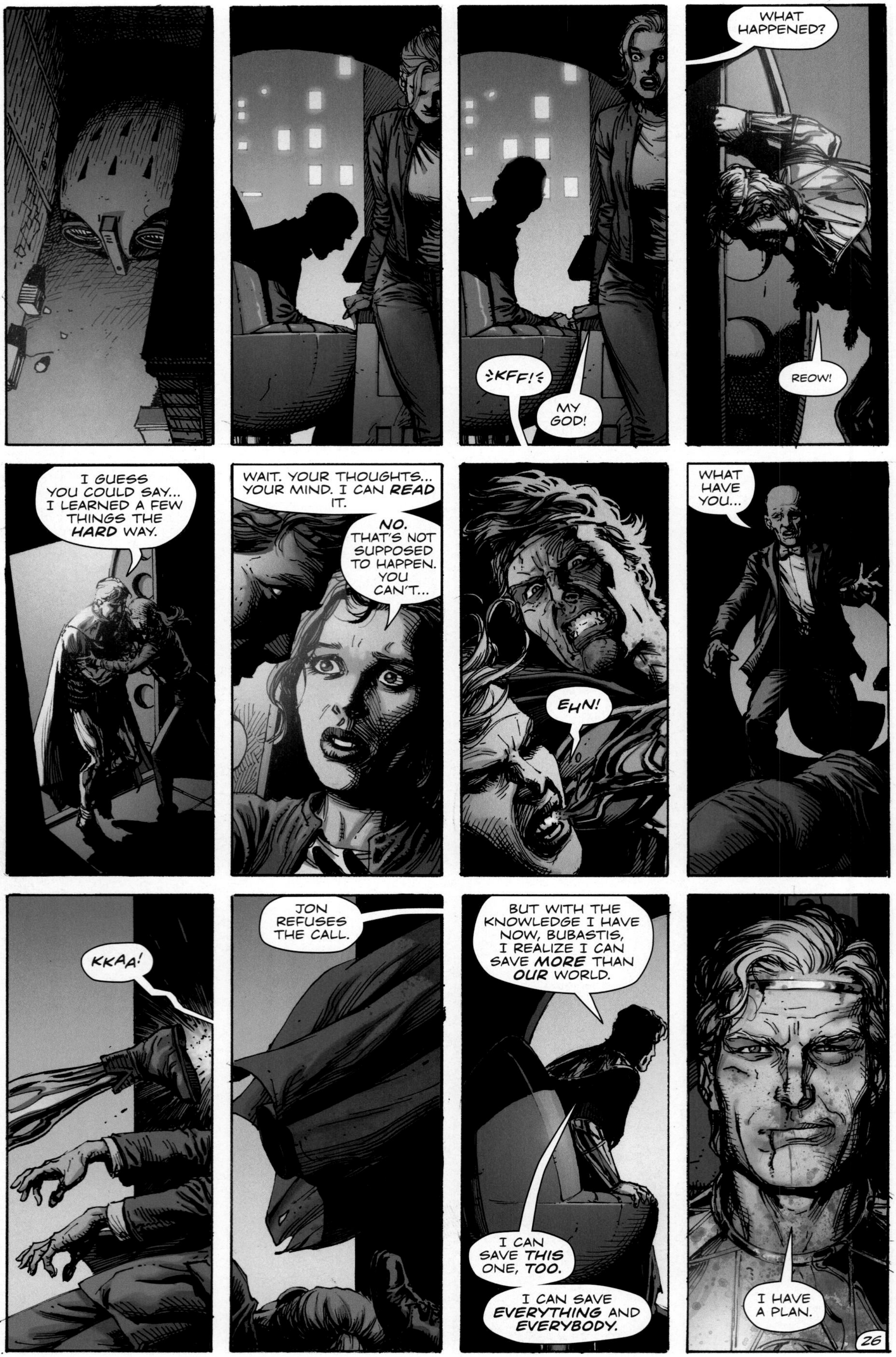

KFF!
MY GOD!
WHAT HAPPENED?
REOW!
I GUESS YOU COULD SAY... I LEARNED A FEW THINGS THE **HARD** WAY.
WAIT. YOUR THOUGHTS... YOUR MIND. I CAN **READ** IT.
NO. THAT'S NOT SUPPOSED TO HAPPEN. YOU CAN'T...
EHN!
WHAT HAVE YOU...
KKAA!
JON REFUSES THE CALL.
BUT WITH THE KNOWLEDGE I HAVE NOW, BUBASTIS, I REALIZE I CAN SAVE **MORE** THAN **OUR** WORLD.
I CAN SAVE **THIS** ONE, **TOO.**
I CAN SAVE **EVERYTHING** AND **EVERYBODY.**
I HAVE A PLAN.

"WHAT DO YOU SEE?"

I SEE BLACK ADAM! HE'S ENTERED JERUSALEM AND...

"JAKE, WE NEED TO TAKE COVER!

"THIS IS SERIOUS.

"WE'RE EXPOSED OUT HERE.

"WHAT'S THAT?

LOIS LANE
C/O THE DAILY PLANET
2525 BROADWAY
METROPOLIS, NY 10025

"SOMETHING'S CREEPING THROUGH THE DARKNESS.

"I THINK IT'S FOLLOWING US."

"HAHAHAHAHAHA!

"BEWARE THE CREEPER!"

"EEEYAAAAAA..."

"MARK? MARK, ARE YOU THERE?"

TWO MEN WERE PLAYING CHESS.

NONE CAME OUT ALIVE.

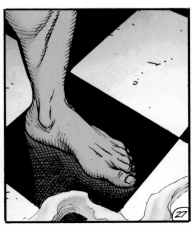

27

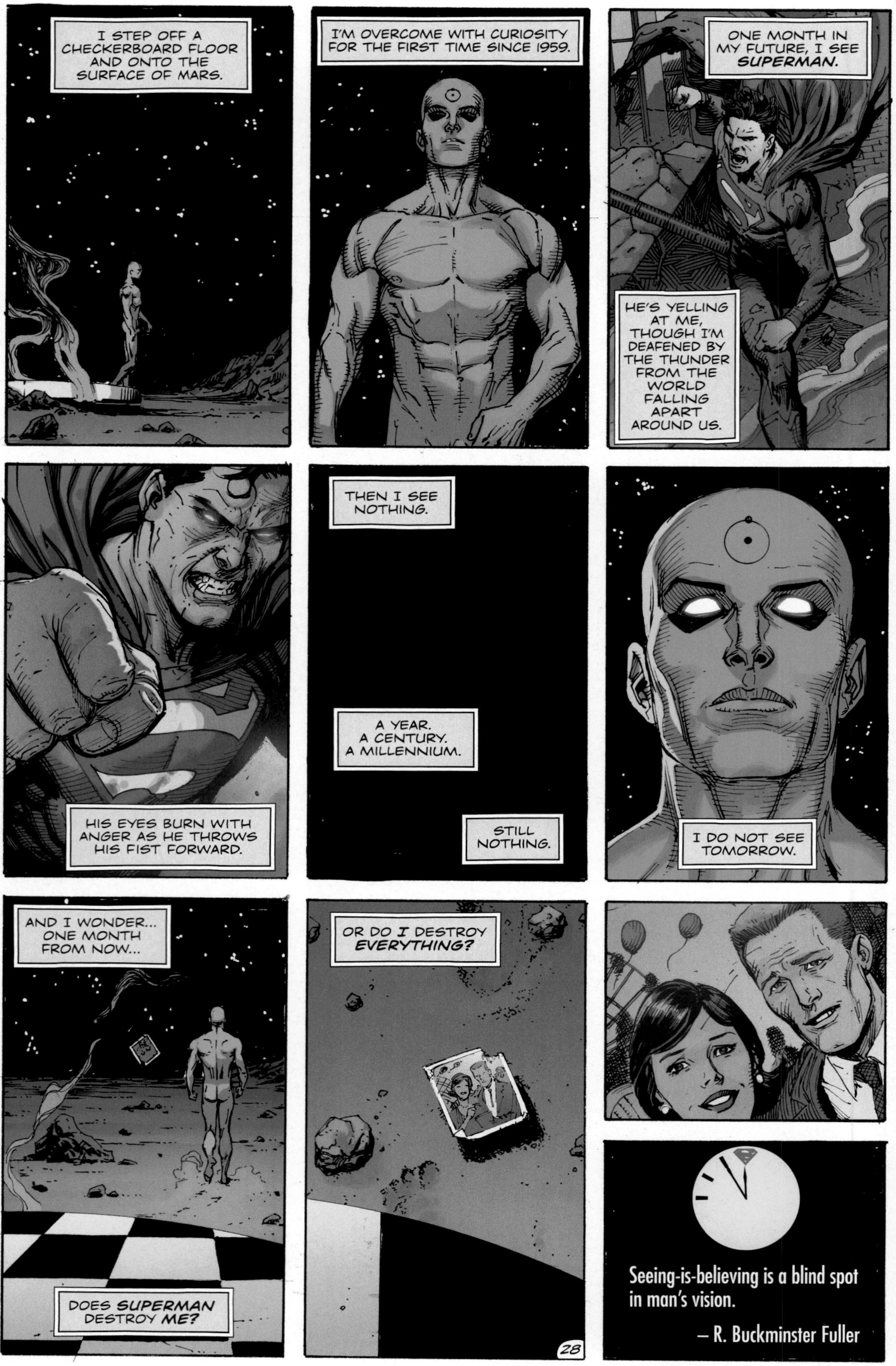
I STEP OFF A CHECKERBOARD FLOOR AND ONTO THE SURFACE OF MARS.
I'M OVERCOME WITH CURIOSITY FOR THE FIRST TIME SINCE 1959.
ONE MONTH IN MY FUTURE, I SEE *SUPERMAN.*
HE'S YELLING AT ME, THOUGH I'M DEAFENED BY THE THUNDER FROM THE WORLD FALLING APART AROUND US.
HIS EYES BURN WITH ANGER AS HE THROWS HIS FIST FORWARD.
THEN I SEE NOTHING.
A YEAR. A CENTURY. A MILLENNIUM.
STILL NOTHING.
I DO NOT SEE TOMORROW.
AND I WONDER... ONE MONTH FROM NOW...
DOES *SUPERMAN* DESTROY *ME?*
OR DO *I* DESTROY *EVERYTHING?*
28
Seeing-is-believing is a blind spot in man's vision.
– R. Buckminster Fuller

VEIDT

Adrian Veidt
President and C.E.O.

November 7, 1985

Kelley Popham
Vice President Public Relations and Communications

Dear Kelley,

As you have heard by now my loyal and dear friend Bubastis has died. I had theorized her unique genetics had left her vulnerable to the psychic backlash in Manhattan. After some investigation, I'm sorry to confirm she is indeed one of the victims of the New York Massacre. Gratefully, I do not believe she suffered in any way. However, to say I am devastated by her death would be an understatement. As the world mourns, I too mourn the only family I had.

In honor of Bubastis, Veidt Industries will put every resource it has into saving all endangered species. We will create groundbreaking sanctuaries throughout the world and fund unparalleled research in curing prevalent and painful diseases that affect them. I would also like to find an artist of rising importance to consign a statue of Bubastis; perhaps Jeff Koons as I have enjoyed his work greatly over years.

I have organized a meeting with my executive team to discuss the above. I w want press there. Before the meeting, I ask you to speak with our head of t Non-Profit Animal Services Division, Marti Kheel. I am sure you will be as impressed with her as I am.

ove to you and your family,

Adrian Veidt
rian Veidt

29

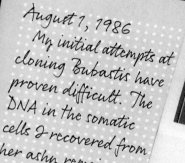

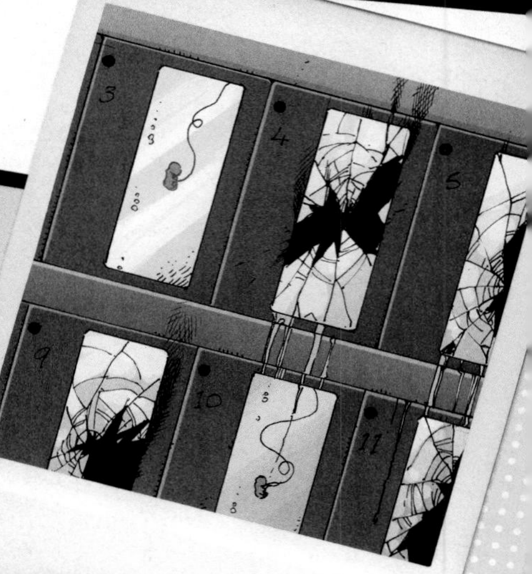

2

Satur
stud

9

August 7, 1986
My initial attempts at cloning Bubastis have proven difficult. The DNA in the somatic cells I recovered from her ashy remains had been unexpectedly altered by the intrinsic field subtractor that killed her. The first eggs to be "fertilized" grew quickly, but every fetus died at week 15.

October 4, 1986
I had forgotten the animated series featuring myself and Bubastis was due to premiere this morning. It is a silly cartoon, even sillier in the wake of last year, but it has made me nostalgic for my old friend.
I find myself once again attempting to re-create Bubastis. I have isolated the missing links in her DNA and will search for a compatible animal that might fill them. Although this will take time, I have hope that one day it will prove successful.

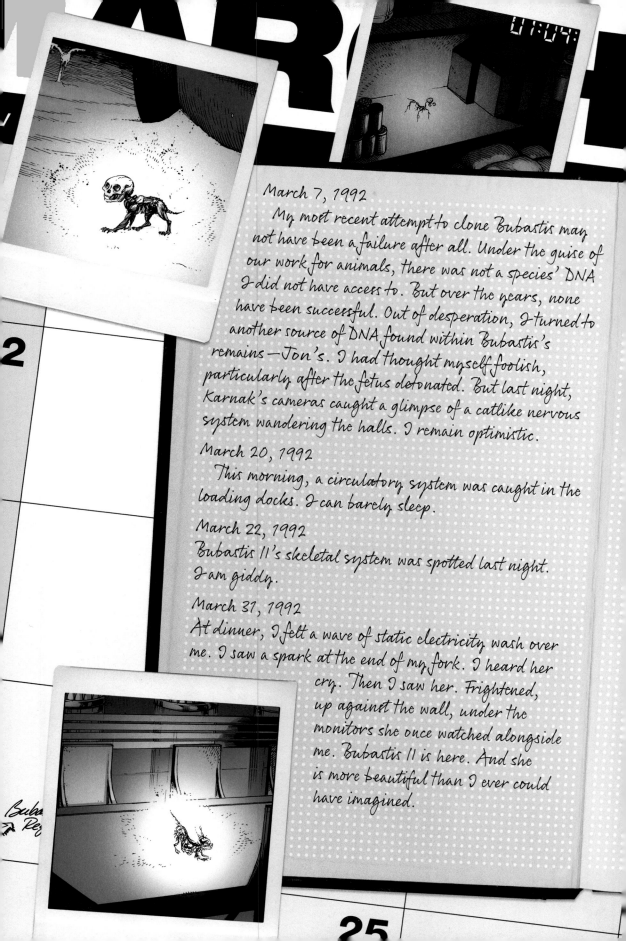

March 7, 1992

My most recent attempt to clone Bubastis may not have been a failure after all. Under the guise of our work for animals, there was not a species' DNA I did not have access to. But over the years, none have been successful. Out of desperation, I turned to another source of DNA found within Bubastis's remains — Jon's. I had thought myself foolish, particularly after the fetus detonated. But last night, Karnak's cameras caught a glimpse of a catlike nervous system wandering the halls. I remain optimistic.

March 20, 1992

This morning, a circulatory system was caught in the loading docks. I can barely sleep.

March 22, 1992

Bubastis II's skeletal system was spotted last night. I am giddy.

March 31, 1992

At dinner, I felt a wave of static electricity wash over me. I saw a spark at the end of my fork. I heard her cry. Then I saw her. Frightened, up against the wall, under the monitors she once watched alongside me. Bubastis II is here. And she is more beautiful than I ever could have imagined.

November 18, 1992

   The Owlship is now capable of locating and traveling to the universe Jon has retreated to, but once there finding him could prove difficult. Thankfully, I have Bubastis.

   Bubastis will function much like the tachyon particles I once used to blur Jon's temporal vision. She gives off a similar energy, though isolated. Jon will not be able to see her or things around her as clearly as the rest of the world. She is a living blind spot.

   Bubastis will also lead me to Jon. She will be able to track and collect the tachyon particles Jon himself leaves behind. And once she absorbs enough of them, Jon will be unable to ignore her. He will be drawn to her. To me.

Bubastis is going to help me save the world. And this time I will do anything so that she may live to see it.

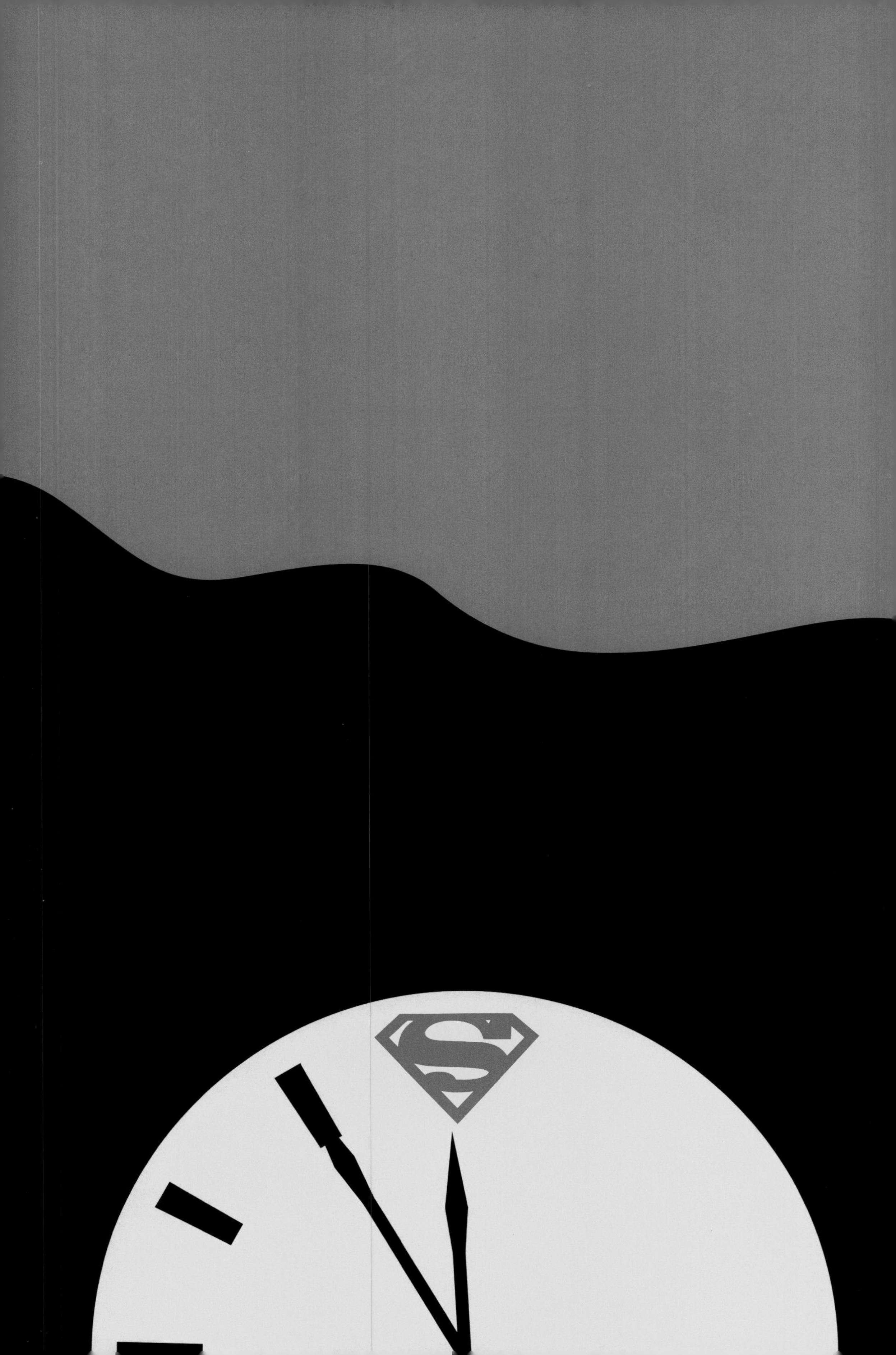

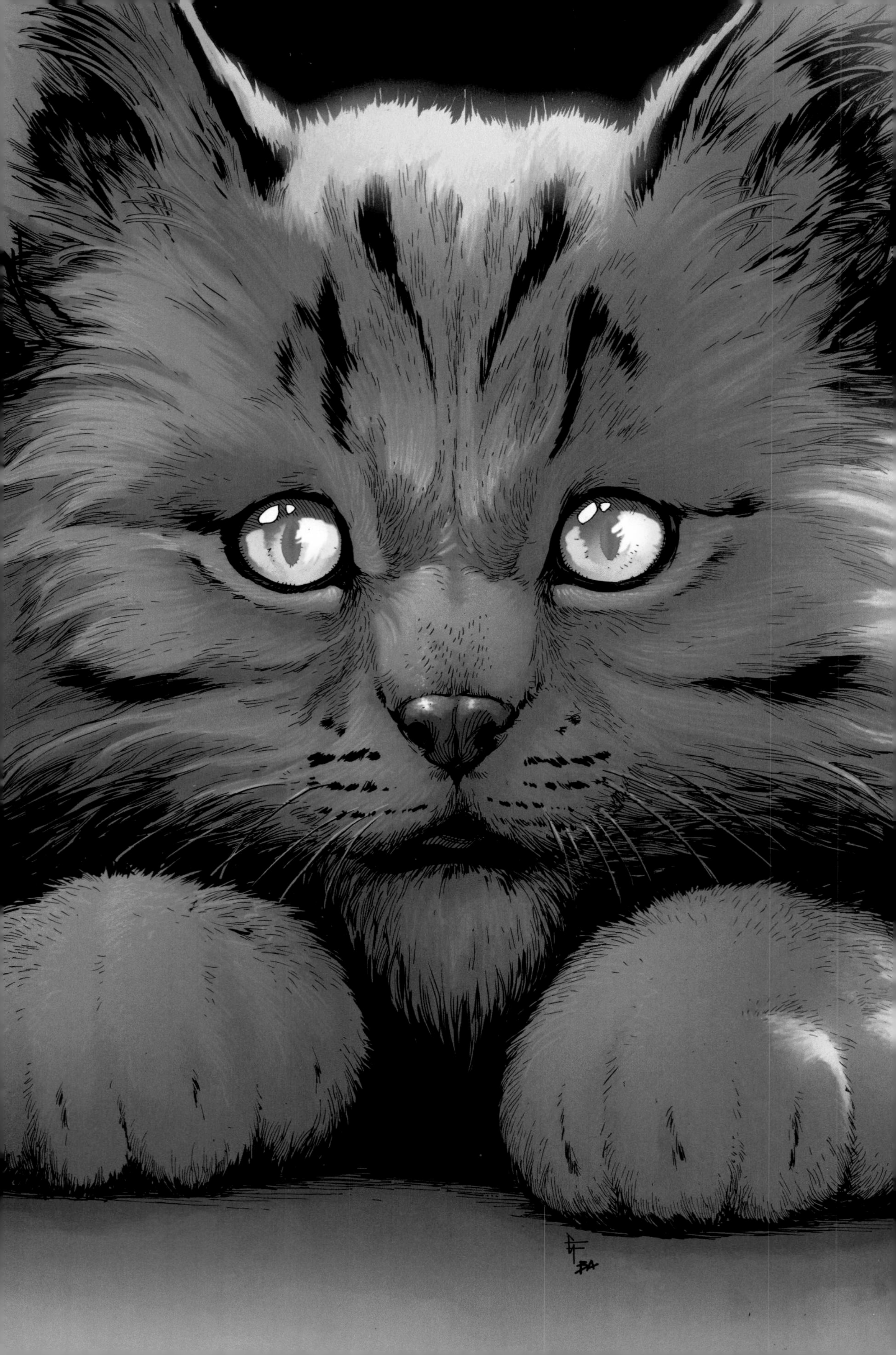

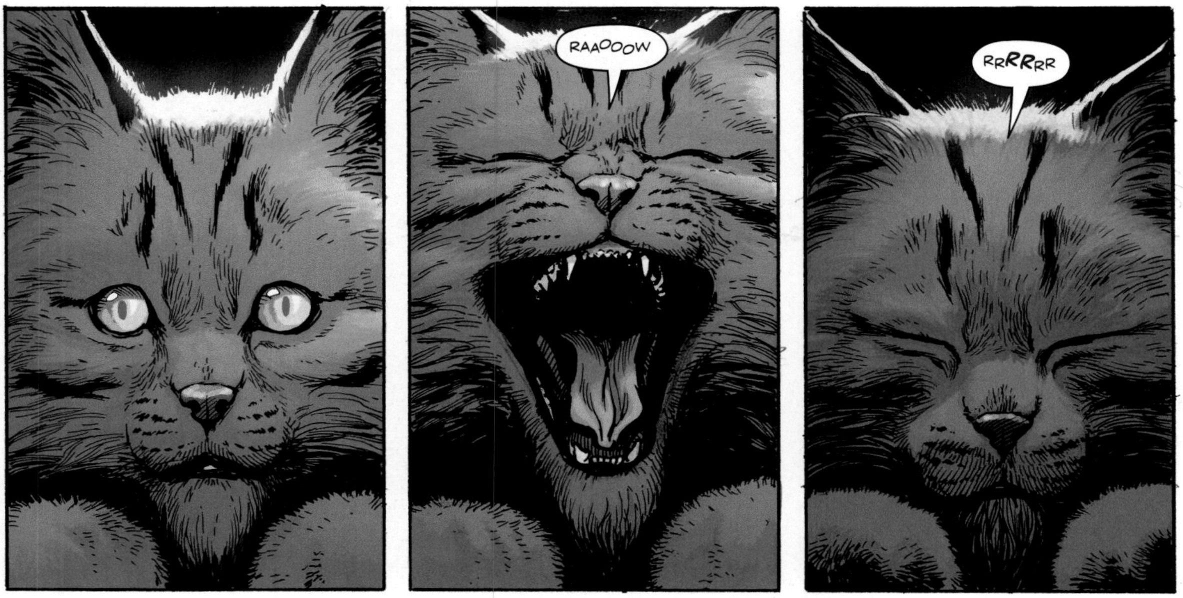
RAAOOOW
RRRRRR

SAVE HUMANITY

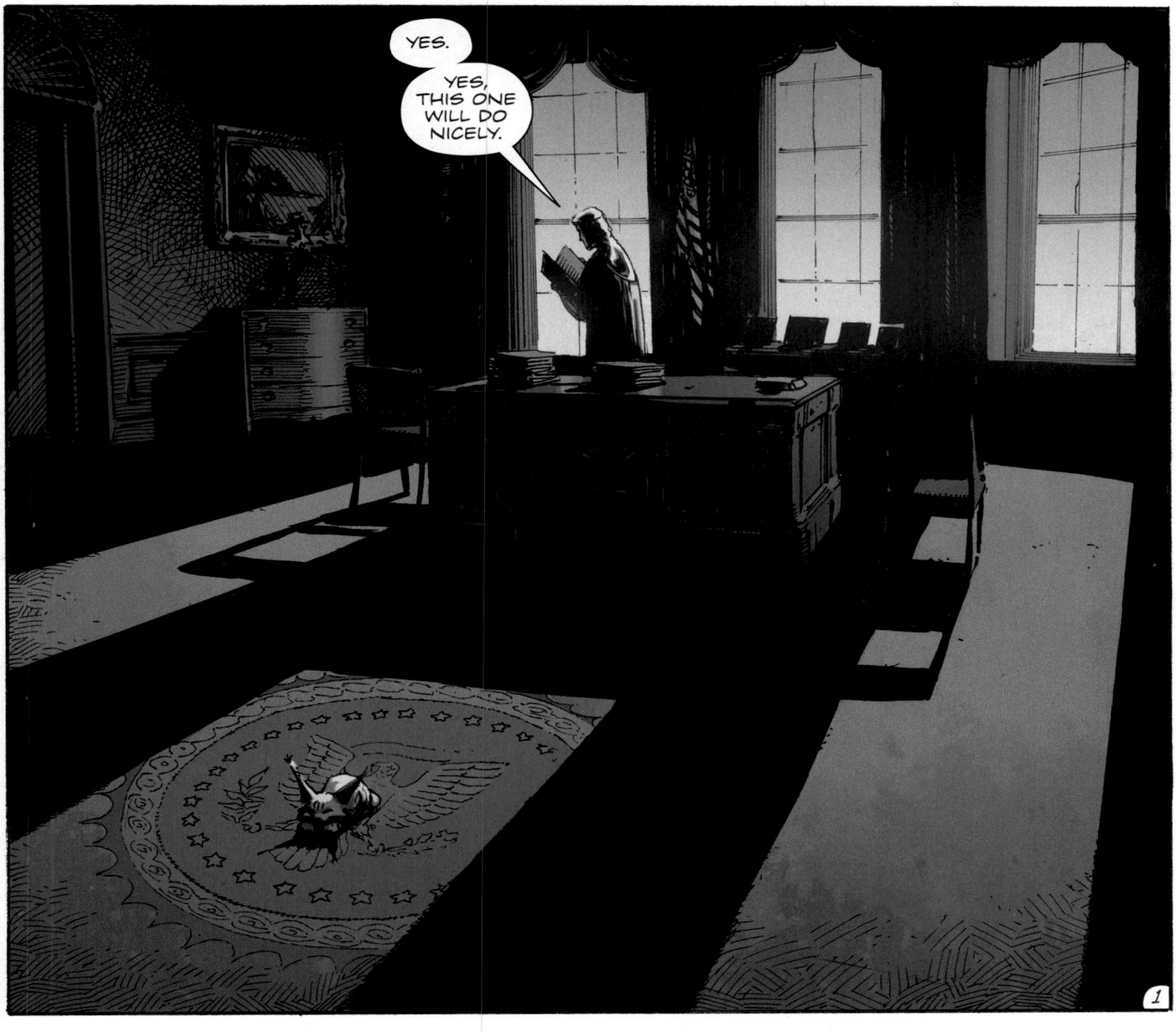
YES.
YES, THIS ONE WILL DO NICELY.

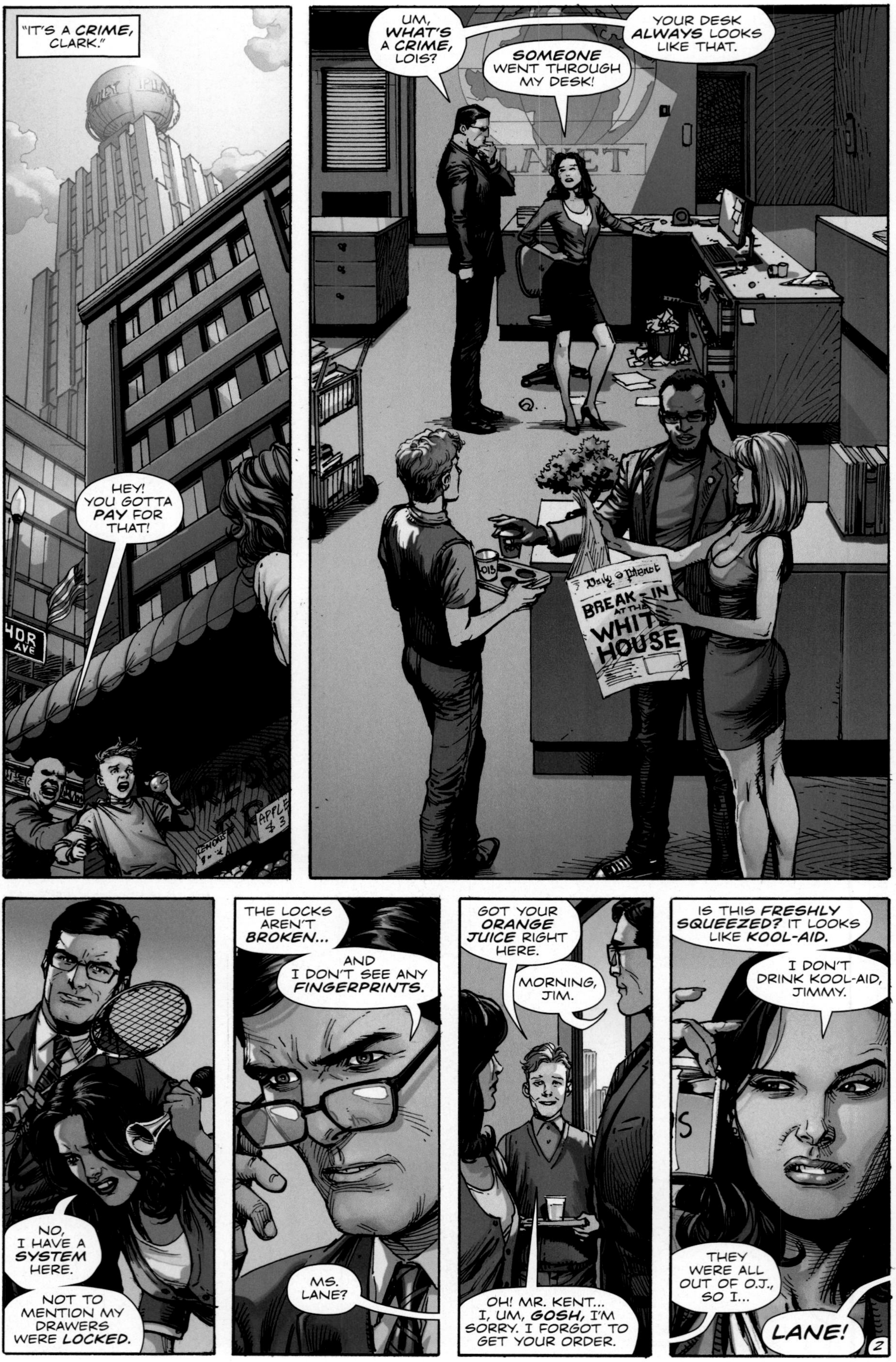
"IT'S A CRIME, CLARK."
HEY! YOU GOTTA PAY FOR THAT!
APPLE $3
UM, WHAT'S A CRIME, LOIS?
SOMEONE WENT THROUGH MY DESK!
YOUR DESK ALWAYS LOOKS LIKE THAT.
Daily Planet
BREAK-IN AT THE WHITE HOUSE
NO, I HAVE A SYSTEM HERE.
NOT TO MENTION MY DRAWERS WERE LOCKED.
THE LOCKS AREN'T BROKEN...
AND I DON'T SEE ANY FINGERPRINTS.
MS. LANE?
GOT YOUR ORANGE JUICE RIGHT HERE.
MORNING, JIM.
OH! MR. KENT... I, UM, GOSH, I'M SORRY. I FORGOT TO GET YOUR ORDER.
IS THIS FRESHLY SQUEEZED? IT LOOKS LIKE KOOL-AID.
I DON'T DRINK KOOL-AID, JIMMY.
THEY WERE ALL OUT OF O.J., SO I...
LANE!

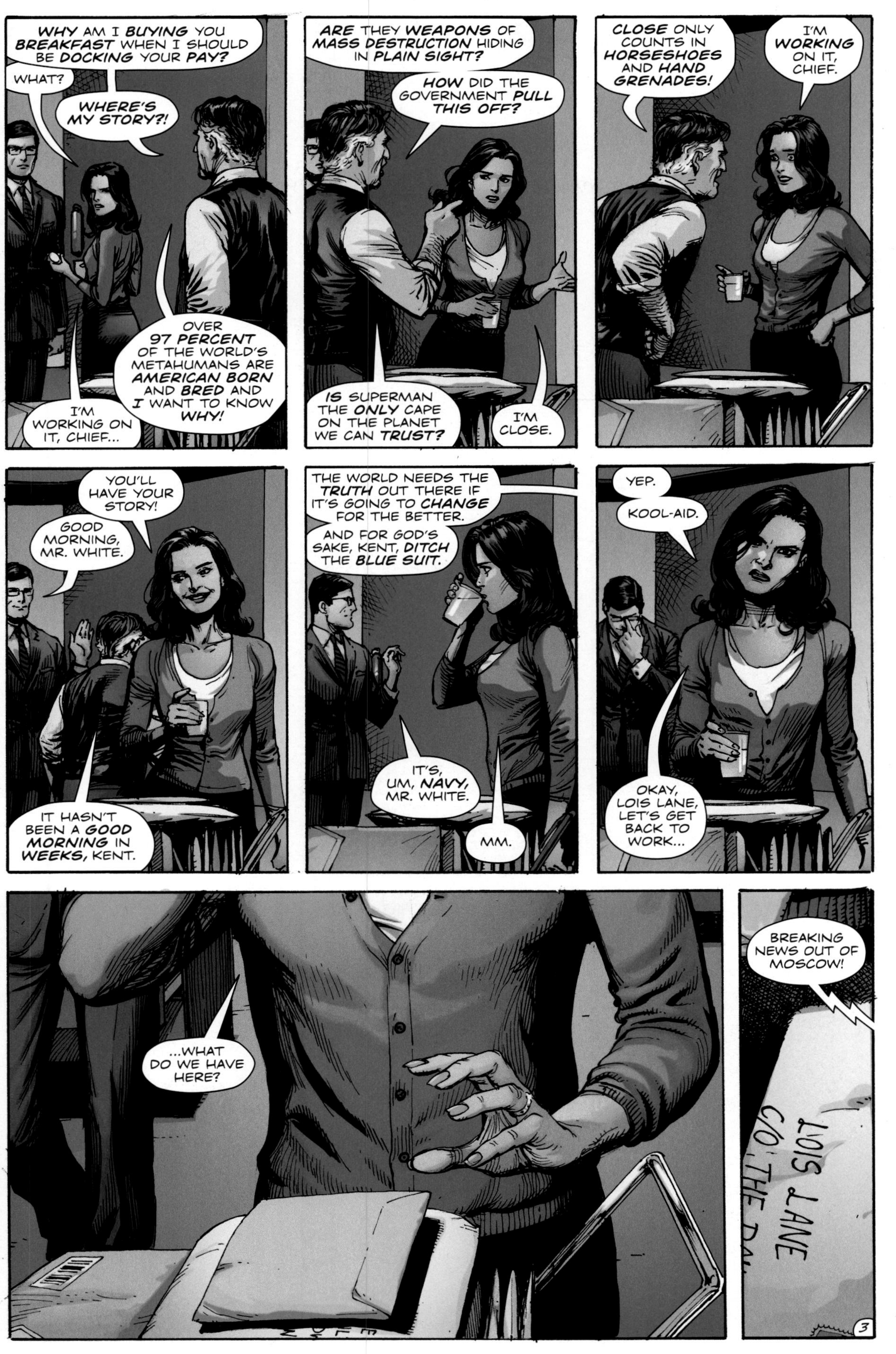
WHY AM I BUYING YOU BREAKFAST WHEN I SHOULD BE DOCKING YOUR PAY?
WHAT?
WHERE'S MY STORY?!
I'M WORKING ON IT, CHIEF...
OVER 97 PERCENT OF THE WORLD'S METAHUMANS ARE AMERICAN BORN AND BRED AND I WANT TO KNOW WHY!
ARE THEY WEAPONS OF MASS DESTRUCTION HIDING IN PLAIN SIGHT?
HOW DID THE GOVERNMENT PULL THIS OFF?
IS SUPERMAN THE ONLY CAPE ON THE PLANET WE CAN TRUST?
I'M CLOSE.
CLOSE ONLY COUNTS IN HORSESHOES AND HAND GRENADES!
I'M WORKING ON IT, CHIEF.
YOU'LL HAVE YOUR STORY!
GOOD MORNING, MR. WHITE.
IT HASN'T BEEN A GOOD MORNING IN WEEKS, KENT.
THE WORLD NEEDS THE TRUTH OUT THERE IF IT'S GOING TO CHANGE FOR THE BETTER.
AND FOR GOD'S SAKE, KENT, DITCH THE BLUE SUIT.
IT'S, UM, NAVY, MR. WHITE.
MM.
YEP.
KOOL-AID.
OKAY, LOIS LANE, LET'S GET BACK TO WORK...
...WHAT DO WE HAVE HERE?
BREAKING NEWS OUT OF MOSCOW!
LOIS LANE
C/O THE

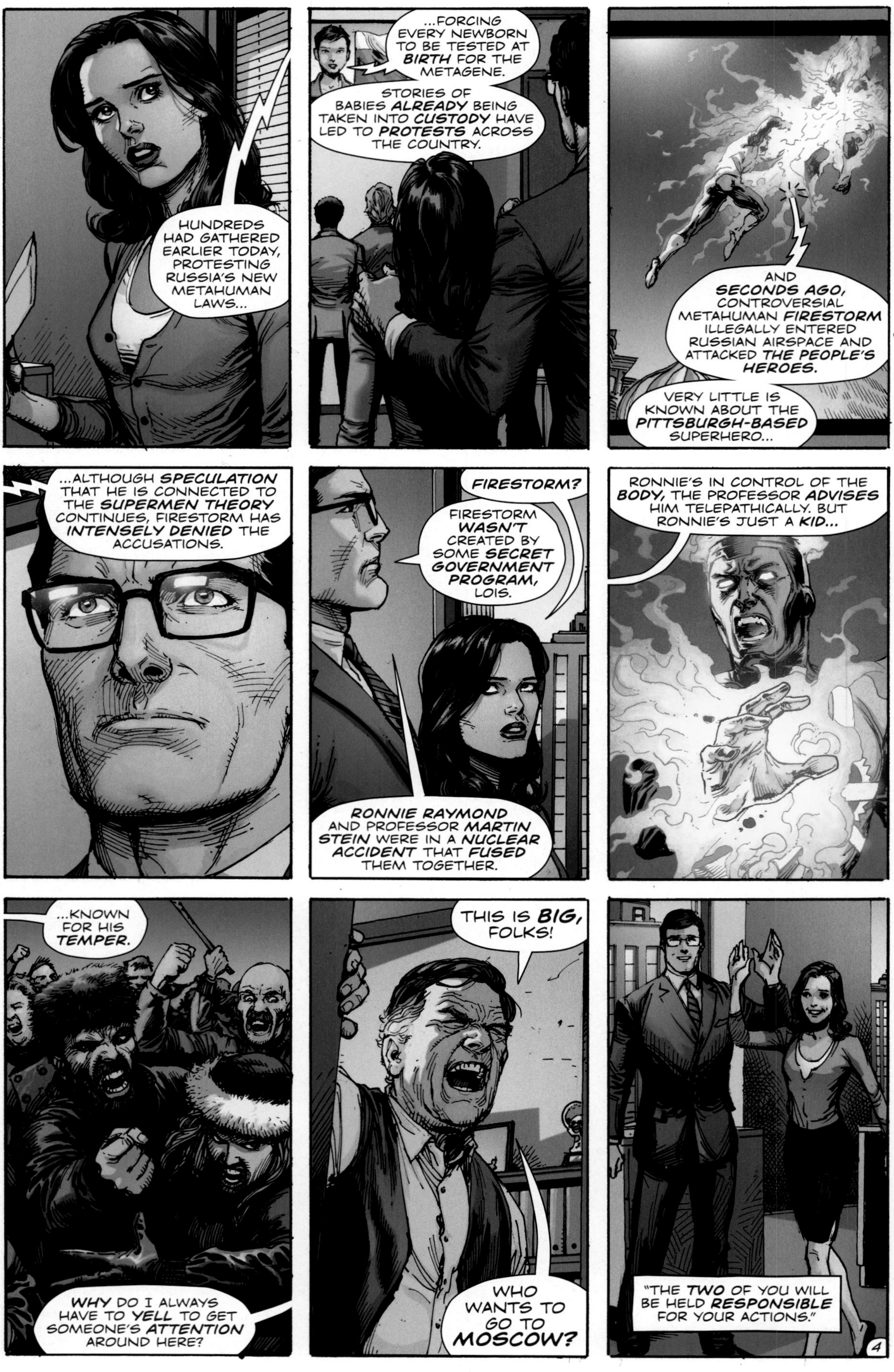
HUNDREDS HAD GATHERED EARLIER TODAY, PROTESTING RUSSIA'S NEW METAHUMAN LAWS...
...FORCING EVERY NEWBORN TO BE TESTED AT BIRTH FOR THE METAGENE.
STORIES OF BABIES ALREADY BEING TAKEN INTO CUSTODY HAVE LED TO PROTESTS ACROSS THE COUNTRY.
AND SECONDS AGO, CONTROVERSIAL METAHUMAN FIRESTORM ILLEGALLY ENTERED RUSSIAN AIRSPACE AND ATTACKED THE PEOPLE'S HEROES.
VERY LITTLE IS KNOWN ABOUT THE PITTSBURGH-BASED SUPERHERO...
...ALTHOUGH SPECULATION THAT HE IS CONNECTED TO THE SUPERMEN THEORY CONTINUES, FIRESTORM HAS INTENSELY DENIED THE ACCUSATIONS.
FIRESTORM?
FIRESTORM WASN'T CREATED BY SOME SECRET GOVERNMENT PROGRAM, LOIS.
RONNIE RAYMOND AND PROFESSOR MARTIN STEIN WERE IN A NUCLEAR ACCIDENT THAT FUSED THEM TOGETHER.
RONNIE'S IN CONTROL OF THE BODY, THE PROFESSOR ADVISES HIM TELEPATHICALLY. BUT RONNIE'S JUST A KID...
...KNOWN FOR HIS TEMPER.
WHY DO I ALWAYS HAVE TO YELL TO GET SOMEONE'S ATTENTION AROUND HERE?
THIS IS BIG, FOLKS!
WHO WANTS TO GO TO MOSCOW?
"THE TWO OF YOU WILL BE HELD RESPONSIBLE FOR YOUR ACTIONS."
4

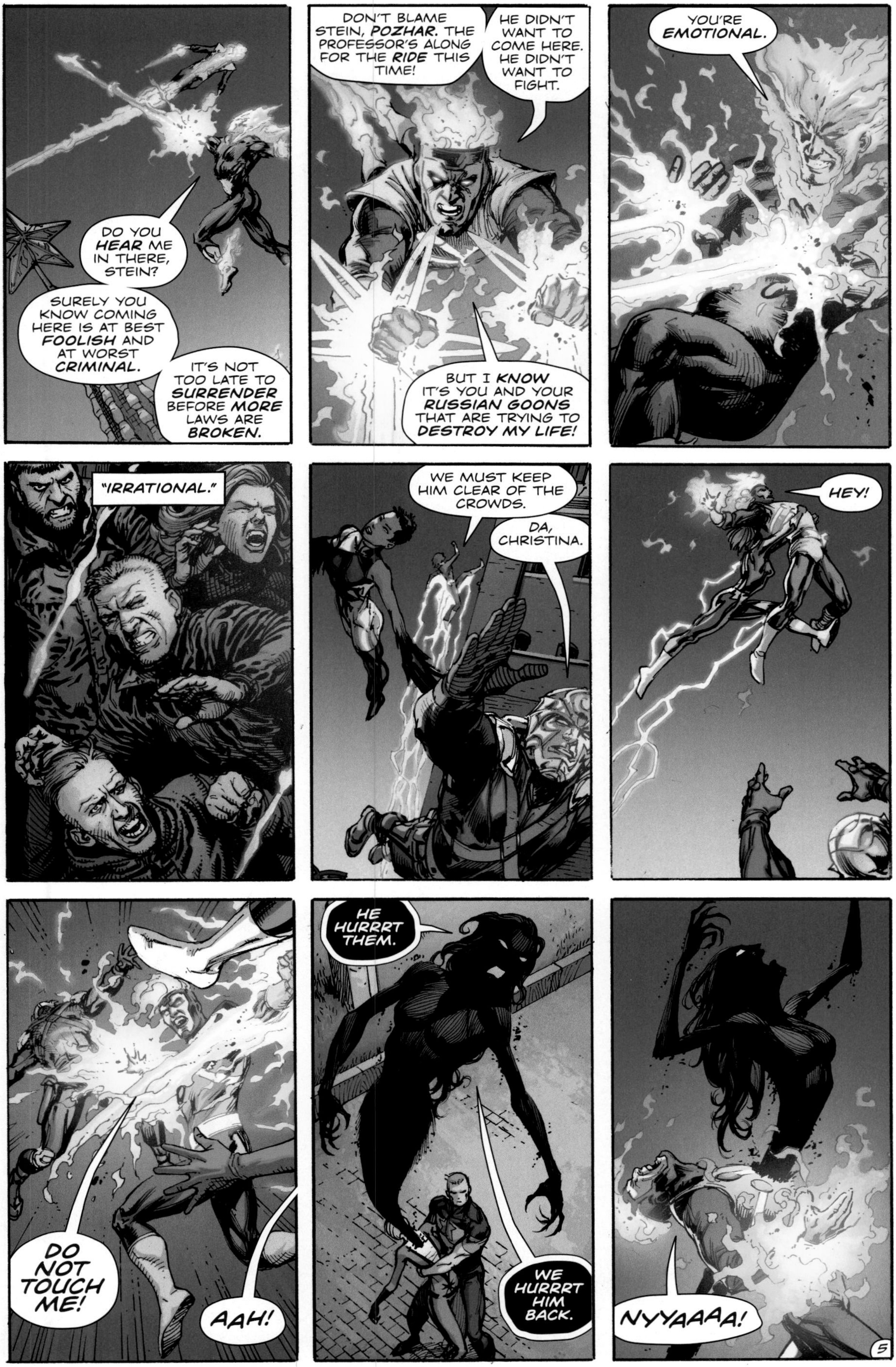
DO YOU HEAR ME IN THERE, STEIN?
SURELY YOU KNOW COMING HERE IS AT BEST FOOLISH AND AT WORST CRIMINAL.
IT'S NOT TOO LATE TO SURRENDER BEFORE MORE LAWS ARE BROKEN.
DON'T BLAME STEIN, POZHAR. THE PROFESSOR'S ALONG FOR THE RIDE THIS TIME!
HE DIDN'T WANT TO COME HERE. HE DIDN'T WANT TO FIGHT.
BUT I KNOW IT'S YOU AND YOUR RUSSIAN GOONS THAT ARE TRYING TO DESTROY MY LIFE!
YOU'RE EMOTIONAL.
"IRRATIONAL."
WE MUST KEEP HIM CLEAR OF THE CROWDS.
DA, CHRISTINA.
HEY!
DO NOT TOUCH ME!
AAH!
HE HURRRT THEM.
WE HURRRT HIM BACK.
NYYAAAA!

PRUH-PROFESSOR?! I CUH-CAN'T HEAR YOU!

PLEASE, ANSWER ME!

I NUH... NEED YOU...

YOU'RE SO QUIET, BUT...

GET BACK ON MY FEET, YEAH. BACK IN THE SKY, I...I'M TRYING. THE FIRE'S OUT, BUT I...

NO! LET GO!

LET GO OF ME!

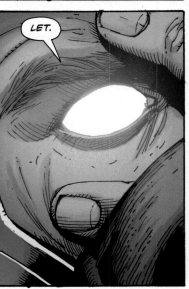

LET.

GO.

6

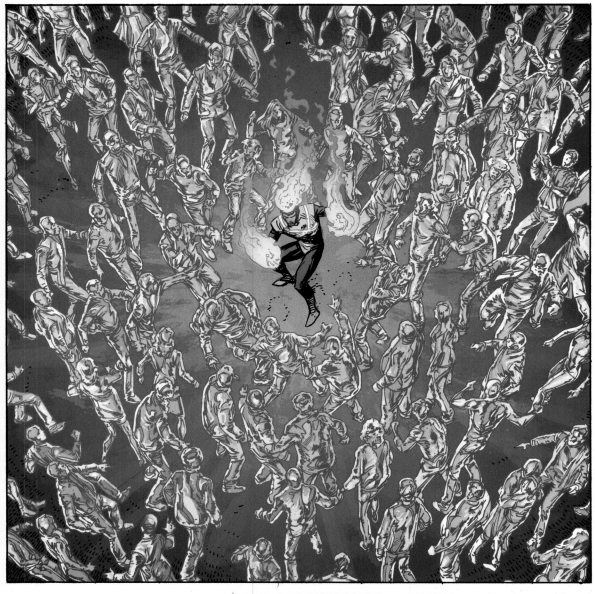

PROFESSOR...

OH MY GOD. I...I DIDN'T MEAN TO...

WHAT DID I DO?

DID HE... DID HE **KILL** ALL THOSE PEOPLE?

WHERE'S HE **GOING?**

PRIME MINISTER MEDVEDEV IS CALLING THIS A **CALCULATED TERRORIST ATTACK** CARRIED OUT BY ONE OF THE **UNITED STATES'** MOST **DANGEROUS METAHUMAN** AGENTS...

ROM MOSCOW

IT CAN'T BE WHAT IT LOOKS LIKE.

CAN IT, CLARK?

CLARK?

THE WHITE HOUSE IS **ALREADY** DENYING **ANY** RELATIONSHIP EXISTS BETWEEN FIRESTORM AND THE DEPARTMENT OF METAHUMAN AFFAIRS.

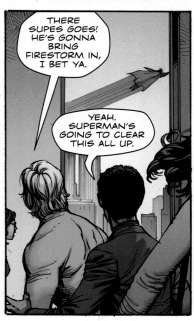

THERE SUPES GOES! HE'S GONNA BRING FIRESTORM IN, I BET YA.

YEAH. SUPERMAN'S GOING TO CLEAR THIS ALL UP.

"AND EVERYTHING WILL BE OKAY."

8

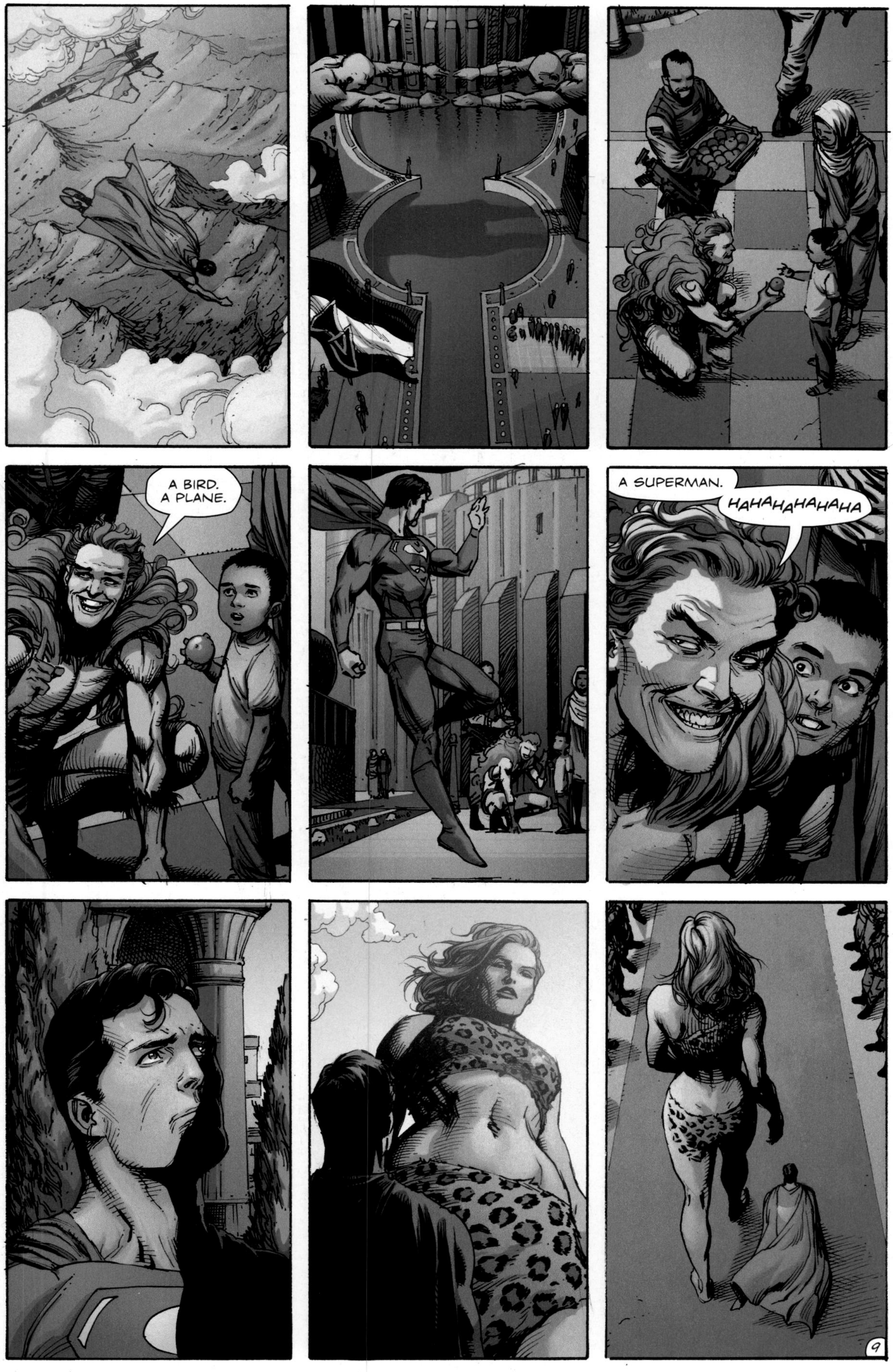
A BIRD.
A PLANE.
A SUPERMAN.
HAHAHAHAHAHAHA

HELLO, SUPERMAN.

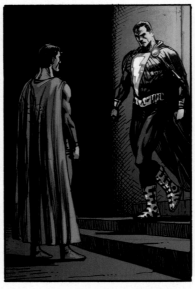

WELCOME TO KAHNDAQ.

10

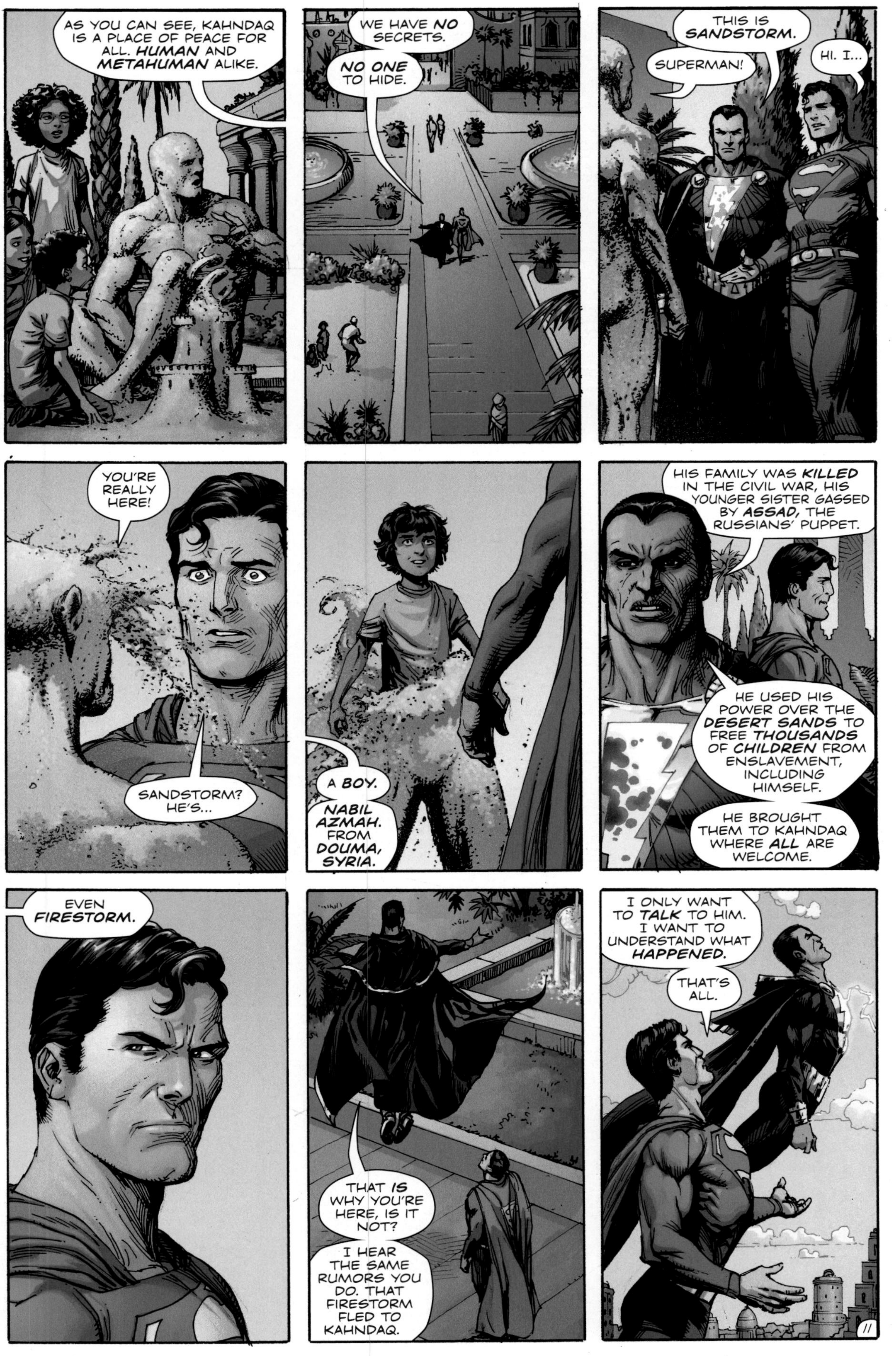
AS YOU CAN SEE, KAHNDAQ IS A PLACE OF PEACE FOR ALL. HUMAN AND METAHUMAN ALIKE.
WE HAVE NO SECRETS.
NO ONE TO HIDE.
THIS IS SANDSTORM.
SUPERMAN!
HI. I...
YOU'RE REALLY HERE!
SANDSTORM? HE'S...
A BOY.
NABIL AZMAH. FROM DOUMA, SYRIA.
HIS FAMILY WAS KILLED IN THE CIVIL WAR, HIS YOUNGER SISTER GASSED BY ASSAD, THE RUSSIANS' PUPPET.
HE USED HIS POWER OVER THE DESERT SANDS TO FREE THOUSANDS OF CHILDREN FROM ENSLAVEMENT, INCLUDING HIMSELF.
HE BROUGHT THEM TO KAHNDAQ WHERE ALL ARE WELCOME.
EVEN FIRESTORM.
THAT IS WHY YOU'RE HERE, IS IT NOT?
I HEAR THE SAME RUMORS YOU DO. THAT FIRESTORM FLED TO KAHNDAQ.
I ONLY WANT TO TALK TO HIM. I WANT TO UNDERSTAND WHAT HAPPENED.
THAT'S ALL.
11

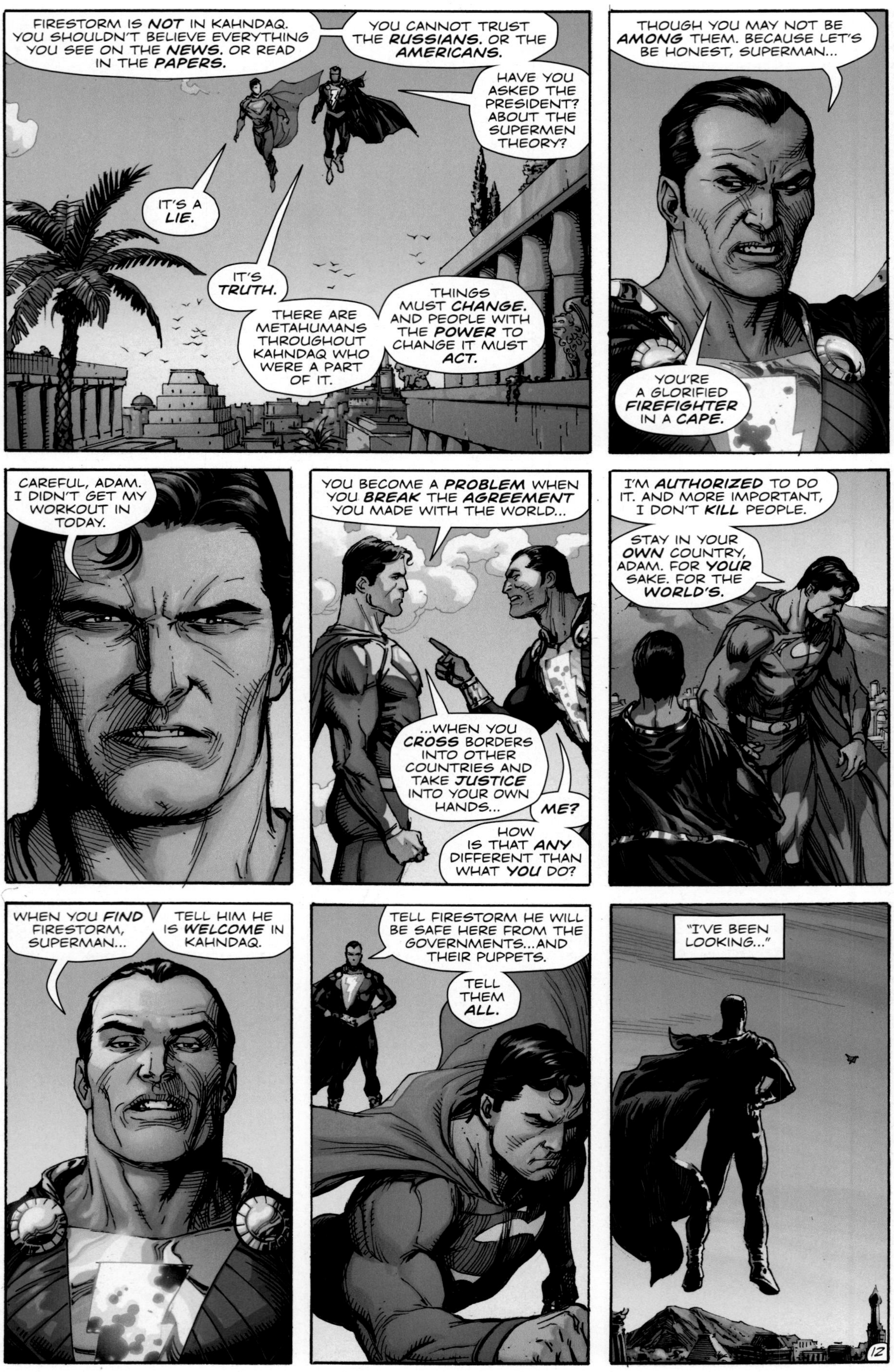
FIRESTORM IS NOT IN KAHNDAQ. YOU SHOULDN'T BELIEVE EVERYTHING YOU SEE ON THE NEWS. OR READ IN THE PAPERS.
YOU CANNOT TRUST THE RUSSIANS. OR THE AMERICANS.
HAVE YOU ASKED THE PRESIDENT? ABOUT THE SUPERMEN THEORY?
IT'S A LIE.
IT'S TRUTH.
THERE ARE METAHUMANS THROUGHOUT KAHNDAQ WHO WERE A PART OF IT.
THINGS MUST CHANGE. AND PEOPLE WITH THE POWER TO CHANGE IT MUST ACT.
THOUGH YOU MAY NOT BE AMONG THEM. BECAUSE LET'S BE HONEST, SUPERMAN...
YOU'RE A GLORIFIED FIREFIGHTER IN A CAPE.
CAREFUL, ADAM. I DIDN'T GET MY WORKOUT IN TODAY.
YOU BECOME A PROBLEM WHEN YOU BREAK THE AGREEMENT YOU MADE WITH THE WORLD...
...WHEN YOU CROSS BORDERS INTO OTHER COUNTRIES AND TAKE JUSTICE INTO YOUR OWN HANDS...
ME?
HOW IS THAT ANY DIFFERENT THAN WHAT YOU DO?
I'M AUTHORIZED TO DO IT. AND MORE IMPORTANT, I DON'T KILL PEOPLE.
STAY IN YOUR OWN COUNTRY, ADAM. FOR YOUR SAKE. FOR THE WORLD'S.
WHEN YOU FIND FIRESTORM, SUPERMAN...
TELL HIM HE IS WELCOME IN KAHNDAQ.
TELL FIRESTORM HE WILL BE SAFE HERE FROM THE GOVERNMENTS...AND THEIR PUPPETS.
TELL THEM ALL.
"I'VE BEEN LOOKING..."

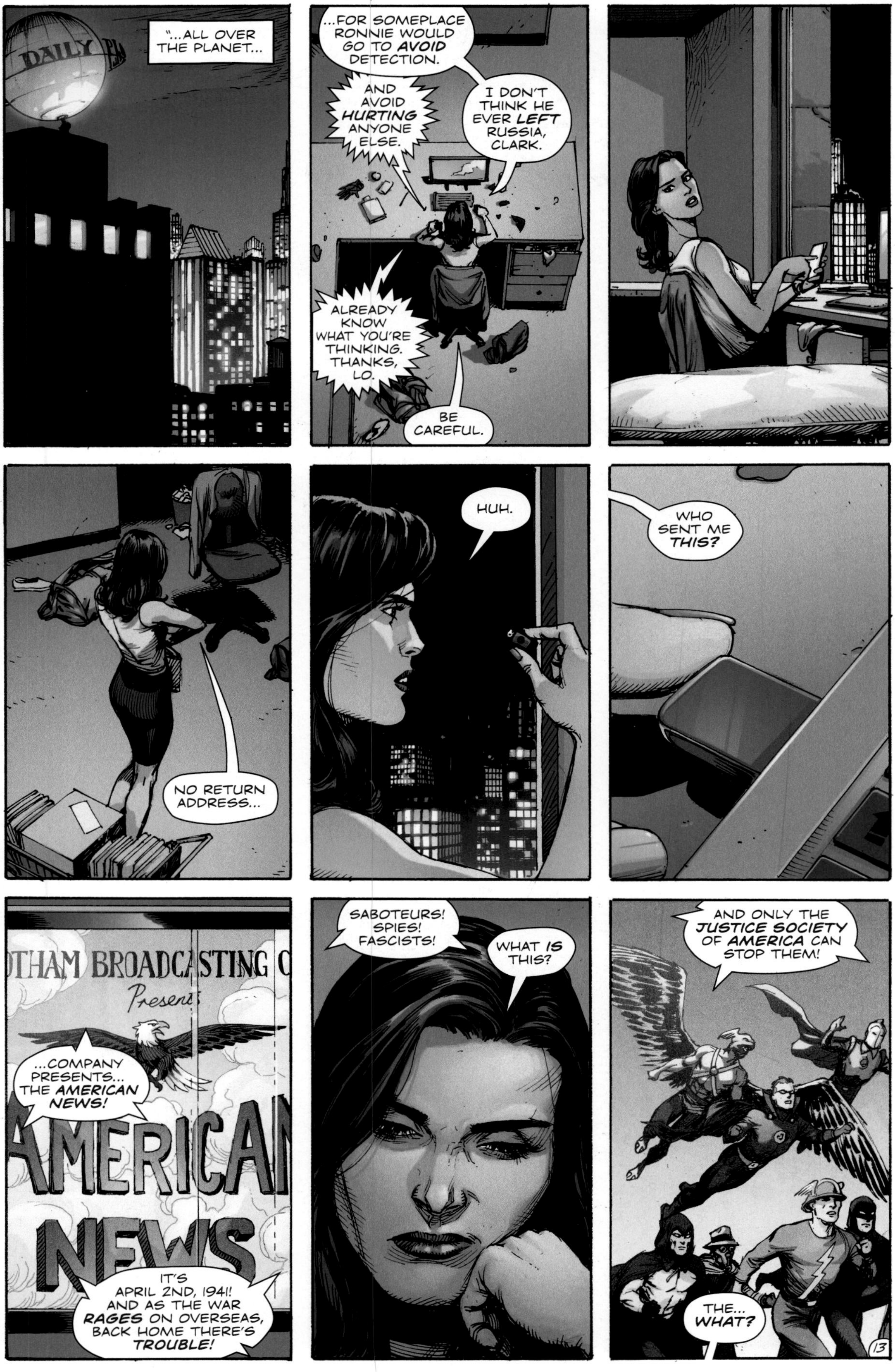
"...ALL OVER THE PLANET...
DAILY
...FOR SOMEPLACE RONNIE WOULD GO TO AVOID DETECTION.
AND AVOID HURTING ANYONE ELSE.
I DON'T THINK HE EVER LEFT RUSSIA, CLARK.
ALREADY KNOW WHAT YOU'RE THINKING. THANKS, LO.
BE CAREFUL.
NO RETURN ADDRESS...
HUH.
WHO SENT ME THIS?
OTHAM BROADCASTING C
Presents
...COMPANY PRESENTS... THE AMERICAN NEWS!
AMERICAN
NEWS
IT'S APRIL 2ND, 1941! AND AS THE WAR RAGES ON OVERSEAS, BACK HOME THERE'S TROUBLE!
SABOTEURS! SPIES! FASCISTS!
WHAT IS THIS?
AND ONLY THE JUSTICE SOCIETY OF AMERICA CAN STOP THEM!
THE... WHAT?

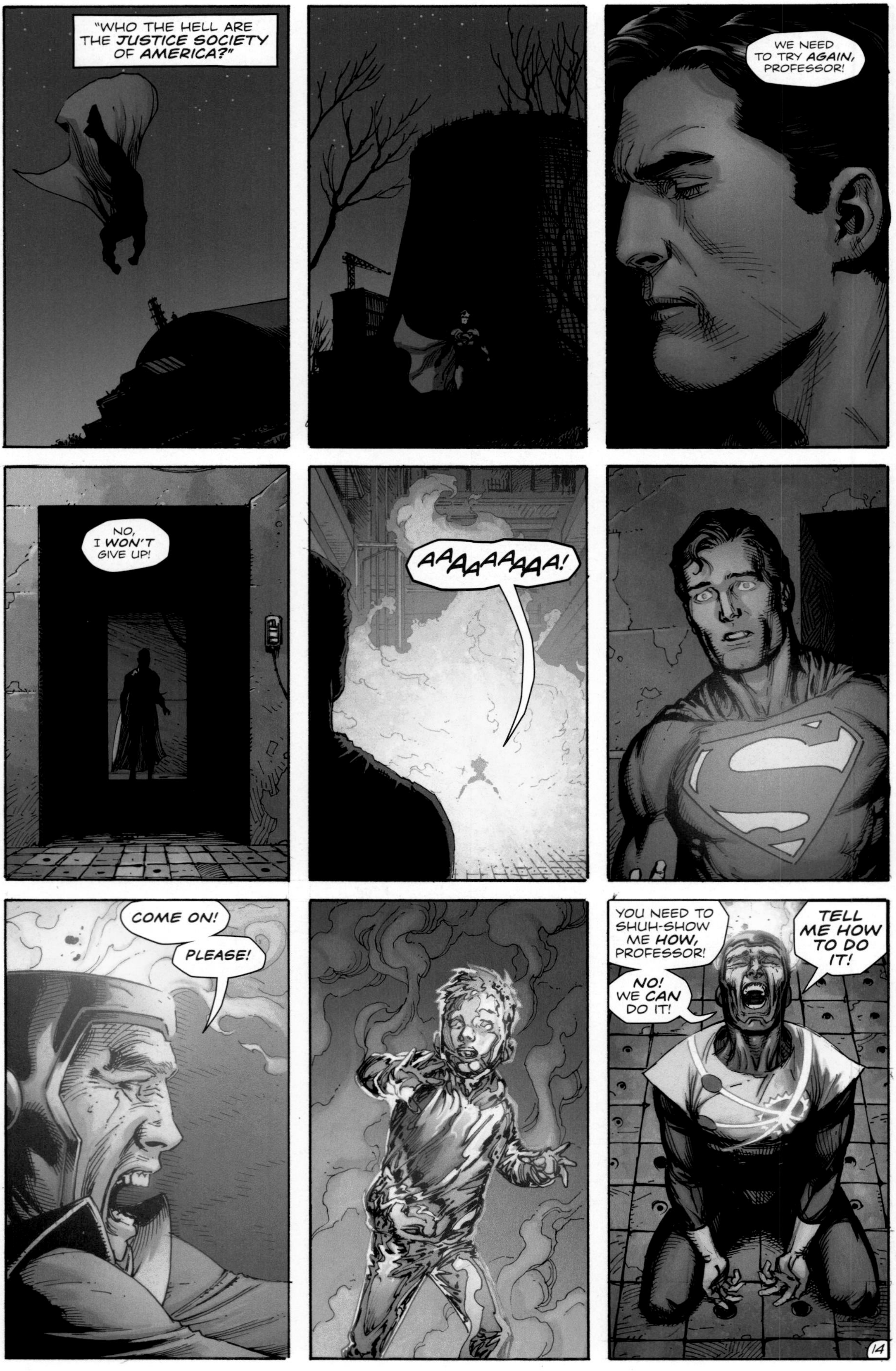
"WHO THE HELL ARE THE JUSTICE SOCIETY OF AMERICA?"
WE NEED TO TRY AGAIN, PROFESSOR!
NO, I WON'T GIVE UP!
AAAAAAAAA!
COME ON!
PLEASE!
YOU NEED TO SHUH-SHOW ME HOW, PROFESSOR!
TELL ME HOW TO DO IT!
NO! WE CAN DO IT!
14

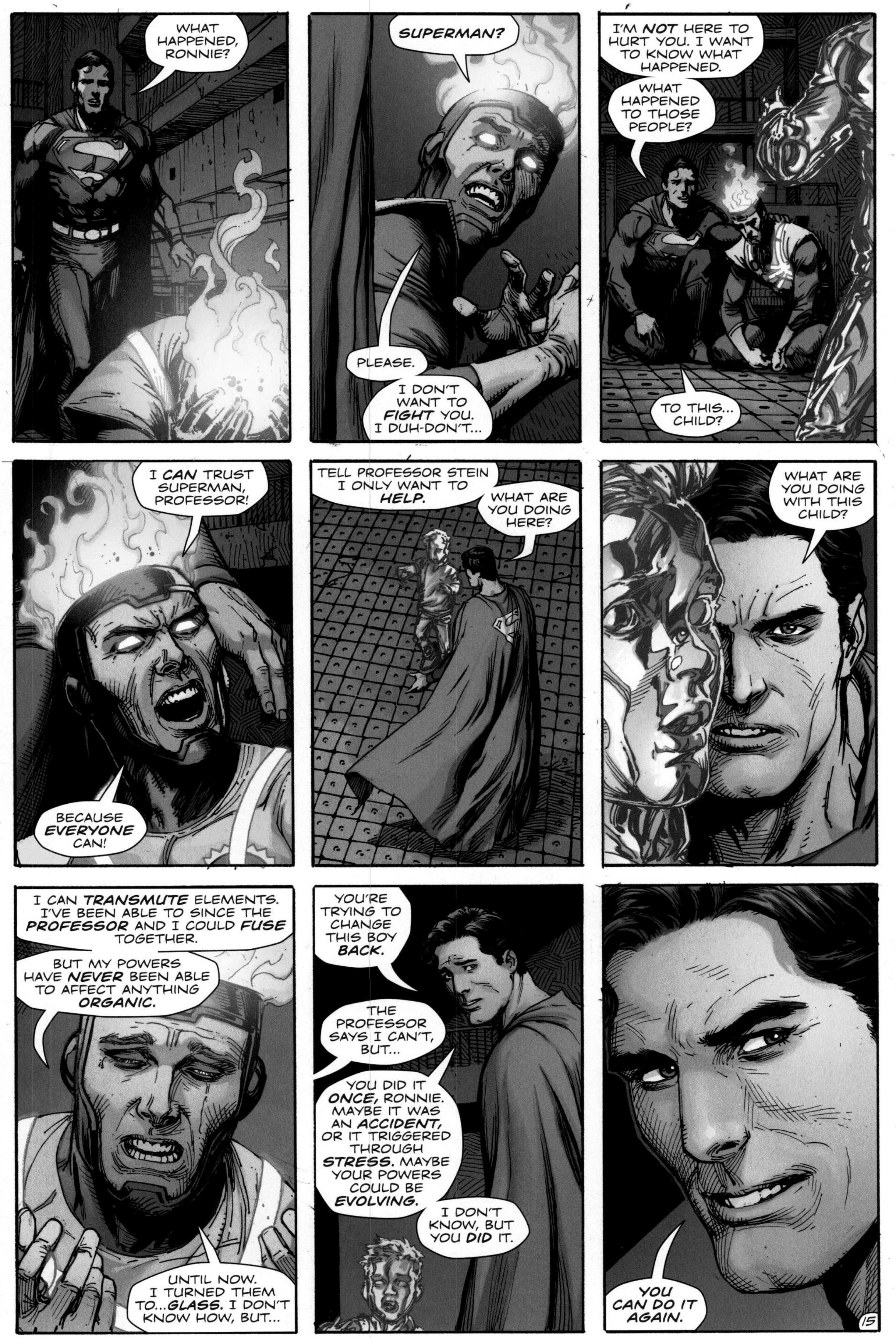

WHAT HAPPENED, RONNIE?
SUPERMAN?
PLEASE.
I DON'T WANT TO FIGHT YOU. I DUH-DON'T...
I'M NOT HERE TO HURT YOU. I WANT TO KNOW WHAT HAPPENED.
WHAT HAPPENED TO THOSE PEOPLE?
TO THIS... CHILD?
I CAN TRUST SUPERMAN, PROFESSOR!
BECAUSE EVERYONE CAN!
TELL PROFESSOR STEIN I ONLY WANT TO HELP.
WHAT ARE YOU DOING HERE?
WHAT ARE YOU DOING WITH THIS CHILD?
I CAN TRANSMUTE ELEMENTS. I'VE BEEN ABLE TO SINCE THE PROFESSOR AND I COULD FUSE TOGETHER.
BUT MY POWERS HAVE NEVER BEEN ABLE TO AFFECT ANYTHING ORGANIC.
UNTIL NOW. I TURNED THEM TO...GLASS. I DON'T KNOW HOW, BUT...
YOU'RE TRYING TO CHANGE THIS BOY BACK.
THE PROFESSOR SAYS I CAN'T, BUT...
YOU DID IT ONCE, RONNIE. MAYBE IT WAS AN ACCIDENT, OR IT TRIGGERED THROUGH STRESS. MAYBE YOUR POWERS COULD BE EVOLVING.
I DON'T KNOW, BUT YOU DID IT.
YOU CAN DO IT AGAIN.

YEAH, I... I CAN TRY.

BUT THE PROFESSOR IS RIGHT. YOU NEED TO LEAVE. PUSHING MYSELF LIKE THIS, I'LL BECOME UNSTABLE.

I COULD DETONATE.

I'M NOT LEAVING YOU.

BUT...

I'LL BE FINE.

OKAY. YEAH. LET'S TRY THIS...

THINK POSITIVE, PROFESSOR! OKAY? OKAY...

YYAAAAA!!

GOD, PLEASE.

PLEASE LET THIS WORRRRRR

KKKKKAAAEEEE!

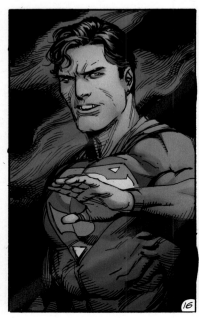

16

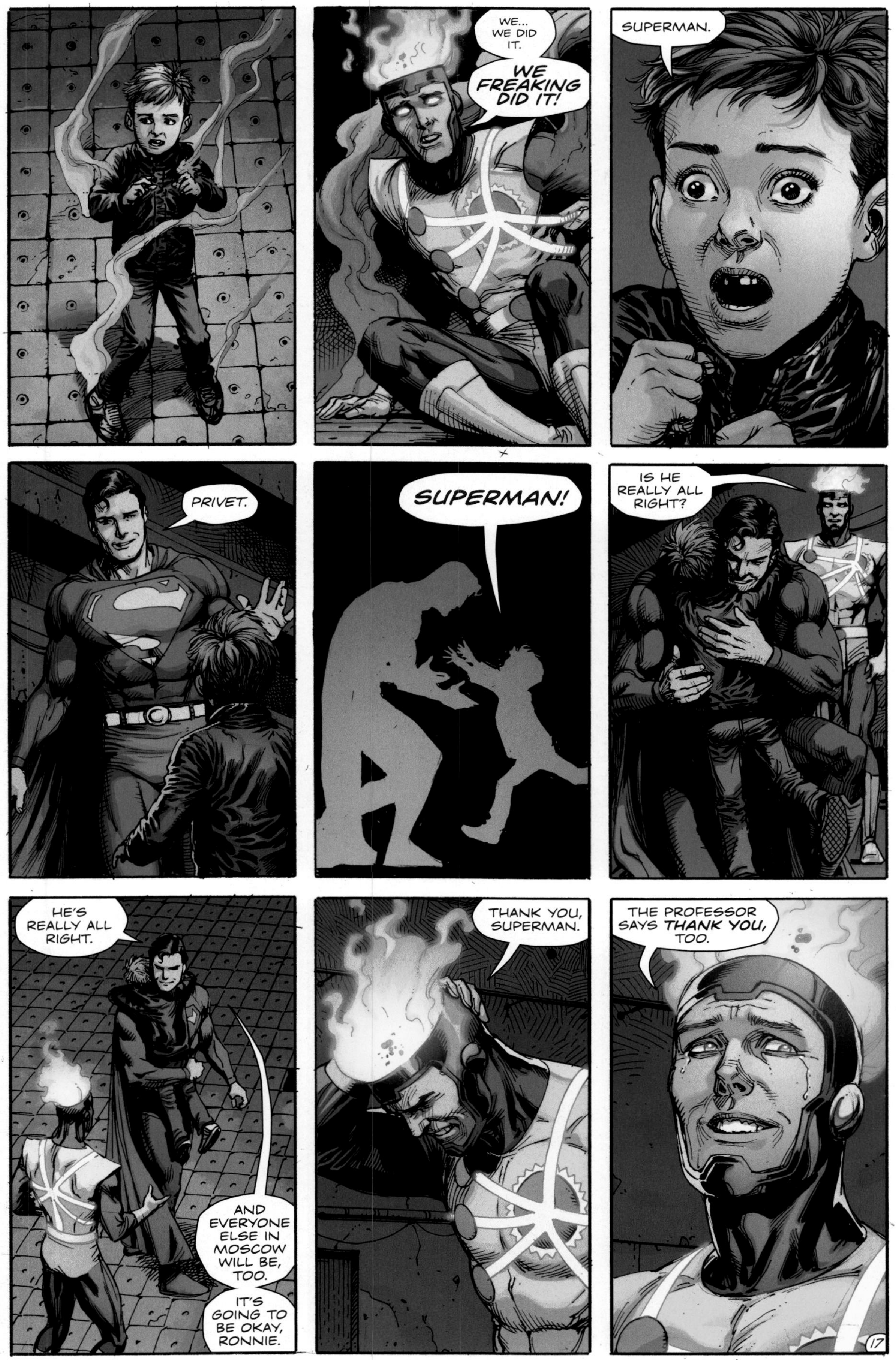
WE... WE DID IT.
WE FREAKING DID IT!
SUPERMAN.
PRIVET.
SUPERMAN!
IS HE REALLY ALL RIGHT?
HE'S REALLY ALL RIGHT.
AND EVERYONE ELSE IN MOSCOW WILL BE, TOO.
IT'S GOING TO BE OKAY, RONNIE.
THANK YOU, SUPERMAN.
THE PROFESSOR SAYS **THANK YOU,** TOO.
17

THIS IS A MESSAGE TO AMERICA FOR ALL THE WORLD TO HEAR.

WE ARE AT A VIOLENT CROSSROADS, WHERE THE DIRECTION WE TURN WILL DETERMINE THE FUTURE OF OUR WORLD.

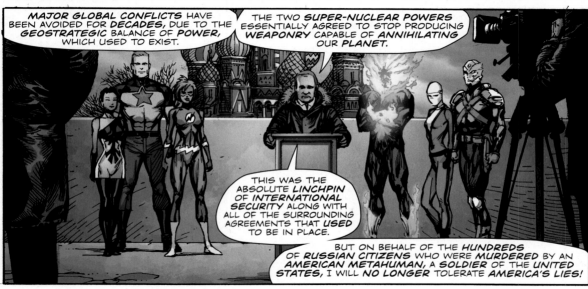

MAJOR GLOBAL CONFLICTS HAVE BEEN AVOIDED FOR DECADES, DUE TO THE GEOSTRATEGIC BALANCE OF POWER, WHICH USED TO EXIST.

THE TWO SUPER-NUCLEAR POWERS ESSENTIALLY AGREED TO STOP PRODUCING WEAPONRY CAPABLE OF ANNIHILATING OUR PLANET.

THIS WAS THE ABSOLUTE LINCHPIN OF INTERNATIONAL SECURITY ALONG WITH ALL OF THE SURROUNDING AGREEMENTS THAT USED TO BE IN PLACE.

BUT ON BEHALF OF THE HUNDREDS OF RUSSIAN CITIZENS WHO WERE MURDERED BY AN AMERICAN METAHUMAN, A SOLDIER OF THE UNITED STATES, I WILL NO LONGER TOLERATE AMERICA'S LIES!

THEY HAVE BEEN AMASSING AN ARMY COVERTLY FOR MORE THAN A DECADE.

FORCING US TO AMASS OUR OWN.

FIRESTORM WILL BE FOUND WHEREVER HE IS. ALONG WITH EVERYONE CONNECTED TO HIS CREATION.

INCLUDING MEMBERS OF THE UNITED STATES GOVERNMENT.

WE ARE AT WAR...

18

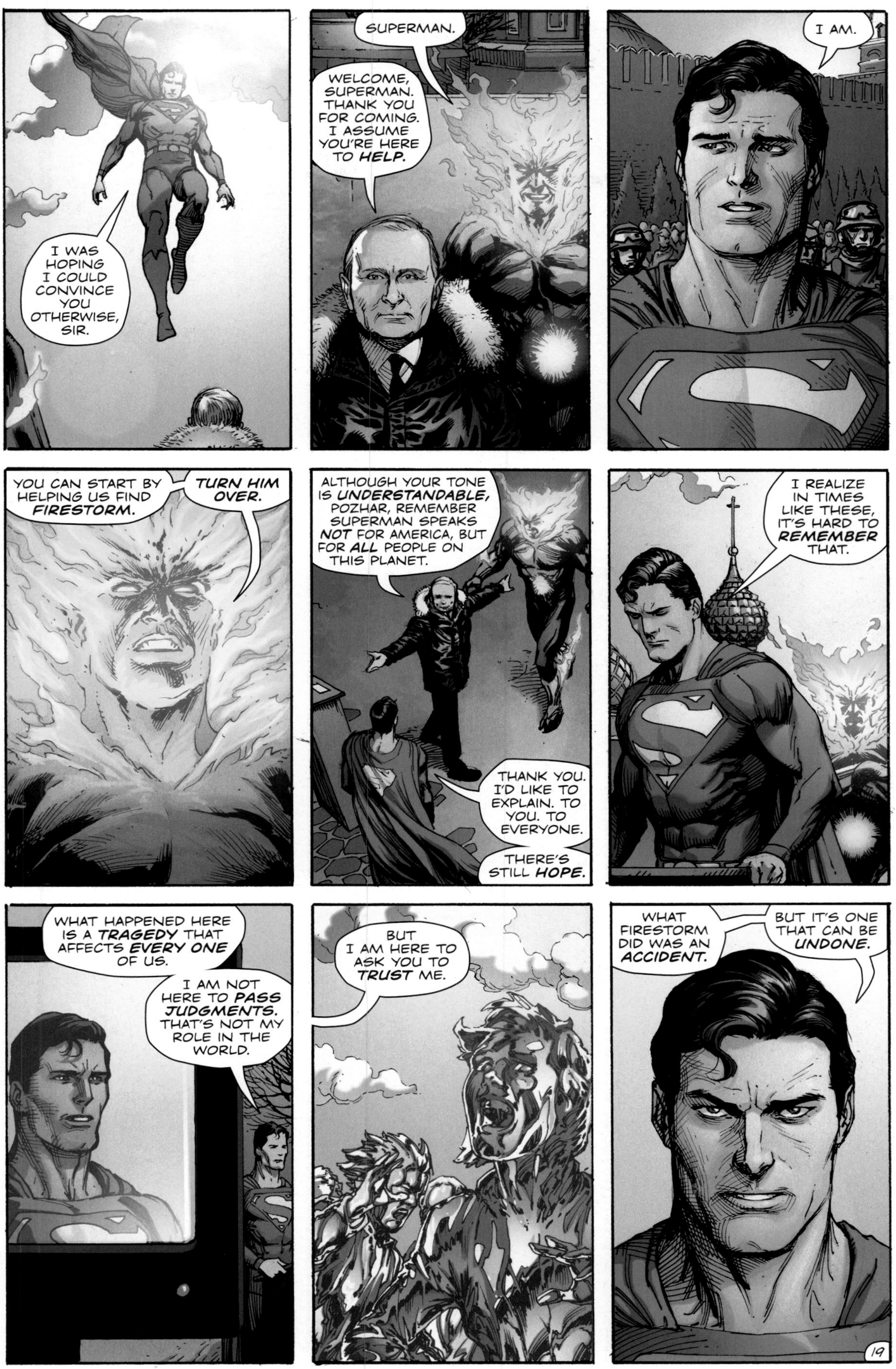
I WAS HOPING I COULD CONVINCE YOU OTHERWISE, SIR.
SUPERMAN.
WELCOME, SUPERMAN. THANK YOU FOR COMING. I ASSUME YOU'RE HERE TO HELP.
I AM.
YOU CAN START BY HELPING US FIND FIRESTORM.
TURN HIM OVER.
ALTHOUGH YOUR TONE IS UNDERSTANDABLE, POZHAR, REMEMBER SUPERMAN SPEAKS NOT FOR AMERICA, BUT FOR ALL PEOPLE ON THIS PLANET.
THANK YOU. I'D LIKE TO EXPLAIN. TO YOU. TO EVERYONE.
THERE'S STILL HOPE.
I REALIZE IN TIMES LIKE THESE, IT'S HARD TO REMEMBER THAT.
WHAT HAPPENED HERE IS A TRAGEDY THAT AFFECTS EVERY ONE OF US.
I AM NOT HERE TO PASS JUDGMENTS. THAT'S NOT MY ROLE IN THE WORLD.
BUT I AM HERE TO ASK YOU TO TRUST ME.
WHAT FIRESTORM DID WAS AN ACCIDENT.
BUT IT'S ONE THAT CAN BE UNDONE.

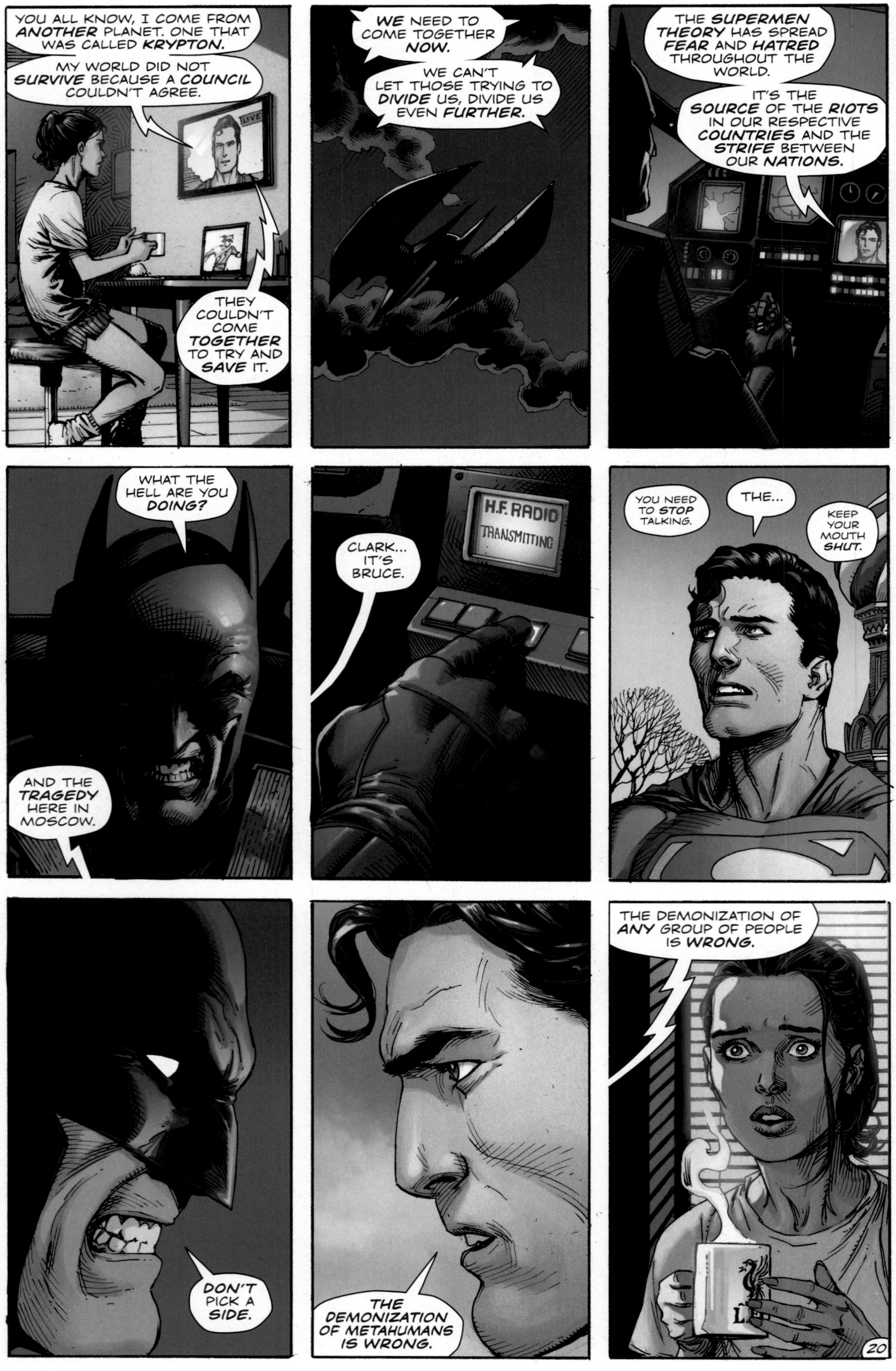
YOU ALL KNOW, I COME FROM ANOTHER PLANET. ONE THAT WAS CALLED KRYPTON.
MY WORLD DID NOT SURVIVE BECAUSE A COUNCIL COULDN'T AGREE.
LIVE
THEY COULDN'T COME TOGETHER TO TRY AND SAVE IT.
WE NEED TO COME TOGETHER NOW.
WE CAN'T LET THOSE TRYING TO DIVIDE US, DIVIDE US EVEN FURTHER.
THE SUPERMEN THEORY HAS SPREAD FEAR AND HATRED THROUGHOUT THE WORLD.
IT'S THE SOURCE OF THE RIOTS IN OUR RESPECTIVE COUNTRIES AND THE STRIFE BETWEEN OUR NATIONS.
WHAT THE HELL ARE YOU DOING?
AND THE TRAGEDY HERE IN MOSCOW.
H.F. RADIO
TRANSMITTING
CLARK... IT'S BRUCE.
YOU NEED TO STOP TALKING.
THE...
KEEP YOUR MOUTH SHUT.
DON'T PICK A SIDE.
THE DEMONIZATION OF METAHUMANS IS WRONG.
THE DEMONIZATION OF ANY GROUP OF PEOPLE IS WRONG.

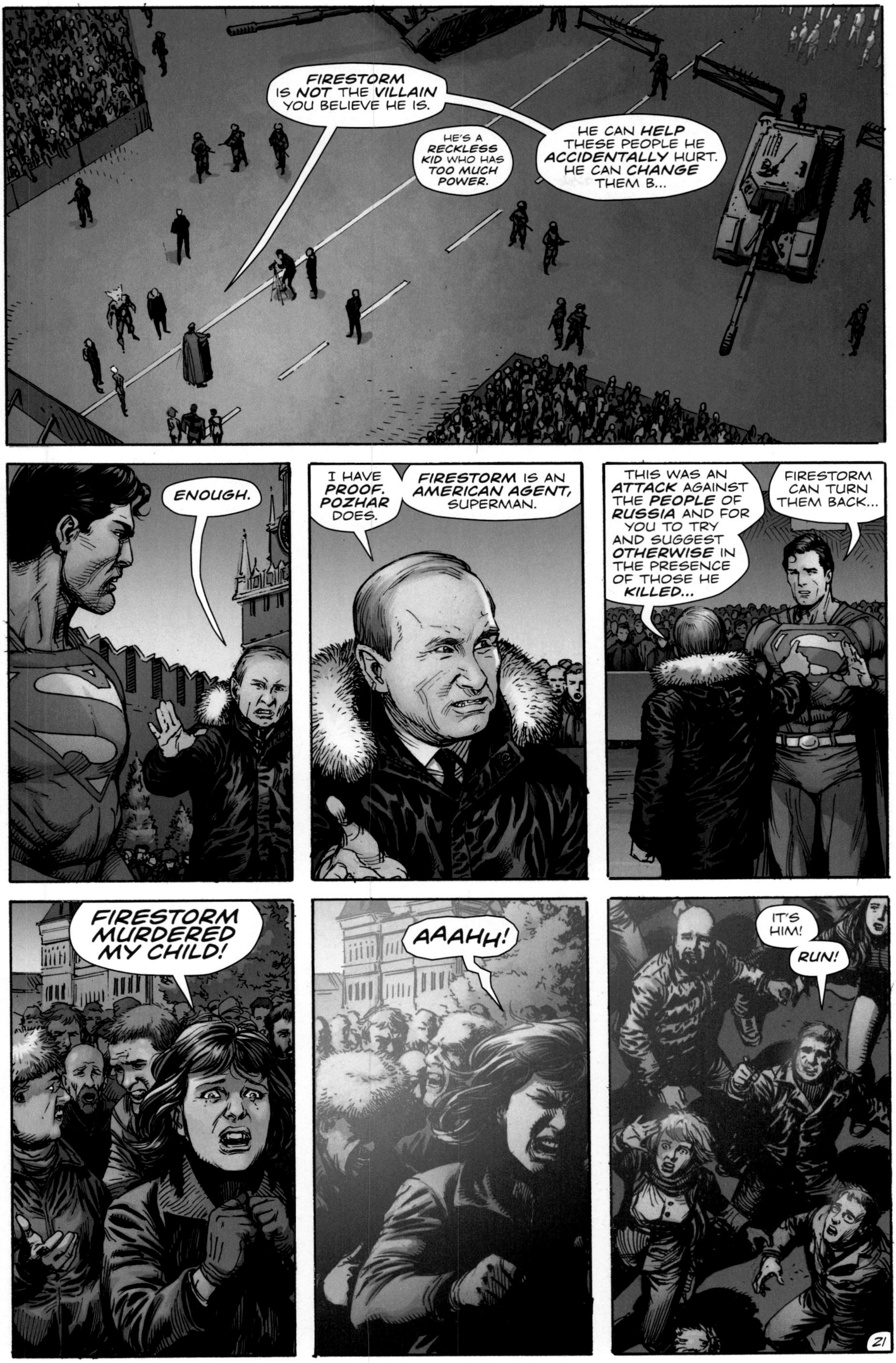
FIRESTORM IS NOT THE VILLAIN YOU BELIEVE HE IS.
HE'S A RECKLESS KID WHO HAS TOO MUCH POWER.
HE CAN HELP THESE PEOPLE HE ACCIDENTALLY HURT. HE CAN CHANGE THEM B...
ENOUGH.
I HAVE PROOF. POZHAR DOES.
FIRESTORM IS AN AMERICAN AGENT, SUPERMAN.
THIS WAS AN ATTACK AGAINST THE PEOPLE OF RUSSIA AND FOR YOU TO TRY AND SUGGEST OTHERWISE IN THE PRESENCE OF THOSE HE KILLED...
FIRESTORM CAN TURN THEM BACK...
FIRESTORM MURDERED MY CHILD!
AAAHH!
IT'S HIM!
RUN!
21

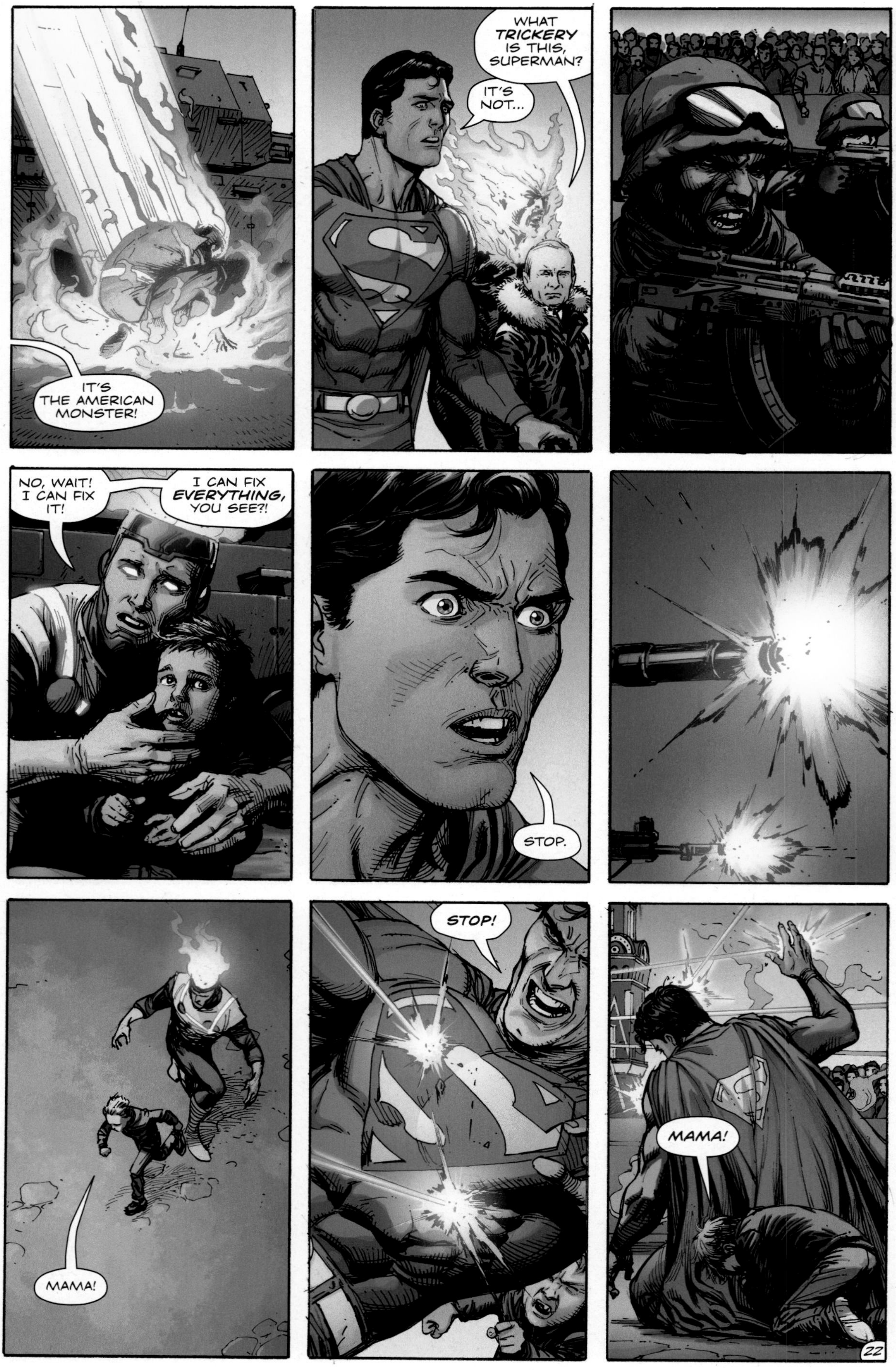
IT'S THE AMERICAN MONSTER!
WHAT TRICKERY IS THIS, SUPERMAN?
IT'S NOT...
NO, WAIT! I CAN FIX IT!
I CAN FIX EVERYTHING, YOU SEE?!
STOP.
MAMA!
STOP!
MAMA!
22

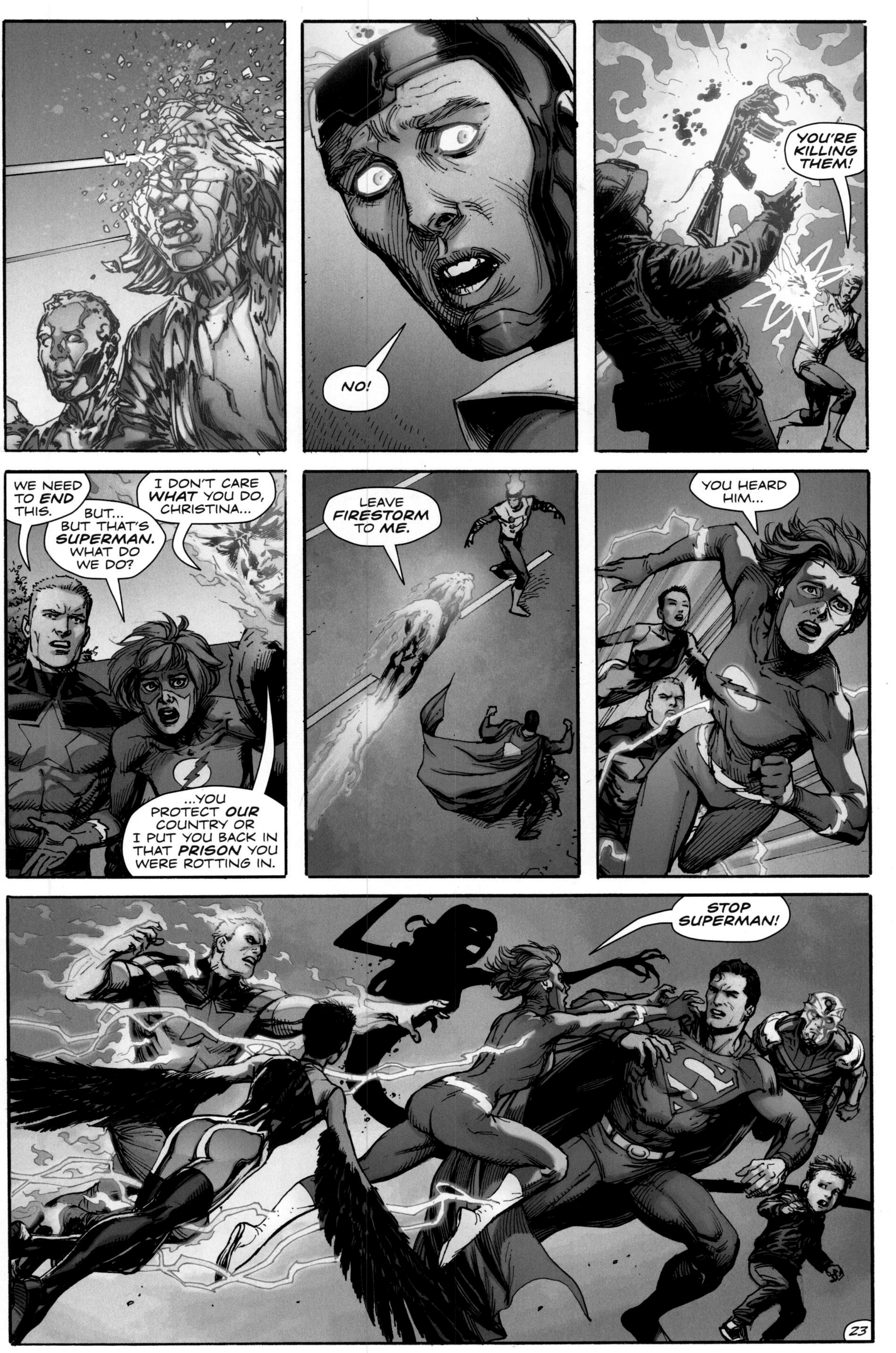
NO!
YOU'RE KILLING THEM!
WE NEED TO END THIS.
BUT... BUT THAT'S SUPERMAN. WHAT DO WE DO?
I DON'T CARE WHAT YOU DO, CHRISTINA...
...YOU PROTECT OUR COUNTRY OR I PUT YOU BACK IN THAT PRISON YOU WERE ROTTING IN.
LEAVE FIRESTORM TO ME.
YOU HEARD HIM...
STOP SUPERMAN!

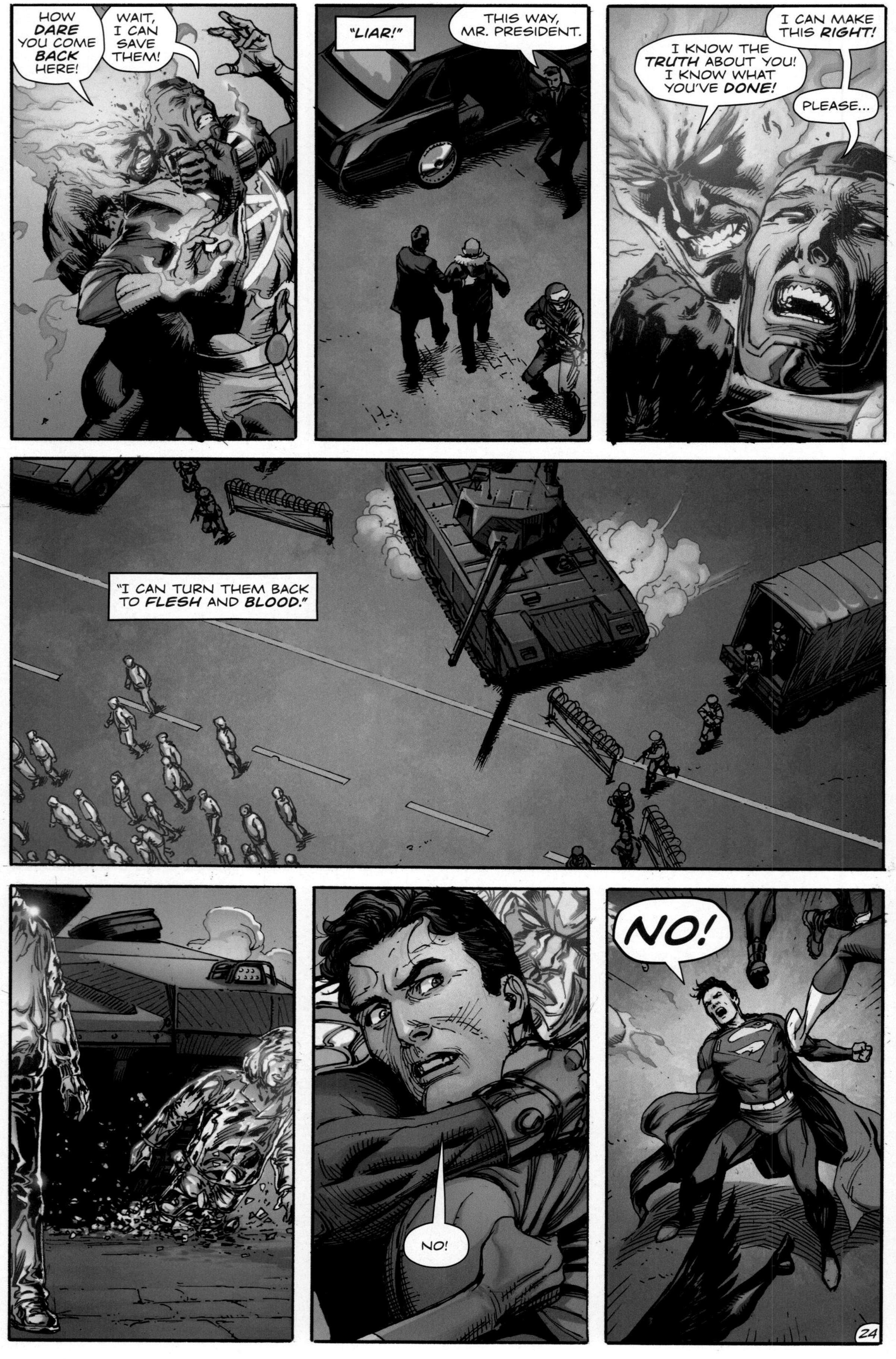

HOW DARE YOU COME BACK HERE!
WAIT, I CAN SAVE THEM!
"LIAR!"
THIS WAY, MR. PRESIDENT.
I CAN MAKE THIS RIGHT!
I KNOW THE TRUTH ABOUT YOU! I KNOW WHAT YOU'VE DONE!
PLEASE...
"I CAN TURN THEM BACK TO FLESH AND BLOOD."
NO!
NO!
24

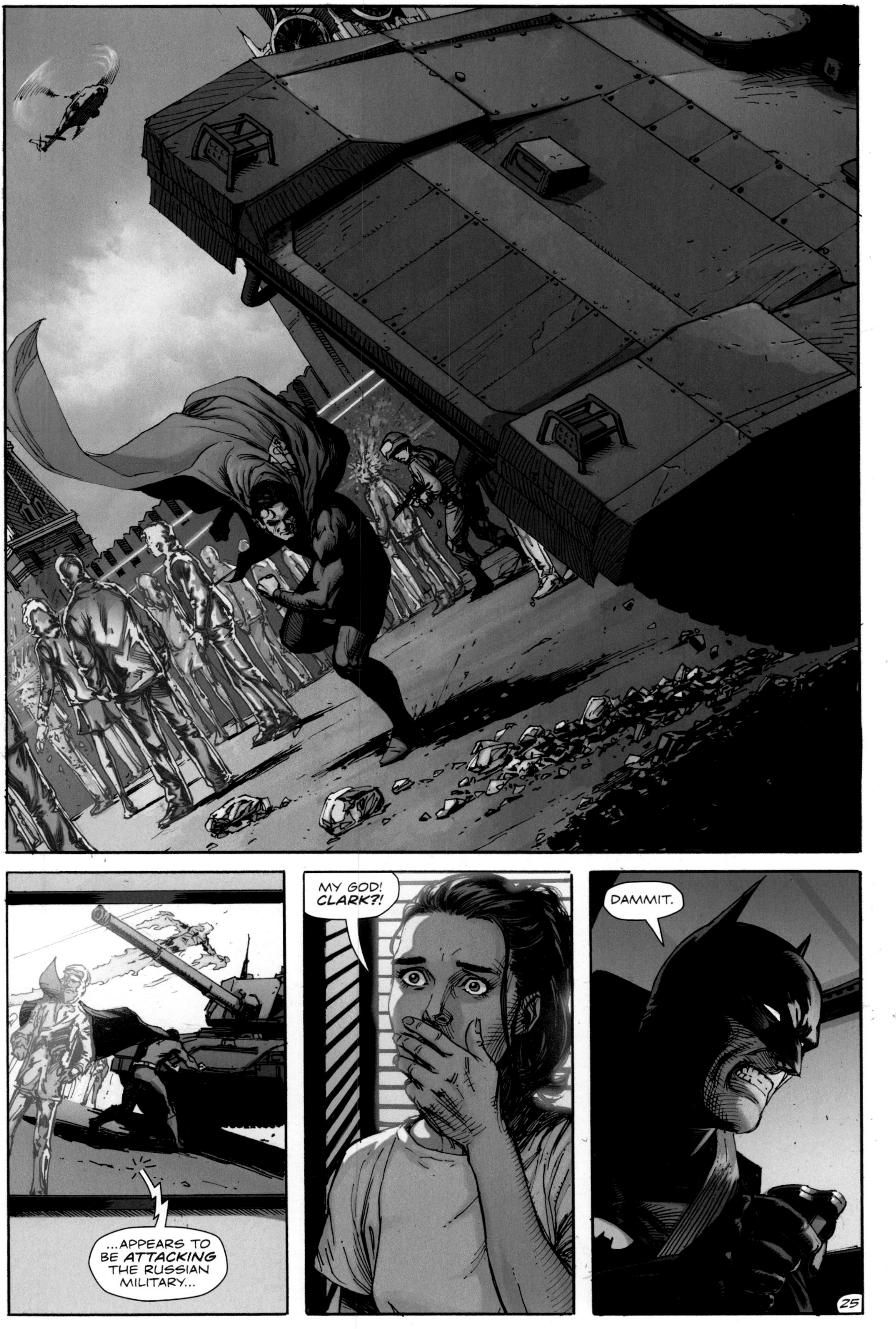
...APPEARS TO BE ATTACKING THE RUSSIAN MILITARY...
MY GOD! CLARK?!
DAMMIT.

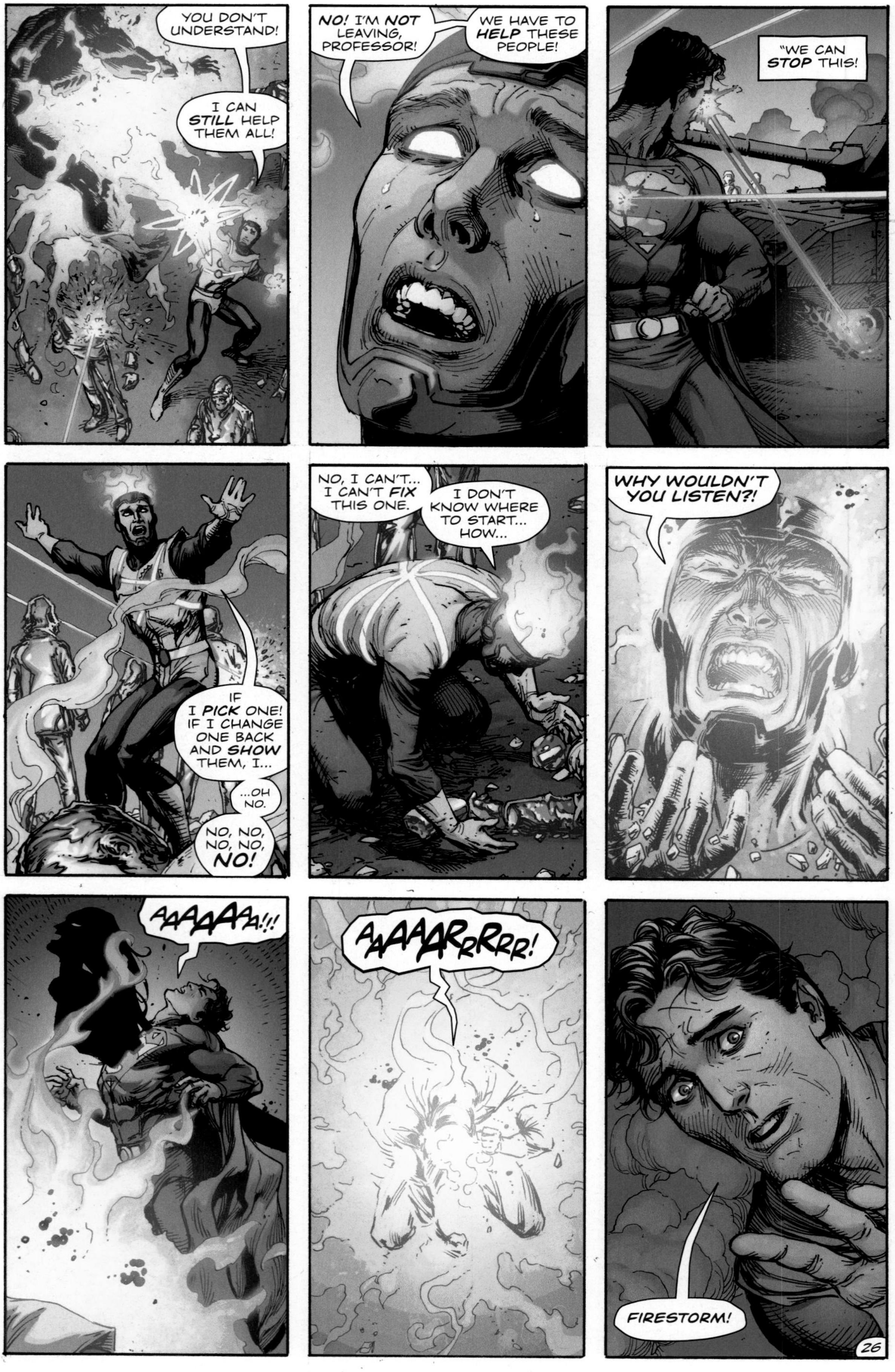
YOU DON'T UNDERSTAND!
I CAN STILL HELP THEM ALL!
NO! I'M NOT LEAVING, PROFESSOR!
WE HAVE TO HELP THESE PEOPLE!
"WE CAN STOP THIS!
IF I PICK ONE! IF I CHANGE ONE BACK AND SHOW THEM, I...
...OH NO.
NO, NO, NO, NO, NO!
NO, I CAN'T... I CAN'T FIX THIS ONE.
I DON'T KNOW WHERE TO START... HOW...
WHY WOULDN'T YOU LISTEN?!
AAAAAAA!!!
AAAAARRRRR!
FIRESTORM!

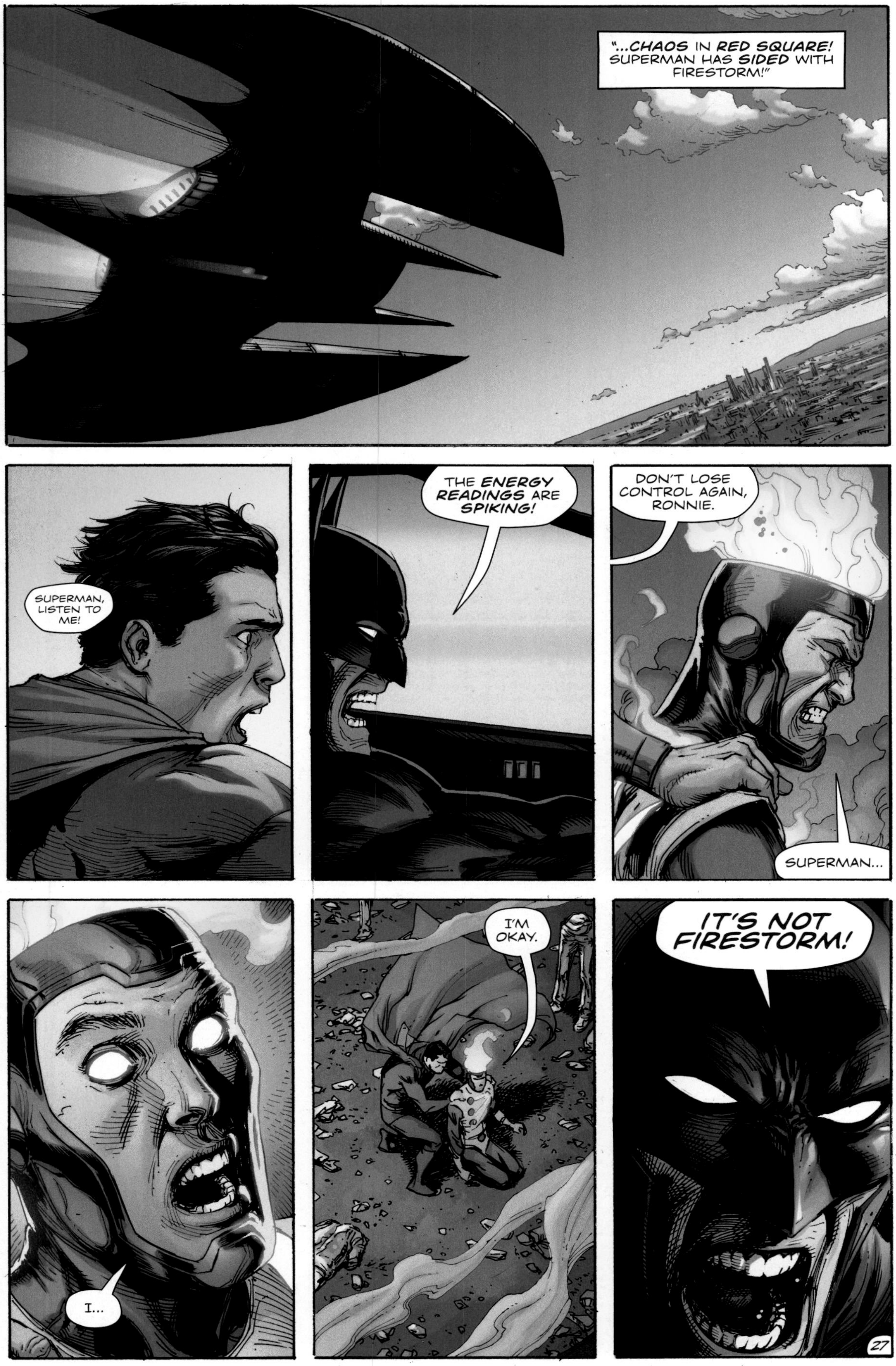
"...CHAOS IN RED SQUARE! SUPERMAN HAS SIDED WITH FIRESTORM!"
SUPERMAN, LISTEN TO ME!
THE ENERGY READINGS ARE SPIKING!
DON'T LOSE CONTROL AGAIN, RONNIE.
SUPERMAN...
I...
I'M OKAY.
IT'S NOT FIRESTORM!

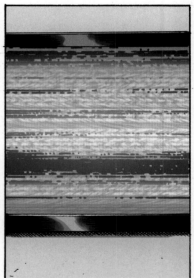

YES.

IT BEGINS.

The urge to save humanity is almost always a false front for the urge to rule.

—H.L. Mencken

28

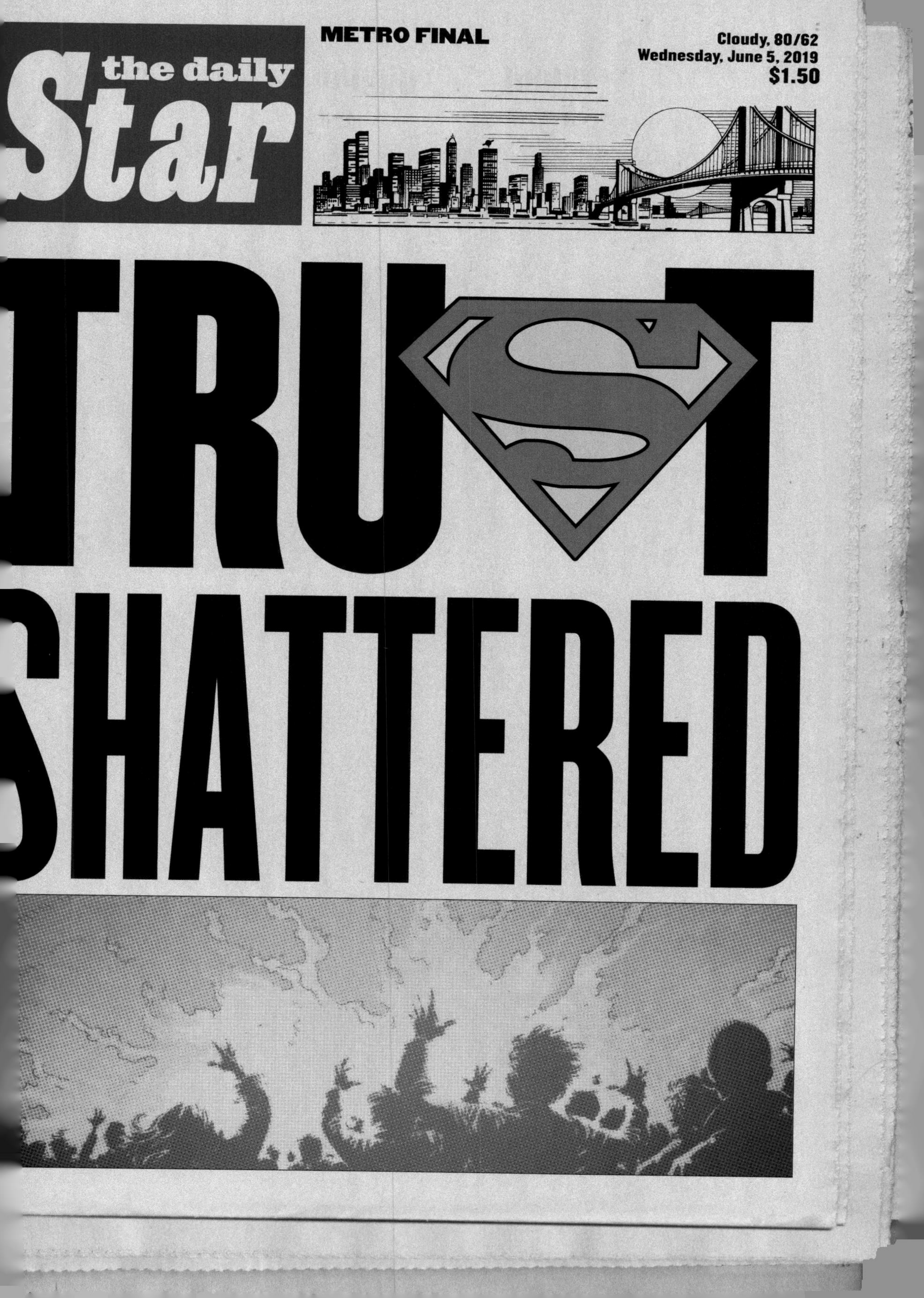

the daily Star
METRO FINAL
Cloudy, 80/62
Wednesday, June 5, 2019
$1.50
TRU T
SHATTERED

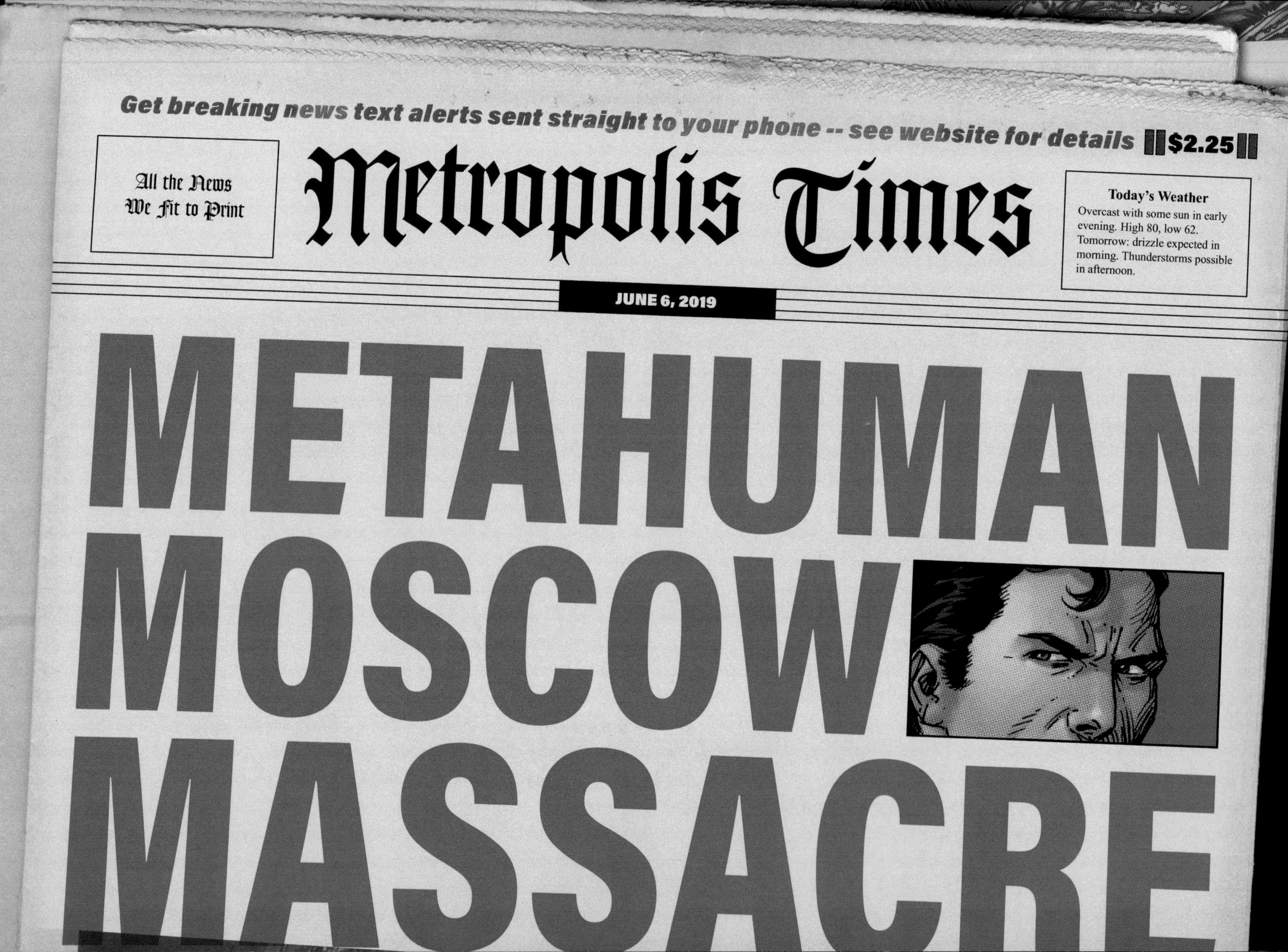
Get breaking news text alerts sent straight to your phone -- see website for details
$2.25
All the News We Fit to Print
Metropolis Times
Today's Weather
Overcast with some sun in early evening. High 80, low 62. Tomorrow: drizzle expected in morning. Thunderstorms possible in afternoon.
JUNE 6, 2019
METAHUMAN MOSCOW MASSACRE

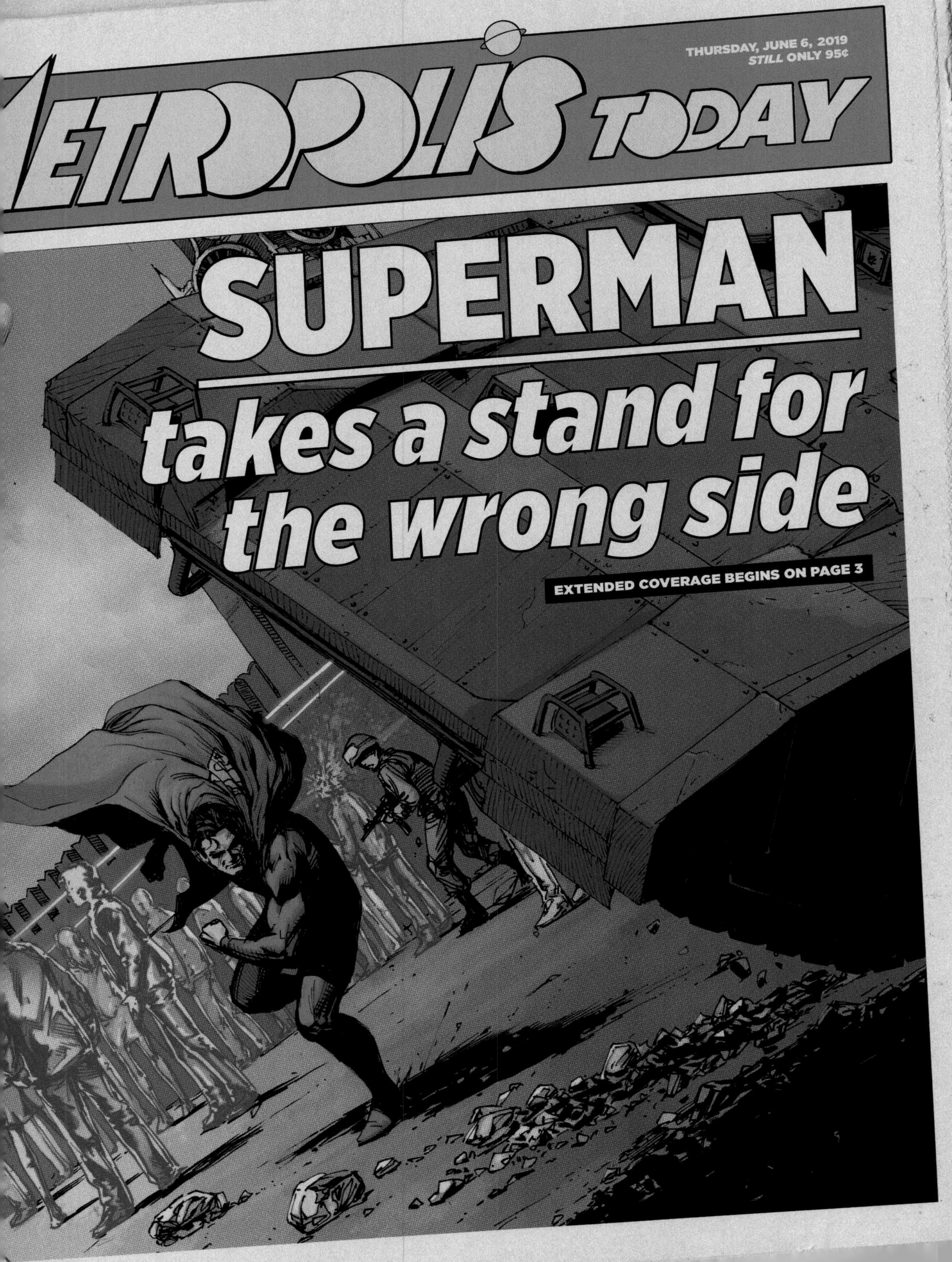

THURSDAY, JUNE 6, 2019
STILL ONLY 95¢
METROPOLIS TODAY
SUPERMAN
takes a stand for the wrong side
EXTENDED COVERAGE BEGINS ON PAGE 3

DAILY PLANET

THE VOICE OF METROPOLIS

EVENING METRO EDITION

THURSDAY, JUNE 6, 2019

$1.50

SUPERMAN MISSING

The Truth We Don't Know

BY PERRY WHITE

Although it's been confirmed Firestorm is responsible for the deaths of dozens in Moscow after transforming them into glass, the exact source of the detonation that later left hundreds dead and Superman and Firestorm missing has come into question. The obvious assumption was yet another outburst from the rash and seemingly unstable Firestorm. But as the world, in this editor's opinion, unjustly began to blame Superman, suspicions of his own "solar flare" eruptions from the past came into question. Was the Man of Steel, the most trusted metahuman in the world, behind it? Or was it a third party? An unseen force that has been speculated by one of the top physicists in the world, Professor Ray Palmer. Could there be an-

Who Attacked Who?

BY RON TROUPE

Government leaders from across the world have quickly moved to denounce Superman for his part in the horrible tragedy at Moscow that has left hundreds dead, but the truth is Superman's exact role in this event is still unclear. By all accounts, prior to the outbreak of violence, Superman was addressing the Russian people, and the world, reflecting upon the destruction of his own home planet and how, in many ways, the inability of its leaders to work together to save Krypton mirror our own troubles here on Earth. Despite reports from media outlets claiming Superman was the first to attack the Russian army, analysis of footage from Red Square reveals a young boy in the line of gunfire from Ru-

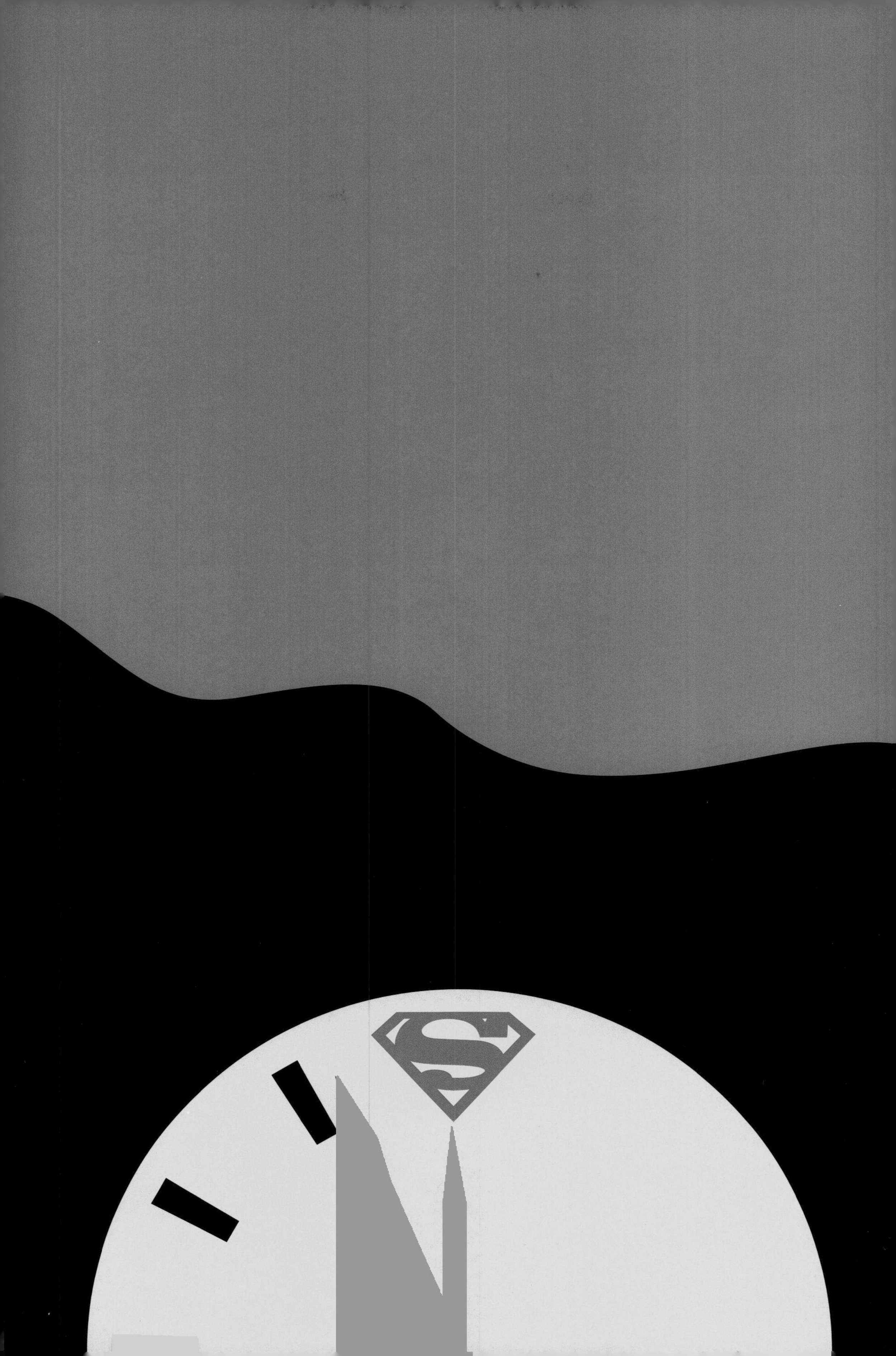

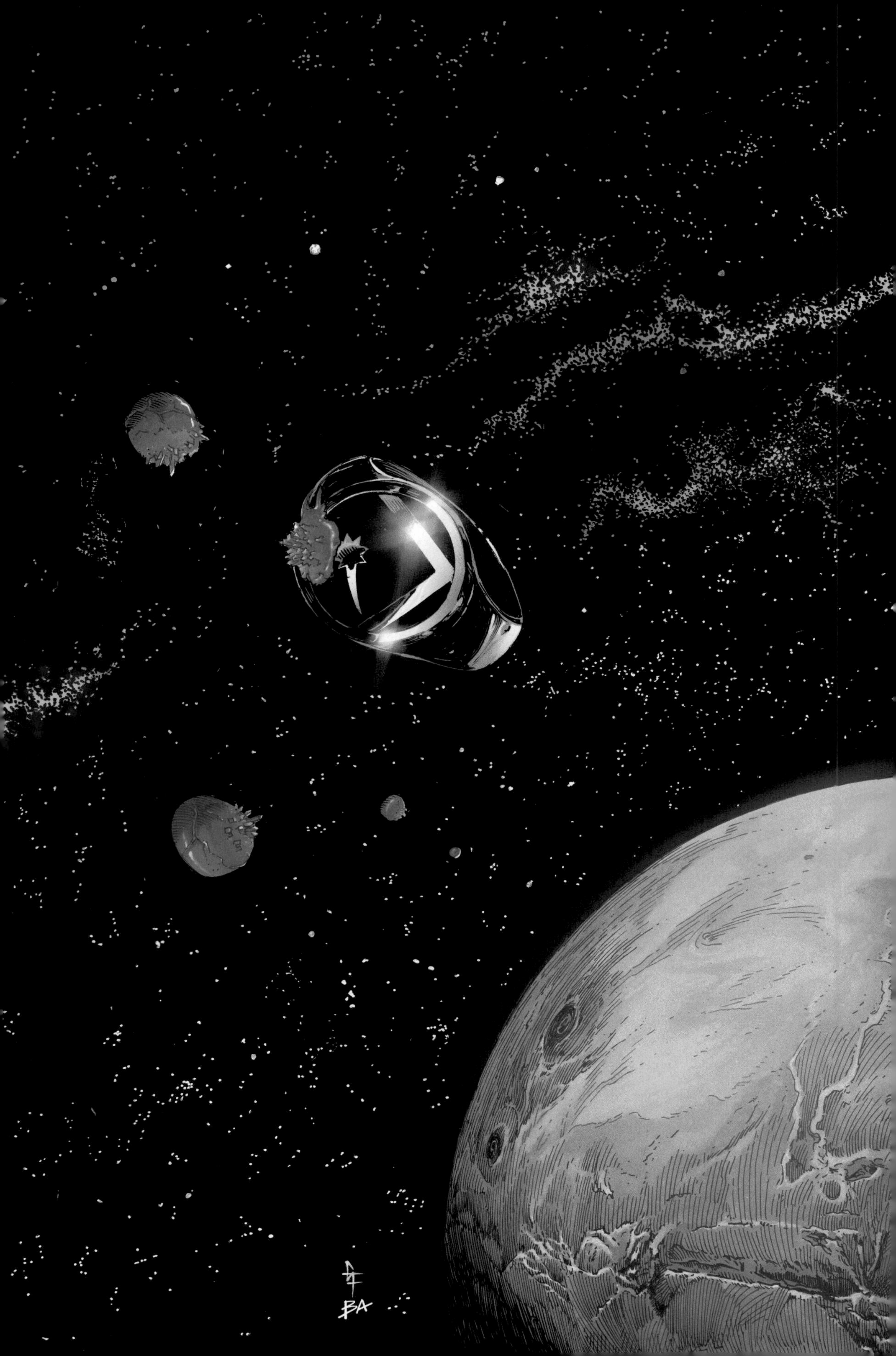

IT'S DECEMBER 27TH, 3019.

A BOY *SACRIFICES* HIS LIFE TO SAVE *EARTH'S SUN.* ALTHOUGH HIS BODY IS DESTROYED, HIS *RING* SURVIVES.

THE EXPLOSION SENDS THE RING CAREENING BACK THROUGH TIME LIKE A *TACHYON PARTICLE.*

IT'S DECEMBER 20TH, 3019. THE DEAD BOY IS ALIVE.

HE SWEATS UNDER HIS IRON MASK, AUDITIONING TO JOIN A LEGION OF OTHERS DEDICATED TO UNITING THE UNIVERSE.

THE DEAD BOY'S RING IS IN MY HAND.

IT'S JULY 16TH, 1940. I MOVE THE LANTERN SIX INCHES OUT OF ALAN SCOTT'S REACH.

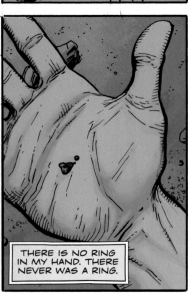

THERE IS NO RING IN MY HAND. THERE NEVER WAS A RING.

IT'S DECEMBER 27TH, 3019.

THERE IS NOTHING BUT DARKNESS.

IT'S NOVEMBER, 3002. THERE IS NOTHING.

MARCH, 2984. FEBRUARY, 2430. AUGUST, 2192. MAY, 2030.

NOTHING.

ONE WEEK FROM NOW, THE LAST THING I SEE IS SUPERMAN IN A RAGE. HIS CAPE IS TORN AND HIS HANDS STAINED WITH BLOOD.

I STAND ON MARS UNABLE TO ANSWER BUT A SINGLE QUESTION: *DOES SUPERMAN DESTROY ME...*

...OR DO I DESTROY EVERYTHING?

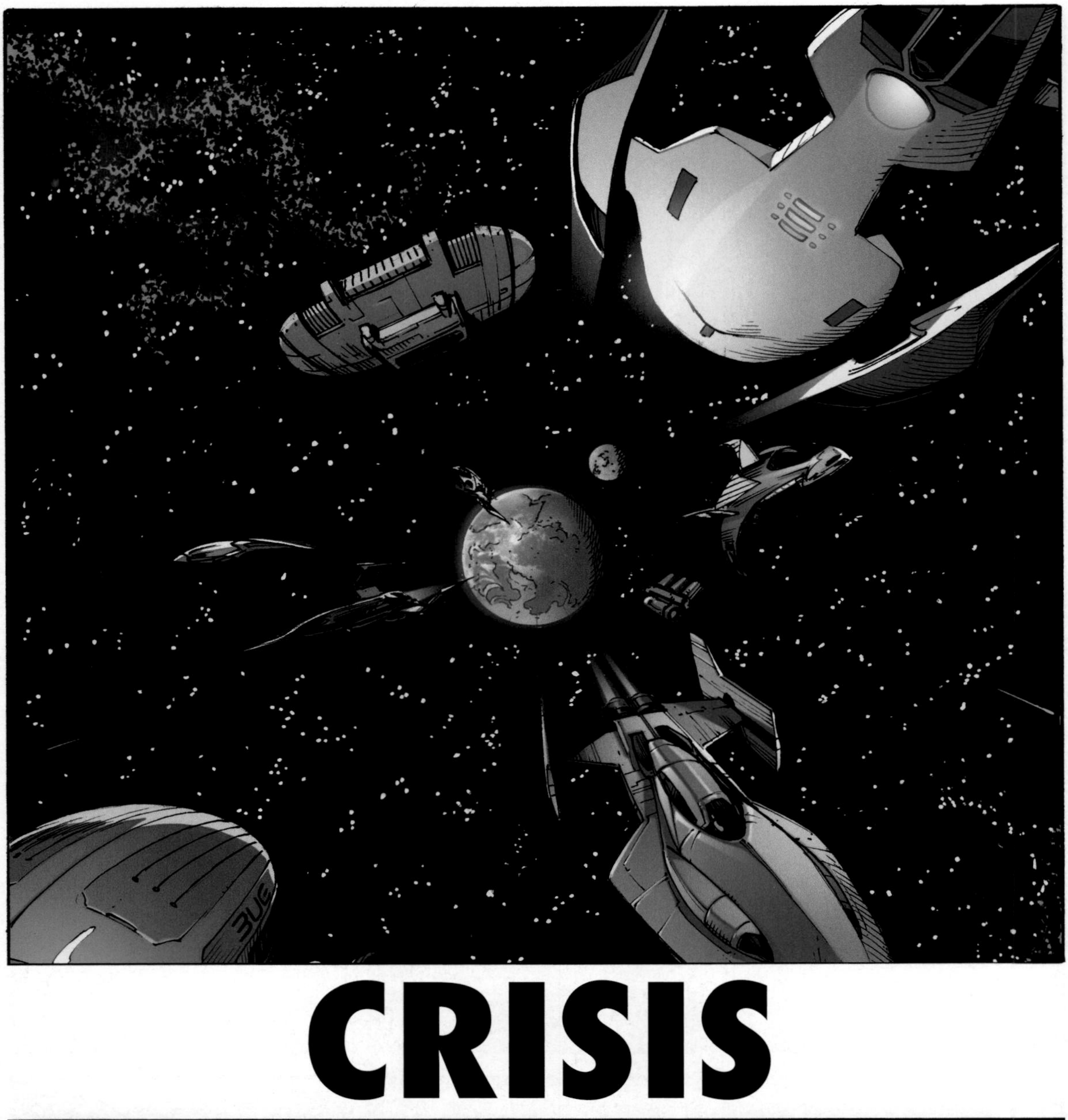

CRISIS

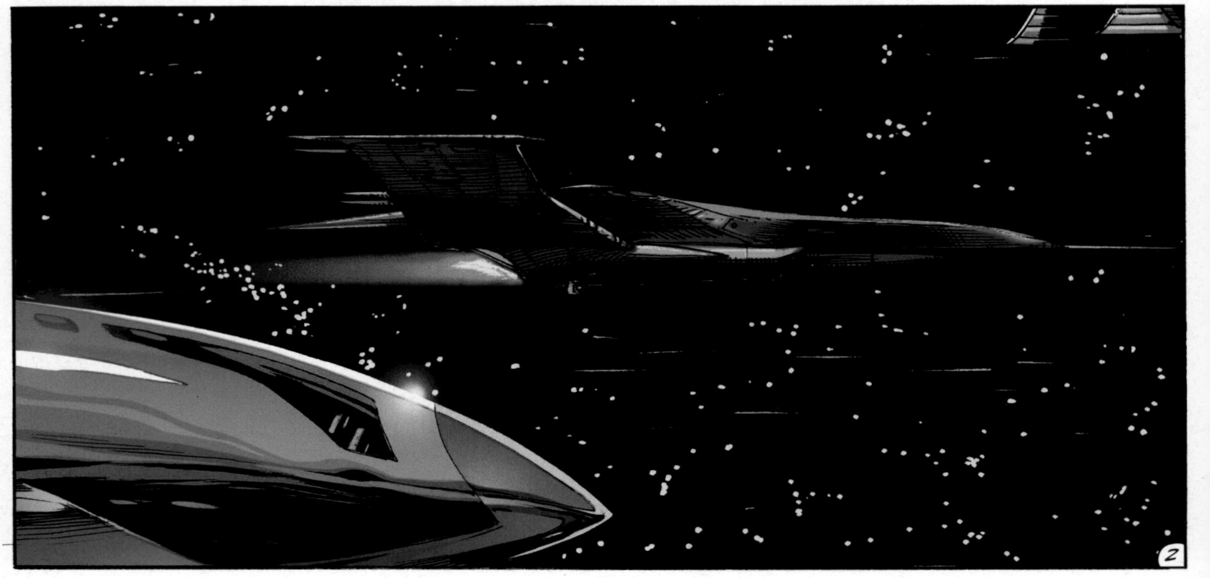

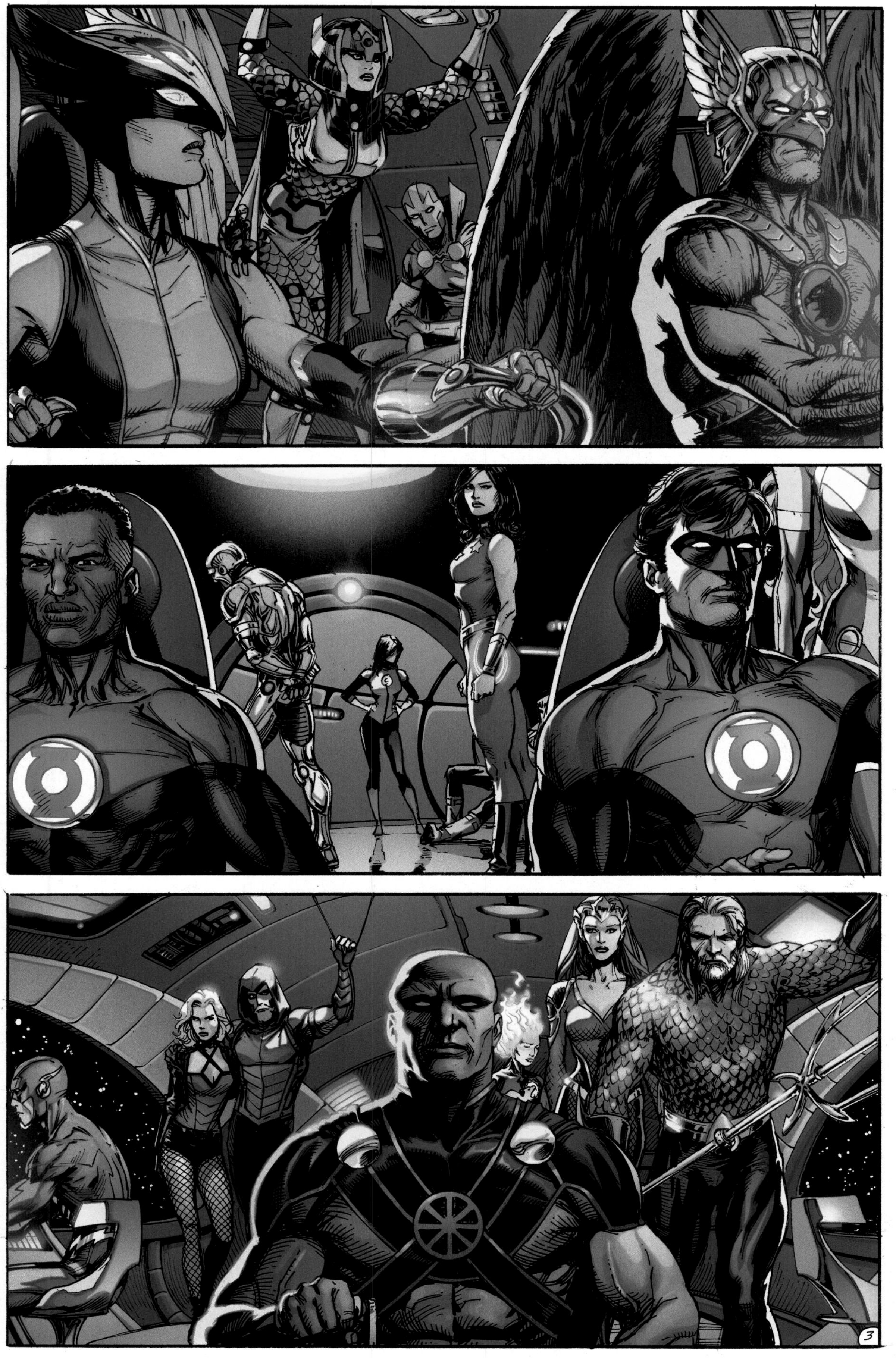

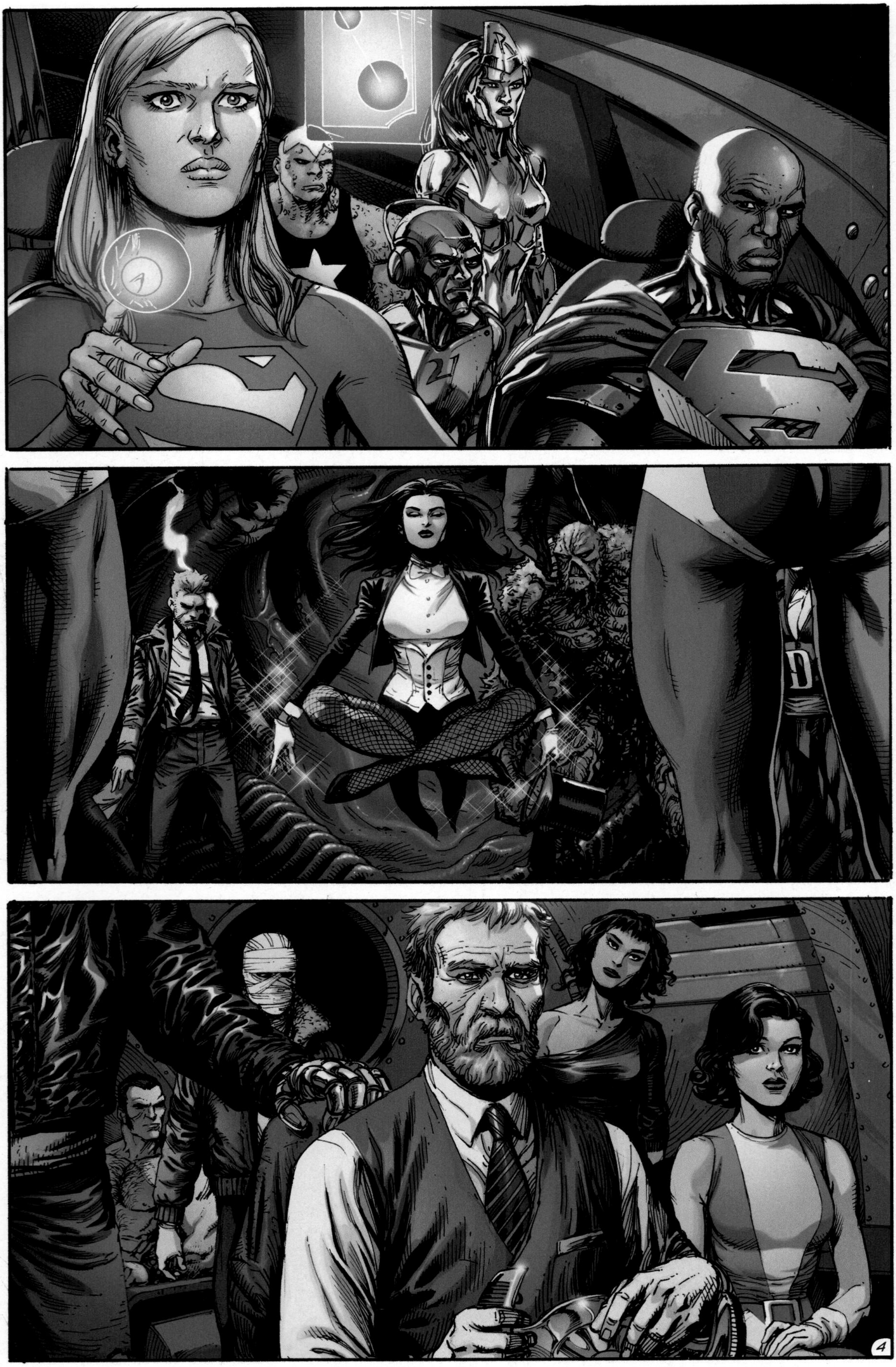

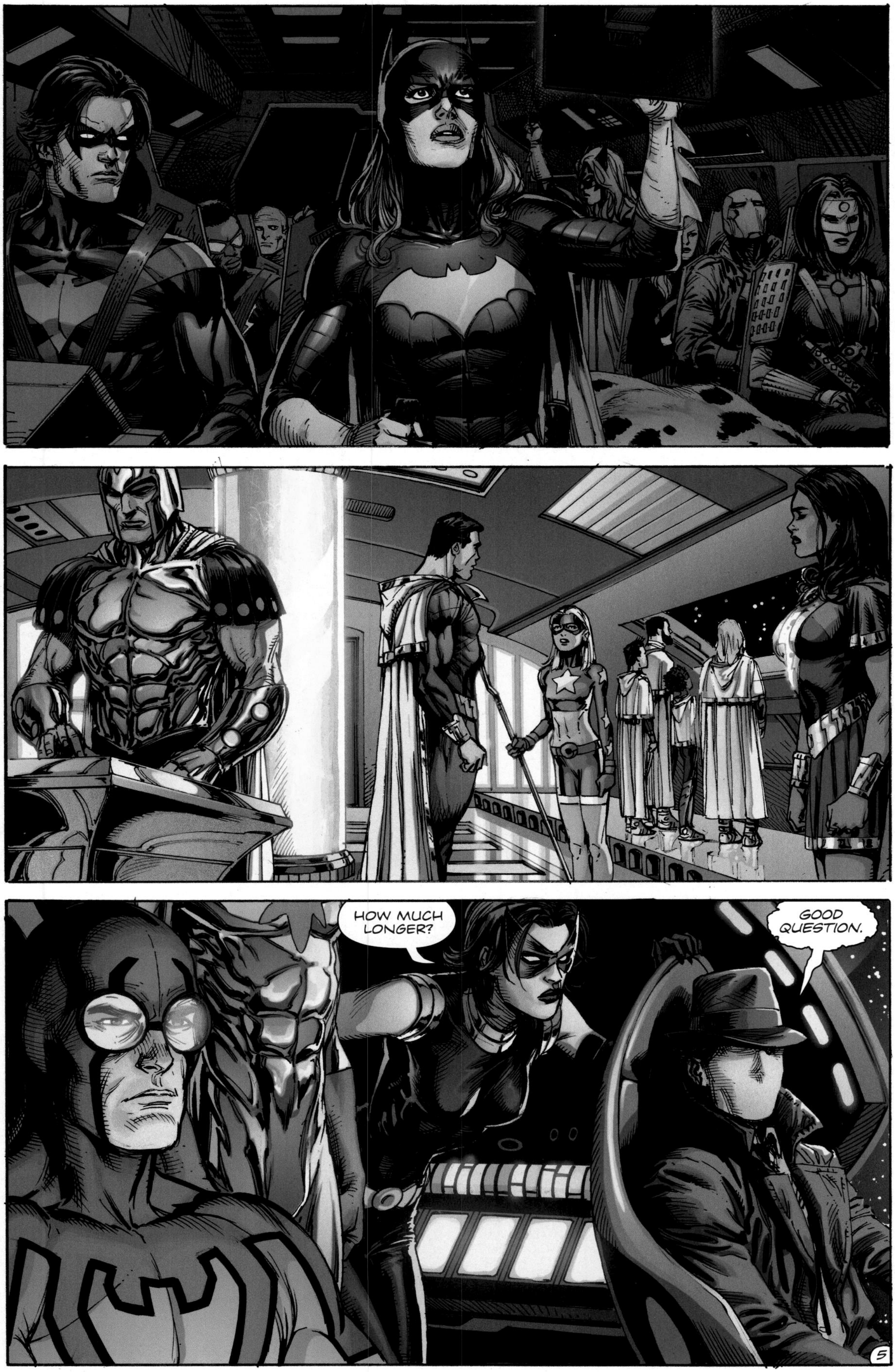
HOW MUCH LONGER?
GOOD QUESTION.

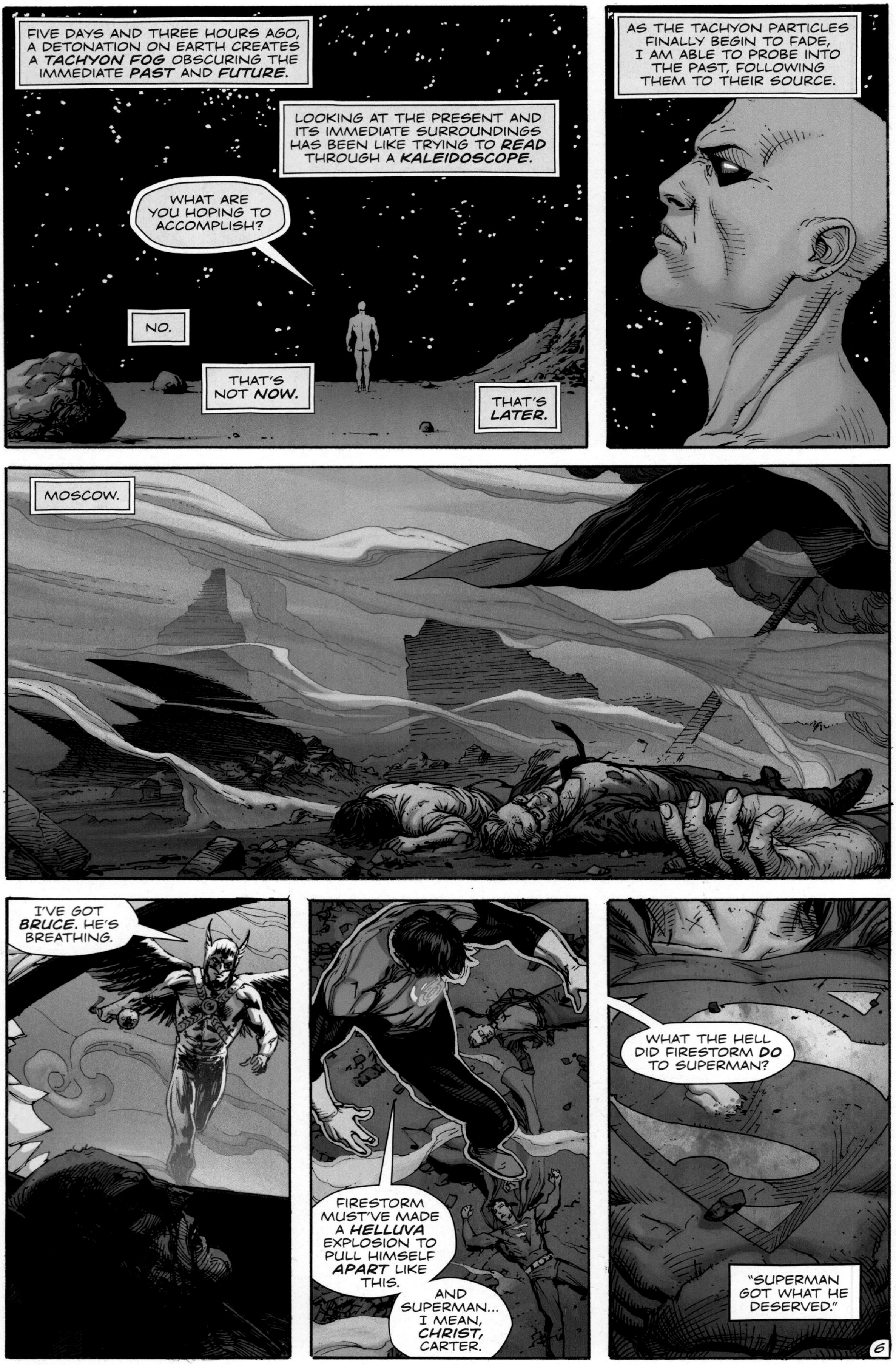
FIVE DAYS AND THREE HOURS AGO, A DETONATION ON EARTH CREATES A TACHYON FOG OBSCURING THE IMMEDIATE PAST AND FUTURE.
LOOKING AT THE PRESENT AND ITS IMMEDIATE SURROUNDINGS HAS BEEN LIKE TRYING TO READ THROUGH A KALEIDOSCOPE.
WHAT ARE YOU HOPING TO ACCOMPLISH?
NO.
THAT'S NOT NOW.
THAT'S LATER.
AS THE TACHYON PARTICLES FINALLY BEGIN TO FADE, I AM ABLE TO PROBE INTO THE PAST, FOLLOWING THEM TO THEIR SOURCE.
MOSCOW.
I'VE GOT BRUCE. HE'S BREATHING.
FIRESTORM MUST'VE MADE A HELLUVA EXPLOSION TO PULL HIMSELF APART LIKE THIS.
AND SUPERMAN... I MEAN, CHRIST, CARTER.
WHAT THE HELL DID FIRESTORM DO TO SUPERMAN?
"SUPERMAN GOT WHAT HE DESERVED."

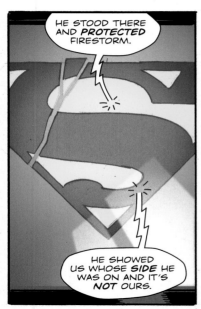

HE STOOD THERE AND *PROTECTED* FIRESTORM.

HE SHOWED US WHOSE *SIDE* HE WAS ON AND IT'S *NOT* OURS.

"...THE *MARCH AGAINST METAHUMANS* CULMINATED IN FRONT OF THE *JUSTICE LEAGUE OF AMERICA'S* HEADQUARTERS HERE IN WASHINGTON, D.C., WHERE IT'S *RUMORED* SUPERMAN HAS TAKEN *REFUGE.*

"*ANTI-SUPERMAN SENTIMENT* CONTINUES TO GROW AS SUPERMAN HAS CHOSEN *NOT* TO *RESPOND* TO THE ALLEGATIONS OF *COLLUSION, FRAUD* AND *ACCESSORY TO MURDER.*

"WE CAN ONLY *GUESS* AS TO *WHY* SUPERMAN *REFUSES* TO TALK TO THE *PRESS.*"

7

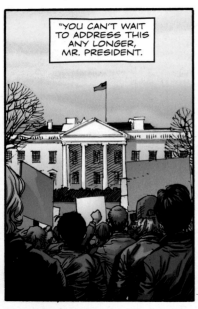

"YOU CAN'T WAIT TO ADDRESS THIS ANY LONGER, MR. PRESIDENT.

YOU HAVE GOT TO GET OUT THERE AND *CONDEMN* SUPERMAN'S ACTIONS.

CONDEMN THEM? I'LL BE *GIVING UP* THE *BIGGEST DETERRENT* TO *FOREIGN ATTACK* I'VE GOT.

IT'S A *HUGE* THING, WHAT YOU'RE ASKING. *HUGE.*

HE'S A *LIABILITY* NOW, MR. PRESIDENT. YOU STAND BY SUPERMAN *TODAY,* YOU LOSE THE WHITE HOUSE *TOMORROW.*

I SHOULD THROW *THIS* FAILURE TO THE WOLVES, TOO. ARROGANT AND *VERY DUMB.*

FIRESTORM

I WOULD ADVISE *AGAINST* THAT. NO ONE WANTS TO GO TO *PRISON.*

"YOU NEED TO SHOW THE AMERICAN PEOPLE *YOU'RE* THEIR SAVIOR NOW."

You see what you want to see

"OUR HEROES CAN NO LONGER WEAR MASKS...

THEY MUST *REVEAL* THEMSELVES AND THEIR *TRUE LOYALTIES* TO THE WORLD.

RUSSIA *DEMANDS* IT.

"...REPORT OF A *MASS EXODUS* OF AMERICAN METAHUMANS. *HUNDREDS* WERE SEEN GATHERING AROUND *SEVERAL SHIPS* OUTSIDE OF WASHINGTON, D.C., LAST NIGHT..."

...PRESIDENT ALSO TWEETED, "THE U.S. CANNOT SUPPORT SUPERMAN ANY LONGER! I'VE DONE MORE FOR THE WORLD ANYWAY AND WILL CONTINUE TO!"

@POT

$899.99

8

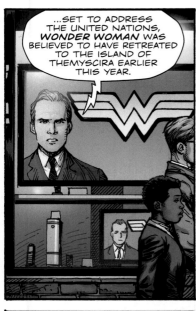

...SET TO ADDRESS THE UNITED NATIONS, **WONDER WOMAN** WAS BELIEVED TO HAVE RETREATED TO THE ISLAND OF THEMYSCIRA EARLIER THIS YEAR.

HER REAPPEARANCE COINCIDES WITH THE DISAPPEARANCE OF THE REST OF THE JUSTICE LEAGUE.

≷HHN...≷

MASTER WAYNE?

ALFRED?

RRN.

WHAT'S GOING ON? WHERE'S CLARK?

HE'S RECOVERING, SECURED WITHIN THE HALL OF JUSTICE.

HE'S SAFE.

AND FIRESTORM?

9

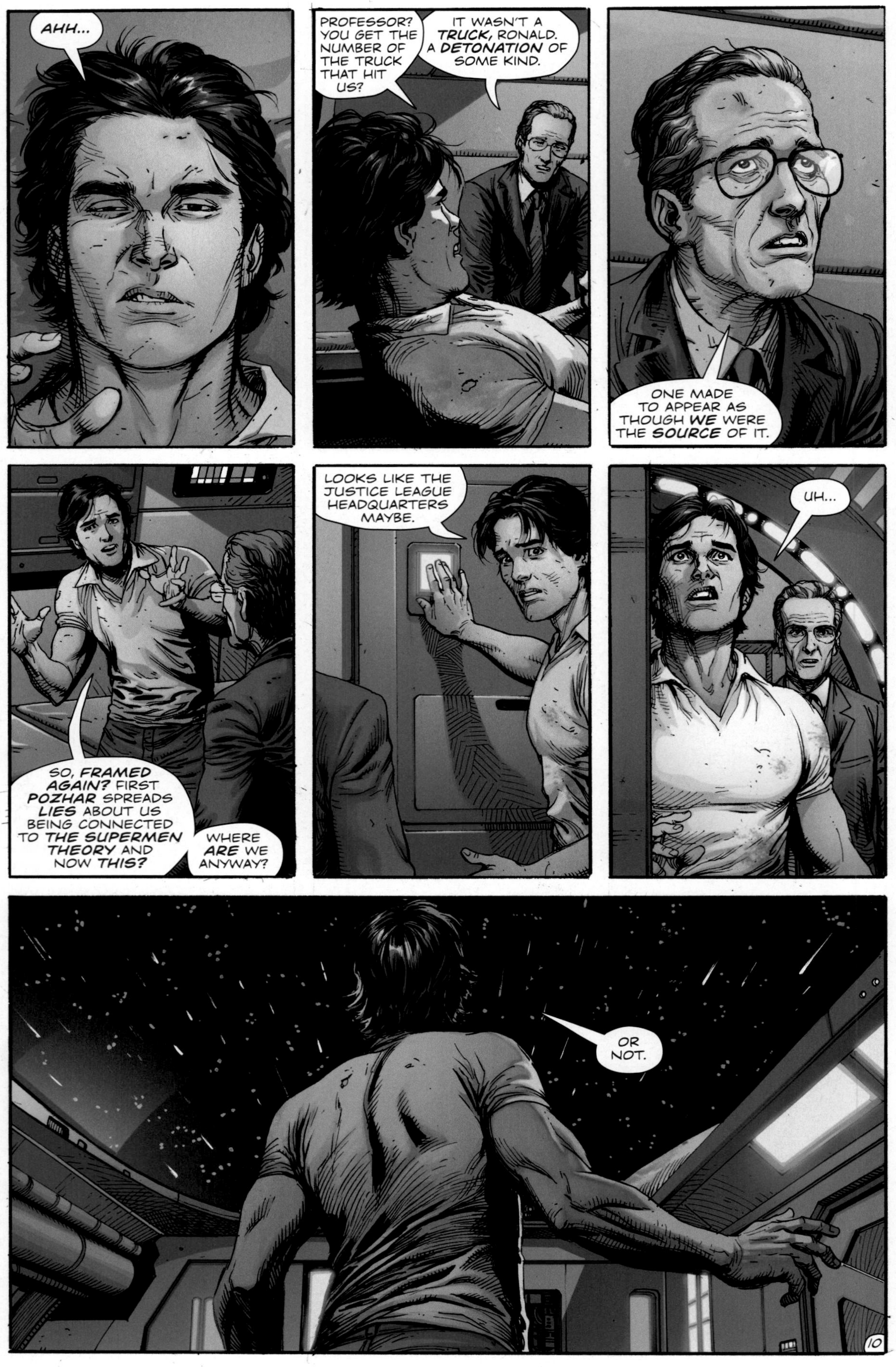
AHH...
PROFESSOR? YOU GET THE NUMBER OF THE TRUCK THAT HIT US?
IT WASN'T A TRUCK, RONALD. A DETONATION OF SOME KIND.
ONE MADE TO APPEAR AS THOUGH WE WERE THE SOURCE OF IT.
SO, FRAMED AGAIN? FIRST POZHAR SPREADS LIES ABOUT US BEING CONNECTED TO THE SUPERMEN THEORY AND NOW THIS?
WHERE ARE WE ANYWAY?
LOOKS LIKE THE JUSTICE LEAGUE HEADQUARTERS MAYBE.
UH...
OR NOT.
10

WHY WOULD THEY **ALL** LEAVE THE PLANET?

...YEAH, YOU CAN QUOTE ME. **NONE** OF YOU BARKING PUNDITS ARE WORTH **SUPERMAN'S PISS!**

HELL, YOU AREN'T WORTH **MINE!**

...THE LEAGUE SENT THE VERY **BEST** TO ANALYZE AND CONTAIN ANY ENVIRONMENTAL DAMAGE FROM FIRESTORM'S DETONATION.

THE GREEN LANTERNS, THE ATOM... EVEN **JOHN CONSTANTINE** VOLUNTEERED.

AND THEY DISCOVERED IT **WASN'T** FIRESTORM WHO CAUSED THE EXPLOSION.

IT WAS SOMEONE **ELSE.** SOMEONE THEY BELIEVE WAS TRYING TO **KILL** SUPERMAN.

"IT WAS AN **ENERGY** THEY'D NEVER ENCOUNTERED.

"AND THEY TRACED IT TO **MARS.**"

THEY'RE BEING PLAYED.

PLAYED? EXCUSE ME, SIR? I BELIEVE YOUR LAST WORDS TO SUPERMAN BEFORE THE EXPLOSION WERE, "IT ISN'T FIRESTORM."

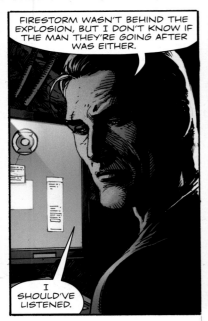

FIRESTORM WASN'T BEHIND THE EXPLOSION, BUT I DON'T KNOW IF THE MAN THEY'RE GOING AFTER WAS EITHER.

I SHOULD'VE LISTENED.

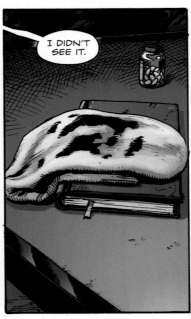

I DIDN'T SEE IT.

COMPUTER? HOW LONG FOR A MESSAGE TO REACH MARS?

11

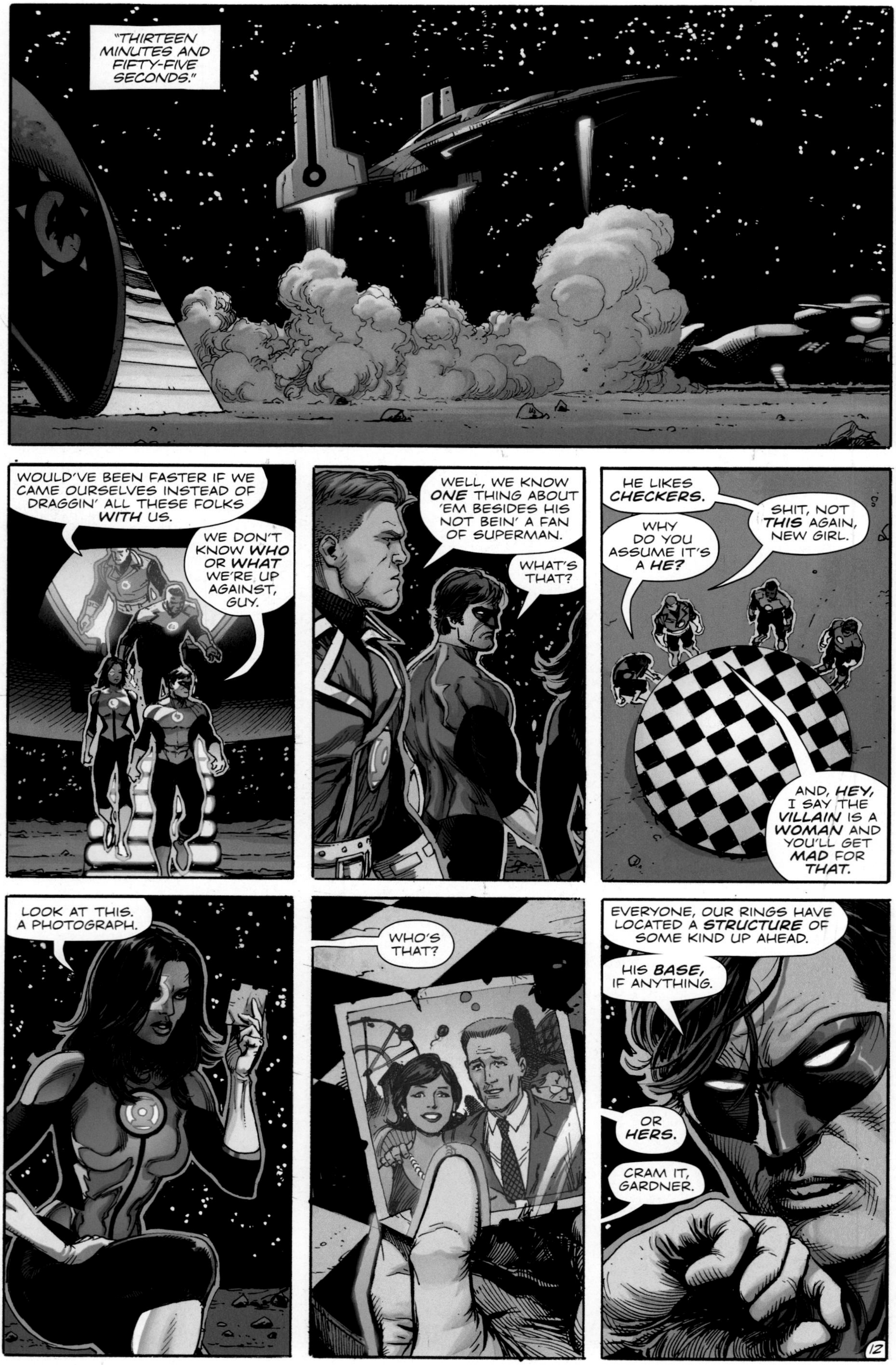
"THIRTEEN MINUTES AND FIFTY-FIVE SECONDS."
WOULD'VE BEEN FASTER IF WE CAME OURSELVES INSTEAD OF DRAGGIN' ALL THESE FOLKS WITH US.
WE DON'T KNOW WHO OR WHAT WE'RE UP AGAINST, GUY.
WELL, WE KNOW ONE THING ABOUT 'EM BESIDES HIS NOT BEIN' A FAN OF SUPERMAN.
WHAT'S THAT?
HE LIKES CHECKERS.
WHY DO YOU ASSUME IT'S A HE?
SHIT, NOT THIS AGAIN, NEW GIRL.
AND, HEY, I SAY THE VILLAIN IS A WOMAN AND YOU'LL GET MAD FOR THAT.
LOOK AT THIS. A PHOTOGRAPH.
WHO'S THAT?
EVERYONE, OUR RINGS HAVE LOCATED A STRUCTURE OF SOME KIND UP AHEAD.
HIS BASE, IF ANYTHING.
OR HERS.
CRAM IT, GARDNER.
12

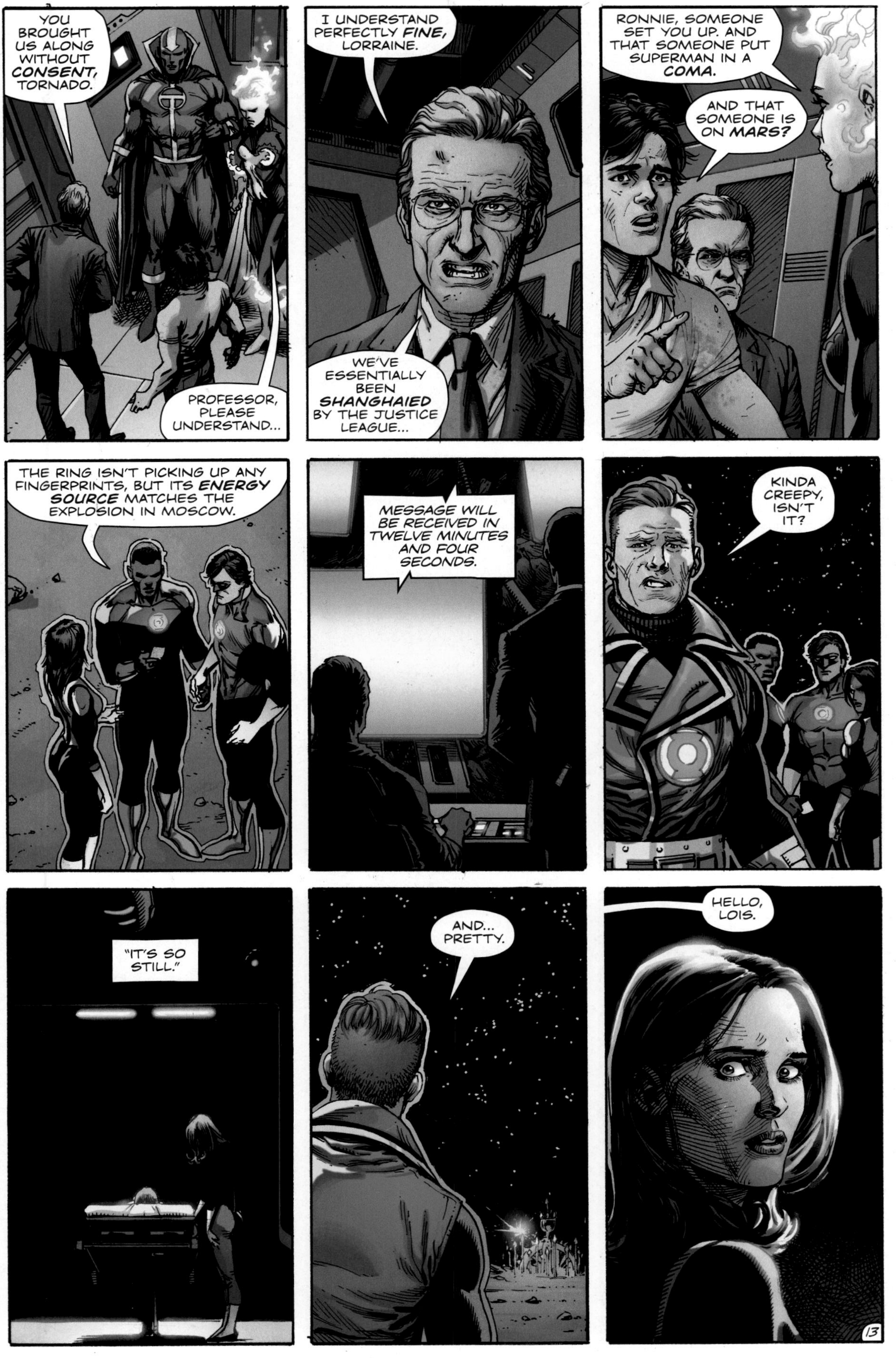
YOU BROUGHT US ALONG WITHOUT CONSENT, TORNADO.
PROFESSOR, PLEASE UNDERSTAND...
I UNDERSTAND PERFECTLY FINE, LORRAINE.
WE'VE ESSENTIALLY BEEN SHANGHAIED BY THE JUSTICE LEAGUE...
RONNIE, SOMEONE SET YOU UP. AND THAT SOMEONE PUT SUPERMAN IN A COMA.
AND THAT SOMEONE IS ON MARS?
THE RING ISN'T PICKING UP ANY FINGERPRINTS, BUT ITS ENERGY SOURCE MATCHES THE EXPLOSION IN MOSCOW.
MESSAGE WILL BE RECEIVED IN TWELVE MINUTES AND FOUR SECONDS.
KINDA CREEPY, ISN'T IT?
"IT'S SO STILL."
AND... PRETTY.
HELLO, LOIS.
13

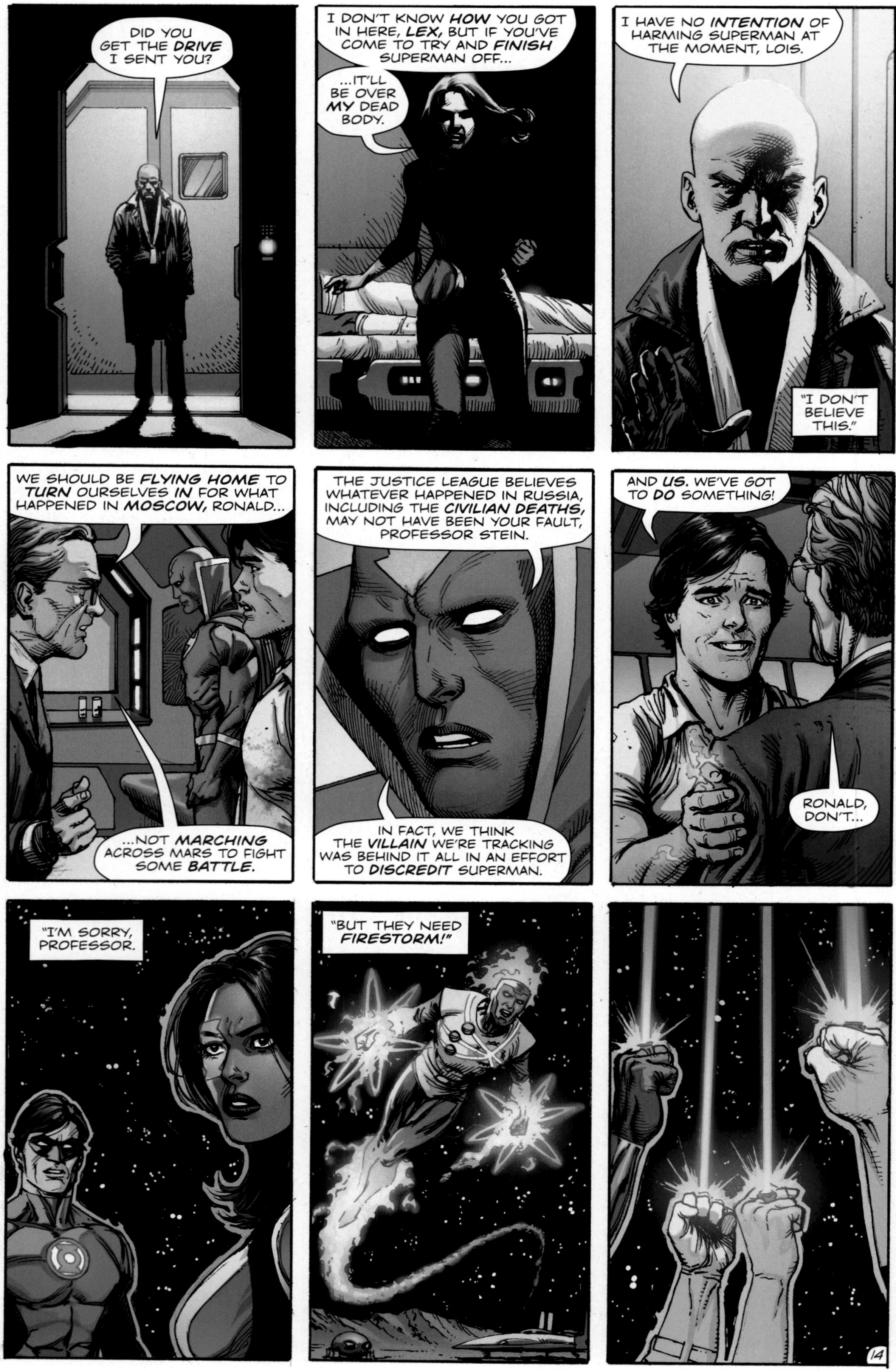
DID YOU GET THE DRIVE I SENT YOU?
I DON'T KNOW HOW YOU GOT IN HERE, LEX, BUT IF YOU'VE COME TO TRY AND FINISH SUPERMAN OFF...
...IT'LL BE OVER MY DEAD BODY.
I HAVE NO INTENTION OF HARMING SUPERMAN AT THE MOMENT, LOIS.
"I DON'T BELIEVE THIS."
WE SHOULD BE FLYING HOME TO TURN OURSELVES IN FOR WHAT HAPPENED IN MOSCOW, RONALD...
...NOT MARCHING ACROSS MARS TO FIGHT SOME BATTLE.
THE JUSTICE LEAGUE BELIEVES WHATEVER HAPPENED IN RUSSIA, INCLUDING THE CIVILIAN DEATHS, MAY NOT HAVE BEEN YOUR FAULT, PROFESSOR STEIN.
IN FACT, WE THINK THE VILLAIN WE'RE TRACKING WAS BEHIND IT ALL IN AN EFFORT TO DISCREDIT SUPERMAN.
AND US. WE'VE GOT TO DO SOMETHING!
RONALD, DON'T...
"I'M SORRY, PROFESSOR.
"BUT THEY NEED FIRESTORM!"
14

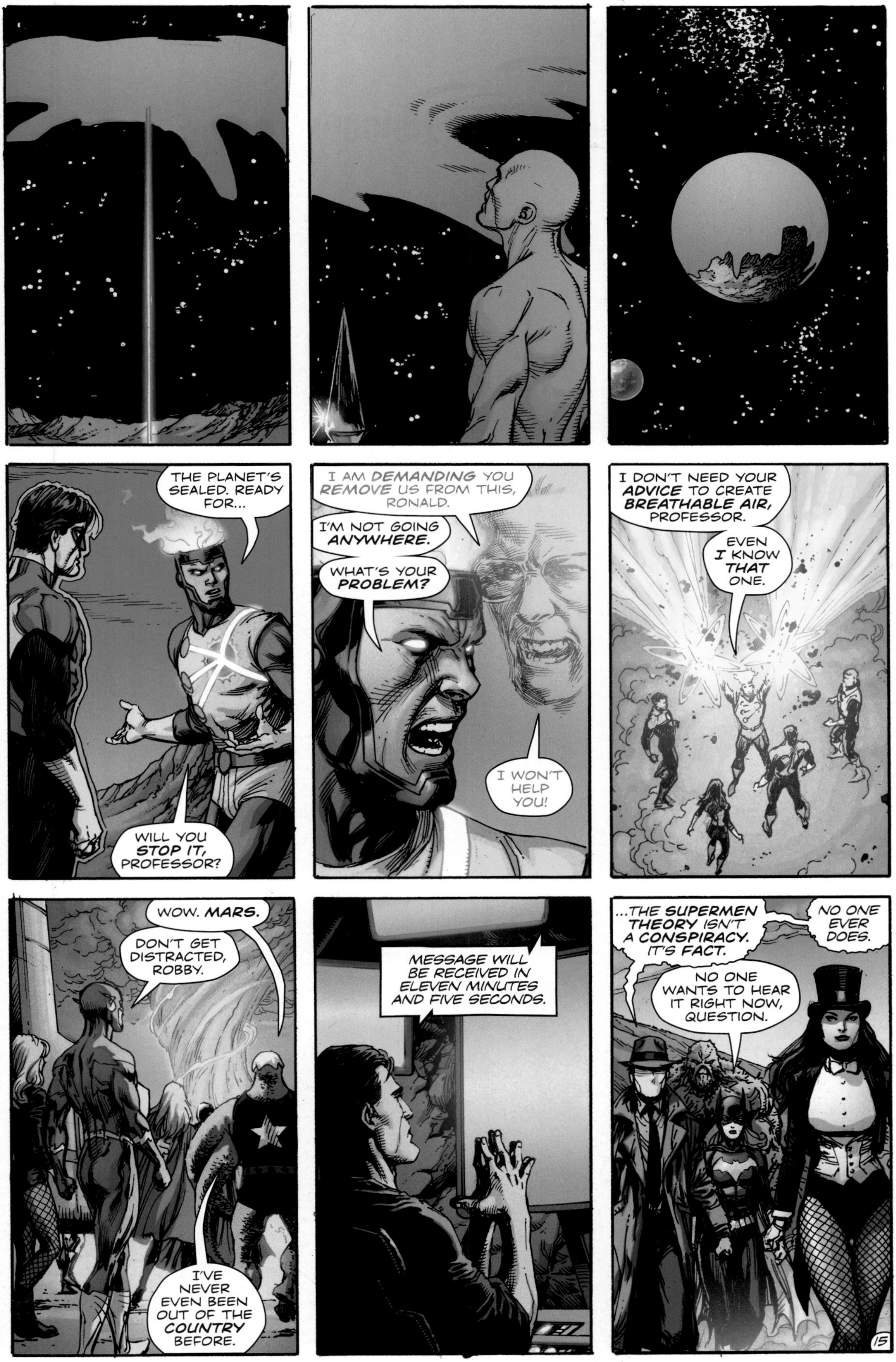
THE PLANET'S SEALED. READY FOR...
WILL YOU STOP IT, PROFESSOR?
I AM DEMANDING YOU REMOVE US FROM THIS, RONALD.
I'M NOT GOING ANYWHERE.
WHAT'S YOUR PROBLEM?
I WON'T HELP YOU!
I DON'T NEED YOUR ADVICE TO CREATE BREATHABLE AIR, PROFESSOR.
EVEN I KNOW THAT ONE.
WOW. MARS.
DON'T GET DISTRACTED, ROBBY.
I'VE NEVER EVEN BEEN OUT OF THE COUNTRY BEFORE.
MESSAGE WILL BE RECEIVED IN ELEVEN MINUTES AND FIVE SECONDS.
...THE SUPERMEN THEORY ISN'T A CONSPIRACY. IT'S FACT.
NO ONE EVER DOES.
NO ONE WANTS TO HEAR IT RIGHT NOW, QUESTION.
15

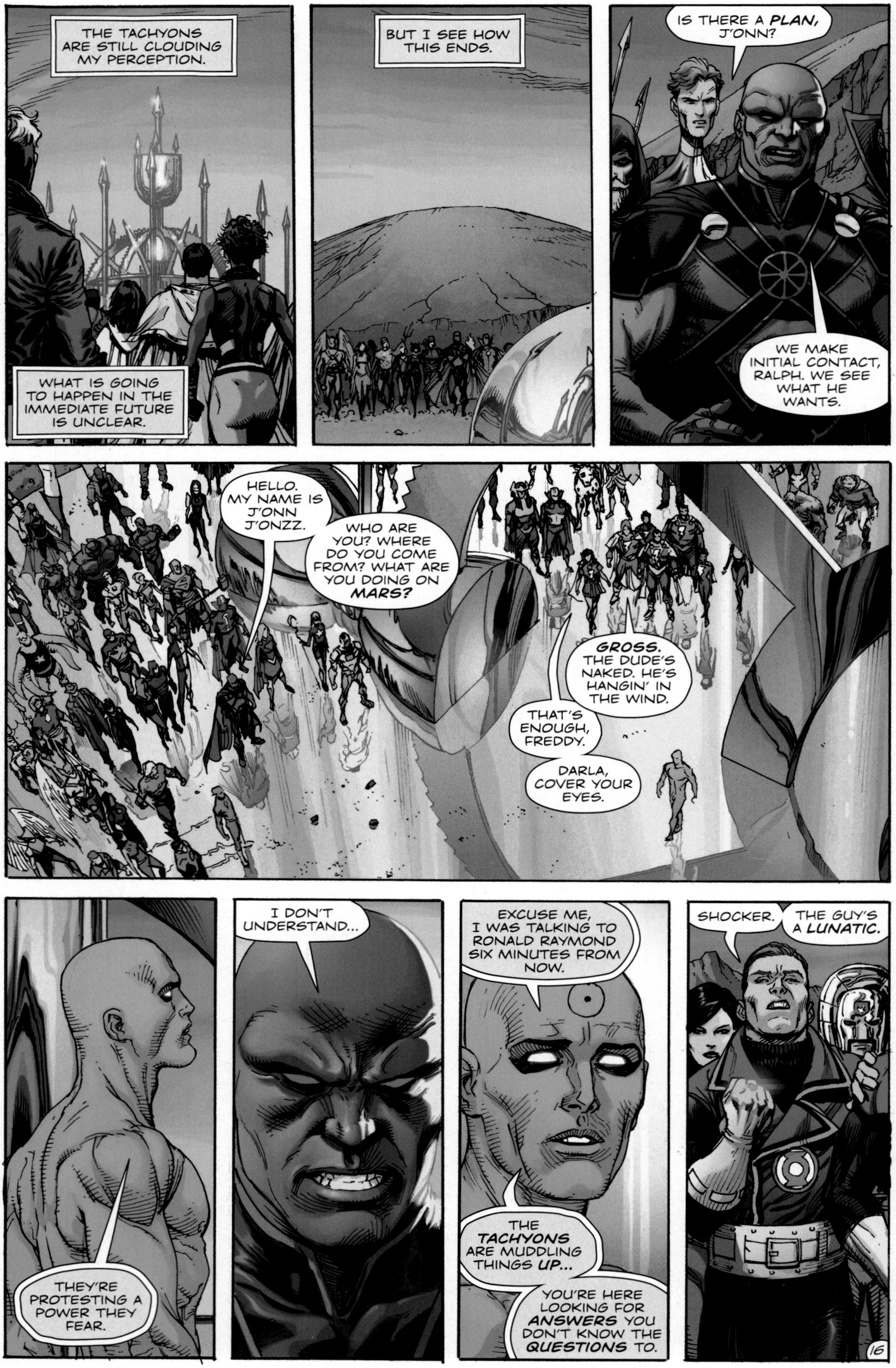
THE TACHYONS ARE STILL CLOUDING MY PERCEPTION.
WHAT IS GOING TO HAPPEN IN THE IMMEDIATE FUTURE IS UNCLEAR.
BUT I SEE HOW THIS ENDS.
IS THERE A PLAN, J'ONN?
WE MAKE INITIAL CONTACT, RALPH. WE SEE WHAT HE WANTS.
HELLO. MY NAME IS J'ONN J'ONZZ.
WHO ARE YOU? WHERE DO YOU COME FROM? WHAT ARE YOU DOING ON MARS?
GROSS. THE DUDE'S NAKED. HE'S HANGIN' IN THE WIND.
THAT'S ENOUGH, FREDDY.
DARLA, COVER YOUR EYES.
THEY'RE PROTESTING A POWER THEY FEAR.
I DON'T UNDERSTAND...
EXCUSE ME, I WAS TALKING TO RONALD RAYMOND SIX MINUTES FROM NOW.
THE TACHYONS ARE MUDDLING THINGS UP...
YOU'RE HERE LOOKING FOR ANSWERS YOU DON'T KNOW THE QUESTIONS TO.
SHOCKER.
THE GUY'S A LUNATIC.
16

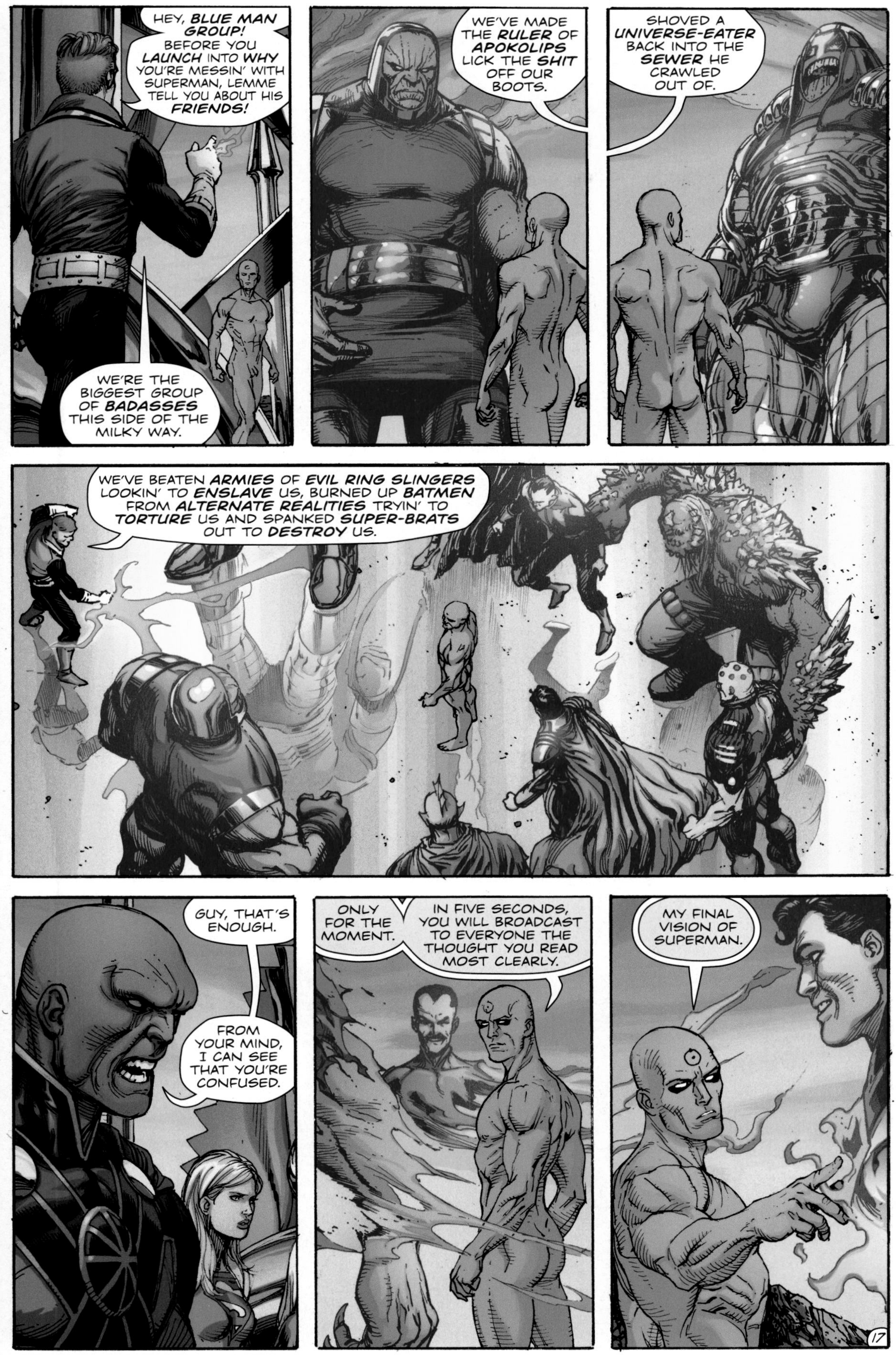
HEY, BLUE MAN GROUP! BEFORE YOU LAUNCH INTO WHY YOU'RE MESSIN' WITH SUPERMAN, LEMME TELL YOU ABOUT HIS FRIENDS!
WE'RE THE BIGGEST GROUP OF BADASSES THIS SIDE OF THE MILKY WAY.
WE'VE MADE THE RULER OF APOKOLIPS LICK THE SHIT OFF OUR BOOTS.
SHOVED A UNIVERSE-EATER BACK INTO THE SEWER HE CRAWLED OUT OF.
WE'VE BEATEN ARMIES OF EVIL RING SLINGERS LOOKIN' TO ENSLAVE US, BURNED UP BATMEN FROM ALTERNATE REALITIES TRYIN' TO TORTURE US AND SPANKED SUPER-BRATS OUT TO DESTROY US.
GUY, THAT'S ENOUGH.
FROM YOUR MIND, I CAN SEE THAT YOU'RE CONFUSED.
ONLY FOR THE MOMENT.
IN FIVE SECONDS, YOU WILL BROADCAST TO EVERYONE THE THOUGHT YOU READ MOST CLEARLY.
MY FINAL VISION OF SUPERMAN.
17

YOU THINK HE'S GOING TO *DESTROY* YOU SO YOU'RE OUT TO DESTROY HIM *FIRST?*

AND ALL OF US *WITH* HIM.

YOU ALL *SAW* WHAT J'ONN DID, RIGHT? THIS *FREAK* THINKS IT'S THE *END* OF THE *UNIVERSE!*

SHIT, THAT'S ENOUGH FOR ME!

TALK IS OVER. LET'S PUT SOME UNDERWEAR ON THIS GUY!

AAAAHHHH!

WAIT. IS THAT *IT?*

CHRIST, I DIDN'T MEAN TO *KILL* HIM OUTRIGHT, BUT HE *HAD* IT COMIN'...

HEY.

WHERE'D HE GO?

18

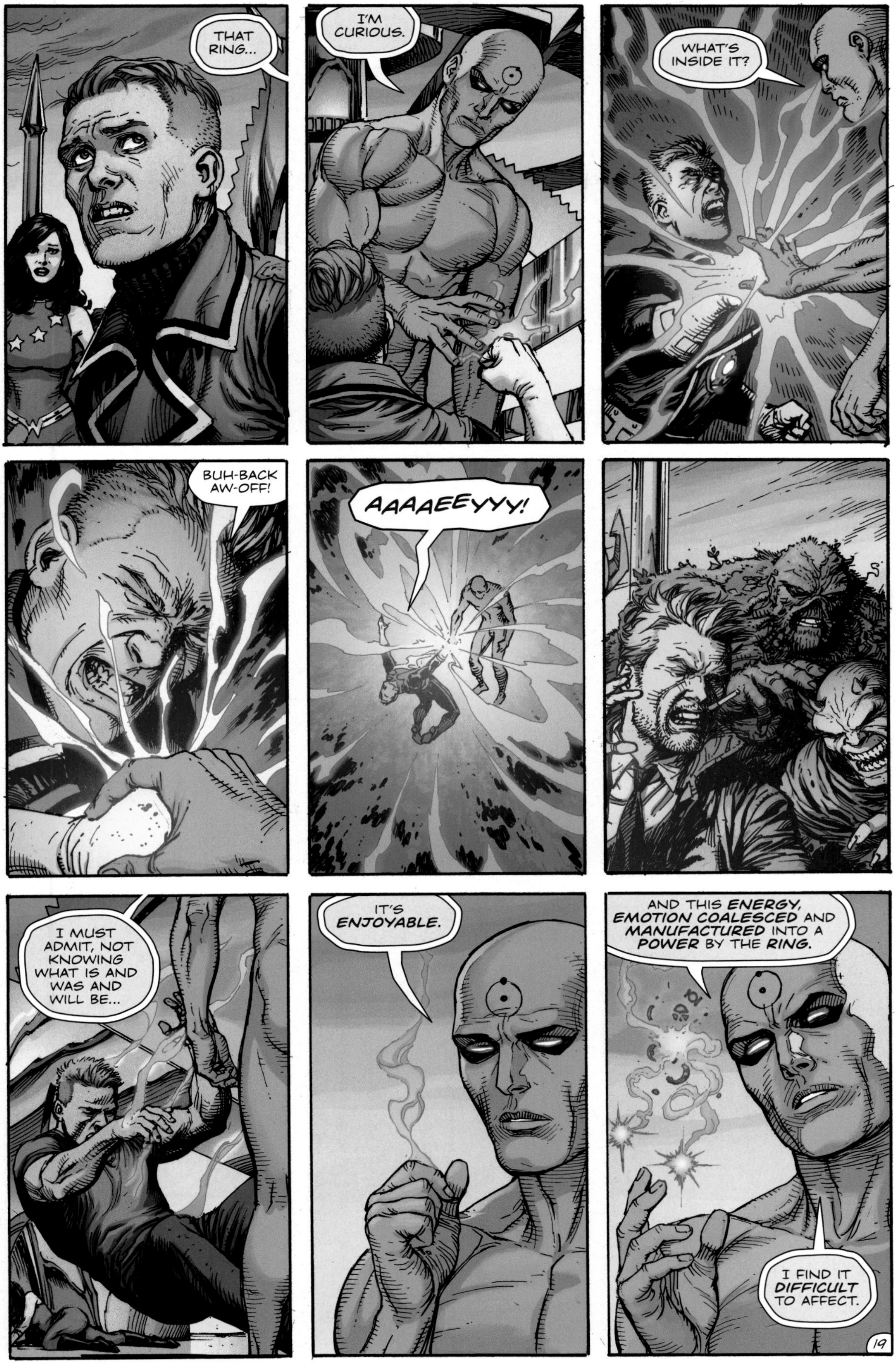

THAT RING...
I'M CURIOUS.
WHAT'S INSIDE IT?
BUH-BACK AW-OFF!
AAAAEEYYY!
I MUST ADMIT, NOT KNOWING WHAT IS AND WAS AND WILL BE...
IT'S ENJOYABLE.
AND THIS ENERGY, EMOTION COALESCED AND MANUFACTURED INTO A POWER BY THE RING.
I FIND IT DIFFICULT TO AFFECT.

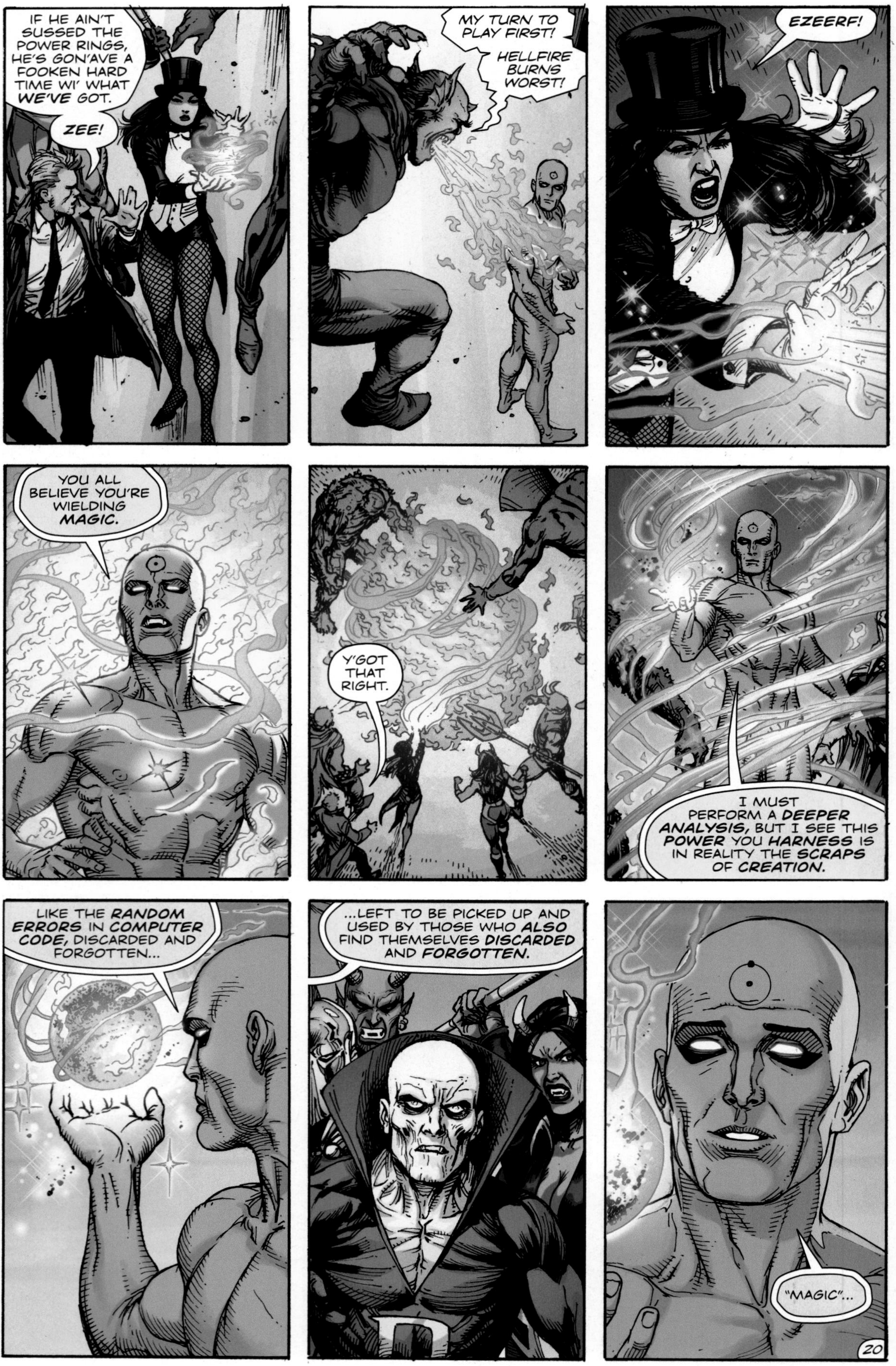
IF HE AIN'T SUSSED THE POWER RINGS, HE'S GON'AVE A FOOKEN HARD TIME WI' WHAT WE'VE GOT.
ZEE!
MY TURN TO PLAY FIRST!
HELLFIRE BURNS WORST!
EZEERF!
YOU ALL BELIEVE YOU'RE WIELDING MAGIC.
Y'GOT THAT RIGHT.
I MUST PERFORM A DEEPER ANALYSIS, BUT I SEE THIS POWER YOU HARNESS IS IN REALITY THE SCRAPS OF CREATION.
LIKE THE RANDOM ERRORS IN COMPUTER CODE, DISCARDED AND FORGOTTEN...
...LEFT TO BE PICKED UP AND USED BY THOSE WHO ALSO FIND THEMSELVES DISCARDED AND FORGOTTEN.
"MAGIC"...

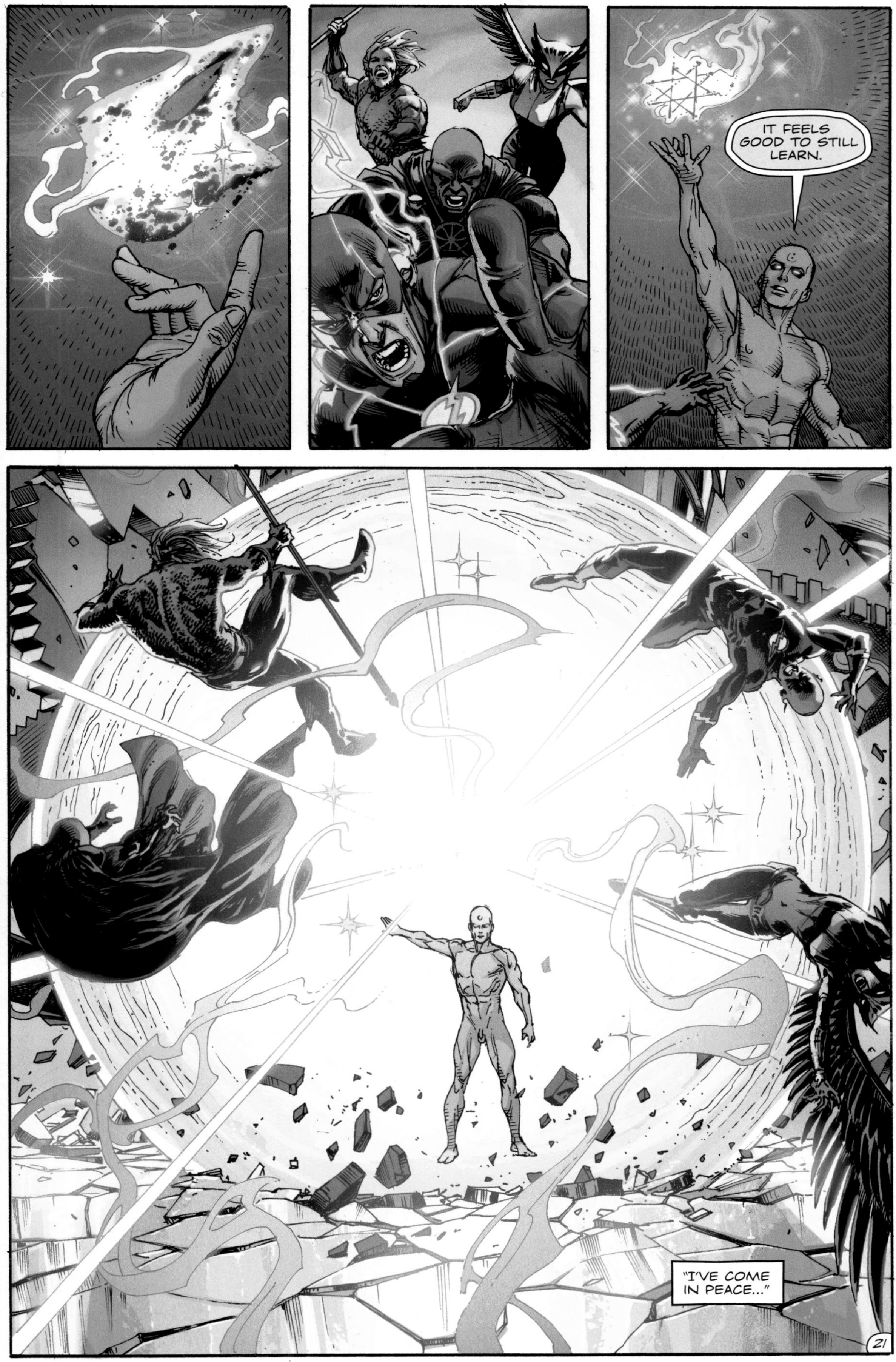
IT FEELS GOOD TO STILL LEARN.
"I'VE COME IN PEACE..."

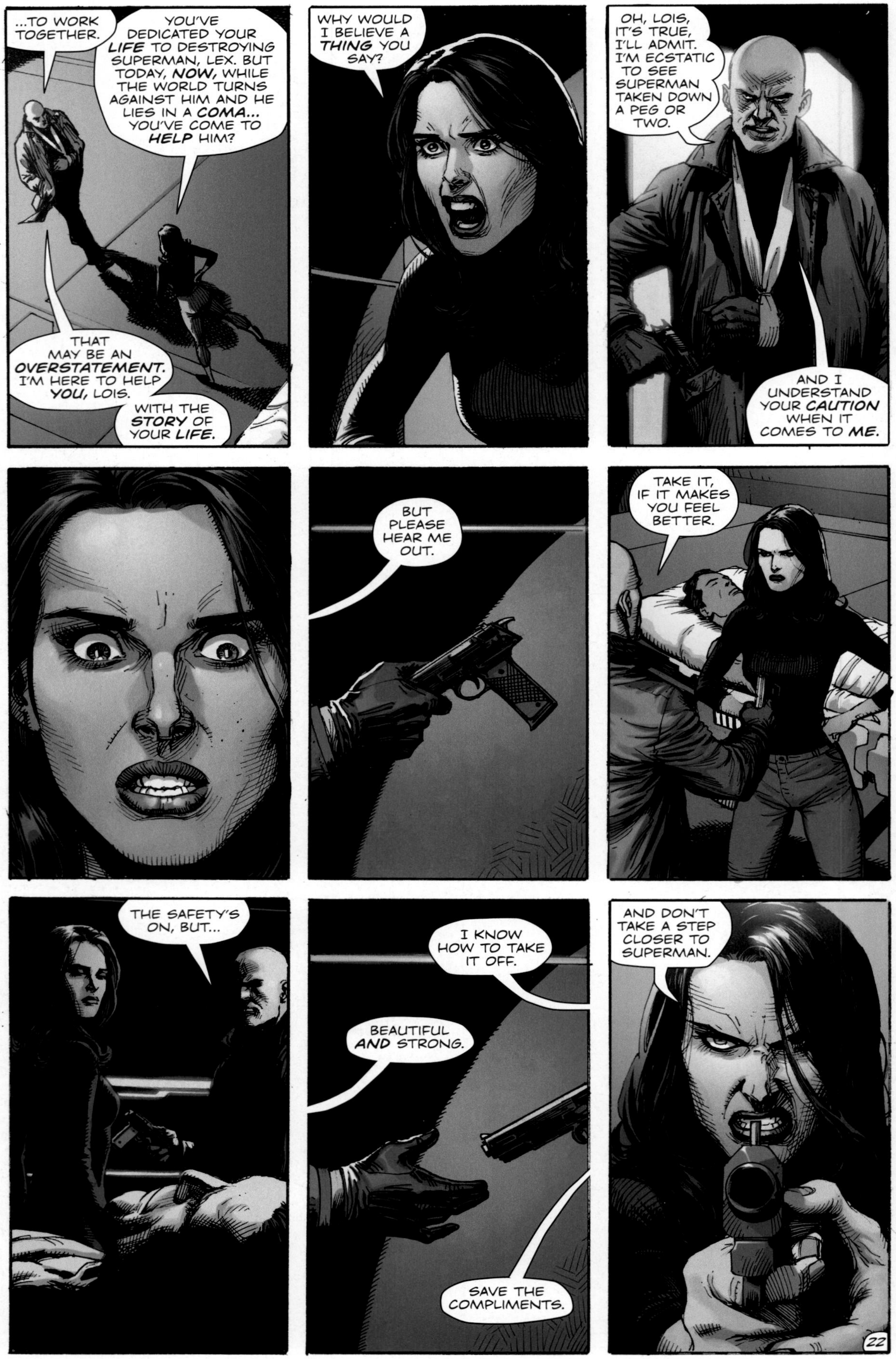
...TO WORK TOGETHER.
YOU'VE DEDICATED YOUR LIFE TO DESTROYING SUPERMAN, LEX. BUT TODAY, NOW, WHILE THE WORLD TURNS AGAINST HIM AND HE LIES IN A COMA... YOU'VE COME TO HELP HIM?
THAT MAY BE AN OVERSTATEMENT. I'M HERE TO HELP YOU, LOIS.
WITH THE STORY OF YOUR LIFE.
WHY WOULD I BELIEVE A THING YOU SAY?
OH, LOIS, IT'S TRUE, I'LL ADMIT. I'M ECSTATIC TO SEE SUPERMAN TAKEN DOWN A PEG OR TWO.
AND I UNDERSTAND YOUR CAUTION WHEN IT COMES TO ME.
BUT PLEASE HEAR ME OUT.
TAKE IT, IF IT MAKES YOU FEEL BETTER.
THE SAFETY'S ON, BUT...
I KNOW HOW TO TAKE IT OFF.
BEAUTIFUL AND STRONG.
SAVE THE COMPLIMENTS.
AND DON'T TAKE A STEP CLOSER TO SUPERMAN.
22

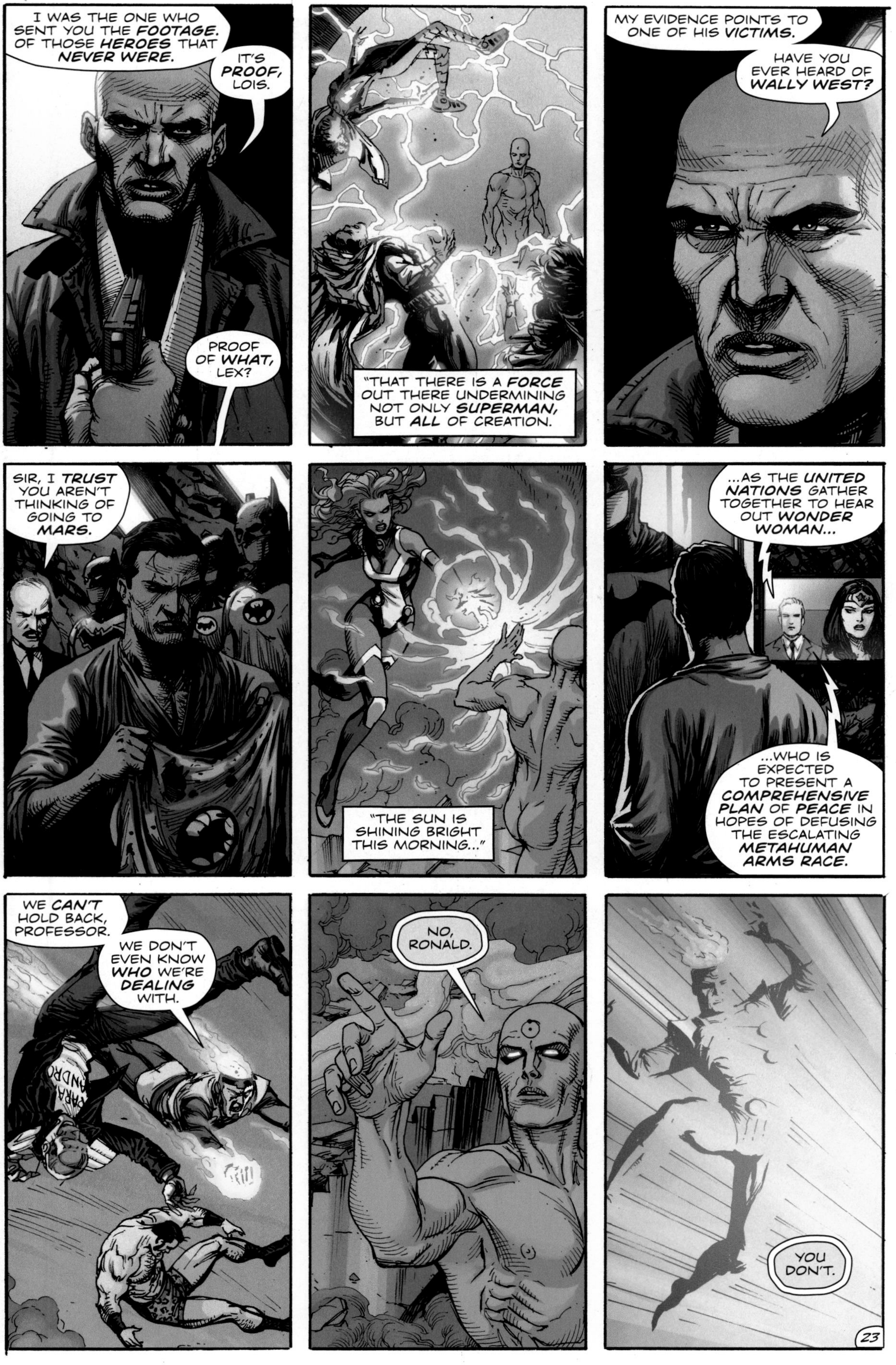
I WAS THE ONE WHO SENT YOU THE FOOTAGE. OF THOSE HEROES THAT NEVER WERE.
IT'S PROOF, LOIS.
PROOF OF WHAT, LEX?
"THAT THERE IS A FORCE OUT THERE UNDERMINING NOT ONLY SUPERMAN, BUT ALL OF CREATION.
MY EVIDENCE POINTS TO ONE OF HIS VICTIMS.
HAVE YOU EVER HEARD OF WALLY WEST?
SIR, I TRUST YOU AREN'T THINKING OF GOING TO MARS.
"THE SUN IS SHINING BRIGHT THIS MORNING..."
...AS THE UNITED NATIONS GATHER TOGETHER TO HEAR OUT WONDER WOMAN...
...WHO IS EXPECTED TO PRESENT A COMPREHENSIVE PLAN OF PEACE IN HOPES OF DEFUSING THE ESCALATING METAHUMAN ARMS RACE.
WE CAN'T HOLD BACK, PROFESSOR.
WE DON'T EVEN KNOW WHO WE'RE DEALING WITH.
NO, RONALD.
YOU DON'T.

WHAT... WHAT HAPPENED? PROFESSOR?

WHERE ARE WE?

YOU ARE SEVEN YEARS, FORTY-SIX DAYS, TWENTY MINUTES AND TEN SECONDS AGO.

OUTSIDE...

THEY'RE PROTESTING A POWER THEY FEAR.

"IN LESS THAN TWO HOURS, THIS FACILITY WILL EXPLODE AND YOU AND PROFESSOR MARTIN STEIN WILL BE FUSED INTO A SINGLE ORGANISM.

"ONE OF THE MOST POWERFUL METAHUMANS I HAVE ENCOUNTERED ON THIS EARTH.

"AND LAID BARE, ONE OF THE MOST DEADLY."

STOP PLAYING GOD

WHERE IS THE PROFESSOR?

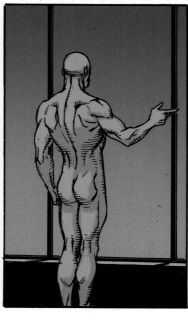

...IT'S ALMOST TIME.

24

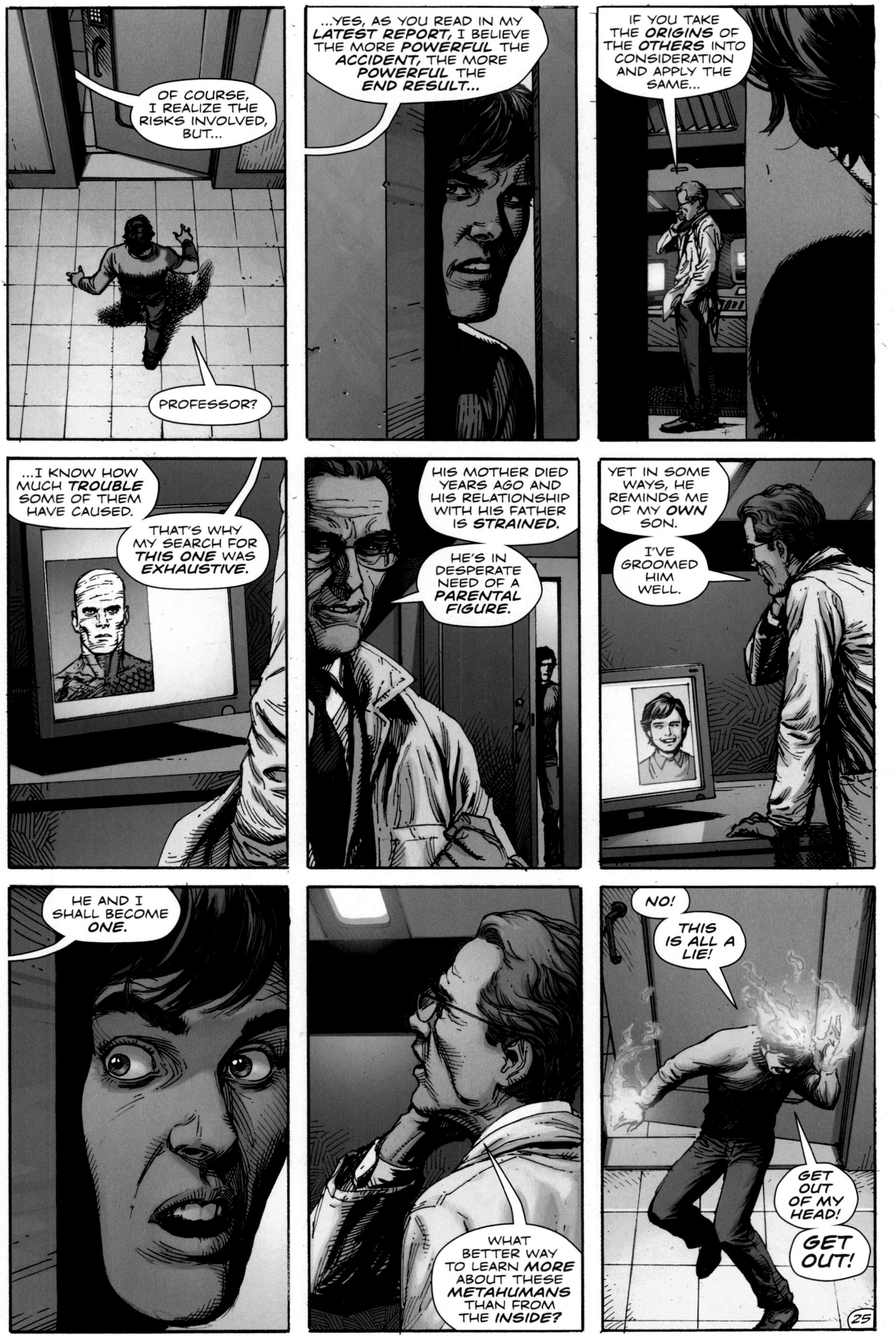
OF COURSE, I REALIZE THE RISKS INVOLVED, BUT...
PROFESSOR?
...YES, AS YOU READ IN MY LATEST REPORT, I BELIEVE THE MORE POWERFUL THE ACCIDENT, THE MORE POWERFUL THE END RESULT...
IF YOU TAKE THE ORIGINS OF THE OTHERS INTO CONSIDERATION AND APPLY THE SAME...
...I KNOW HOW MUCH TROUBLE SOME OF THEM HAVE CAUSED.
THAT'S WHY MY SEARCH FOR THIS ONE WAS EXHAUSTIVE.
HIS MOTHER DIED YEARS AGO AND HIS RELATIONSHIP WITH HIS FATHER IS STRAINED.
HE'S IN DESPERATE NEED OF A PARENTAL FIGURE.
YET IN SOME WAYS, HE REMINDS ME OF MY OWN SON.
I'VE GROOMED HIM WELL.
HE AND I SHALL BECOME ONE.
WHAT BETTER WAY TO LEARN MORE ABOUT THESE METAHUMANS THAN FROM THE INSIDE?
NO!
THIS IS ALL A LIE!
GET OUT OF MY HEAD!
GET OUT!
25

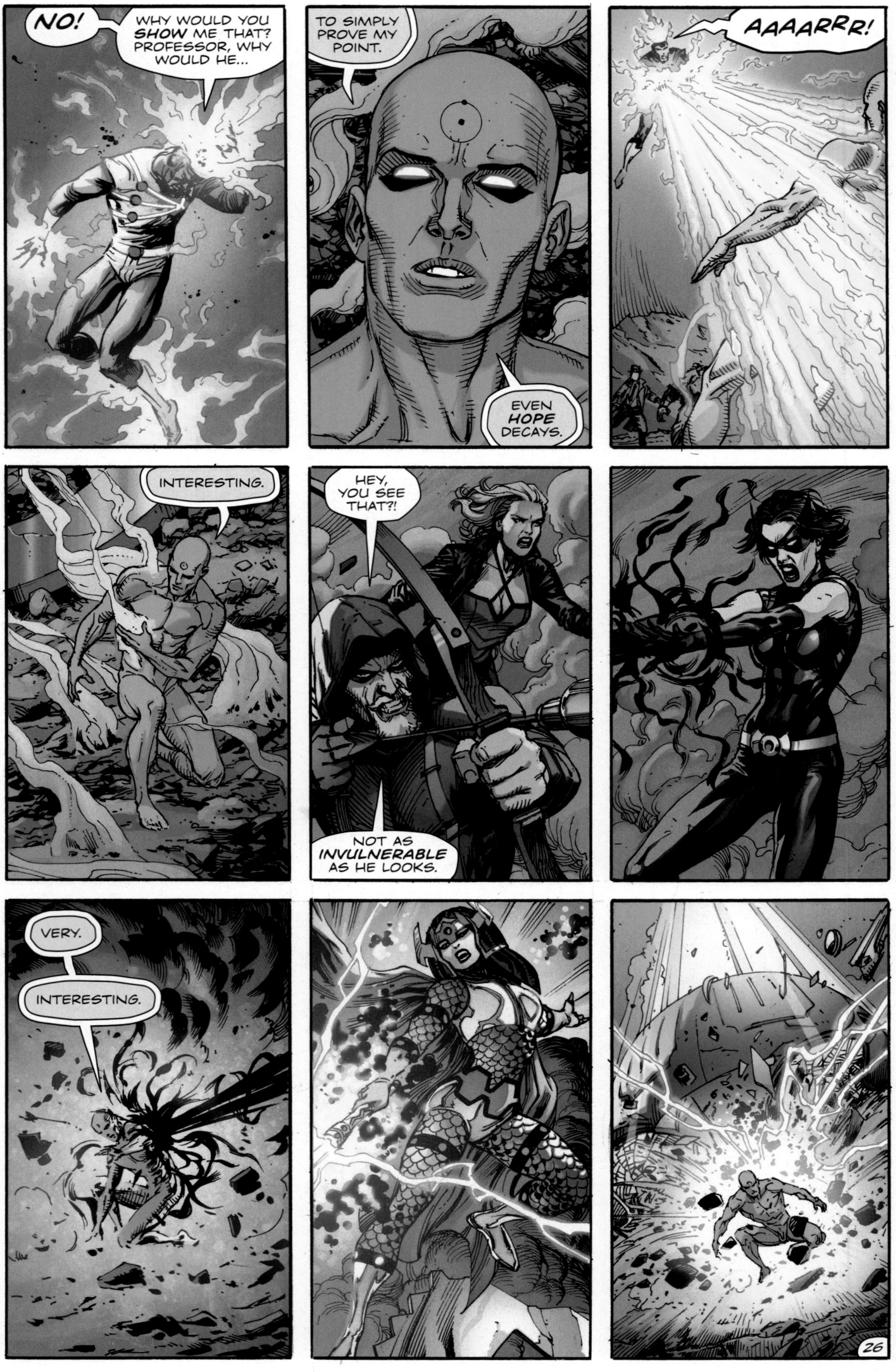
NO!
WHY WOULD YOU SHOW ME THAT? PROFESSOR, WHY WOULD HE...
TO SIMPLY PROVE MY POINT.
EVEN HOPE DECAYS.
AAAARRR!
INTERESTING.
HEY, YOU SEE THAT?!
NOT AS INVULNERABLE AS HE LOOKS.
VERY.
INTERESTING.

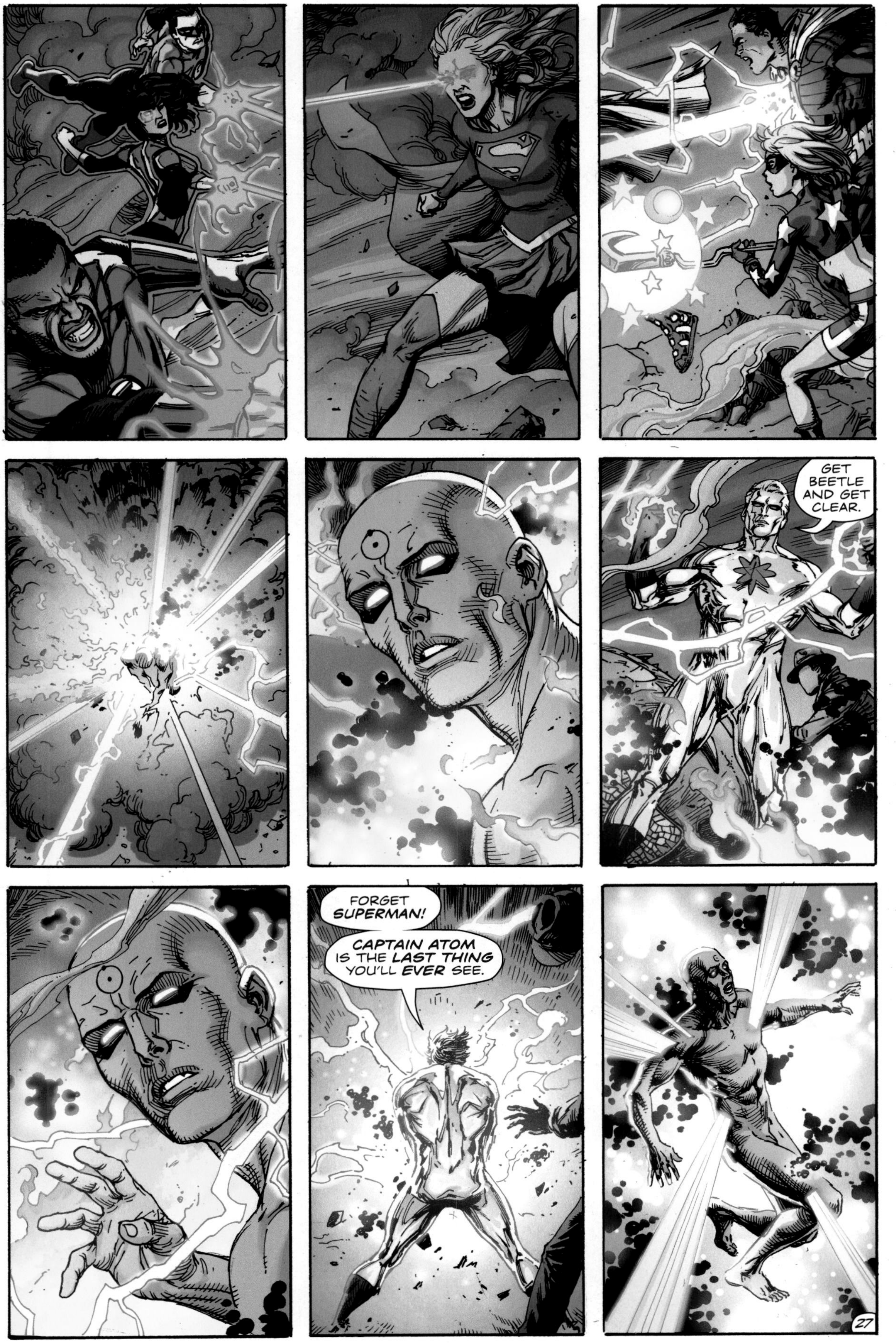
GET BEETLE AND GET CLEAR.
FORGET SUPERMAN!
CAPTAIN ATOM IS THE LAST THING YOU'LL EVER SEE.

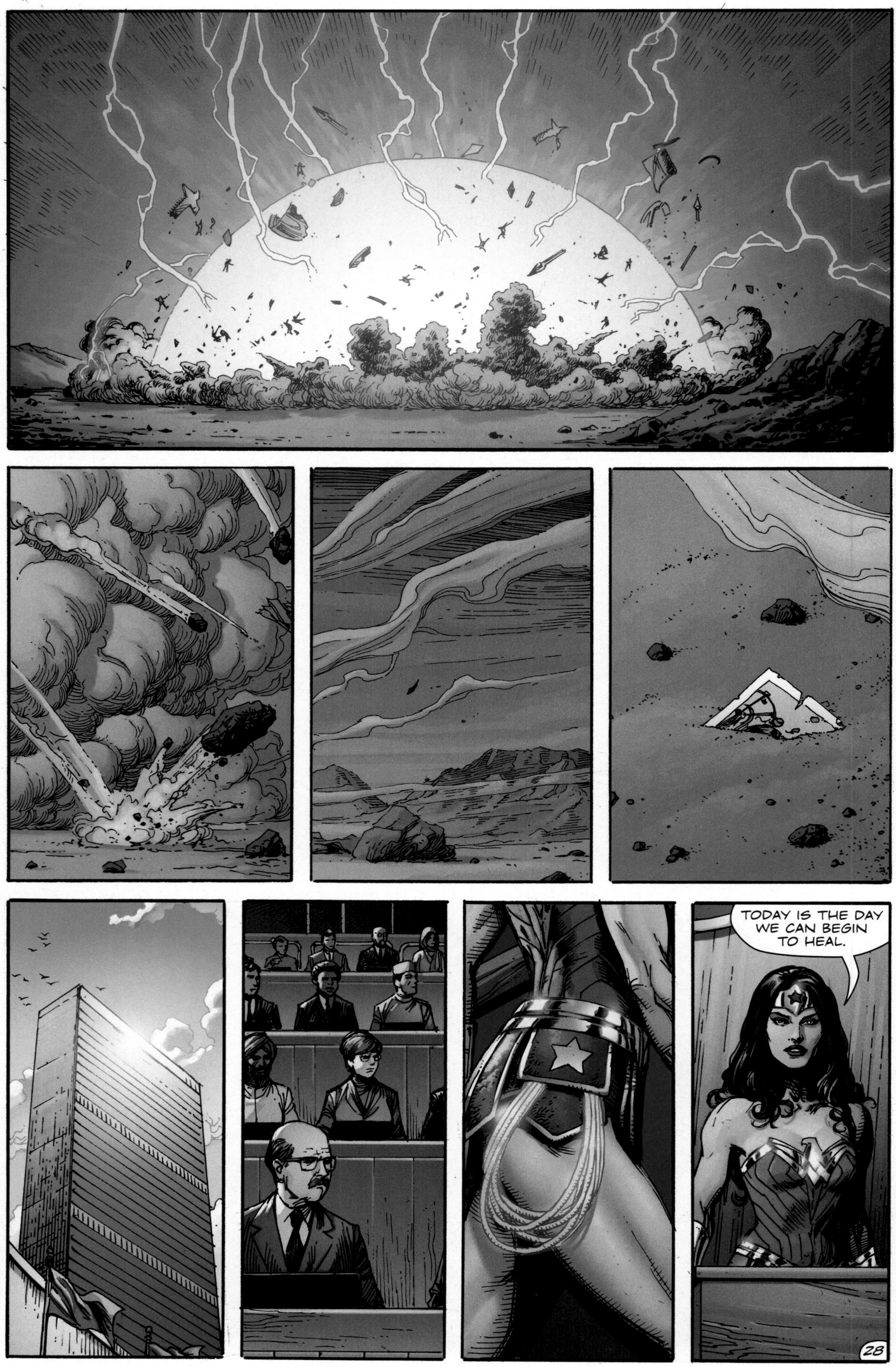
TODAY IS THE DAY WE CAN BEGIN TO HEAL.
28

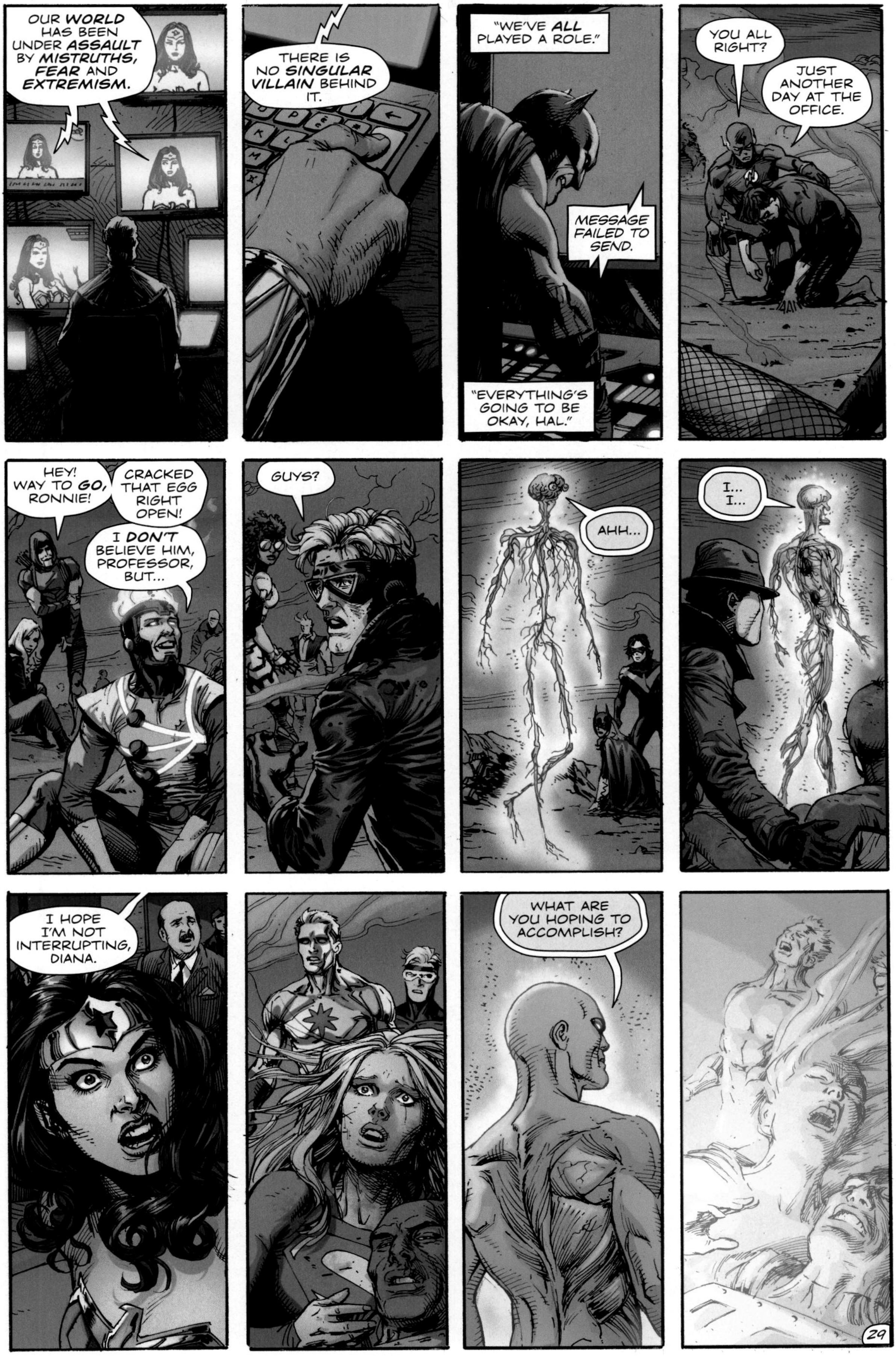
OUR WORLD HAS BEEN UNDER ASSAULT BY MISTRUTHS, FEAR AND EXTREMISM.
THERE IS NO SINGULAR VILLAIN BEHIND IT.
"WE'VE ALL PLAYED A ROLE."
MESSAGE FAILED TO SEND.
"EVERYTHING'S GOING TO BE OKAY, HAL."
YOU ALL RIGHT?
JUST ANOTHER DAY AT THE OFFICE.
HEY! WAY TO GO, RONNIE!
CRACKED THAT EGG RIGHT OPEN!
I DON'T BELIEVE HIM, PROFESSOR, BUT...
GUYS?
AHH...
I... I...
I HOPE I'M NOT INTERRUPTING, DIANA.
WHAT ARE YOU HOPING TO ACCOMPLISH?

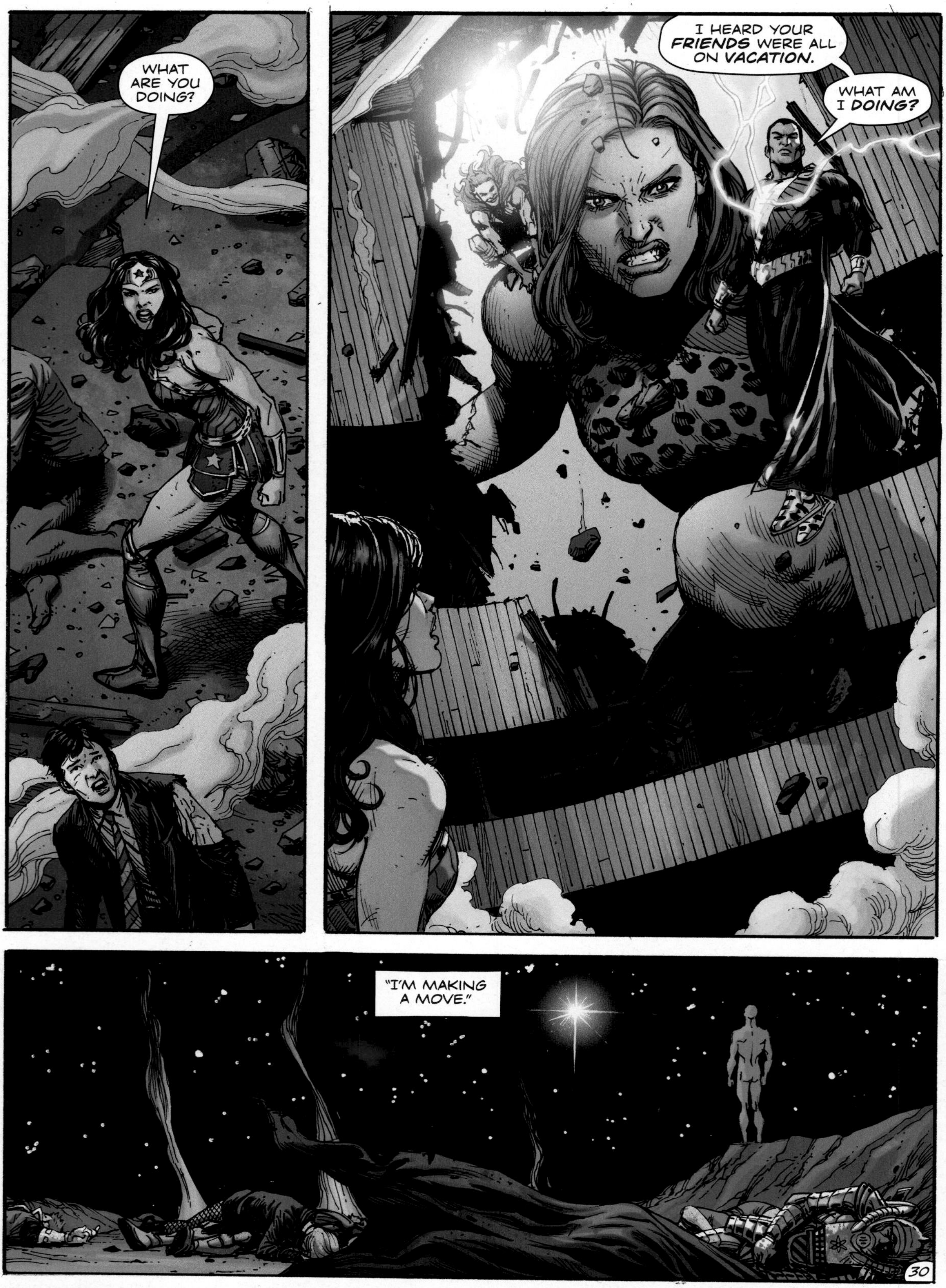
WHAT ARE YOU DOING?
I HEARD YOUR FRIENDS WERE ALL ON VACATION.
WHAT AM I DOING?
"I'M MAKING A MOVE."

Wherever there is a human being, there is an opportunity for crisis.

—Seneca

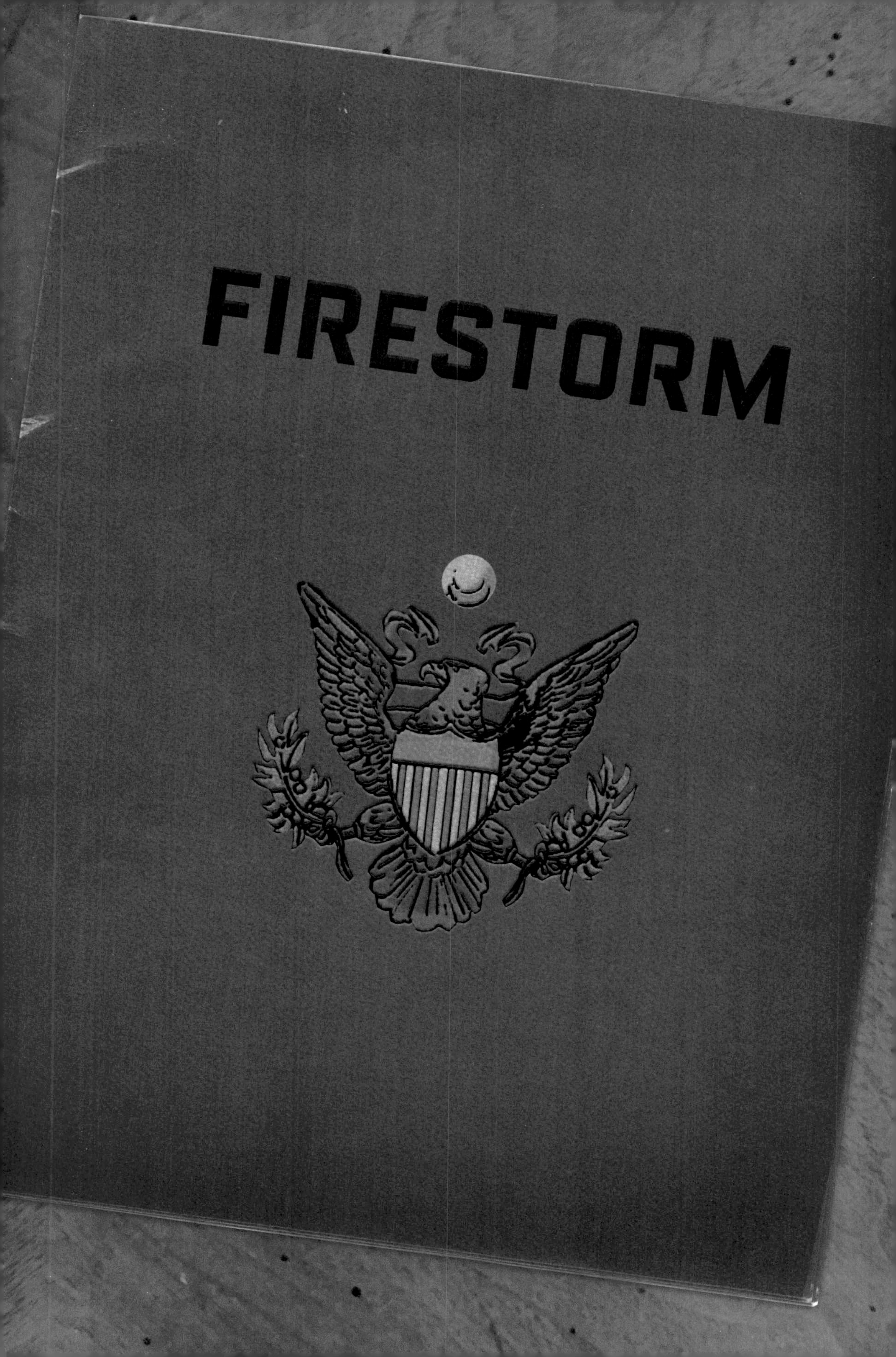
FIRESTORM

DEPARTMENT of METAHUMAN AFFAIRS

THE PENTAGON . . . WASHINGTON, DC . . . 20201

Mr. Secretary,

I believe my son's death could have been prevented had this Department and its agents existed back in his day. My son is why I created this Department and why I've dedicated my life to it. He is also why I'll risk my life for it.

As you are aware, my studies have determined that approximately one in one-thousand Americans are meta-positive, meaning they carry the metagene. A gene that remains a mystery to us. What we do know is that most meta-positives will live out their lives, never realizing they are carriers. In those rare times that a meta-positive is faced with a life-threatening event, the metagene will attempt to "trigger" and "evolve." In most cases, the meta-positive will not survive. But in a rare few cases, the meta-positive will develop fantastic and amazing abilities, most often in correlation to the event. i.e.: the more powerful the accident, the more powerful the metahuman.

As a meta-negative, my research can only take me so far. Rex Mason, Jack Ryder, Kirk Langstrom and the others we've created and put into place have helped us make great leaps forward in our studies. Still, the metahuman community continues to grow at a rapid pace. Only a fraction of them are truly known to us anymore. Even fewer committed to us. I need to personally infiltrate their deepest groups and learn their darkest secrets so that I can protect this great nation. The best way I can do that is to become one of them. And I believe I've found a way with Project Firestorm.

I look forward to discussing more.

With respect,

Martin Stein

Professor Martin Stein
Director, Department of Metahuman Affairs

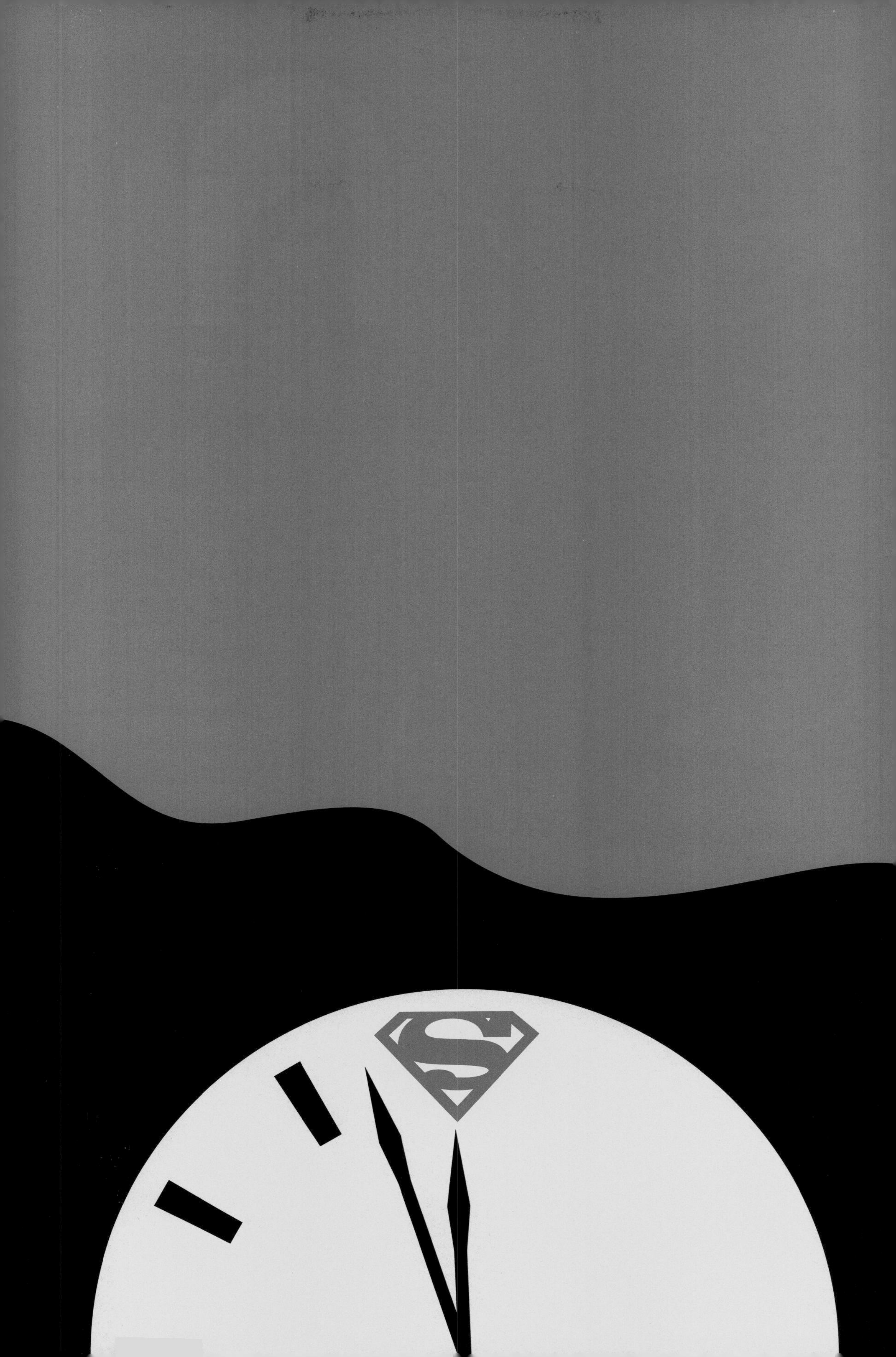

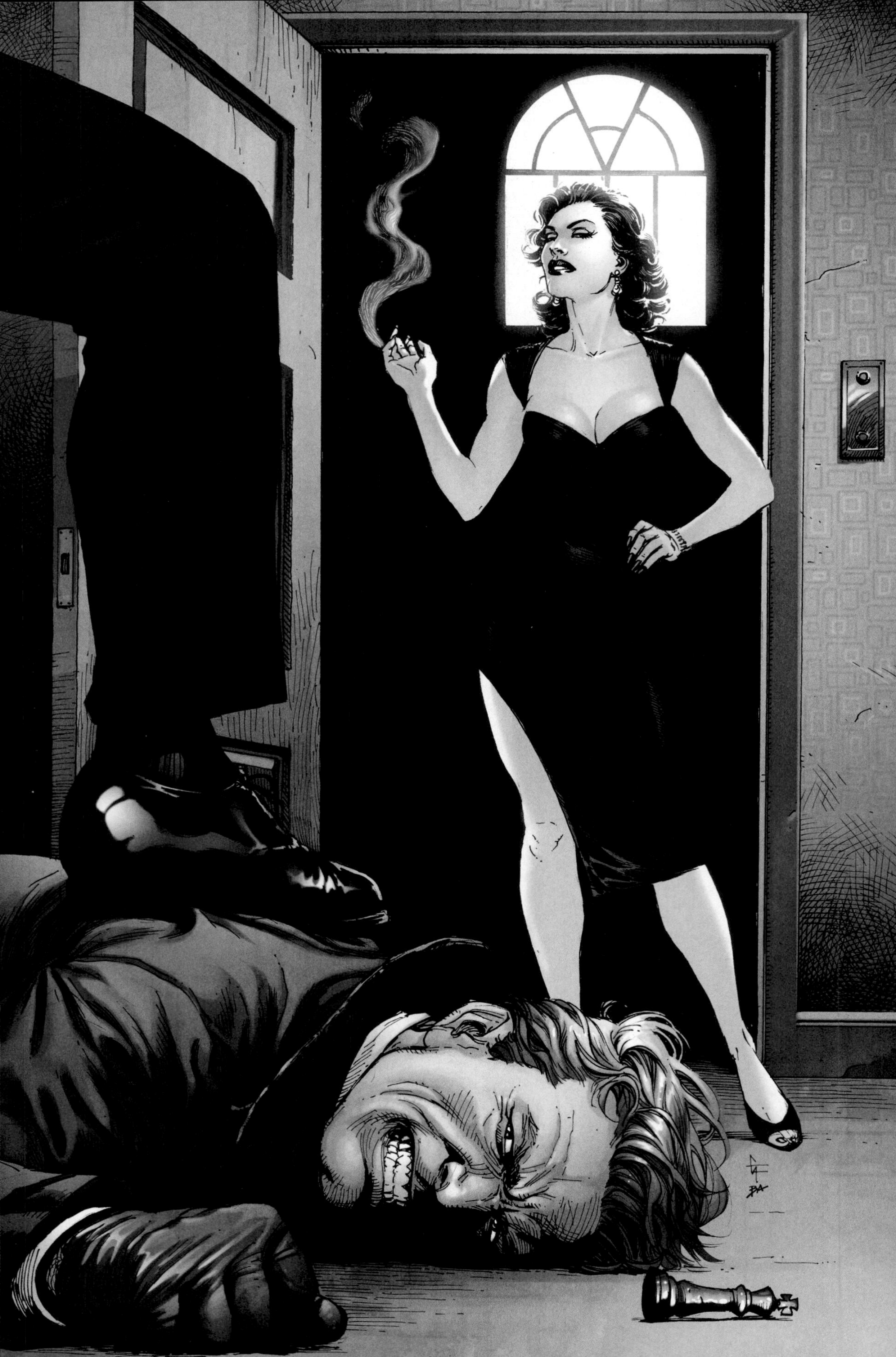

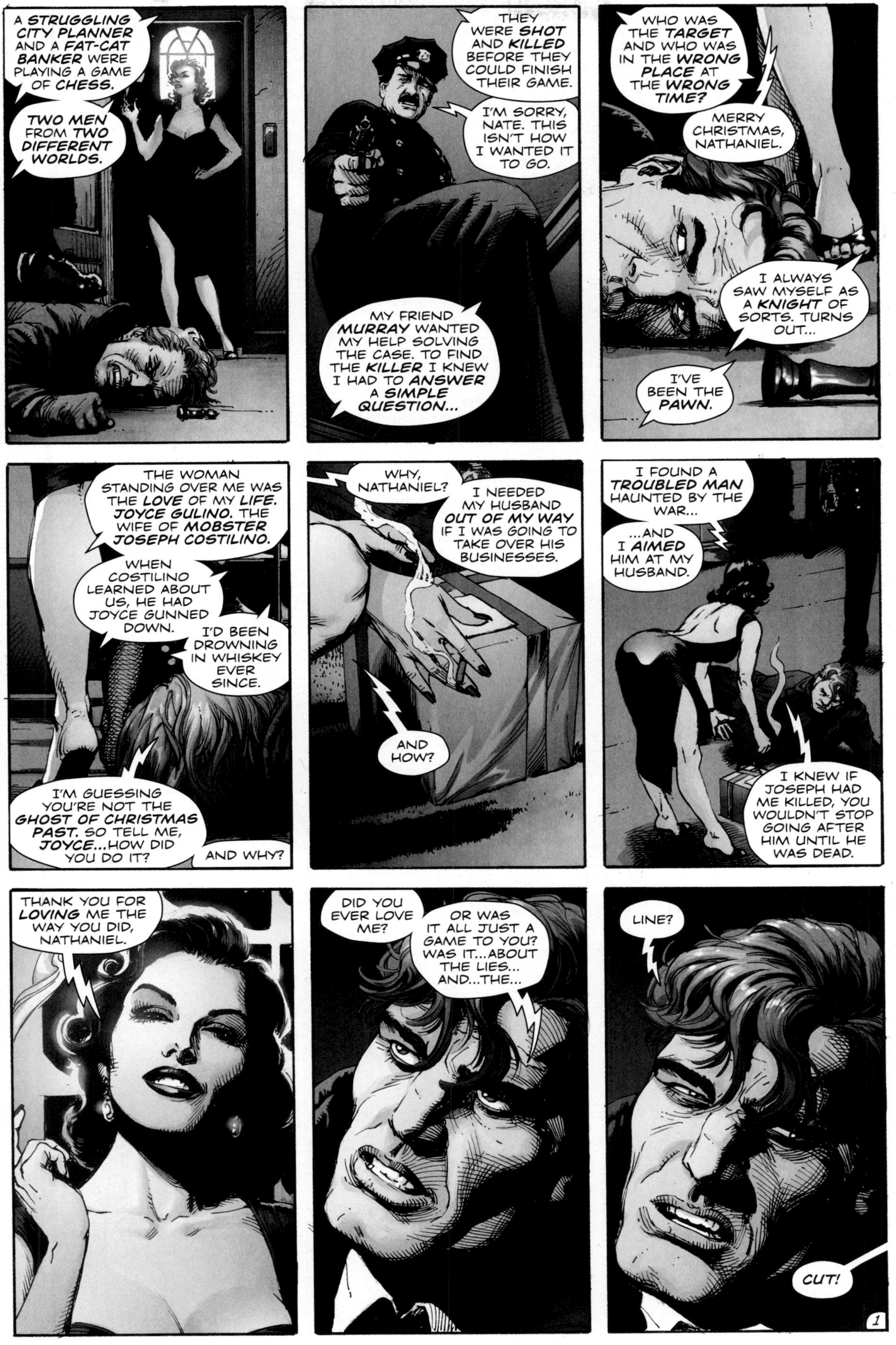
A STRUGGLING CITY PLANNER AND A FAT-CAT BANKER WERE PLAYING A GAME OF CHESS.
TWO MEN FROM TWO DIFFERENT WORLDS.
THEY WERE SHOT AND KILLED BEFORE THEY COULD FINISH THEIR GAME.
I'M SORRY, NATE. THIS ISN'T HOW I WANTED IT TO GO.
MY FRIEND MURRAY WANTED MY HELP SOLVING THE CASE. TO FIND THE KILLER I KNEW I HAD TO ANSWER A SIMPLE QUESTION...
WHO WAS THE TARGET AND WHO WAS IN THE WRONG PLACE AT THE WRONG TIME?
MERRY CHRISTMAS, NATHANIEL.
I ALWAYS SAW MYSELF AS A KNIGHT OF SORTS. TURNS OUT...
I'VE BEEN THE PAWN.
THE WOMAN STANDING OVER ME WAS THE LOVE OF MY LIFE. JOYCE GULINO. THE WIFE OF MOBSTER JOSEPH COSTILINO.
WHEN COSTILINO LEARNED ABOUT US, HE HAD JOYCE GUNNED DOWN.
I'D BEEN DROWNING IN WHISKEY EVER SINCE.
I'M GUESSING YOU'RE NOT THE GHOST OF CHRISTMAS PAST. SO TELL ME, JOYCE...HOW DID YOU DO IT?
AND WHY?
WHY, NATHANIEL?
I NEEDED MY HUSBAND OUT OF MY WAY IF I WAS GOING TO TAKE OVER HIS BUSINESSES.
AND HOW?
I FOUND A TROUBLED MAN HAUNTED BY THE WAR...
...AND I AIMED HIM AT MY HUSBAND.
I KNEW IF JOSEPH HAD ME KILLED, YOU WOULDN'T STOP GOING AFTER HIM UNTIL HE WAS DEAD.
THANK YOU FOR LOVING ME THE WAY YOU DID, NATHANIEL.
DID YOU EVER LOVE ME?
OR WAS IT ALL JUST A GAME TO YOU? WAS IT...ABOUT THE LIES... AND...THE...
LINE?
CUT!

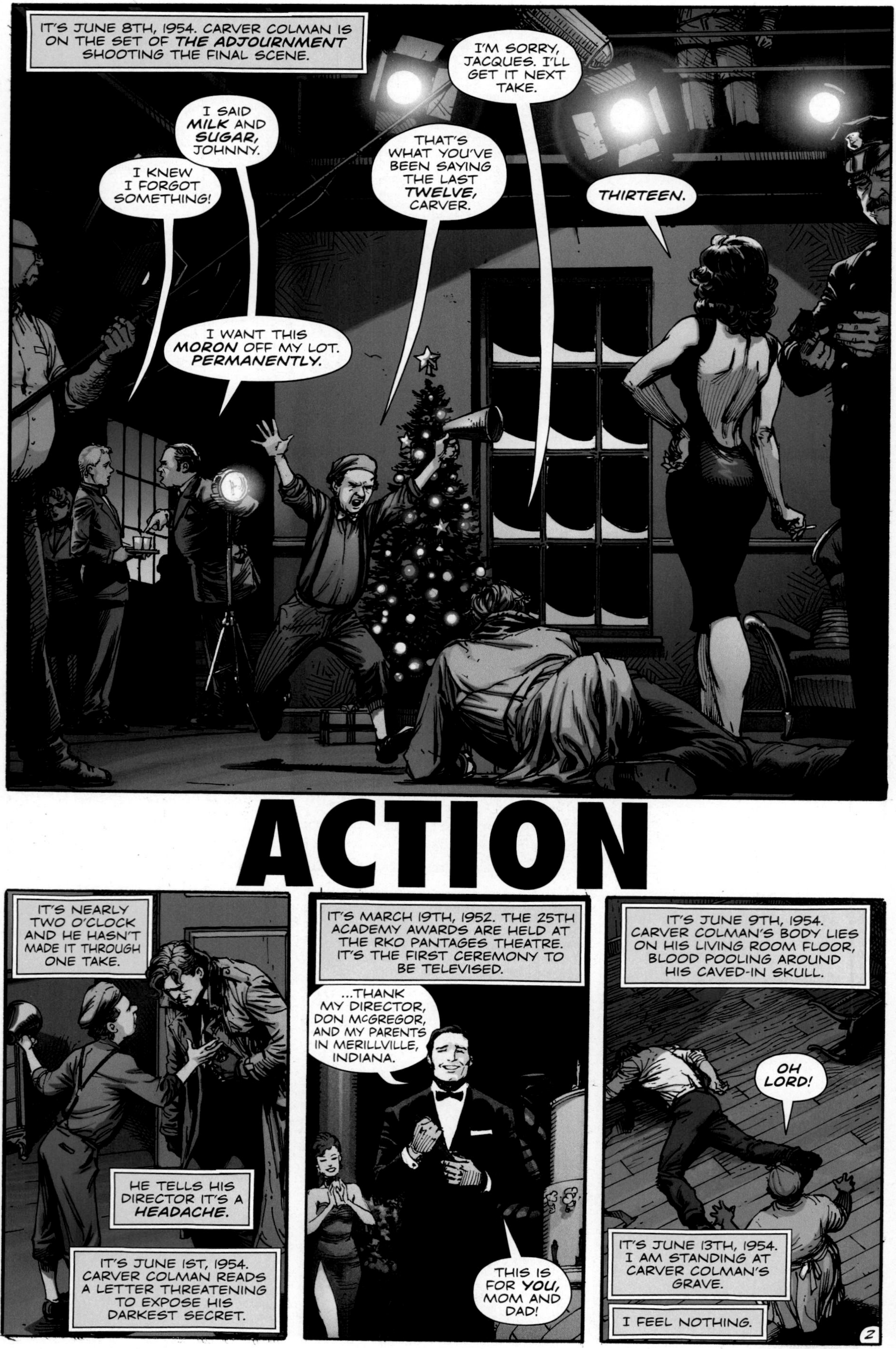

IT'S JUNE 8TH, 1954. CARVER COLMAN IS ON THE SET OF *THE ADJOURNMENT* SHOOTING THE FINAL SCENE.
I SAID *MILK* AND *SUGAR,* JOHNNY.
I KNEW I FORGOT SOMETHING!
I WANT THIS *MORON* OFF MY LOT. *PERMANENTLY.*
I'M SORRY, JACQUES. I'LL GET IT NEXT TAKE.
THAT'S WHAT YOU'VE BEEN SAYING THE LAST *TWELVE,* CARVER.
THIRTEEN.
ACTION
IT'S NEARLY TWO O'CLOCK AND HE HASN'T MADE IT THROUGH ONE TAKE.
HE TELLS HIS DIRECTOR IT'S A *HEADACHE.*
IT'S JUNE 1ST, 1954. CARVER COLMAN READS A LETTER THREATENING TO EXPOSE HIS DARKEST SECRET.
IT'S MARCH 19TH, 1952. THE 25TH ACADEMY AWARDS ARE HELD AT THE RKO PANTAGES THEATRE. IT'S THE FIRST CEREMONY TO BE TELEVISED.
...THANK MY DIRECTOR, DON McGREGOR, AND MY PARENTS IN MERILLVILLE, INDIANA.
THIS IS FOR *YOU,* MOM AND DAD!
IT'S JUNE 9TH, 1954. CARVER COLMAN'S BODY LIES ON HIS LIVING ROOM FLOOR, BLOOD POOLING AROUND HIS CAVED-IN SKULL.
OH LORD!
IT'S JUNE 13TH, 1954. I AM STANDING AT CARVER COLMAN'S GRAVE.
I FEEL NOTHING.

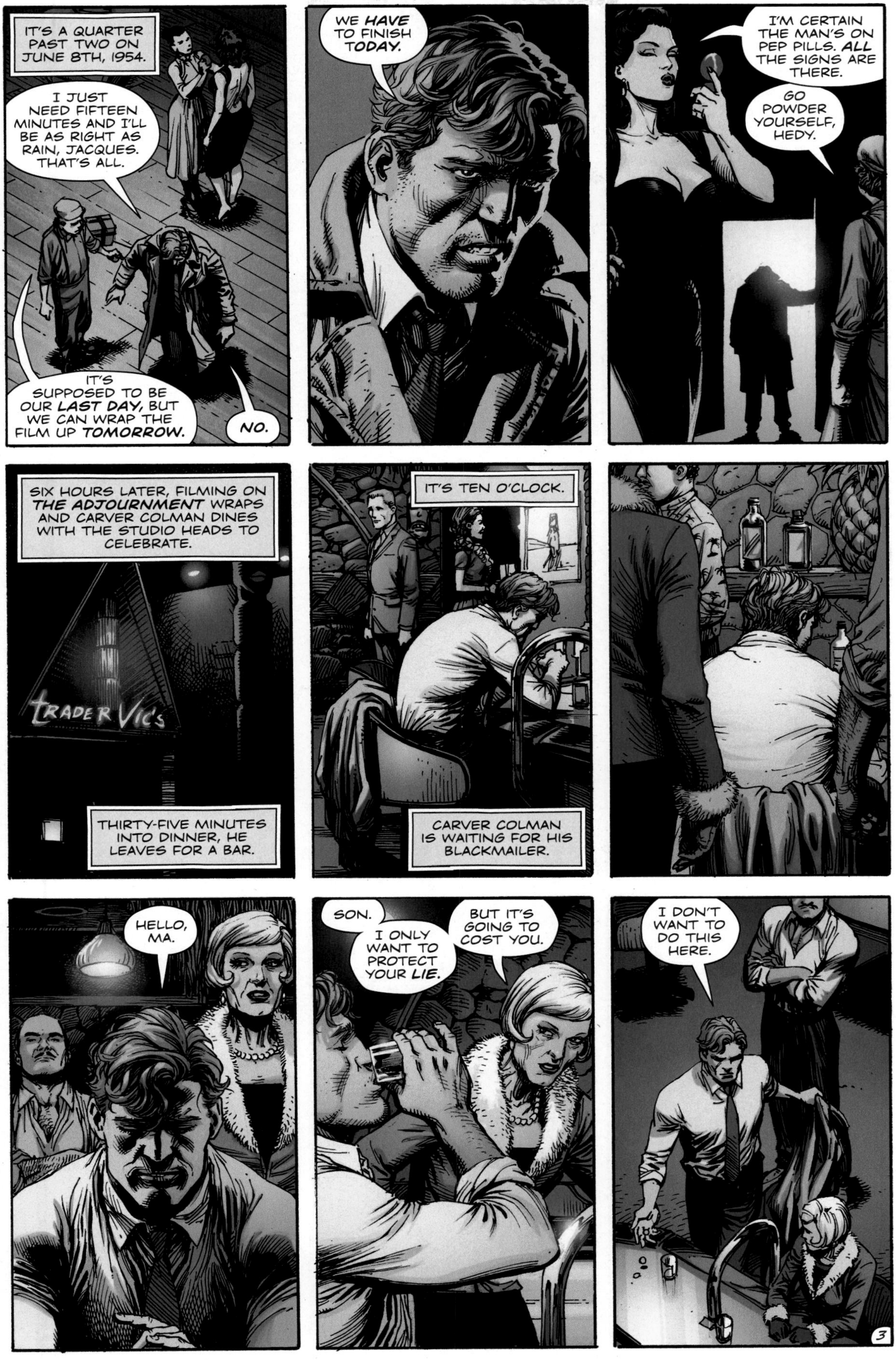
IT'S A QUARTER PAST TWO ON JUNE 8TH, 1954.
I JUST NEED FIFTEEN MINUTES AND I'LL BE AS RIGHT AS RAIN, JACQUES. THAT'S ALL.
IT'S SUPPOSED TO BE OUR **LAST DAY,** BUT WE CAN WRAP THE FILM UP **TOMORROW.**
NO.
WE **HAVE** TO FINISH **TODAY.**
I'M CERTAIN THE MAN'S ON PEP PILLS. **ALL** THE SIGNS ARE THERE.
GO POWDER YOURSELF, HEDY.
SIX HOURS LATER, FILMING ON ***THE ADJOURNMENT*** WRAPS AND CARVER COLMAN DINES WITH THE STUDIO HEADS TO CELEBRATE.
TRADER VIC'S
THIRTY-FIVE MINUTES INTO DINNER, HE LEAVES FOR A BAR.
IT'S TEN O'CLOCK.
CARVER COLMAN IS WAITING FOR HIS BLACKMAILER.
HELLO, MA.
SON.
I ONLY WANT TO PROTECT YOUR **LIE.**
BUT IT'S GOING TO COST YOU.
I DON'T WANT TO DO THIS HERE.
3

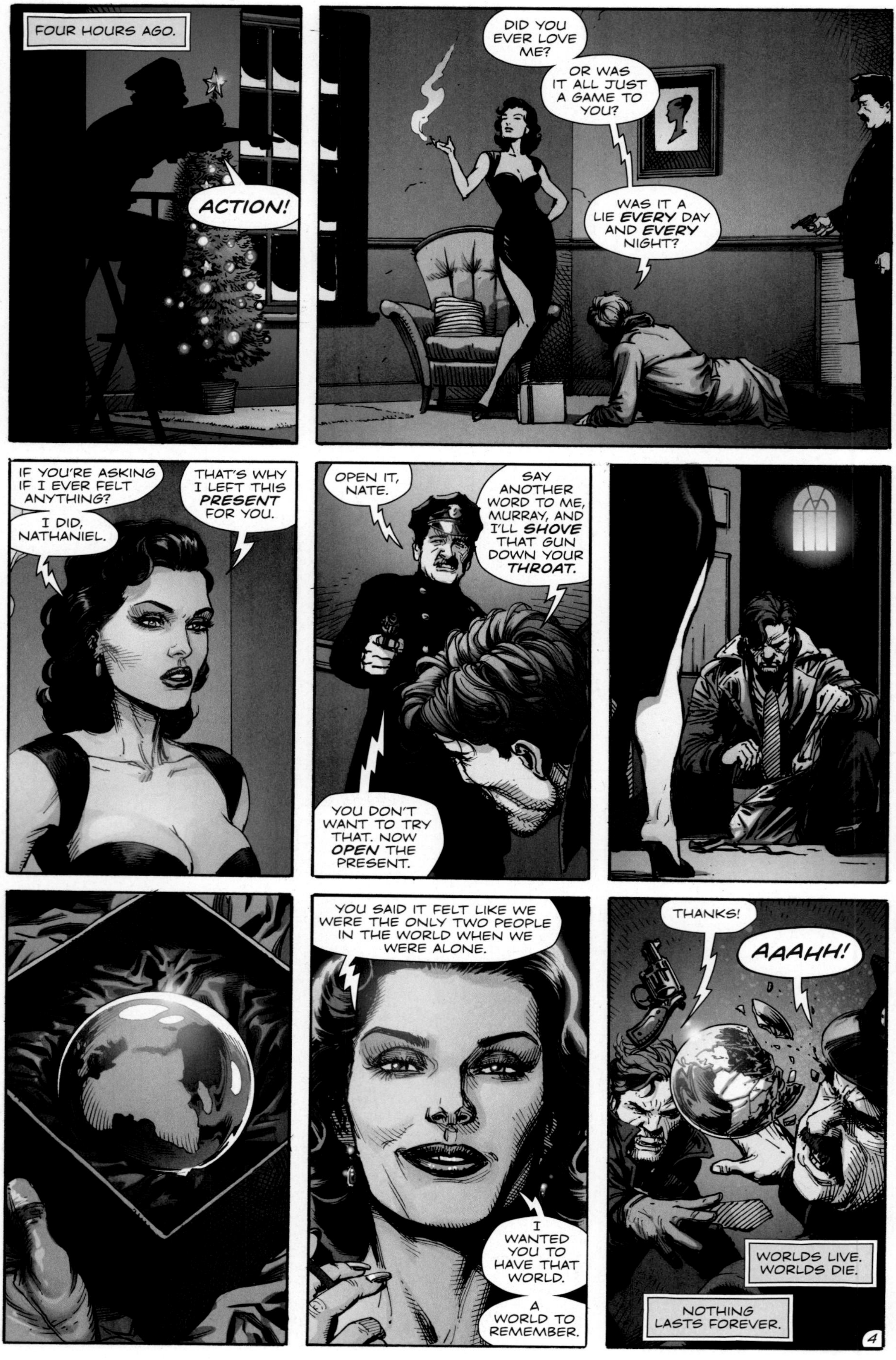
FOUR HOURS AGO.
ACTION!
DID YOU EVER LOVE ME?
OR WAS IT ALL JUST A GAME TO YOU?
WAS IT A LIE EVERY DAY AND EVERY NIGHT?
IF YOU'RE ASKING IF I EVER FELT ANYTHING?
I DID, NATHANIEL.
THAT'S WHY I LEFT THIS PRESENT FOR YOU.
OPEN IT, NATE.
SAY ANOTHER WORD TO ME, MURRAY, AND I'LL SHOVE THAT GUN DOWN YOUR THROAT.
YOU DON'T WANT TO TRY THAT. NOW OPEN THE PRESENT.
YOU SAID IT FELT LIKE WE WERE THE ONLY TWO PEOPLE IN THE WORLD WHEN WE WERE ALONE.
I WANTED YOU TO HAVE THAT WORLD.
A WORLD TO REMEMBER.
THANKS!
AAAHH!
WORLDS LIVE. WORLDS DIE.
NOTHING LASTS FOREVER.

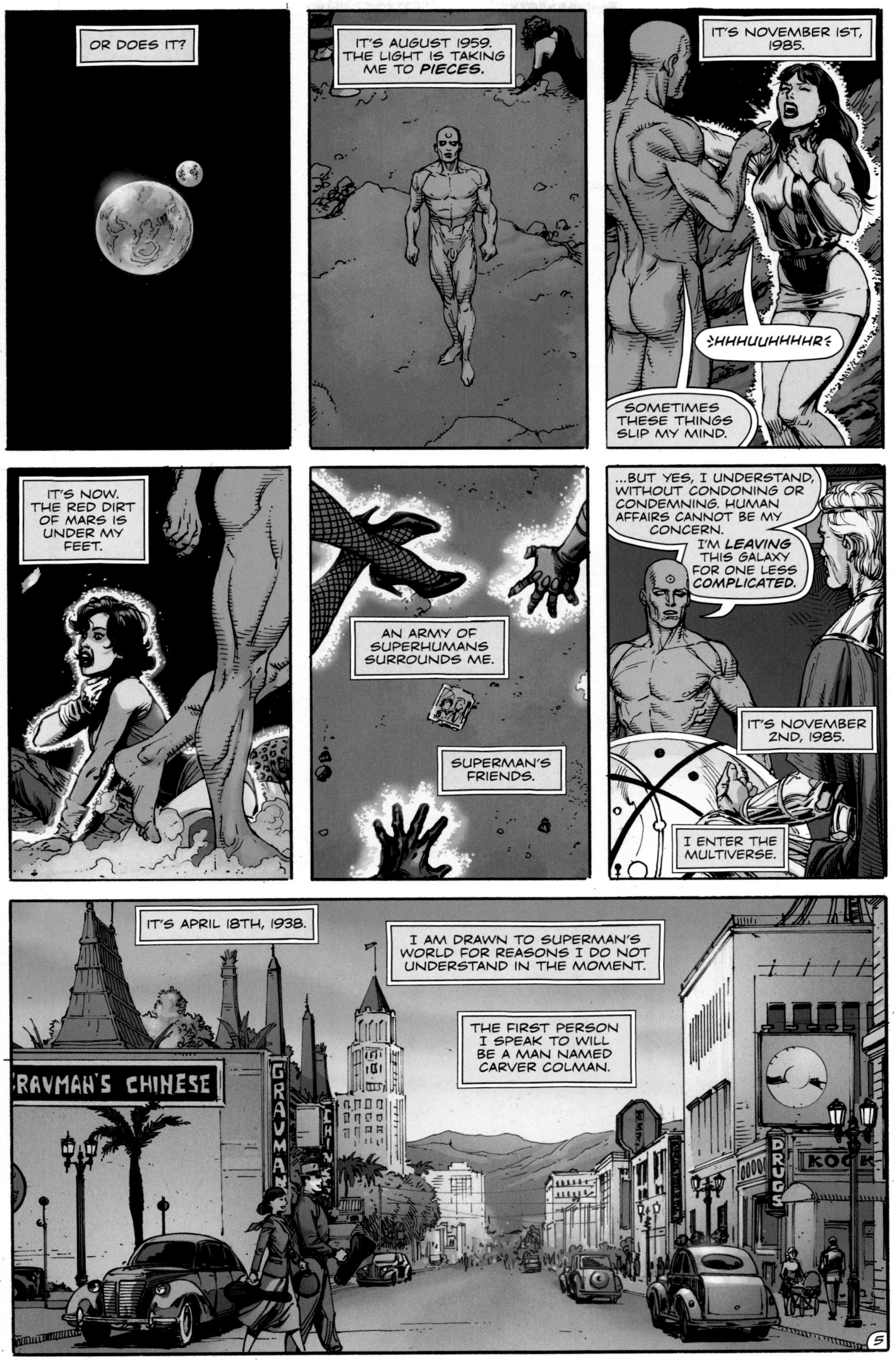
OR DOES IT?
IT'S AUGUST 1959. THE LIGHT IS TAKING ME TO *PIECES.*
IT'S NOVEMBER 1ST, 1985.
HHHUUHHHHR
SOMETIMES THESE THINGS SLIP MY MIND.
IT'S NOW. THE RED DIRT OF MARS IS UNDER MY FEET.
AN ARMY OF SUPERHUMANS SURROUNDS ME.
SUPERMAN'S FRIENDS.
...BUT YES, I UNDERSTAND, WITHOUT CONDONING OR CONDEMNING. HUMAN AFFAIRS CANNOT BE MY CONCERN.
I'M *LEAVING* THIS GALAXY FOR ONE LESS *COMPLICATED.*
IT'S NOVEMBER 2ND, 1985.
I ENTER THE MULTIVERSE.
IT'S APRIL 18TH, 1938.
I AM DRAWN TO SUPERMAN'S WORLD FOR REASONS I DO NOT UNDERSTAND IN THE MOMENT.
THE FIRST PERSON I SPEAK TO WILL BE A MAN NAMED CARVER COLMAN.
GRAUMAN'S CHINESE
GRAUMAN'S
DRUGS

IT'S CHRISTMAS DAY, 1928. CARVER COLMAN SITS IN A DARK THEATER IN PHILADELPHIA WHILE HIS MOTHER DANCES DOWN THE STREET FOR SWEATY MEN AND DIMES.

ANYBODY CAN MAKE A MISTAKE. THAT'S WHY THEY HAVE RUBBERS ON PENCILS.

WHEN SHE BRINGS ONE OF THE MEN HOME, HE DECIDES TO GO WEST.

IT'S DECEMBER 31ST, 1928. CARVER COLMAN ARRIVES IN LOS ANGELES WITH SEVENTEEN DOLLARS AND A CLEAN CHANGE OF CLOTHES.

IT'S JANUARY 19TH, 1930. CARVER COLMAN HAS DELIVERED MAIL AT PARAMOUNT STUDIOS FOR EIGHT MONTHS.

MORNING, JACKIE.

MORNING, CALVIN.

PEOPLE STILL DON'T REMEMBER HIS NAME.

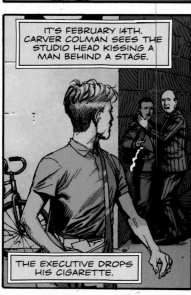

IT'S FEBRUARY 14TH. CARVER COLMAN SEES THE STUDIO HEAD KISSING A MAN BEHIND A STAGE.

THE EXECUTIVE DROPS HIS CIGARETTE.

SEVEN HOURS LATER, THE STAGE WILL BURN TO THE GROUND.

SOUNDPROOF TALKING PICTURE STAGE BURNS

THE STUDIO WILL CLAIM IT WAS DUE TO FAULTY WIRING.

CARVER COLMAN LOSES HIS JOB OVER IT.

IT'S FEBRUARY 12TH, 1937. CARVER COLMAN IS FIRED FROM DAN TANA'S WHEN HE SKIPS WORK TO WAIT IN LINE FOR AN AUDITION THAT NEVER HAPPENS.

HE IS EVICTED ON APRIL 18TH, 1938.

THAT NIGHT, CARVER COLMAN SLEEPS ON THE STREETS OF LOS ANGELES.

TEN TO MIDNIGHT, HE IS WOKEN BY A BLUE LIGHT.

WHY ARE YOU HERE?

6

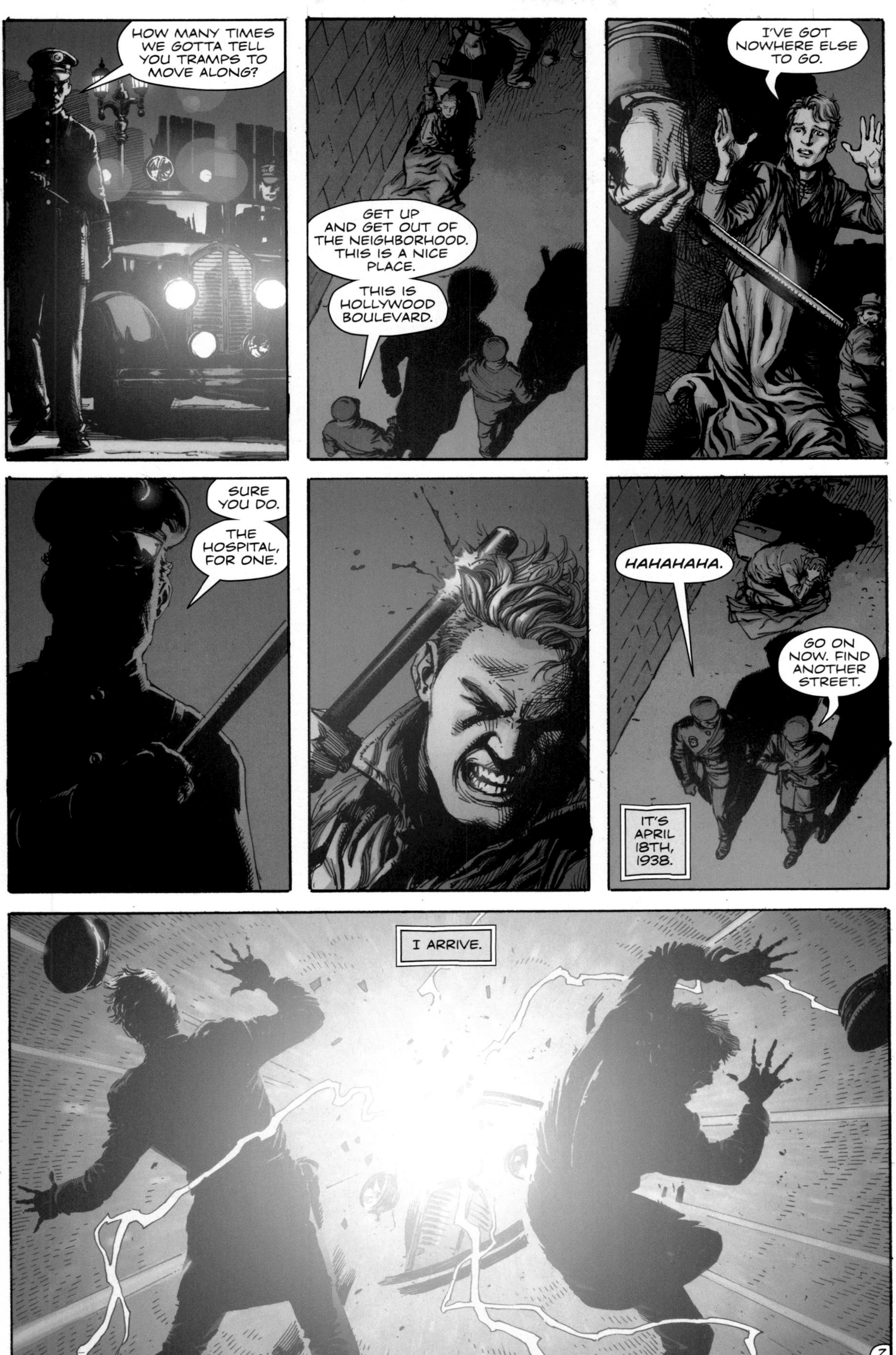
HOW MANY TIMES WE GOTTA TELL YOU TRAMPS TO MOVE ALONG?
GET UP AND GET OUT OF THE NEIGHBORHOOD. THIS IS A NICE PLACE.
THIS IS HOLLYWOOD BOULEVARD.
I'VE GOT NOWHERE ELSE TO GO.
SURE YOU DO.
THE HOSPITAL, FOR ONE.
HAHAHAHA.
GO ON NOW. FIND ANOTHER STREET.
IT'S APRIL 18TH, 1938.
I ARRIVE.
7

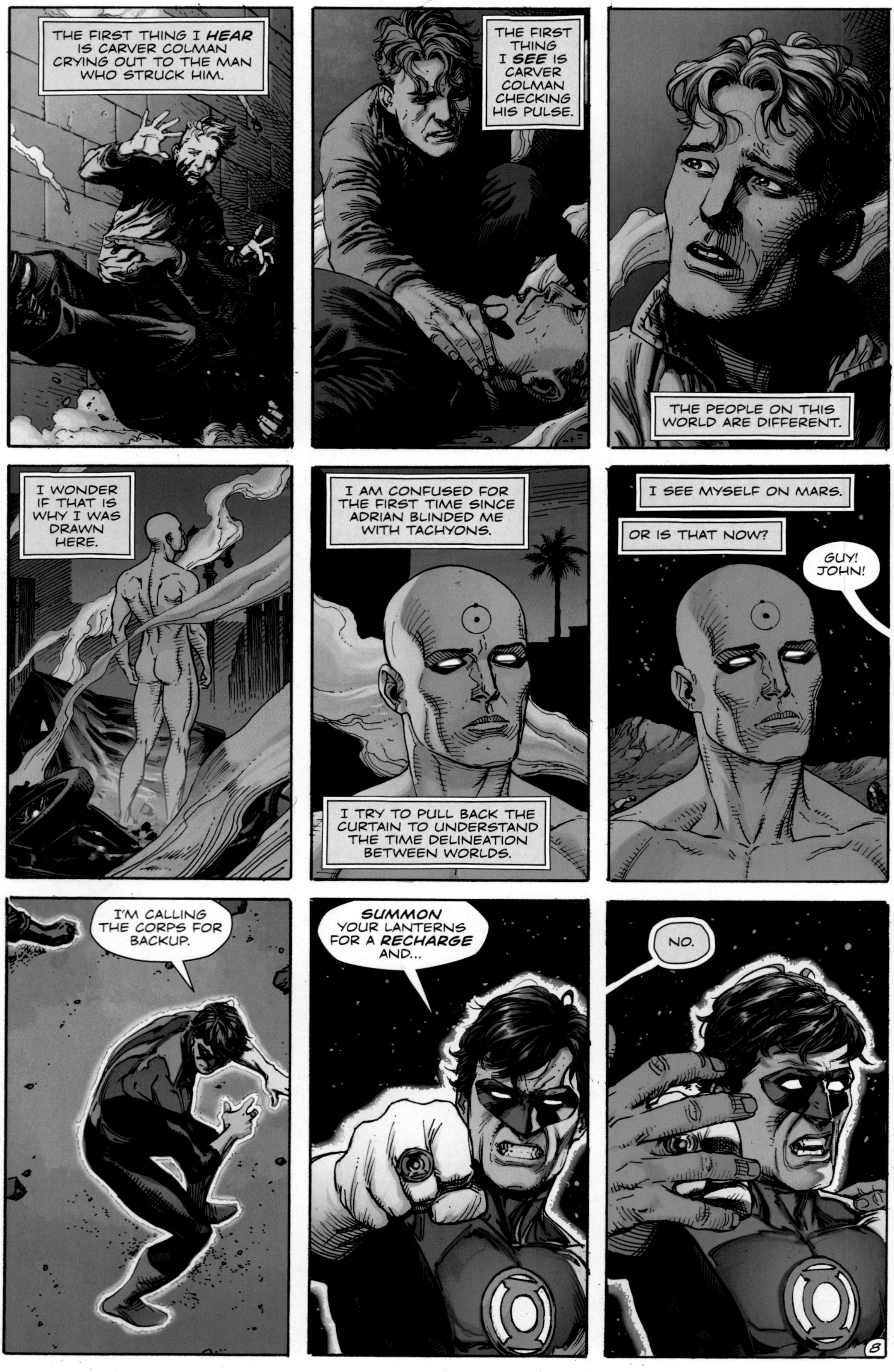
THE FIRST THING I HEAR IS CARVER COLMAN CRYING OUT TO THE MAN WHO STRUCK HIM.
THE FIRST THING I SEE IS CARVER COLMAN CHECKING HIS PULSE.
THE PEOPLE ON THIS WORLD ARE DIFFERENT.
I WONDER IF THAT IS WHY I WAS DRAWN HERE.
I AM CONFUSED FOR THE FIRST TIME SINCE ADRIAN BLINDED ME WITH TACHYONS.
I TRY TO PULL BACK THE CURTAIN TO UNDERSTAND THE TIME DELINEATION BETWEEN WORLDS.
I SEE MYSELF ON MARS.
OR IS THAT NOW?
GUY! JOHN!
I'M CALLING THE CORPS FOR BACKUP.
SUMMON YOUR LANTERNS FOR A RECHARGE AND...
NO.

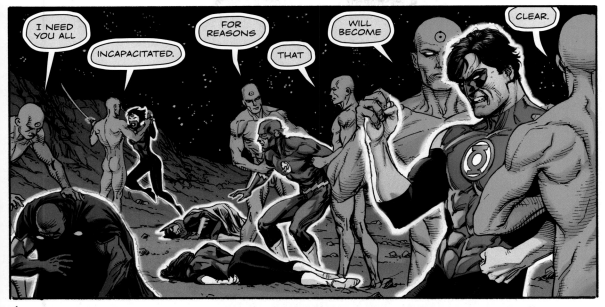

I NEED YOU ALL

INCAPACITATED.

FOR REASONS

THAT

WILL BECOME

CLEAR.

I STAND ON THE SURFACE OF MARS.

WAITING FOR SUPERMAN.

IT'S AUGUST 13TH, 1943. THE FIRST NATHANIEL DUSK PICTURE IS RELEASED.

ALTHOUGH ITS *CONTROVERSIAL CONTENT* BRINGS CRITICISM, IT IS VERNER BROS' MOST *SUCCESSFUL* PICTURE OF THE YEAR.

NATHANIEL
DUSK
PRIVATE INVESTIGATOR

in "NOTHING TO LOSE"

MY NAME IS NATHANIEL DUSK. I'M A *PRIVATE INVESTIGATOR.*

I SERVED IN THE *GREAT WAR* THEN I SERVED ON THE *NEW YORK POLICE FORCE.*

NOW I SERVE WHOEVER HAS THE MONEY.

IT'S APRIL 18TH, 1938. I HAVE ARRIVED.

WHO ARE YOU?

MY NAME IS JON.

9

ARE YOU AN ANGEL?

NO.

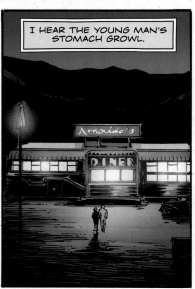

I HEAR THE YOUNG MAN'S STOMACH GROWL.

I DON'T HAVE MONEY...

YOU DON'T NEED ANY.

HI THERE. TABLE FOR TWO?

YES. THANK YOU.

I DON'T UNDERSTAND. WHY ISN'T SHE...

I'M SHIFTING THE LIGHT'S COLOR FREQUENCIES AROUND ME. SHE'S SEEING WHAT I WANT HER TO SEE.

NOW WHAT CAN I GET YOU BOTH?

10

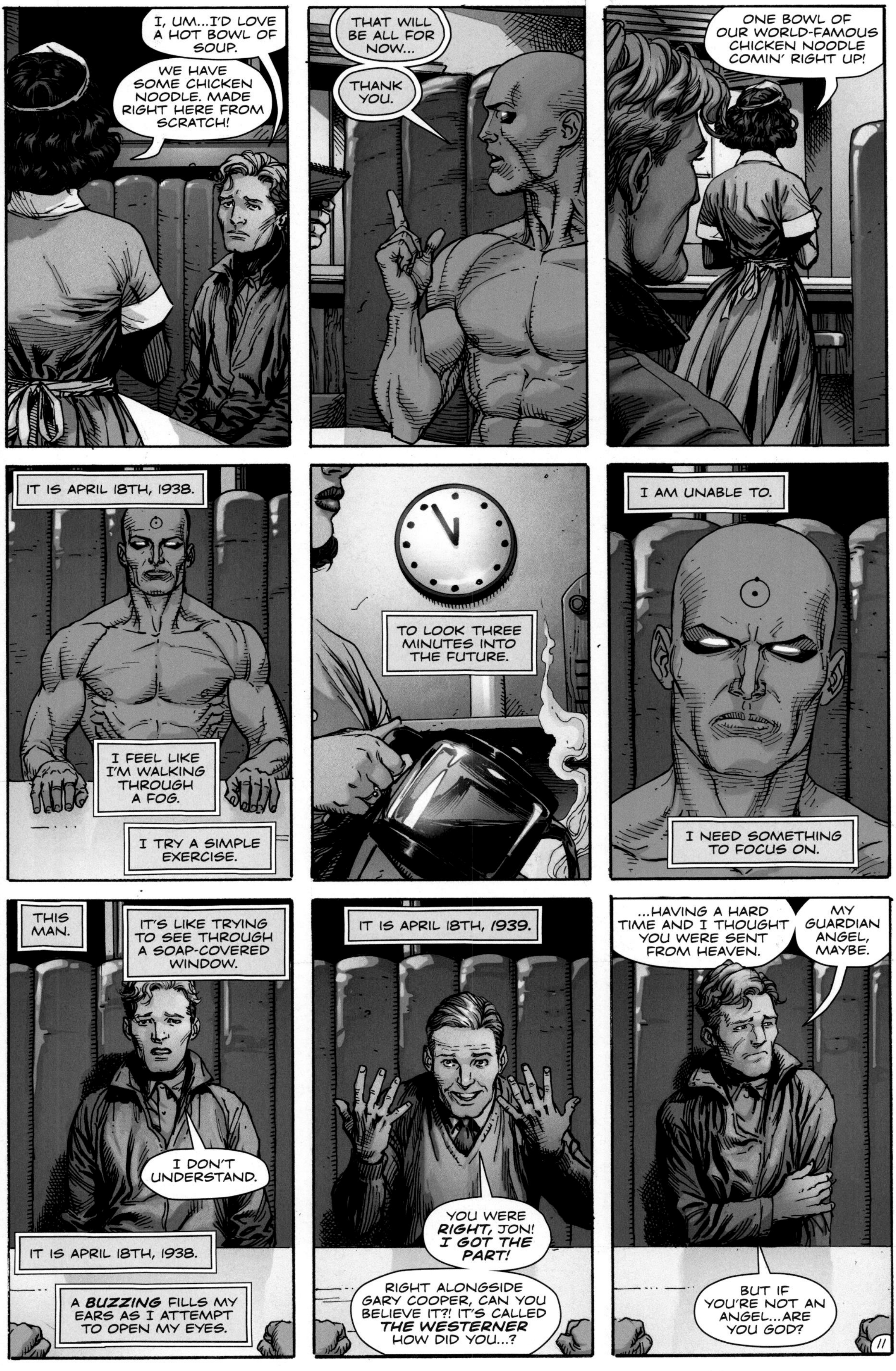
I, UM...I'D LOVE A HOT BOWL OF SOUP.
WE HAVE SOME CHICKEN NOODLE. MADE RIGHT HERE FROM SCRATCH!
THAT WILL BE ALL FOR NOW...
THANK YOU.
ONE BOWL OF OUR WORLD-FAMOUS CHICKEN NOODLE COMIN' RIGHT UP!
IT IS APRIL 18TH, 1938.
I FEEL LIKE I'M WALKING THROUGH A FOG.
I TRY A SIMPLE EXERCISE.
TO LOOK THREE MINUTES INTO THE FUTURE.
I AM UNABLE TO.
I NEED SOMETHING TO FOCUS ON.
THIS MAN.
IT'S LIKE TRYING TO SEE THROUGH A SOAP-COVERED WINDOW.
I DON'T UNDERSTAND.
IT IS APRIL 18TH, 1938.
A BUZZING FILLS MY EARS AS I ATTEMPT TO OPEN MY EYES.
IT IS APRIL 18TH, 1939.
YOU WERE RIGHT, JON! I GOT THE PART!
RIGHT ALONGSIDE GARY COOPER, CAN YOU BELIEVE IT?! IT'S CALLED THE WESTERNER. HOW DID YOU...?
...HAVING A HARD TIME AND I THOUGHT YOU WERE SENT FROM HEAVEN.
MY GUARDIAN ANGEL, MAYBE.
BUT IF YOU'RE NOT AN ANGEL...ARE YOU GOD?
11

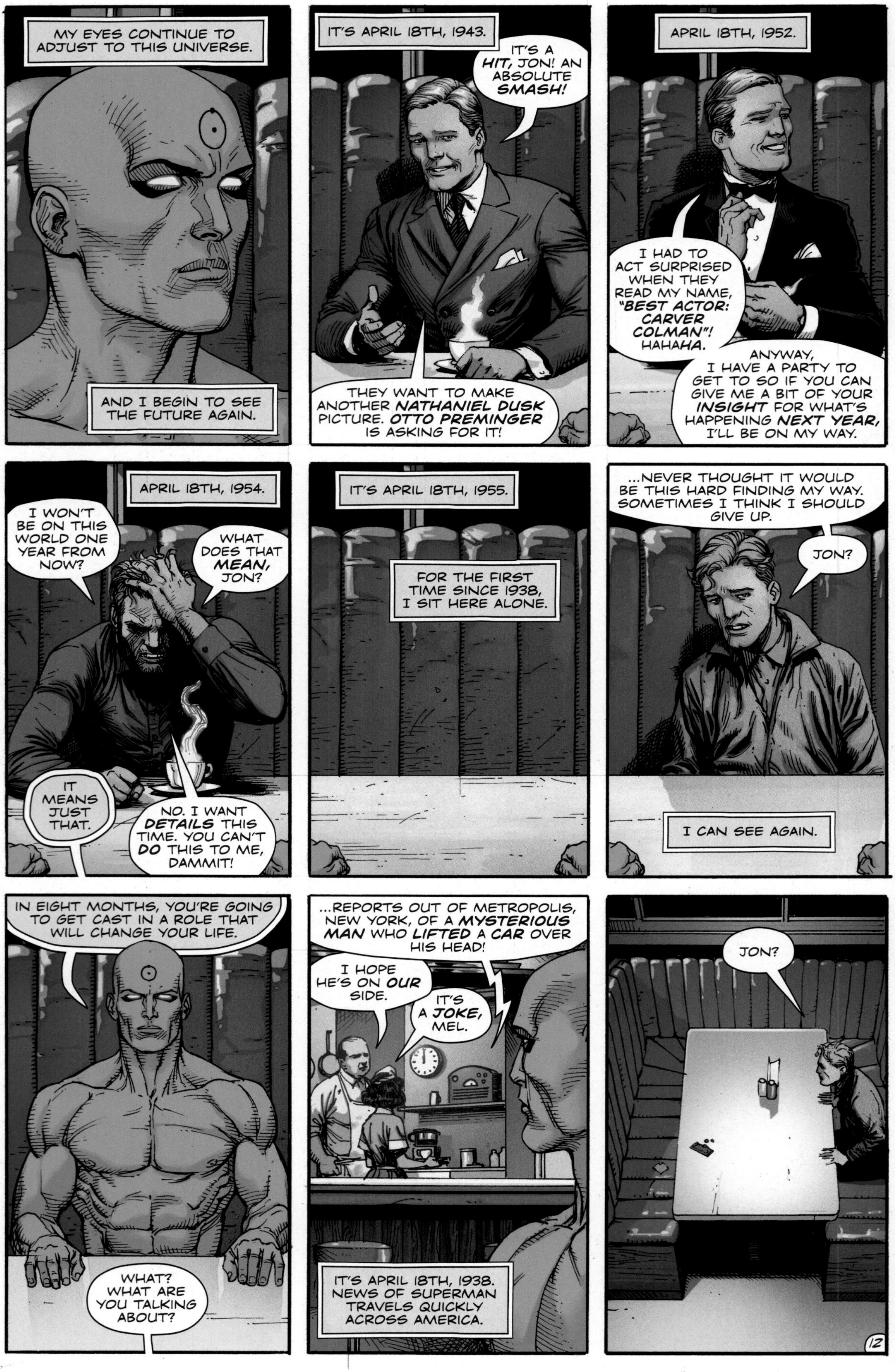

MY EYES CONTINUE TO ADJUST TO THIS UNIVERSE.
AND I BEGIN TO SEE THE FUTURE AGAIN.
IT'S APRIL 18TH, 1943.
IT'S A HIT, JON! AN ABSOLUTE SMASH!
THEY WANT TO MAKE ANOTHER NATHANIEL DUSK PICTURE. OTTO PREMINGER IS ASKING FOR IT!
APRIL 18TH, 1952.
I HAD TO ACT SURPRISED WHEN THEY READ MY NAME, "BEST ACTOR: CARVER COLMAN"! HAHAHA.
ANYWAY, I HAVE A PARTY TO GET TO SO IF YOU CAN GIVE ME A BIT OF YOUR INSIGHT FOR WHAT'S HAPPENING NEXT YEAR, I'LL BE ON MY WAY.
APRIL 18TH, 1954.
I WON'T BE ON THIS WORLD ONE YEAR FROM NOW?
WHAT DOES THAT MEAN, JON?
IT MEANS JUST THAT.
NO. I WANT DETAILS THIS TIME. YOU CAN'T DO THIS TO ME, DAMMIT!
IT'S APRIL 18TH, 1955.
FOR THE FIRST TIME SINCE 1938, I SIT HERE ALONE.
...NEVER THOUGHT IT WOULD BE THIS HARD FINDING MY WAY. SOMETIMES I THINK I SHOULD GIVE UP.
JON?
I CAN SEE AGAIN.
IN EIGHT MONTHS, YOU'RE GOING TO GET CAST IN A ROLE THAT WILL CHANGE YOUR LIFE.
WHAT? WHAT ARE YOU TALKING ABOUT?
...REPORTS OUT OF METROPOLIS, NEW YORK, OF A MYSTERIOUS MAN WHO LIFTED A CAR OVER HIS HEAD!
I HOPE HE'S ON OUR SIDE.
IT'S A JOKE, MEL.
IT'S APRIL 18TH, 1938. NEWS OF SUPERMAN TRAVELS QUICKLY ACROSS AMERICA.
JON?
12

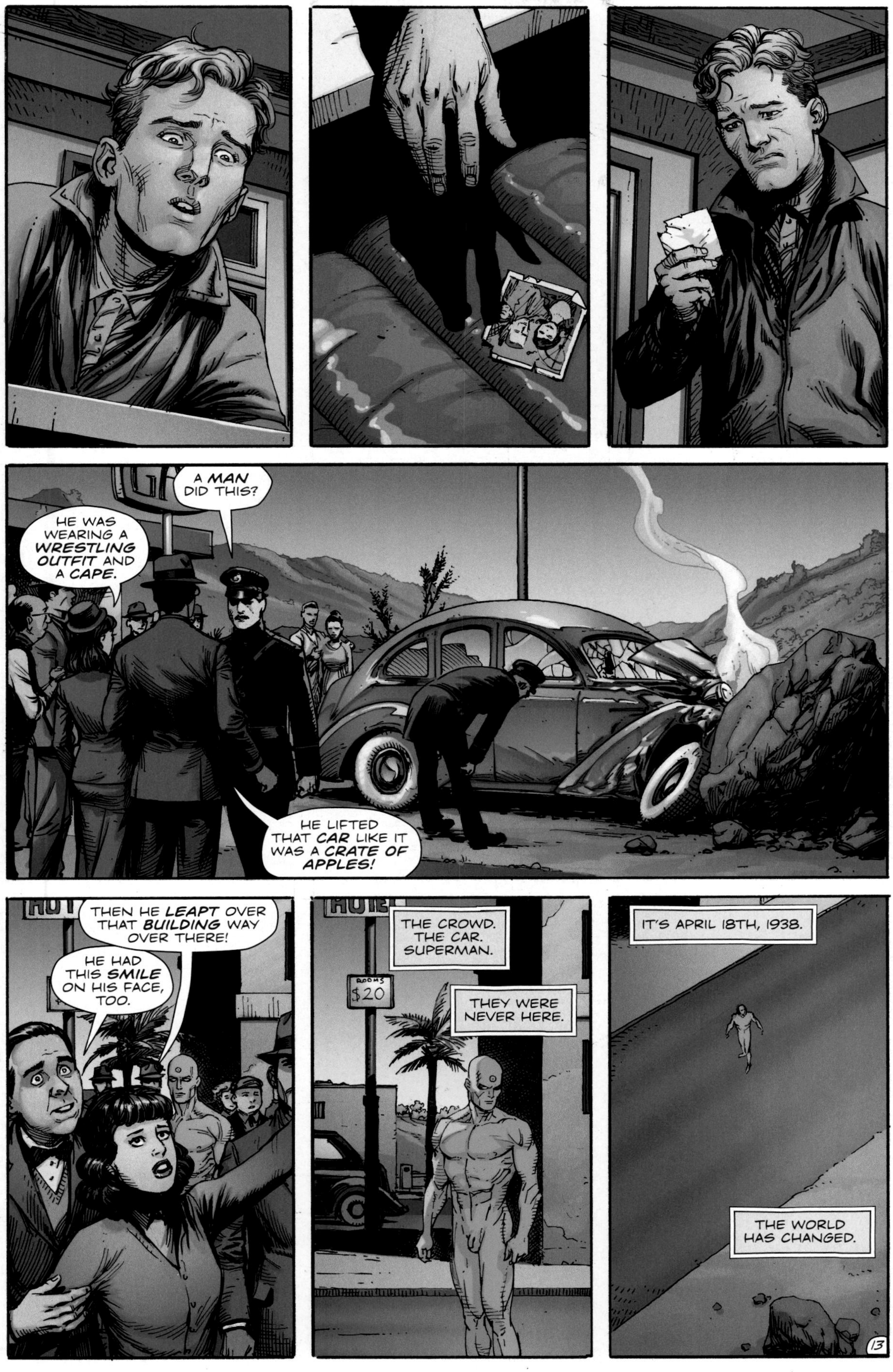
A MAN DID THIS?
HE WAS WEARING A WRESTLING OUTFIT AND A CAPE.
HE LIFTED THAT CAR LIKE IT WAS A CRATE OF APPLES!
THEN HE LEAPT OVER THAT BUILDING WAY OVER THERE!
HE HAD THIS SMILE ON HIS FACE, TOO.
ROOMS
$20
THE CROWD. THE CAR. SUPERMAN.
THEY WERE NEVER HERE.
IT'S APRIL 18TH, 1938.
THE WORLD HAS CHANGED.
13

A THEORETICAL PHYSICIST NAMED **BRYCE DeWITT** HYPOTHESIZED THAT THE UNIVERSE WAS CONSTANTLY **SPLITTING** INTO **ALTERNATE** TIMELINES.

THE MANY WORLDS INTERPRETATION.

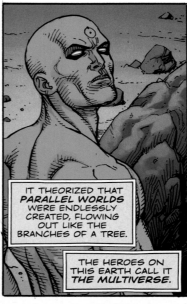

IT THEORIZED THAT **PARALLEL WORLDS** WERE ENDLESSLY CREATED, FLOWING OUT LIKE THE BRANCHES OF A TREE.

THE HEROES ON THIS EARTH CALL IT **THE MULTIVERSE.**

AND THIS WORLD WAS ITS CENTER.

THE WORLD WAS INTRODUCED TO **SUPERMAN** ON APRIL 18TH, 1938.

HE WAS THE FIRST OF THE COSTUMED HEROES.

THE FIRST OF MANY ON THIS WORLD...

IT'S JULY, 1940.

AN ENGINEER NAMED **ALAN SCOTT** IS ON A TRAIN CAREENING OVER A BRIDGE.

HE GRABS ONTO A GREEN LANTERN, UNAWARE OF THE POWER WITHIN.

14

IN JANUARY, A COLLEGE STUDENT NAMED *JAY GARRICK* LIES UNCONSCIOUS IN THE SCHOOL LAB, BREATHING IN HEAVY WATER VAPORS.

BY MORNING, HE WILL BE THE FASTEST MAN ALIVE.

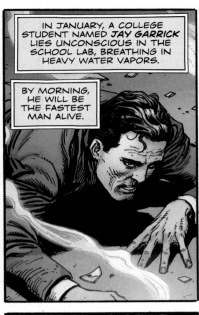

THAT SAME MONTH, ARCHAEOLOGIST *CARTER HALL* COMES INTO CONTACT WITH AN ANCIENT KNIFE THAT AWAKENS HIS PAST LIFE AS AN EGYPTIAN PRINCE.

REMEMBERING THE WARRIOR HE WAS, CARTER WILL SEARCH FOR NOT ONLY THE WEAPONS HE ONCE WIELDED, BUT FOR THE LOVE HE LOST.

IN OCTOBER, FRUSTRATED BY HIS SIZE, *AL PRATT* BEGINS TRAINING UNDER ONE OF THE GREATEST FIGHTERS IN THE WORLD.

IN NOVEMBER, HE WILL SIT AROUND A TABLE AND FEEL THE NEED TO POINT THAT OUT.

IN MAY, A GOLDEN HELMET OF UNKNOWN SUPERNATURAL POWER FALLS INTO THE HANDS OF *KENT NELSON*.

THREE YEARS LATER, HE WILL LEARN THE SPIRIT WITHIN SOUGHT HIM OUT.

IT'S APRIL, 1939. *WESLEY DODDS* AWAKES FROM A NIGHTMARE OF A MURDER ON THE GROUNDS OF THE WORLD'S FAIR.

DONNING A GAS MASK, WESLEY DODDS FINDS THE KILLER.

IN FEBRUARY OF 1940, THE BODY OF *JIM CORRIGAN* LIES STILL.

HE RISES FROM THE DEAD, SEEKING VENGEANCE.

IN MARCH, CHEMIST *REX TYLER* WILL INVENT A PILL THAT INCREASES HIS STRENGTH TENFOLD.

HE BEGINS TRIAL TESTING ON HIMSELF.

IT'S NOVEMBER, 1940.

"I KNOW WE'VE BEEN WAITING FOR SUPERMAN..."

15

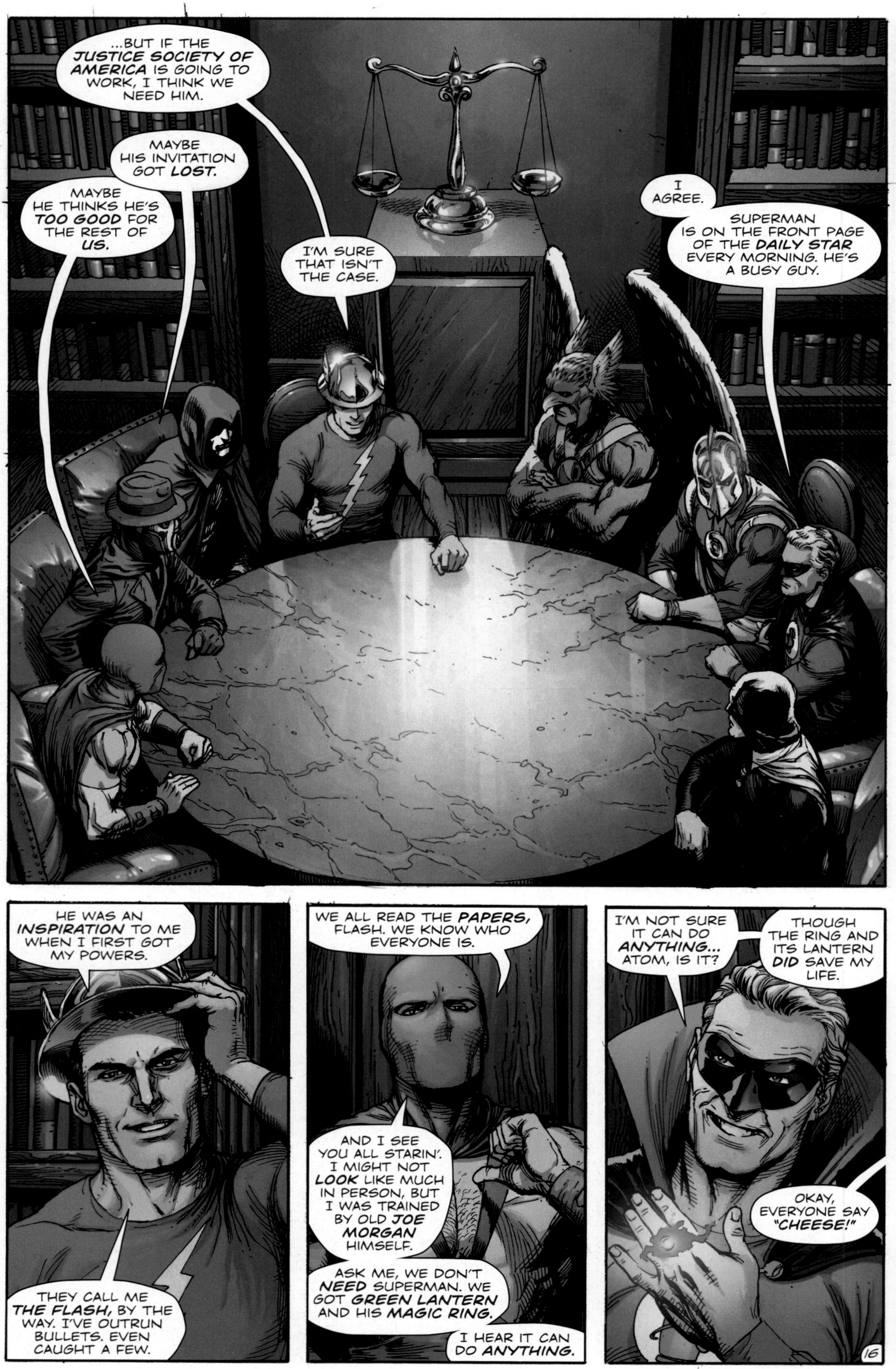
MAYBE HE THINKS HE'S TOO GOOD FOR THE REST OF US.
MAYBE HIS INVITATION GOT LOST.
I'M SURE THAT ISN'T THE CASE.
...BUT IF THE JUSTICE SOCIETY OF AMERICA IS GOING TO WORK, I THINK WE NEED HIM.
I AGREE.
SUPERMAN IS ON THE FRONT PAGE OF THE DAILY STAR EVERY MORNING. HE'S A BUSY GUY.
HE WAS AN INSPIRATION TO ME WHEN I FIRST GOT MY POWERS.
THEY CALL ME THE FLASH, BY THE WAY. I'VE OUTRUN BULLETS. EVEN CAUGHT A FEW.
WE ALL READ THE PAPERS, FLASH. WE KNOW WHO EVERYONE IS.
AND I SEE YOU ALL STARIN'. I MIGHT NOT LOOK LIKE MUCH IN PERSON, BUT I WAS TRAINED BY OLD JOE MORGAN HIMSELF.
ASK ME, WE DON'T NEED SUPERMAN. WE GOT GREEN LANTERN AND HIS MAGIC RING.
I HEAR IT CAN DO ANYTHING.
I'M NOT SURE IT CAN DO ANYTHING... ATOM, IS IT?
THOUGH THE RING AND ITS LANTERN DID SAVE MY LIFE.
OKAY, EVERYONE SAY "CHEESE!"

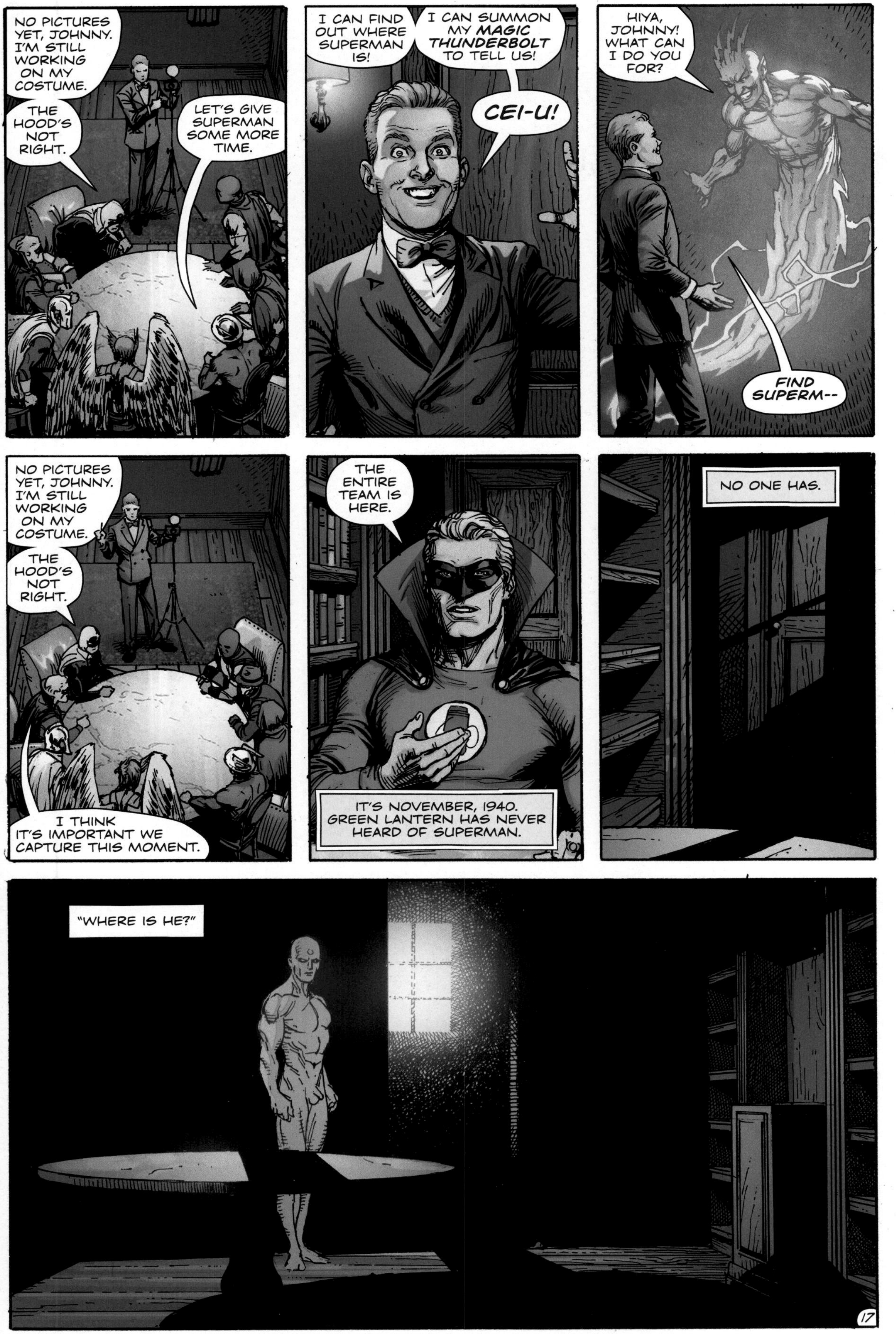
NO PICTURES YET, JOHNNY. I'M STILL WORKING ON MY COSTUME.
THE HOOD'S NOT RIGHT.
LET'S GIVE SUPERMAN SOME MORE TIME.
I CAN FIND OUT WHERE SUPERMAN IS!
I CAN SUMMON MY MAGIC THUNDERBOLT TO TELL US!
CEI-U!
HIYA, JOHNNY! WHAT CAN I DO YOU FOR?
FIND SUPERM--
NO PICTURES YET, JOHNNY. I'M STILL WORKING ON MY COSTUME.
THE HOOD'S NOT RIGHT.
I THINK IT'S IMPORTANT WE CAPTURE THIS MOMENT.
THE ENTIRE TEAM IS HERE.
IT'S NOVEMBER, 1940. GREEN LANTERN HAS NEVER HEARD OF SUPERMAN.
NO ONE HAS.
"WHERE IS HE?"

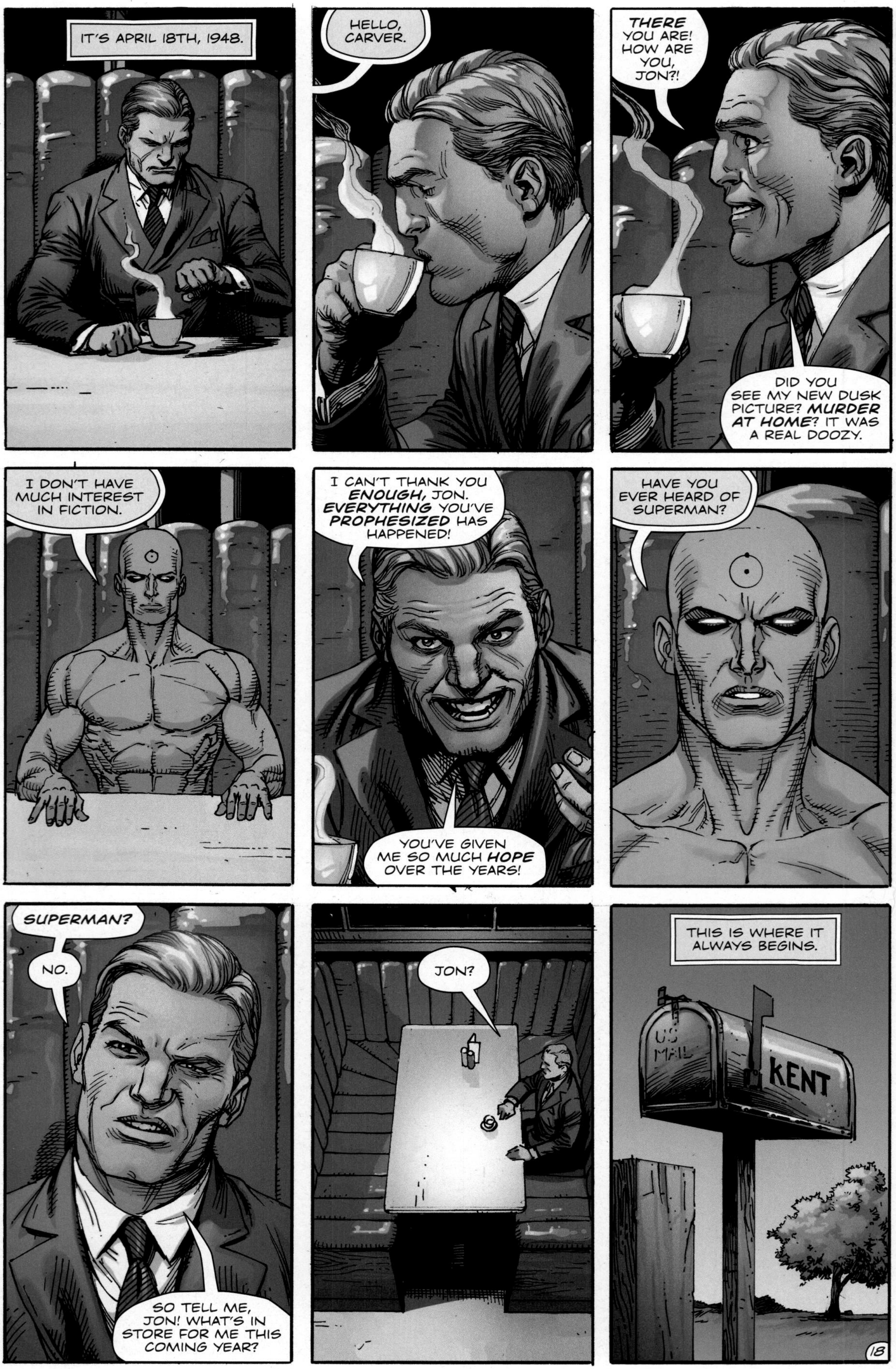

IT'S APRIL 18TH, 1948.
HELLO, CARVER.
THERE YOU ARE! HOW ARE YOU, JON?!
DID YOU SEE MY NEW DUSK PICTURE? MURDER AT HOME? IT WAS A REAL DOOZY.
I DON'T HAVE MUCH INTEREST IN FICTION.
I CAN'T THANK YOU ENOUGH, JON. EVERYTHING YOU'VE PROPHESIZED HAS HAPPENED!
YOU'VE GIVEN ME SO MUCH HOPE OVER THE YEARS!
HAVE YOU EVER HEARD OF SUPERMAN?
SUPERMAN?
NO.
SO TELL ME, JON! WHAT'S IN STORE FOR ME THIS COMING YEAR?
JON?
THIS IS WHERE IT ALWAYS BEGINS.
U.S. MAIL
KENT

IT'S 1956. SUPERMAN IS SEEN IN METROPOLIS FOR THE FIRST TIME.

TWENTY-FIVE YEARS EARLIER, THE WINDS CHANGE ON A FARM IN KANSAS.

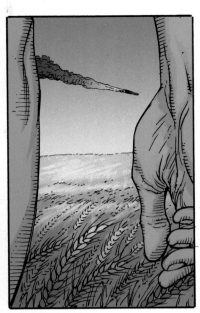

JONATHAN AND MARTHA KENT FIND THE ORPHAN BOY.

GREAT SCOTT! THAT'S A *SPACE ROCKET*!

LAND SAKES! THEN THIS CHILD MUST BE FROM ANOTHER WORLD!

OH, IF ONLY WE HAD A BABY OF OUR OWN AS SWEET AS HE LOOKS!

CARVER COLMAN NEVER HEARD OF SUPERMAN BECAUSE AN *OUTSIDE FORCE* SHIFTED HIS ARRIVAL FORWARD IN TIME.

THE REVERBERATIONS OF THIS CHANGE AFFECT NOT ONLY *THIS* WORLD, BUT *EVERY WORLD* IN THE *MULTIVERSE*.

SUPERMAN IS NO LONGER FIRST SEEN IN 1938. IT'S 1956.

NO.

IT'S OCTOBER, 1986.

HIS ARRIVAL ON EARTH HAS SHIFTED FORWARD AGAIN.

OMIGOSH!

P-PA...?

WHAT *IS* IT?

IT'S WHERE YOU *CAME* FROM, SON.

HIS ARRIVAL CHANGES AGAIN.

AND AGAIN.

...YOU WILL BE *FREE* TO MOVE AMONG THE PEOPLE OF EARTH.

BUT NEVER FORGET, ALTHOUGH YOU *LOOK* LIKE ONE OF THEM...

...YOU ARE *NOT* ONE OF THEM.

19

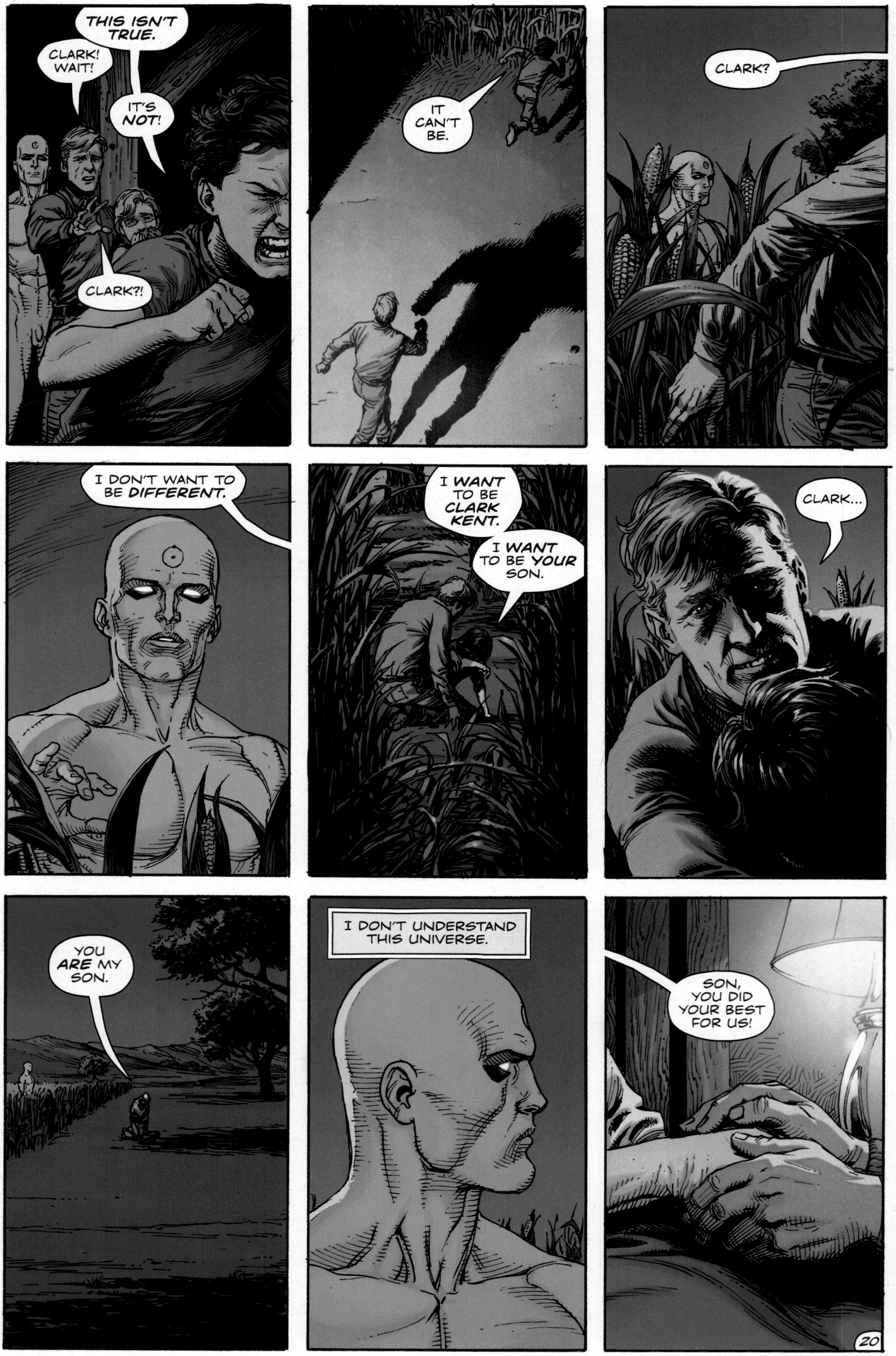
THIS ISN'T TRUE.
CLARK! WAIT!
IT'S NOT!
CLARK?!
IT CAN'T BE.
CLARK?
I DON'T WANT TO BE DIFFERENT.
I WANT TO BE CLARK KENT.
I WANT TO BE YOUR SON.
CLARK...
YOU ARE MY SON.
I DON'T UNDERSTAND THIS UNIVERSE.
SON, YOU DID YOUR BEST FOR US!

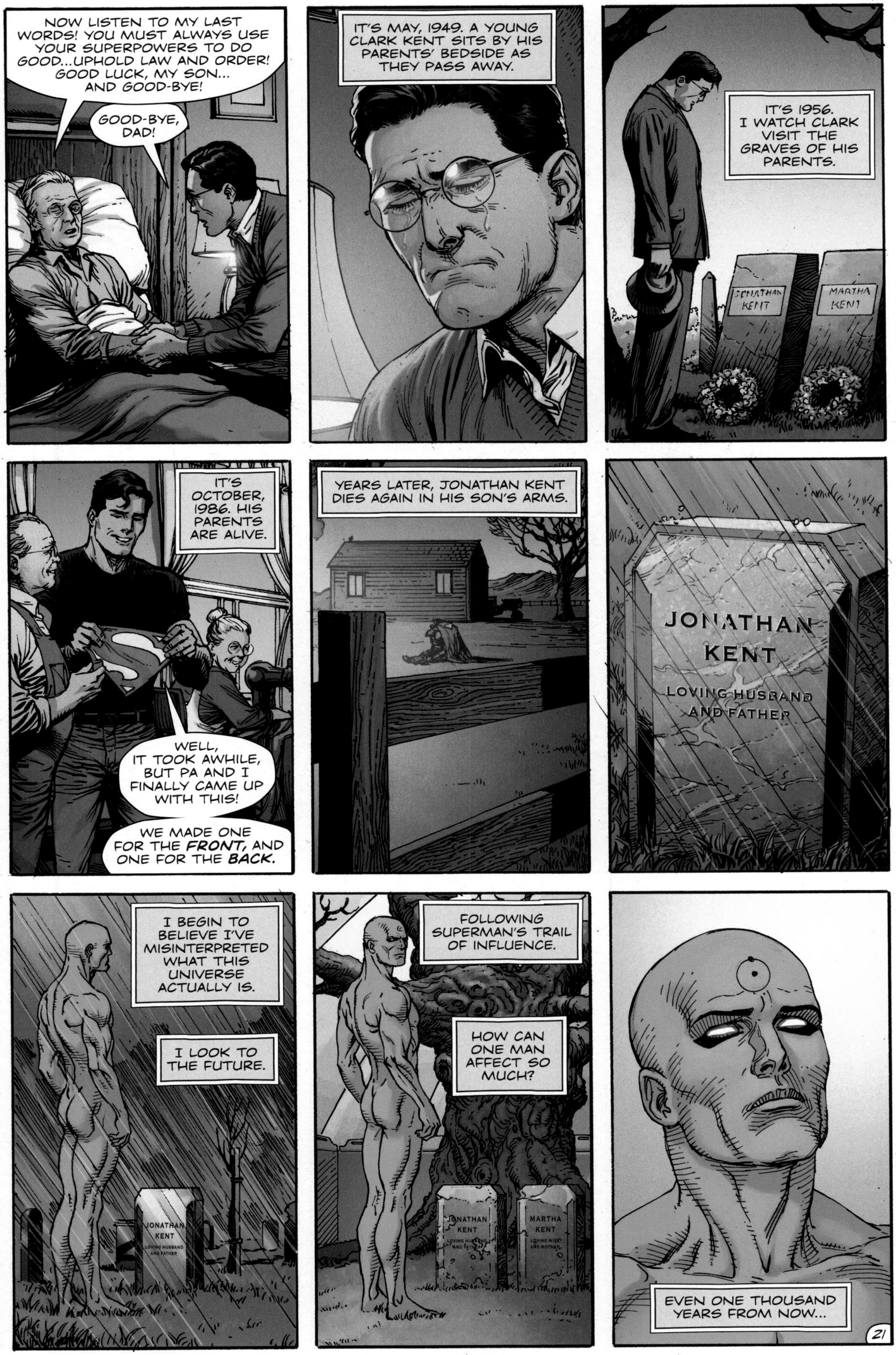
NOW LISTEN TO MY LAST WORDS! YOU MUST ALWAYS USE YOUR SUPERPOWERS TO DO GOOD...UPHOLD LAW AND ORDER! GOOD LUCK, MY SON... AND GOOD-BYE!
GOOD-BYE, DAD!
IT'S MAY, 1949. A YOUNG CLARK KENT SITS BY HIS PARENTS' BEDSIDE AS THEY PASS AWAY.
IT'S 1956. I WATCH CLARK VISIT THE GRAVES OF HIS PARENTS.
JONATHAN KENT
MARTHA KENT
IT'S OCTOBER, 1986. HIS PARENTS ARE ALIVE.
WELL, IT TOOK AWHILE, BUT PA AND I FINALLY CAME UP WITH THIS!
WE MADE ONE FOR THE FRONT, AND ONE FOR THE BACK.
YEARS LATER, JONATHAN KENT DIES AGAIN IN HIS SON'S ARMS.
JONATHAN KENT
LOVING HUSBAND AND FATHER
I BEGIN TO BELIEVE I'VE MISINTERPRETED WHAT THIS UNIVERSE ACTUALLY IS.
I LOOK TO THE FUTURE.
JONATHAN KENT
LOVING HUSBAND AND FATHER
FOLLOWING SUPERMAN'S TRAIL OF INFLUENCE.
HOW CAN ONE MAN AFFECT SO MUCH?
JONATHAN KENT
LOVING HUSBAND AND FATHER
MARTHA KENT
LOVING WIFE AND MOTHER
EVEN ONE THOUSAND YEARS FROM NOW...

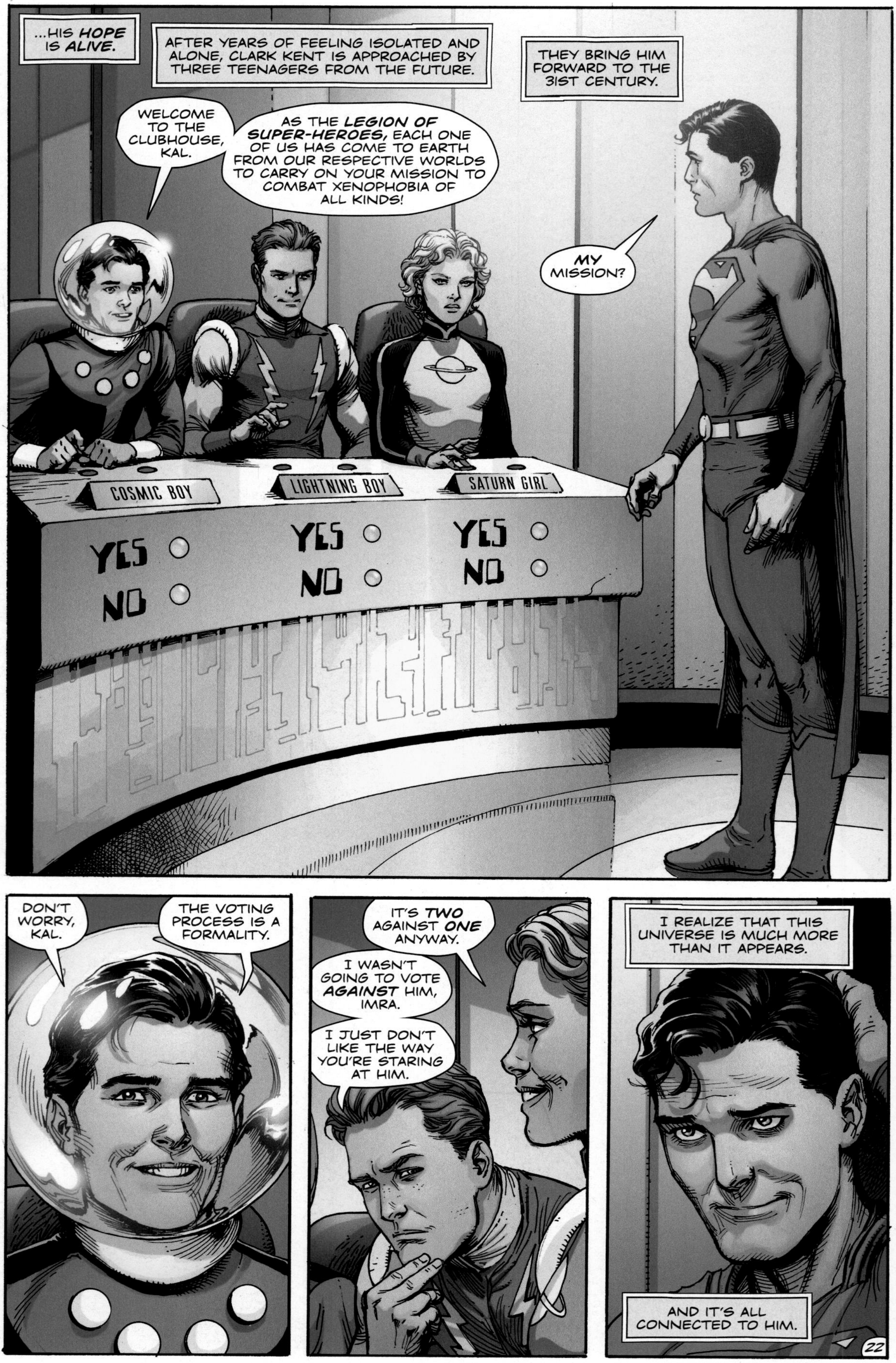
...HIS HOPE IS ALIVE.
AFTER YEARS OF FEELING ISOLATED AND ALONE, CLARK KENT IS APPROACHED BY THREE TEENAGERS FROM THE FUTURE.
WELCOME TO THE CLUBHOUSE, KAL.
AS THE LEGION OF SUPER-HEROES, EACH ONE OF US HAS COME TO EARTH FROM OUR RESPECTIVE WORLDS TO CARRY ON YOUR MISSION TO COMBAT XENOPHOBIA OF ALL KINDS!
THEY BRING HIM FORWARD TO THE 31ST CENTURY.
MY MISSION?
COSMIC BOY
LIGHTNING BOY
SATURN GIRL
YES
NO
YES
NO
YES
NO
DON'T WORRY, KAL.
THE VOTING PROCESS IS A FORMALITY.
IT'S TWO AGAINST ONE ANYWAY.
I WASN'T GOING TO VOTE AGAINST HIM, IMRA.
I JUST DON'T LIKE THE WAY YOU'RE STARING AT HIM.
I REALIZE THAT THIS UNIVERSE IS MUCH MORE THAN IT APPEARS.
AND IT'S ALL CONNECTED TO HIM.
22

WHY IS HE THE CENTER OF THIS UNIVERSE?

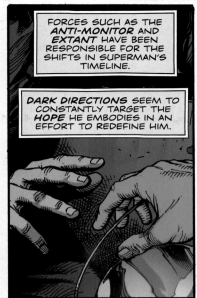

FORCES SUCH AS THE *ANTI-MONITOR* AND *EXTANT* HAVE BEEN RESPONSIBLE FOR THE SHIFTS IN SUPERMAN'S TIMELINE.

DARK DIRECTIONS SEEM TO CONSTANTLY TARGET THE *HOPE* HE EMBODIES IN AN EFFORT TO REDEFINE HIM.

I GROW CURIOUS.

AS OTHERS HAVE DONE, I MOVE TO RESHAPE THIS UNIVERSE SO THAT I MIGHT SEE HOW IT FORMS AROUND SUPERMAN.

I CHANGE THE PAST TO CHALLENGE THE FUTURE.

AND AS I WATCH REALITY COME CRASHING DOWN, I REALIZE THAT *THIS* UNIVERSE IS NOT A PART OF THE *MULTIVERSE* AS OTHERS BELIEVE.

THE MULTIVERSE *REACTS* TO THIS UNIVERSE. THERE HAVE BEEN ENDLESS PARALLEL WORLDS, NONE, FIFTY-TWO, DARK MULTIVERSES, ALL CREATED BY CHANGES TO *THIS* UNIVERSE.

THIS UNIVERSE *STANDS APART* FROM THE MULTIVERSE.

IT IS THE *METAVERSE.*

AND IT IS IN A *CONSTANT* STATE OF *CHANGE.*

AND AS I *REMOVE* THE LINCHPIN TO THE *JUSTICE SOCIETY OF AMERICA,* I CHANGE SUPERMAN ONCE AGAIN.

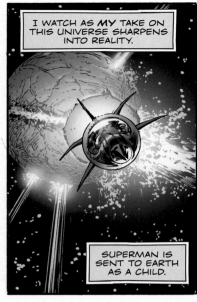

I WATCH AS *MY* TAKE ON THIS UNIVERSE SHARPENS INTO REALITY.

SUPERMAN IS SENT TO EARTH AS A CHILD.

I *LOST* OUR BABY.

OUR *LAST* CHANCE AT... AT A...

WHAT *IS* THAT, JONATHAN?

...IT WAS LIKE *CRYING.*

I KNOW HOW THAT *SOUNDS,* BUT I KNOW WHAT I *HEARD...*

LOOKS LIKE SOME KIND OF *PLANE* OR *SPACE* EXPERIMENT.

JONNY, IT'S...

IT'S A BABY.

ON THE EVE OF CLARK KENT'S HIGH SCHOOL PROM, JONATHAN AND MARTHA ARE KILLED IN A CAR ACCIDENT.

24

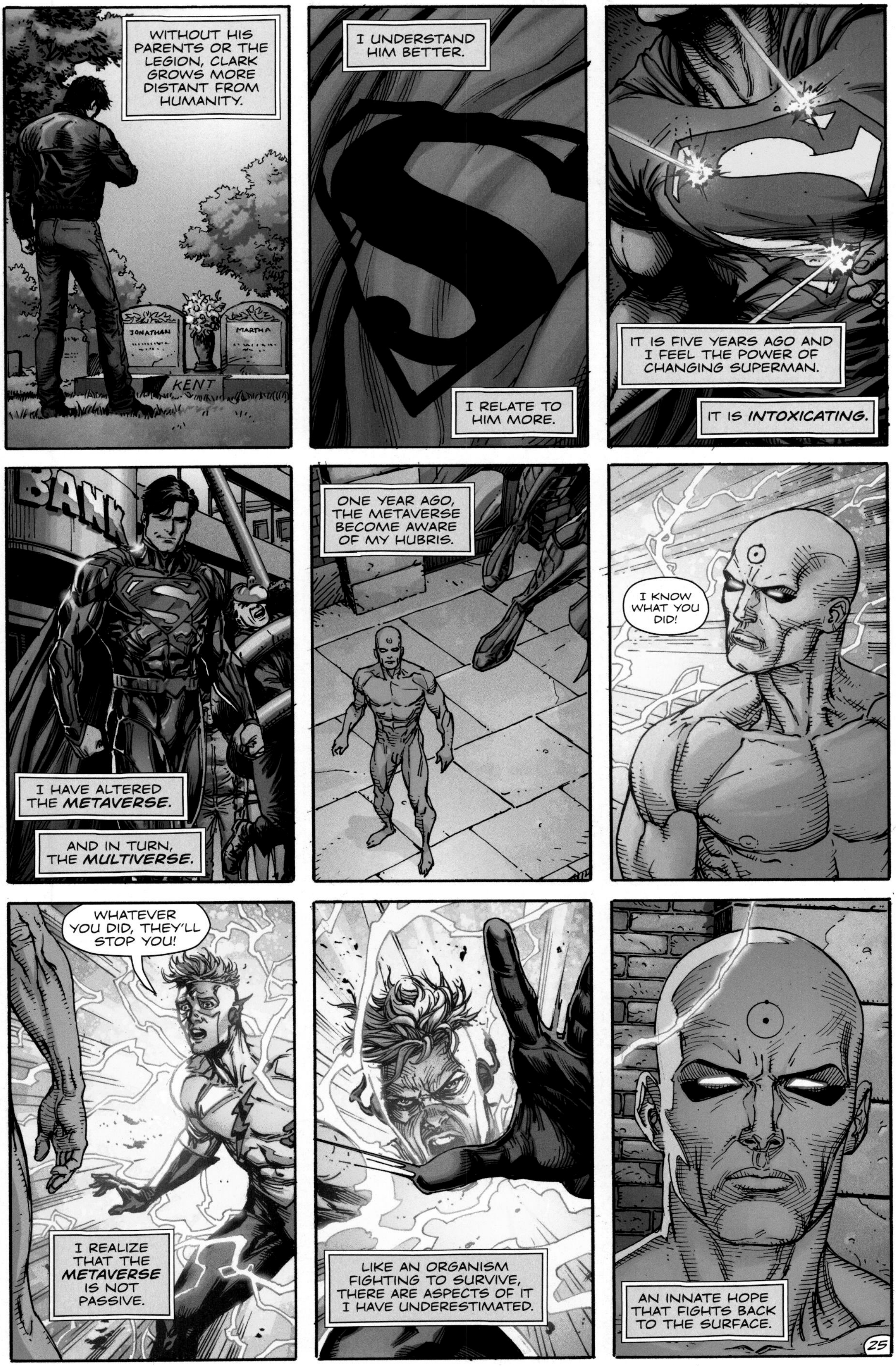
WITHOUT HIS PARENTS OR THE LEGION, CLARK GROWS MORE DISTANT FROM HUMANITY.
JONATHAN
MARTHA
KENT
I UNDERSTAND HIM BETTER.
I RELATE TO HIM MORE.
IT IS FIVE YEARS AGO AND I FEEL THE POWER OF CHANGING SUPERMAN.
IT IS INTOXICATING.
BANK
I HAVE ALTERED THE METAVERSE.
AND IN TURN, THE MULTIVERSE.
ONE YEAR AGO, THE METAVERSE BECOME AWARE OF MY HUBRIS.
I KNOW WHAT YOU DID!
WHATEVER YOU DID, THEY'LL STOP YOU!
I REALIZE THAT THE METAVERSE IS NOT PASSIVE.
LIKE AN ORGANISM FIGHTING TO SURVIVE, THERE ARE ASPECTS OF IT I HAVE UNDERESTIMATED.
AN INNATE HOPE THAT FIGHTS BACK TO THE SURFACE.

JON, TELL ME WHAT YOU SEE!

IT IS APRIL 18, 1938.

I HAVE RE-CREATED THE METAVERSE.

AND IT HAS TURNED AGAINST ME.

I SEE A VISION OF SUPERMAN IN THE FUTURE.

HE HAS FOUND ME.

AND HE DESTROYS ME.

OR I DESTROY THE METAVERSE.

JON?

JON? ARE YOU OKAY?

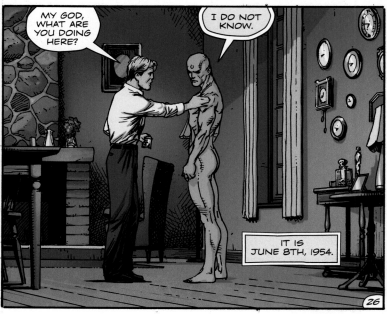

MY GOD, WHAT ARE YOU DOING HERE?

I DO NOT KNOW.

IT IS JUNE 8TH, 1954.

26

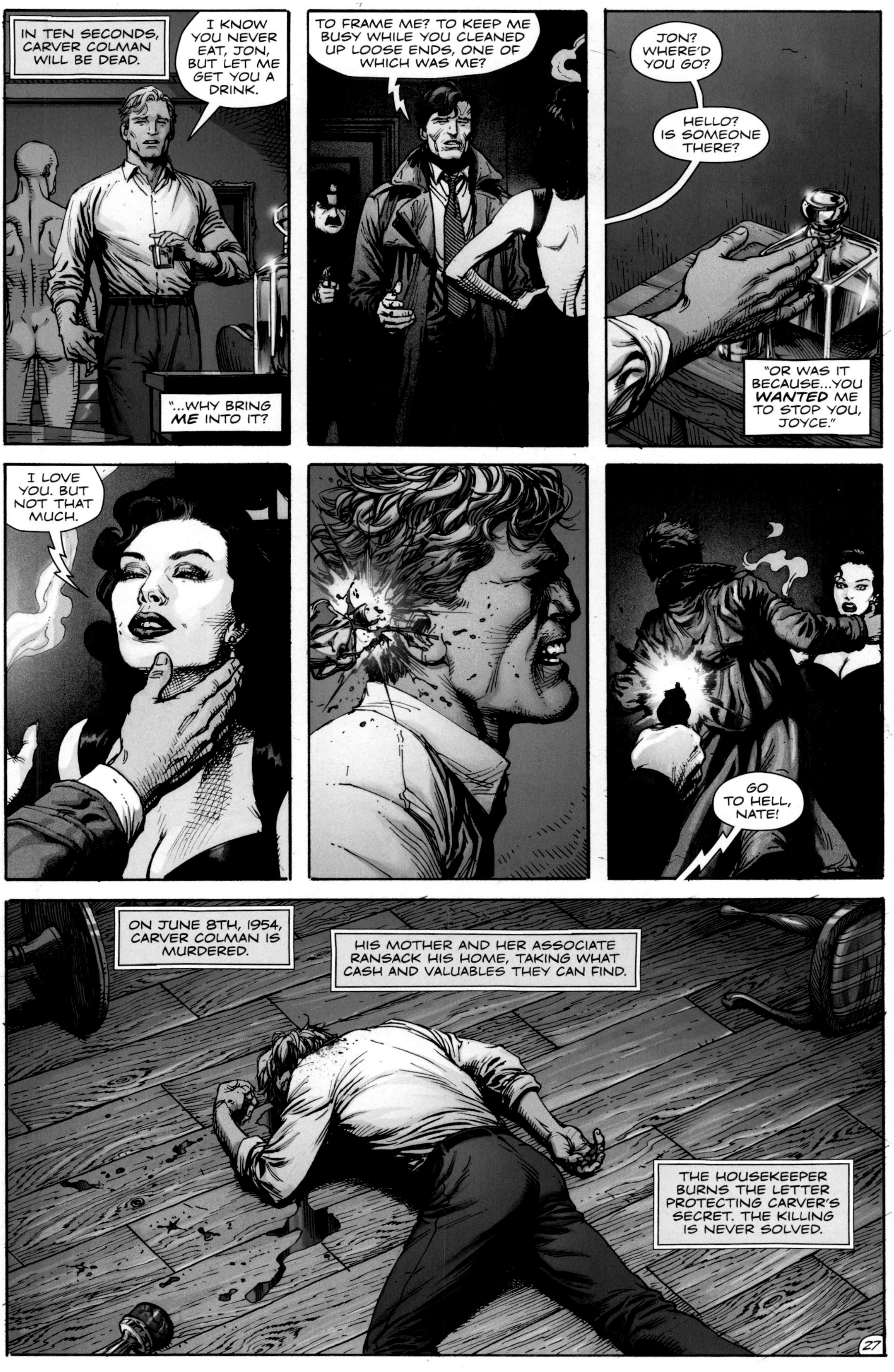
IN TEN SECONDS, CARVER COLMAN WILL BE DEAD.
I KNOW YOU NEVER EAT, JON, BUT LET ME GET YOU A DRINK.
"...WHY BRING ME INTO IT?
TO FRAME ME? TO KEEP ME BUSY WHILE YOU CLEANED UP LOOSE ENDS, ONE OF WHICH WAS ME?
JON? WHERE'D YOU GO?
HELLO? IS SOMEONE THERE?
"OR WAS IT BECAUSE...YOU WANTED ME TO STOP YOU, JOYCE."
I LOVE YOU. BUT NOT THAT MUCH.
GO TO HELL, NATE!
ON JUNE 8TH, 1954, CARVER COLMAN IS MURDERED.
HIS MOTHER AND HER ASSOCIATE RANSACK HIS HOME, TAKING WHAT CASH AND VALUABLES THEY CAN FIND.
THE HOUSEKEEPER BURNS THE LETTER PROTECTING CARVER'S SECRET. THE KILLING IS NEVER SOLVED.

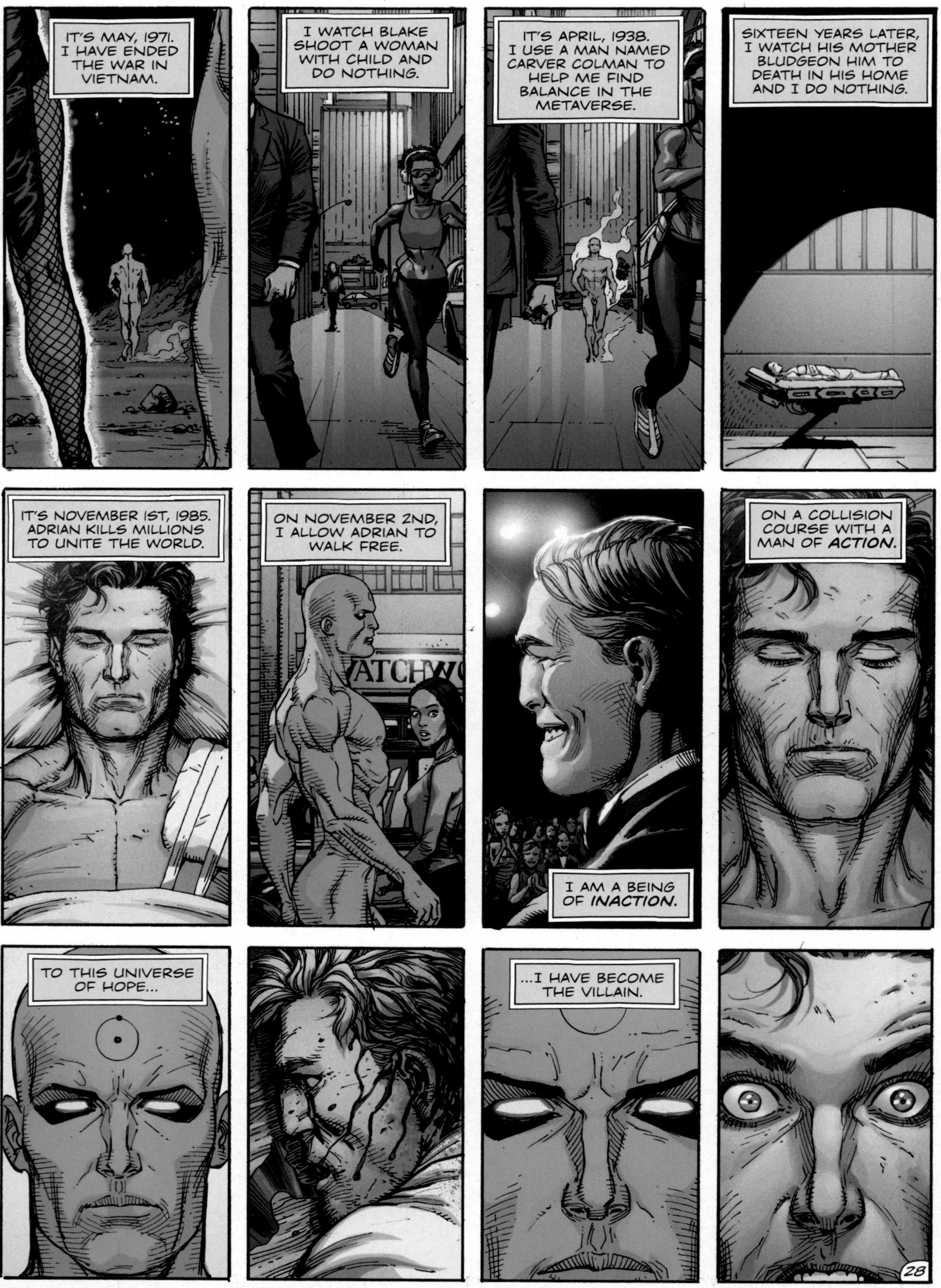
IT'S MAY, 1971. I HAVE ENDED THE WAR IN VIETNAM.
I WATCH BLAKE SHOOT A WOMAN WITH CHILD AND DO NOTHING.
IT'S APRIL, 1938. I USE A MAN NAMED CARVER COLMAN TO HELP ME FIND BALANCE IN THE METAVERSE.
SIXTEEN YEARS LATER, I WATCH HIS MOTHER BLUDGEON HIM TO DEATH IN HIS HOME AND I DO NOTHING.
IT'S NOVEMBER 1ST, 1985. ADRIAN KILLS MILLIONS TO UNITE THE WORLD.
ON NOVEMBER 2ND, I ALLOW ADRIAN TO WALK FREE.
ATCHW
I AM A BEING OF *INACTION*.
ON A COLLISION COURSE WITH A MAN OF *ACTION*.
TO THIS UNIVERSE OF HOPE...
...I HAVE BECOME THE VILLAIN.

Every action has its pleasures and its price.

—Socrates

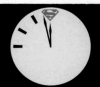

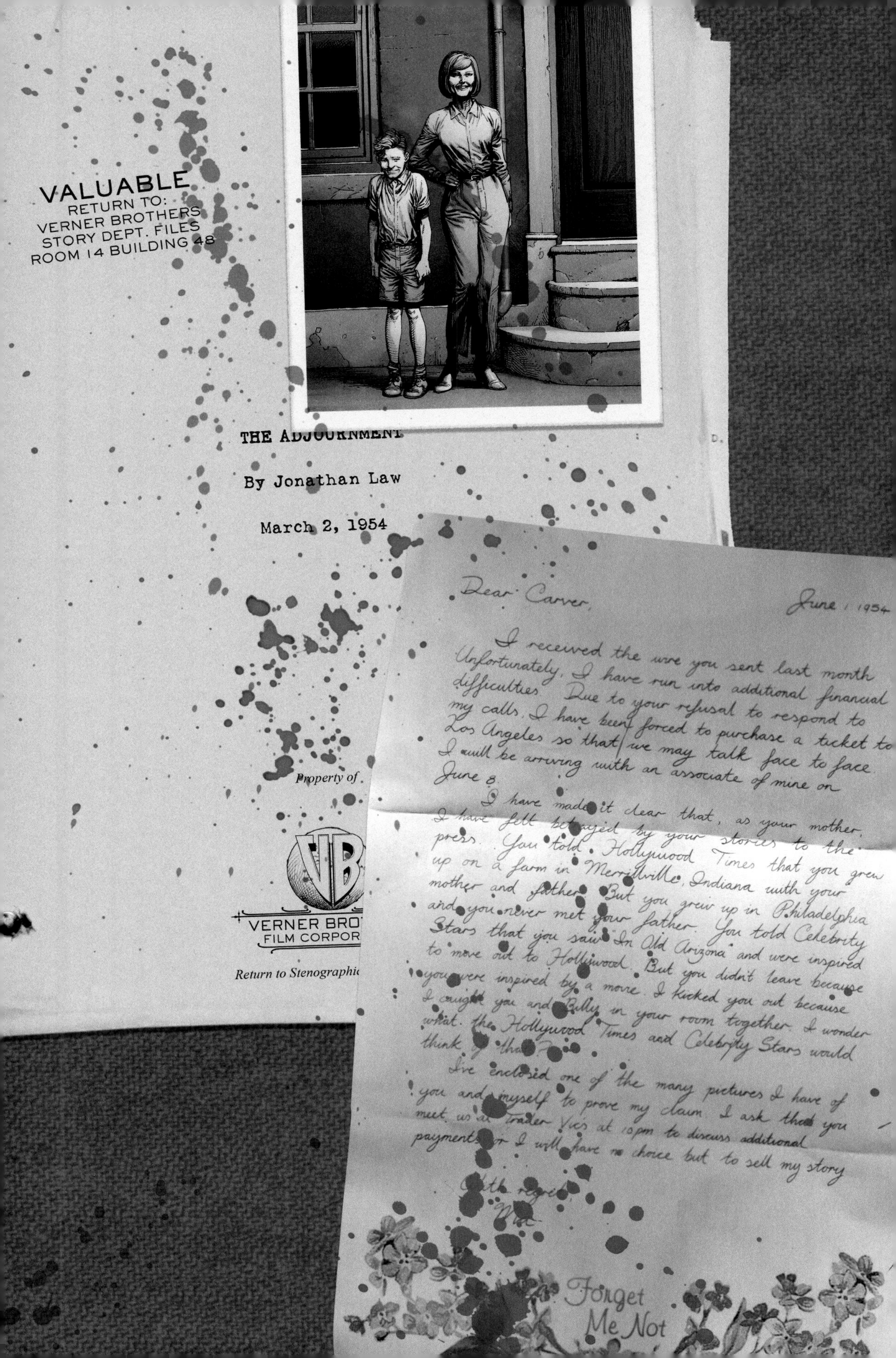

VALUABLE
RETURN TO:
VERNER BROTHERS
STORY DEPT. FILES
ROOM 14 BUILDING 48

THE ADJOURNMENT

By Jonathan Law

March 2, 1954

Property of

VB

VERNER BROT
FILM CORPOR

Return to Stenographic

Dear Carver,

June 1 1954

I received the wire you sent last month
Unfortunately, I have run into additional financial
difficulties. Due to your refusal to respond to
my calls, I have been forced to purchase a ticket to
Los Angeles so that we may talk face to face.
I will be arriving with an associate of mine on
June 8.

I have made it clear that, as your mother,
I have felt betrayed by your stories to the
press. You told Hollywood Times that you grew
up on a farm in Merrillville, Indiana with your
mother and father. But you grew up in Philadelphia
and you never met your father. You told Celebrity
Stars that you saw "In Old Arizona" and were inspired
to move out to Hollywood. But you didn't leave because
you were inspired by a movie. I kicked you out because
I caught you and Billy in your room together. I wonder
what the Hollywood Times and Celebrity Stars would
think of that?

I've enclosed one of the many pictures I have of
you and myself to prove my claim. I ask that you
meet us at Trader Vic's at 10pm to discuss additional
payments or I will have no choice but to sell my story

With regrets,
Mat

Forget
Me Not

FADE IN:

INT. NATHANIEL DUSK'S OFFICE - CHRISTMAS EVE

MOVING ACROSS NATHANIEL DUSK'S DESK; a picture of his (now-deceased) fianceé JOYCE GULINO and her TWO CHILDREN next to a FULL ASH TRAY... and a GLASS OF WHISKEY.

> DUSK (V.O.)
> It's worse at Christmastime. Being without my family.

DUSK'S HAND reaches for the whiskey.

> DUSK (V.O.)
> I lost my girl to her ex-husband, a gangster who got a bullet in his gut but deserved worse. And the kids to her parents in Indiana. The truth is, Joyce and he children were never mind to being with.

Silhouetted by the window, Dusk drinks. It's never enough.

> DUSK (V.O.)
> At least that's what I keep telling myself. Bottle half gone, I'm starting to believe it.

CLOSER ON: Dusk, the lights outside turn on... and off...

> DUSK (V.O.)
> Blinking red and green lights on Maria's soup kitchen make my headache worse. Never been one for charity.

The SHADOW of a FIGURE can be seen through the FROSTED GLASS of Dusk's door. NATHANIEL DUSK, PRIVATE INVESTIGATOR on it.

> DUSK (V.O.)
> That's why I went into business for myself. But on Christmas Eve, business is supposed to be closed.

> MURRAY (BEHIND DOOR)
> Dusk? You in there?

Dusk has no idea it's his old friend, LT. MURRAY ABRAHAMS. The only cop on the force he trusts.

Hunched at Joyce's feet, Dusk opens the present. He looks
inside the box to find: A GLASS GLOBE.

> JOYCE
> You said it felt like we were the
> only people in the world when
> we were alone. I wanted you to have
> that world. A world to remember.

Dusk looks into the reflection in the globe, watching Murray holding his
gun. He spots Murray gazing away for a moment.

> DUSK
> Thanks!

Dusk spins around, throwing the globe at Murray! The globe
shatters, knocking the gun out of Murray's hand! Dusk goes
for the gun, but Joyce kicks it skittering across the floor.
Back into Murray's hands.

> MURRAY
> Nice try. But you lose, Nate.

Suddenly, SIRENS wail outside. The police are here.

> DUSK
> No losers yet, Murray. As much as I
> hate the NYPD... I called them.
> (off Murray's shock)
> Do you really think I'd meet you in
> the dead of night to discuss the
> case without knowing what I was
> walking into?

> MURRAY
> What are you talking about?

> DUSK
> I solved the chess player murders
> 35 minutes ago, Murray.
> I know they were both targets and
> I know Joyce had you kill them.

Joyce and Murray exchange a look, the tables turning.

> DUSK (CONT'D)
> I was so focused on what made the
> two men different... I didn't see
> the obvious. It was what they have
> in common that mattered.

Joyce and Murray hear the police exit their cars outside. As the police
close in, Dusk walks towards Joyce, unafraid.

                    DUSK (CONT'D)
          The city planner, Bentley Farmer,
          was Murray's brother-in-law. I knew
          Murray disliked him, but that
          wasn't what tipped me off. Every
          plan Farmer approved over the last
          year was connected to Costilino's
          businesses. Now your businesses, I
          guess you'd rather I say, Joyce.
          Farmer was on the payroll. And the
          banker, Alastair Tempus, was fronting
          the cash. The only question I have
          left is... why bring me into it? To
          frame me? To keep me busy while you
          cleaned up loose ends, one of which
          was me? Or was it because... you
          wanted me to stop you, Joyce?

                    JOYCE
          I love you. But not that much.

As the cops rush in, Murray shoots Dusk in the back. BANG!

                    MURRAY
          Go to hell, Nate!

The cops tackle Murray and grab Joyce. Dusk lies on the floor,
bleeding. He looks up at Joyce with a smile.

                    DUSK
          I love you, too.

Still smiling, he blacks out.

INT. NEW YORK CITY STREETS - NEW YEAR'S EVE

It's New Year's Eve. People celebrate in the streets as the
clock ticks down. Limping through the crowd we find...
NATHANIEL DUSK on a crutch, healing from the shooting days before.

                    DUSK (V.O.)
          Doc says the limp will put me out
          of the game permanently. I don't
          mind. I was honest. I was loyal.
          And I've learned the greatest
          lesson of all...

He looks up at the clock as it ticks down, people cheering.

                    DUSK (V.O.)
          It's not who wins or loses. It's
          how you played the game.

                         THE END

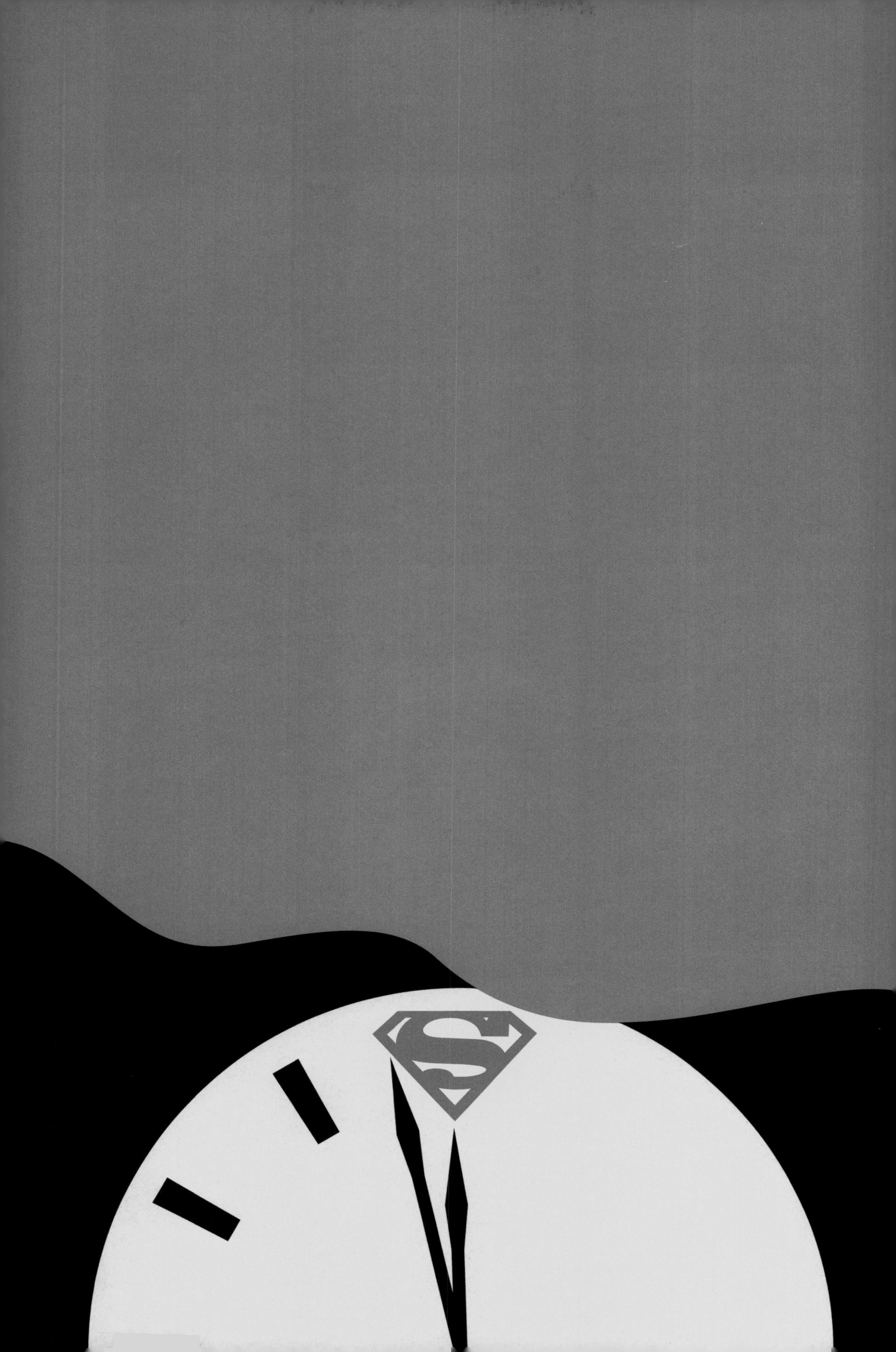

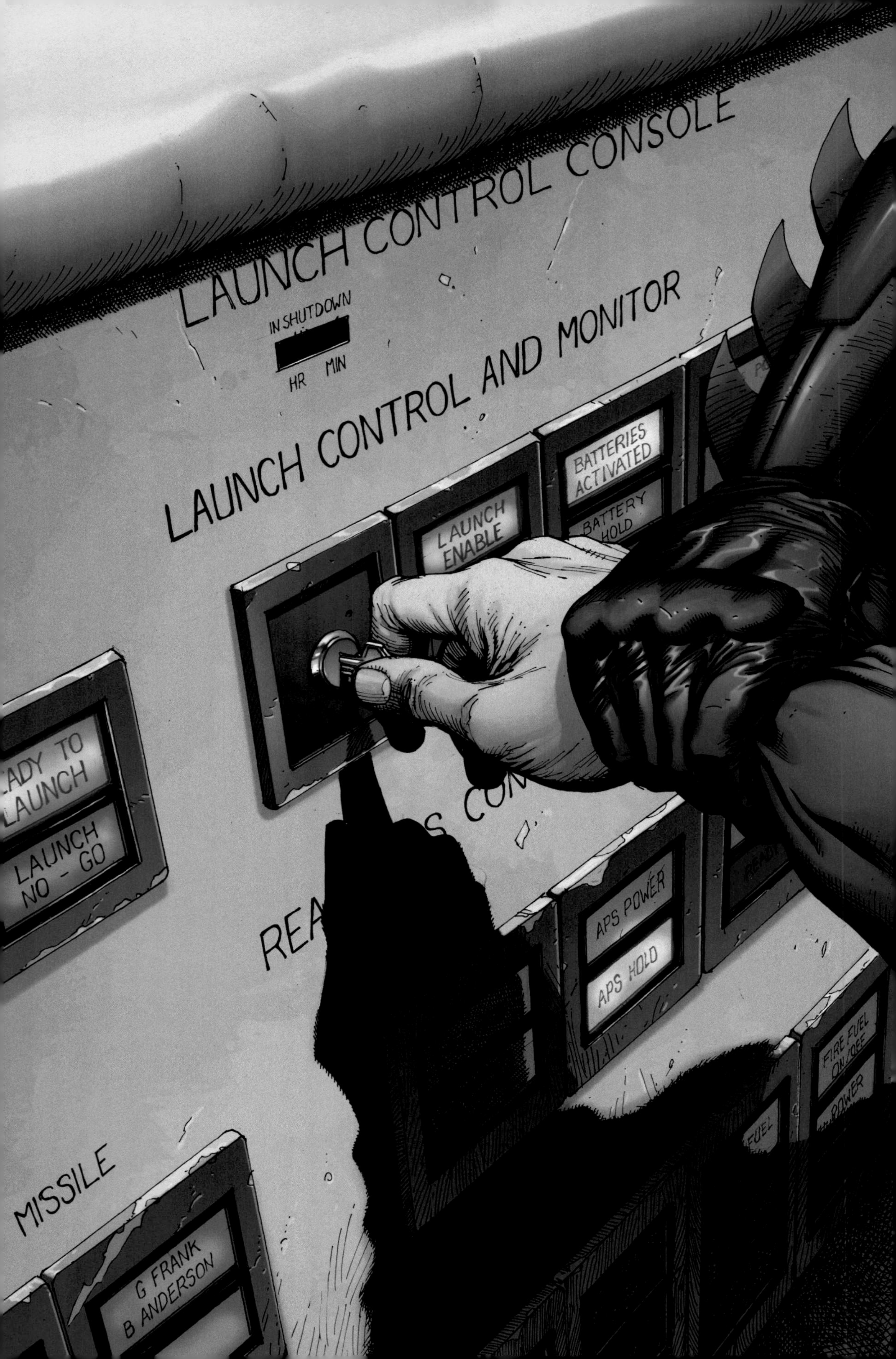
LAUNCH CONTROL CONSOLE
IN SHUTDOWN
HR MIN
LAUNCH CONTROL AND MONITOR
BATTERIES ACTIVATED
BATTERY HOLD
LAUNCH ENABLE
LAUNCH NO - GO
APS POWER
APS HOLD
FIRE FUEL ON/OFF
POWER
MISSILE
G FRANK
B ANDERSON

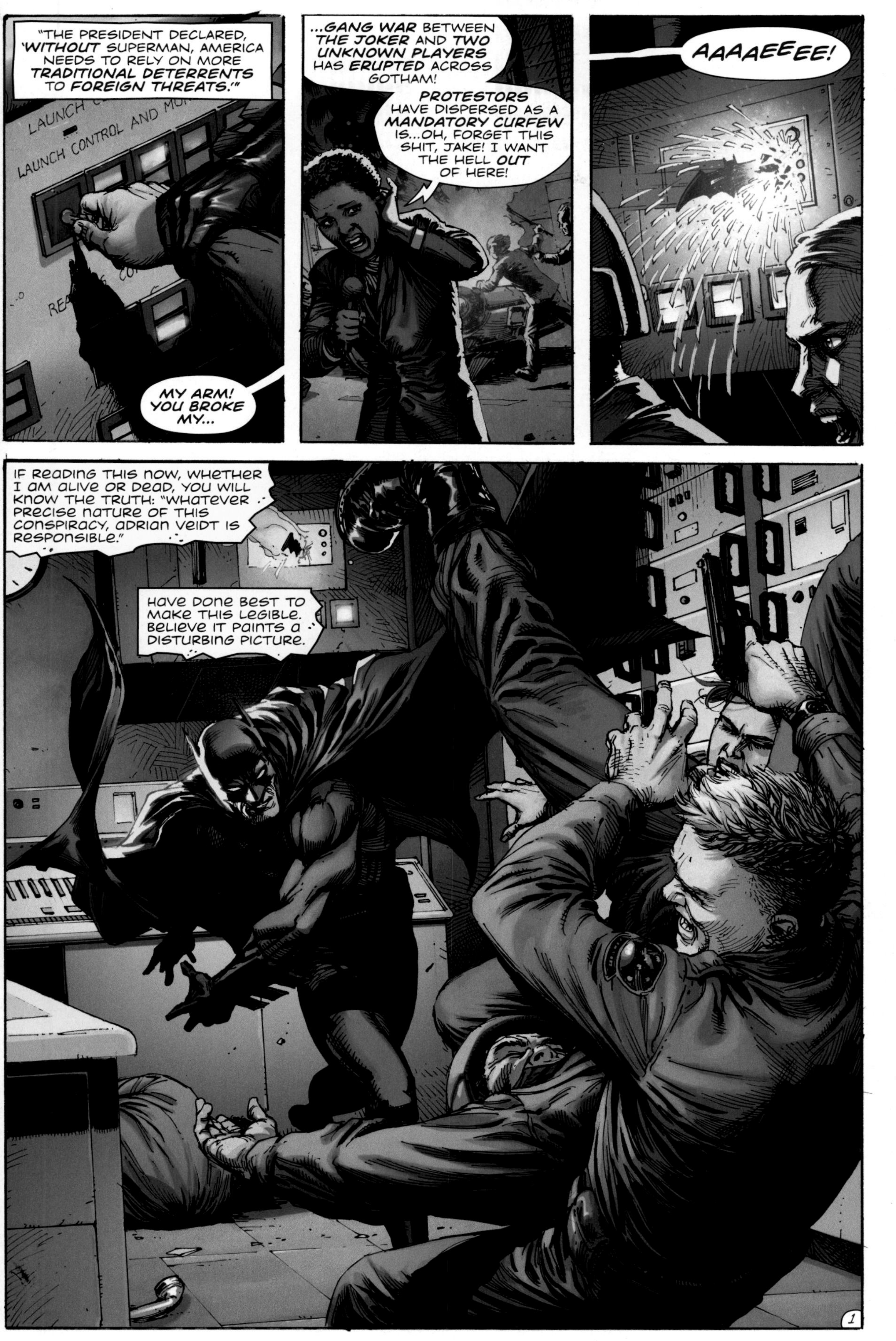
"THE PRESIDENT DECLARED, '*WITHOUT* SUPERMAN, AMERICA NEEDS TO RELY ON MORE *TRADITIONAL DETERRENTS* TO *FOREIGN THREATS.*'"
MY ARM! YOU BROKE MY...
...*GANG WAR* BETWEEN *THE JOKER* AND *TWO UNKNOWN PLAYERS* HAS *ERUPTED* ACROSS GOTHAM!
PROTESTORS HAVE DISPERSED AS A *MANDATORY CURFEW* IS...OH, FORGET THIS SHIT, JAKE! I WANT THE HELL *OUT* OF HERE!
AAAAEEEEE!
IF READING THIS NOW, WHETHER I AM ALIVE OR DEAD, YOU WILL KNOW THE TRUTH: "WHATEVER PRECISE NATURE OF THIS CONSPIRACY, ADRIAN VEIDT IS RESPONSIBLE."
HAVE DONE BEST TO MAKE THIS LEGIBLE. BELIEVE IT PAINTS A DISTURBING PICTURE.

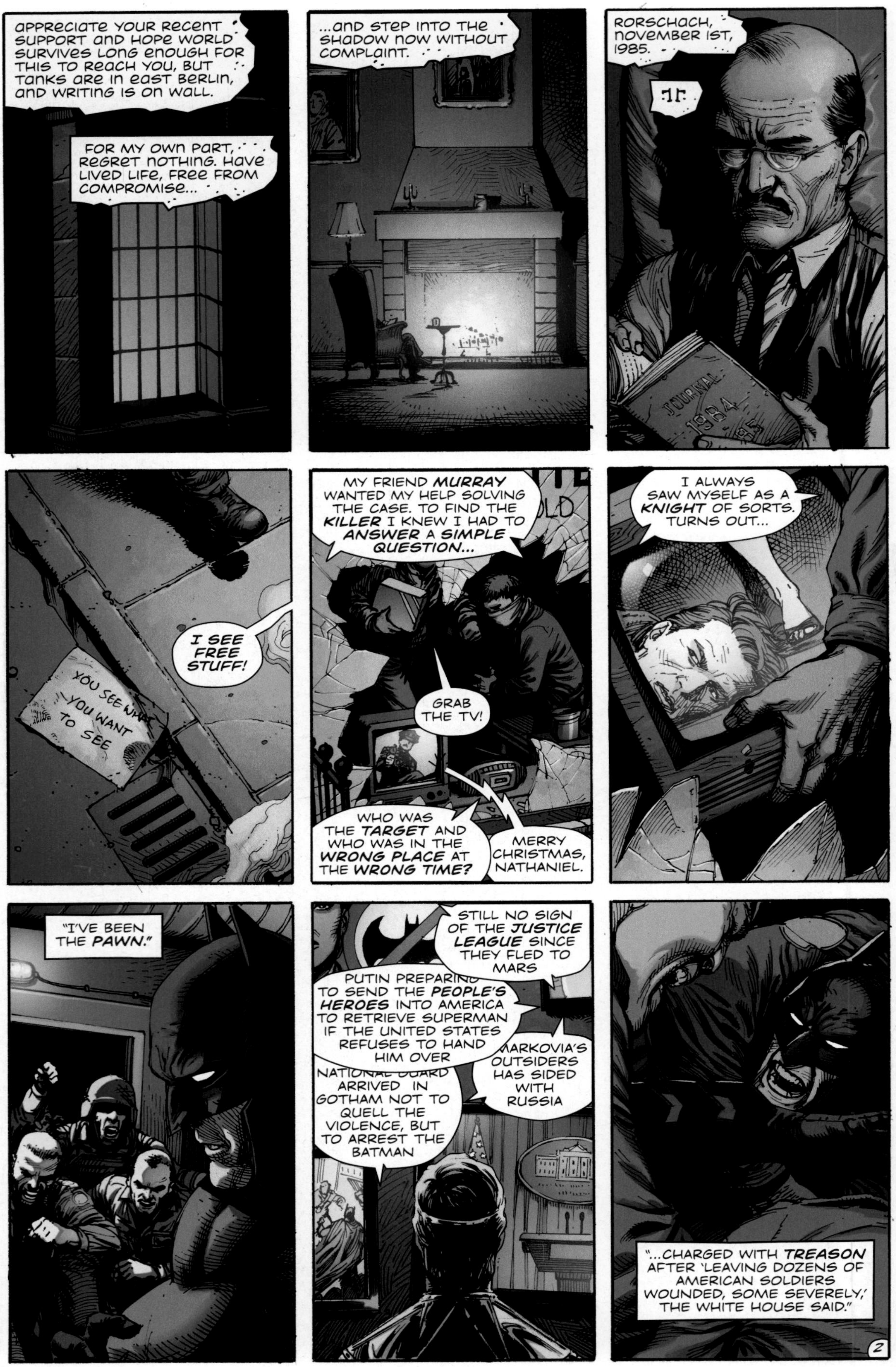
appreciate your recent support and hope world survives long enough for this to reach you, but tanks are in east berlin, and writing is on wall.
FOR MY OWN PART, Regret nothing. Have lived life, free from compromise...
...and step into the shadow now without complaint.
RORSCHACH, november 1st, 1985.
MY FRIEND MURRAY WANTED MY HELP SOLVING THE CASE. TO FIND THE KILLER I KNEW I HAD TO ANSWER A SIMPLE QUESTION...
I ALWAYS SAW MYSELF AS A KNIGHT OF SORTS. TURNS OUT...
I SEE FREE STUFF!
YOU SEE WHAT YOU WANT TO SEE
GRAB THE TV!
WHO WAS THE TARGET AND WHO WAS IN THE WRONG PLACE AT THE WRONG TIME?
MERRY CHRISTMAS, NATHANIEL.
"I'VE BEEN THE PAWN."
STILL NO SIGN OF THE JUSTICE LEAGUE SINCE THEY FLED TO MARS
PUTIN PREPARING TO SEND THE PEOPLE'S HEROES INTO AMERICA TO RETRIEVE SUPERMAN IF THE UNITED STATES REFUSES TO HAND HIM OVER
MARKOVIA'S OUTSIDERS HAS SIDED WITH RUSSIA
NATIONAL GUARD ARRIVED IN GOTHAM NOT TO QUELL THE VIOLENCE, BUT TO ARREST THE BATMAN
"...CHARGED WITH TREASON AFTER 'LEAVING DOZENS OF AMERICAN SOLDIERS WOUNDED, SOME SEVERELY,' THE WHITE HOUSE SAID."
2

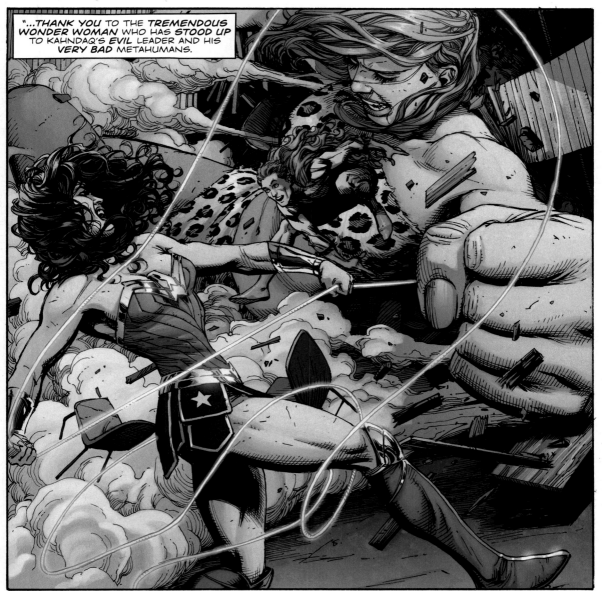

"...THANK YOU TO THE *TREMENDOUS WONDER WOMAN* WHO HAS *STOOD UP* TO KAHNDAQ'S *EVIL* LEADER AND HIS *VERY BAD* METAHUMANS.

"BLACK ADAM IS A *HUGE TERRORIST THREAT* TO THE WORLD. BUT AMERICA WILL *WIN.* THE *BIGGER* THEY ARE...

"...THE *BIGGER* THEY'LL FALL."

"IT'S HARDER, MR. PRESIDENT."

AAAAAAAA!

YOU PREACH OF *PEACE* AS IF THAT'S WHAT THE LEADERS OF THIS *BLOATED, SELFISH, FRIGHTENED* COUNTRY *WANT.*

3

THEY ARE THE **DESCENDANTS** OF THOSE WHO **ENSLAVED** YOUR PEOPLE, DIANA. WHO **RAPED** AND **KILLED** SO MANY OF YOU.

THEY FIGHT FOR THE **PRIVILEGED**.

I FIGHT FOR THE **OPPRESSED**.

I NEED TO KNOW, RIGHT NOW...

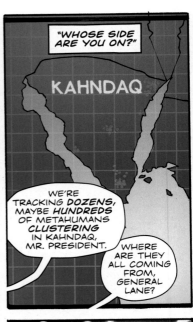

"WHOSE SIDE ARE YOU ON?"

KAHNDAQ

WE'RE TRACKING **DOZENS**, MAYBE **HUNDREDS** OF METAHUMANS **CLUSTERING** IN KAHNDAQ, MR. PRESIDENT.

WHERE ARE THEY ALL COMING FROM, GENERAL LANE?

FROM ALL OVER THE **GLOBE**.

THE **SUPERMEN THEORY**, THE **ABDUCTIONS** OF METAHUMANS BY **GOVERNMENTS** AND **TRAFFICKERS**... THESE PEOPLE SEE KAHNDAQ AS THEIR **ONLY OPTION** TO FIND **SAFETY**.

YOU NEED TO **RECONSIDER** YOUR POSITION ON WHETHER WE **ACKNOWLEDGE** PROFESSOR MARTIN STEIN'S WORK OR NOT.

IF WE TELL THE WORLD WE **ARE** RESPONSIBLE FOR A **PERCENTAGE** OF AMERICA'S "SUPERHEROES" AND "SUPER-VILLAINS," IF WE RESTORE **FAITH** IN AT LEAST **SOME** OF THEM...

NO.

"BUT WITH OUR NUCLEAR SYSTEMS **DOWN**, WE HAVE NO **DEFENSES** IN PLACE."

"WON'T THE **AMAZONS** COME TO WONDER WOMAN'S AID?"

WE HAVE **WARSHIPS** WATCHING THE MEDITERRANEAN FOR ANY **SIGNS**, BUT WE DON'T KNOW THE PRECISE LOCATION OF THEIR ISLAND.

OR WHAT THEIR **TRUE** INTENTIONS ARE.

THE ORACLE HAS PREDICTED DIANA WILL BE SEVERELY INJURED IN BATTLE IF IT CONTINUES.

WE MUST BRING HER **BACK** TO THE ISLAND TO THE **PURPLE LIGHT**.

SHE WILL **FIGHT** TO STAY, BUT THIS IS FOR HER OWN PROTECTION.

WHAT OF THE IMPENDING WAR ON MAN'S WORLD?

RETRIBUTION AGAINST BLACK ADAM IS NOT OUR WAY...

4

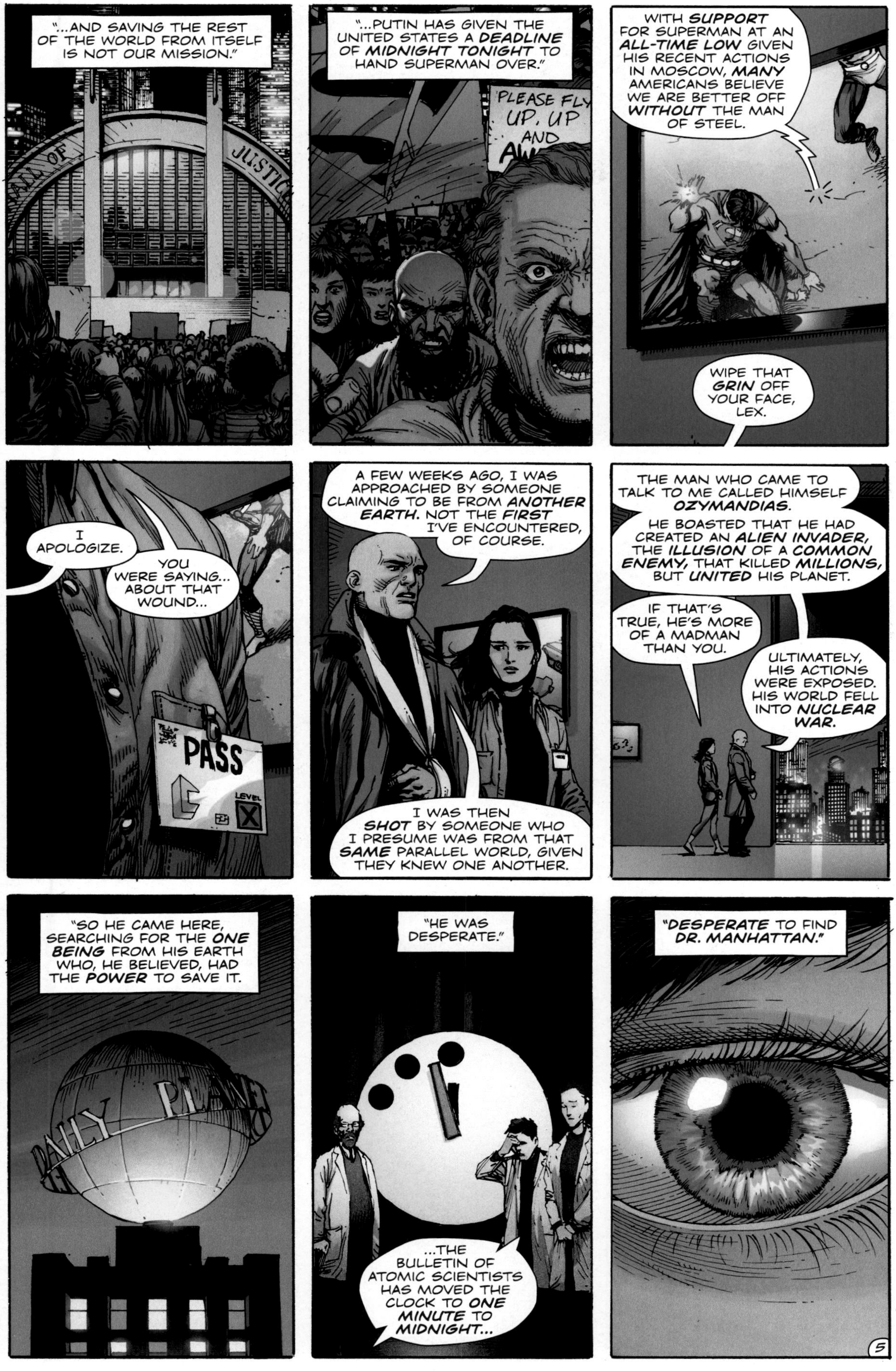
"...AND SAVING THE REST OF THE WORLD FROM ITSELF IS NOT OUR MISSION."
HALL OF JUSTICE
"...PUTIN HAS GIVEN THE UNITED STATES A DEADLINE OF MIDNIGHT TONIGHT TO HAND SUPERMAN OVER."
PLEASE FLY UP, UP AND AW
WITH SUPPORT FOR SUPERMAN AT AN ALL-TIME LOW GIVEN HIS RECENT ACTIONS IN MOSCOW, MANY AMERICANS BELIEVE WE ARE BETTER OFF WITHOUT THE MAN OF STEEL.
WIPE THAT GRIN OFF YOUR FACE, LEX.
I APOLOGIZE.
YOU WERE SAYING... ABOUT THAT WOUND...
PASS
LEVEL
X
A FEW WEEKS AGO, I WAS APPROACHED BY SOMEONE CLAIMING TO BE FROM ANOTHER EARTH. NOT THE FIRST I'VE ENCOUNTERED, OF COURSE.
I WAS THEN SHOT BY SOMEONE WHO I PRESUME WAS FROM THAT SAME PARALLEL WORLD, GIVEN THEY KNEW ONE ANOTHER.
THE MAN WHO CAME TO TALK TO ME CALLED HIMSELF OZYMANDIAS.
HE BOASTED THAT HE HAD CREATED AN ALIEN INVADER, THE ILLUSION OF A COMMON ENEMY, THAT KILLED MILLIONS, BUT UNITED HIS PLANET.
IF THAT'S TRUE, HE'S MORE OF A MADMAN THAN YOU.
ULTIMATELY, HIS ACTIONS WERE EXPOSED. HIS WORLD FELL INTO NUCLEAR WAR.
"SO HE CAME HERE, SEARCHING FOR THE ONE BEING FROM HIS EARTH WHO, HE BELIEVED, HAD THE POWER TO SAVE IT.
DAILY PLANET
"HE WAS DESPERATE."
...THE BULLETIN OF ATOMIC SCIENTISTS HAS MOVED THE CLOCK TO ONE MINUTE TO MIDNIGHT...
"DESPERATE TO FIND DR. MANHATTAN."

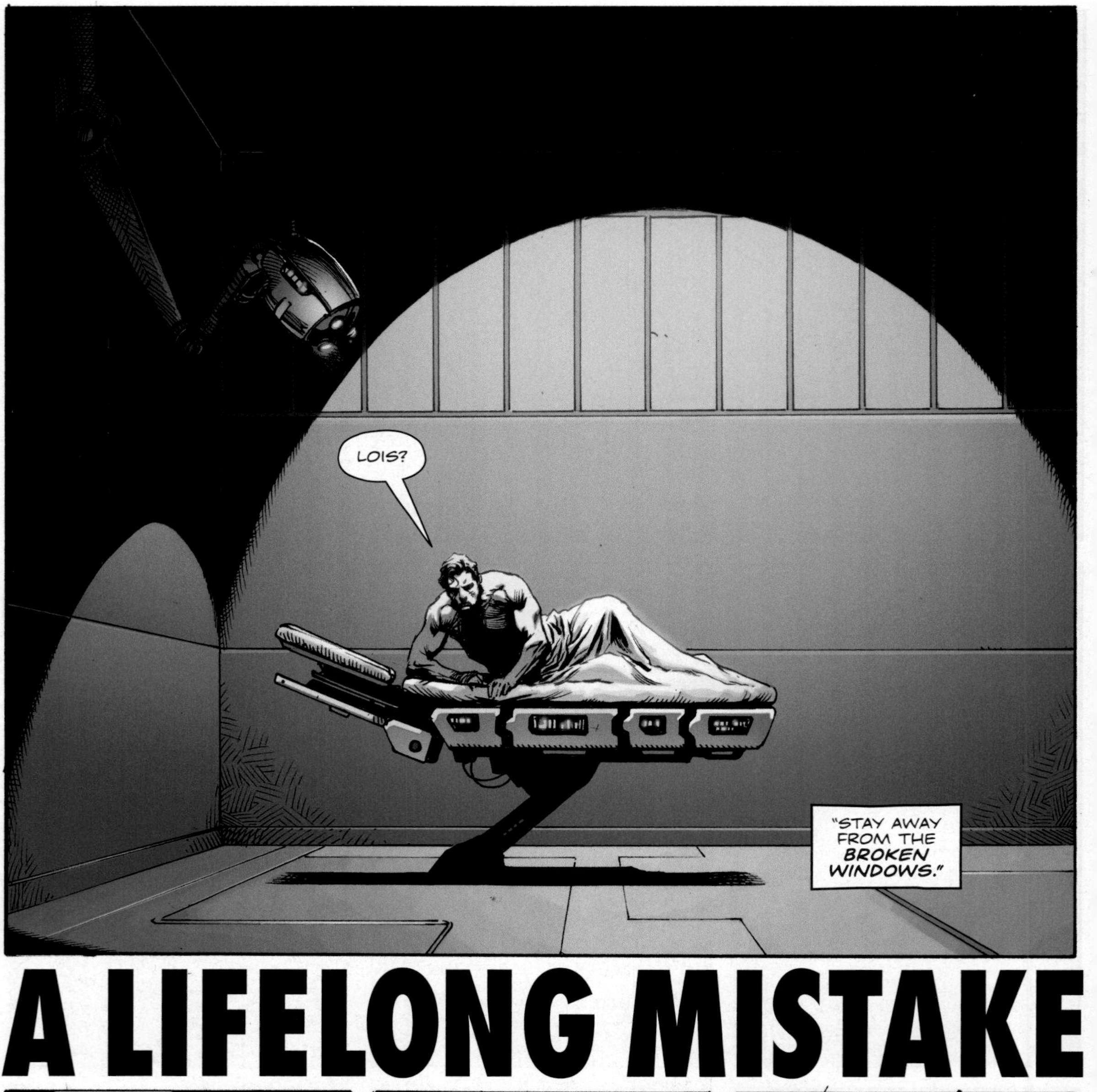
LOIS?
"STAY AWAY FROM THE BROKEN WINDOWS."

A LIFELONG MISTAKE

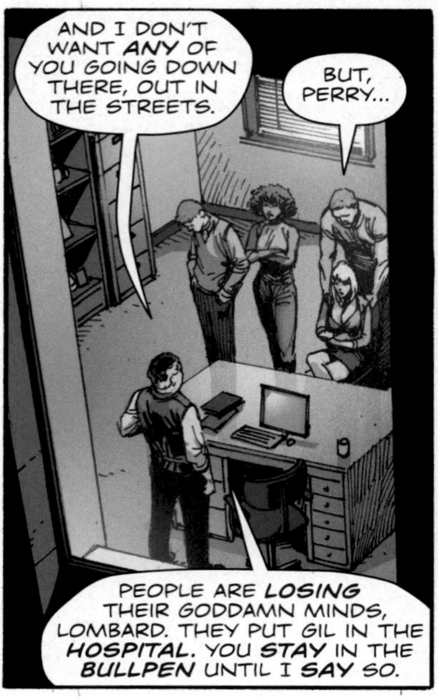
AND I DON'T WANT ANY OF YOU GOING DOWN THERE, OUT IN THE STREETS.
BUT, PERRY...
PEOPLE ARE LOSING THEIR GODDAMN MINDS, LOMBARD. THEY PUT GIL IN THE HOSPITAL. YOU STAY IN THE BULLPEN UNTIL I SAY SO.

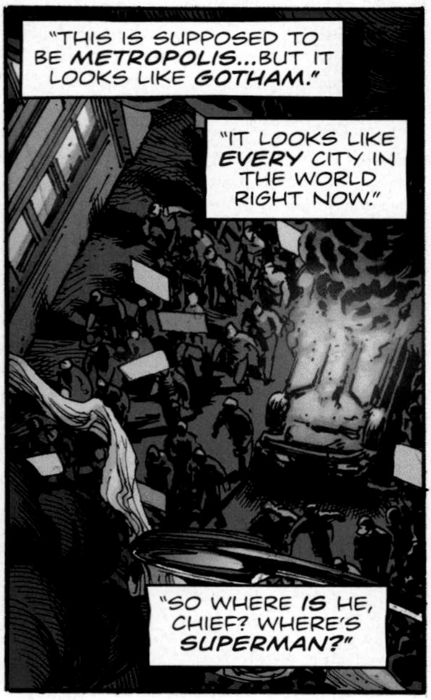
"THIS IS SUPPOSED TO BE METROPOLIS...BUT IT LOOKS LIKE GOTHAM."
"IT LOOKS LIKE EVERY CITY IN THE WORLD RIGHT NOW."
"SO WHERE IS HE, CHIEF? WHERE'S SUPERMAN?"

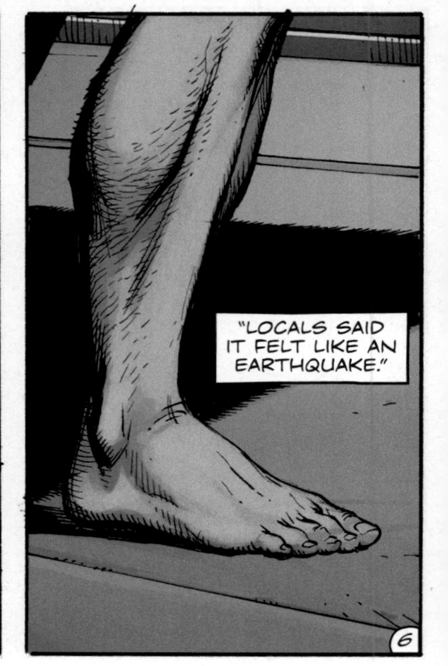
"LOCALS SAID IT FELT LIKE AN EARTHQUAKE."

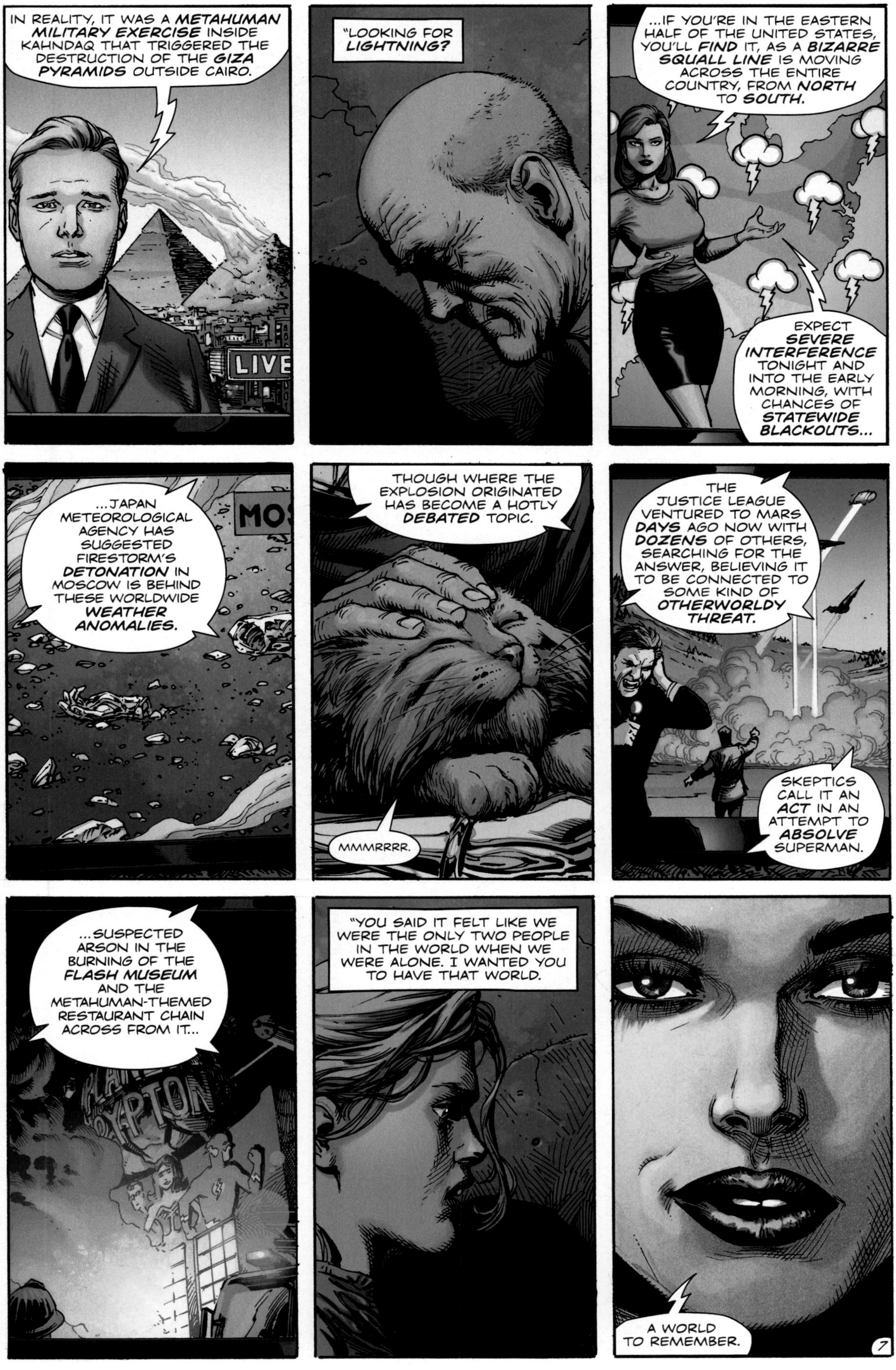
IN REALITY, IT WAS A METAHUMAN MILITARY EXERCISE INSIDE KAHNDAQ THAT TRIGGERED THE DESTRUCTION OF THE GIZA PYRAMIDS OUTSIDE CAIRO.
LIVE
"LOOKING FOR LIGHTNING?
...IF YOU'RE IN THE EASTERN HALF OF THE UNITED STATES, YOU'LL FIND IT, AS A BIZARRE SQUALL LINE IS MOVING ACROSS THE ENTIRE COUNTRY, FROM NORTH TO SOUTH.
EXPECT SEVERE INTERFERENCE TONIGHT AND INTO THE EARLY MORNING, WITH CHANCES OF STATEWIDE BLACKOUTS...
...JAPAN METEOROLOGICAL AGENCY HAS SUGGESTED FIRESTORM'S DETONATION IN MOSCOW IS BEHIND THESE WORLDWIDE WEATHER ANOMALIES.
MOS
THOUGH WHERE THE EXPLOSION ORIGINATED HAS BECOME A HOTLY DEBATED TOPIC.
MMMRRRR.
THE JUSTICE LEAGUE VENTURED TO MARS DAYS AGO NOW WITH DOZENS OF OTHERS, SEARCHING FOR THE ANSWER, BELIEVING IT TO BE CONNECTED TO SOME KIND OF OTHERWORLDY THREAT.
SKEPTICS CALL IT AN ACT IN AN ATTEMPT TO ABSOLVE SUPERMAN.
...SUSPECTED ARSON IN THE BURNING OF THE FLASH MUSEUM AND THE METAHUMAN-THEMED RESTAURANT CHAIN ACROSS FROM IT...
"YOU SAID IT FELT LIKE WE WERE THE ONLY TWO PEOPLE IN THE WORLD WHEN WE WERE ALONE. I WANTED YOU TO HAVE THAT WORLD.
A WORLD TO REMEMBER.

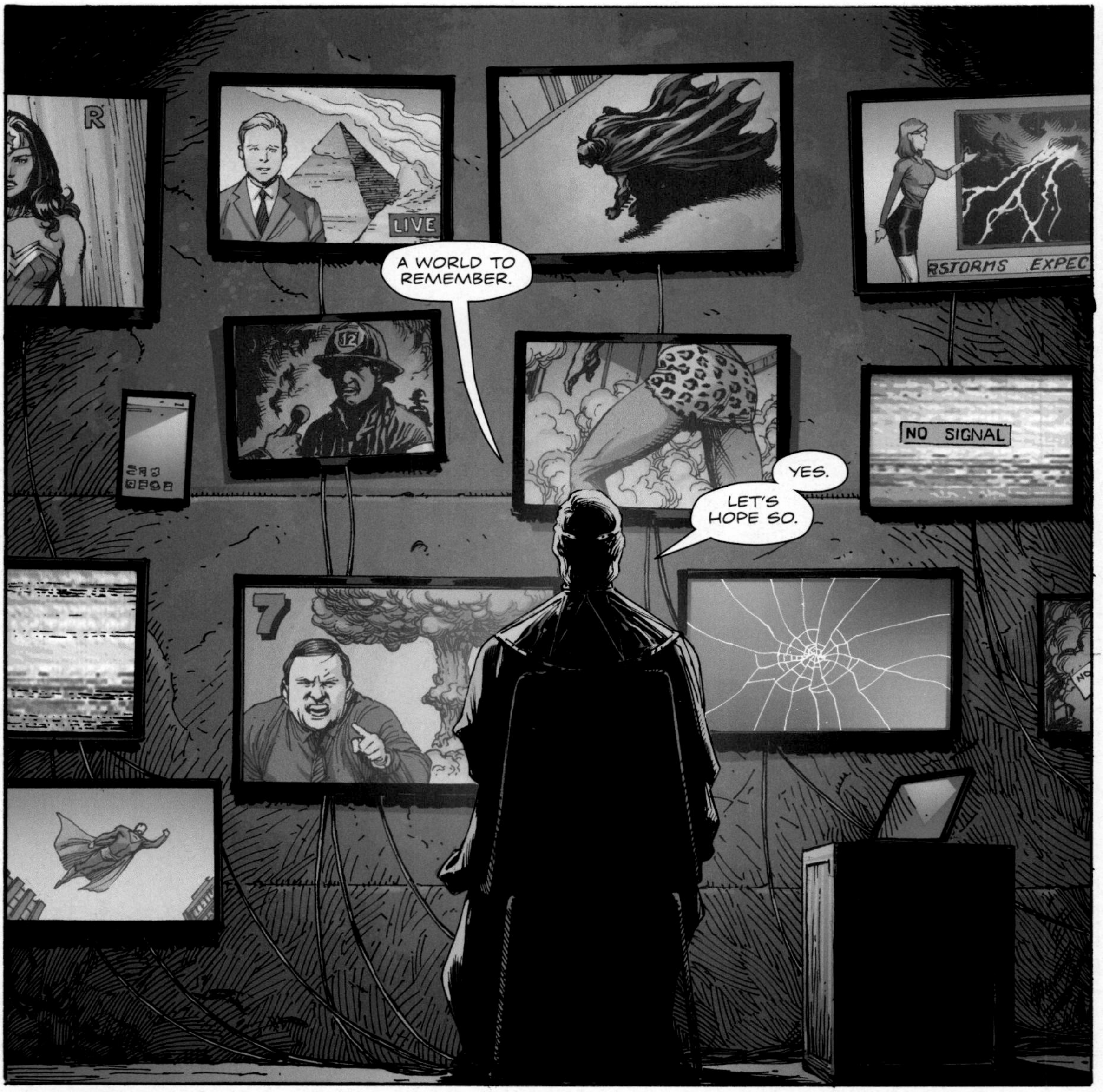
LIVE
RSTORMS EXPEC
A WORLD TO REMEMBER.
NO SIGNAL
YES.
LET'S HOPE SO.
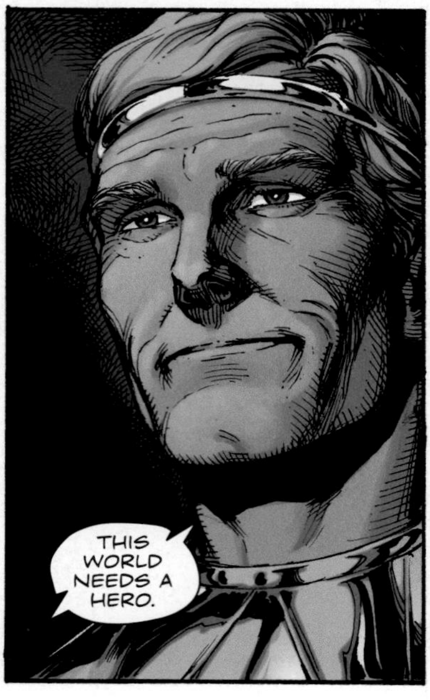
THIS WORLD NEEDS A HERO.
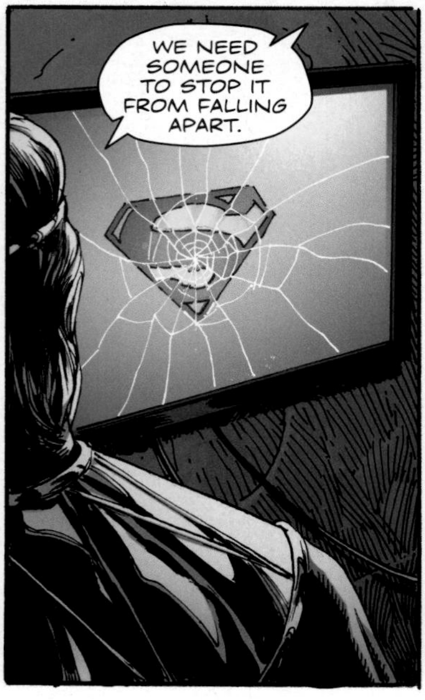
WE NEED SOMEONE TO STOP IT FROM FALLING APART.
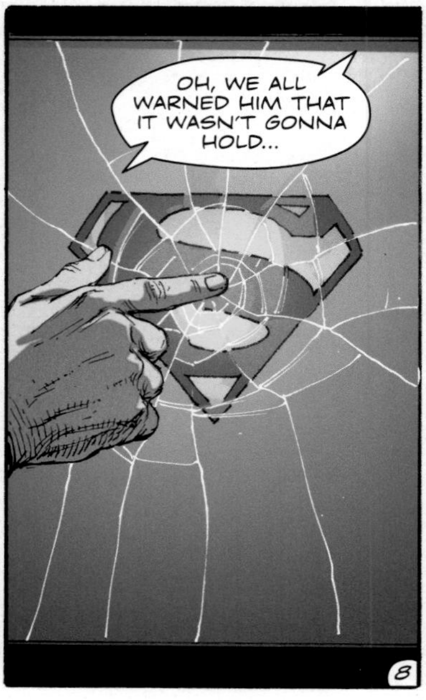
OH, WE ALL WARNED HIM THAT IT WASN'T GONNA HOLD...

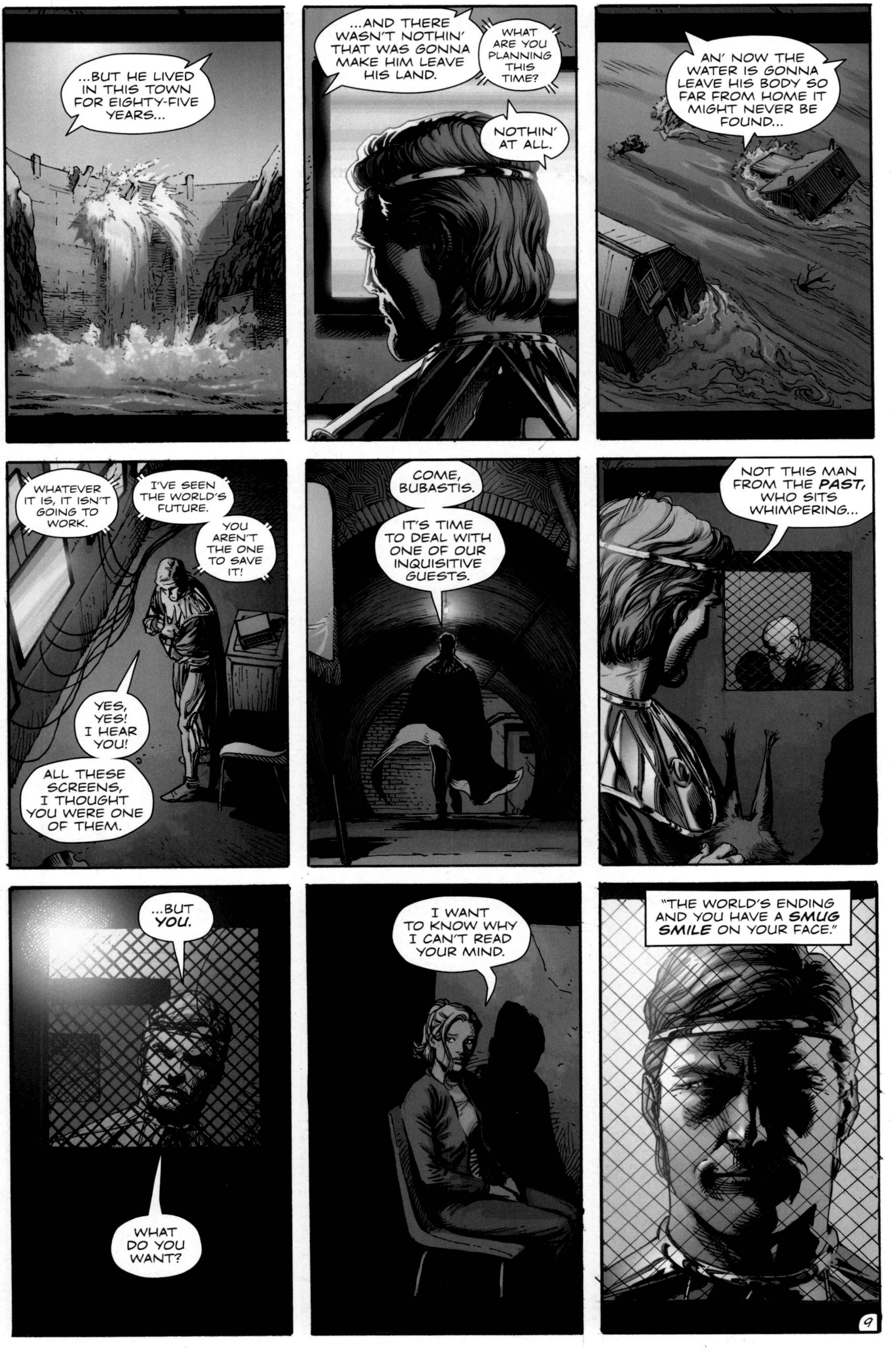
...BUT HE LIVED IN THIS TOWN FOR EIGHTY-FIVE YEARS...
...AND THERE WASN'T NOTHIN' THAT WAS GONNA MAKE HIM LEAVE HIS LAND.
WHAT ARE YOU PLANNING THIS TIME?
NOTHIN' AT ALL.
AN' NOW THE WATER IS GONNA LEAVE HIS BODY SO FAR FROM HOME IT MIGHT NEVER BE FOUND...
WHATEVER IT IS, IT ISN'T GOING TO WORK.
I'VE SEEN THE WORLD'S FUTURE.
YOU AREN'T THE ONE TO SAVE IT!
YES, YES! I HEAR YOU!
ALL THESE SCREENS, I THOUGHT YOU WERE ONE OF THEM.
COME, BUBASTIS.
IT'S TIME TO DEAL WITH ONE OF OUR INQUISITIVE GUESTS.
NOT THIS MAN FROM THE PAST, WHO SITS WHIMPERING...
...BUT YOU.
WHAT DO YOU WANT?
I WANT TO KNOW WHY I CAN'T READ YOUR MIND.
"THE WORLD'S ENDING AND YOU HAVE A SMUG SMILE ON YOUR FACE."
9

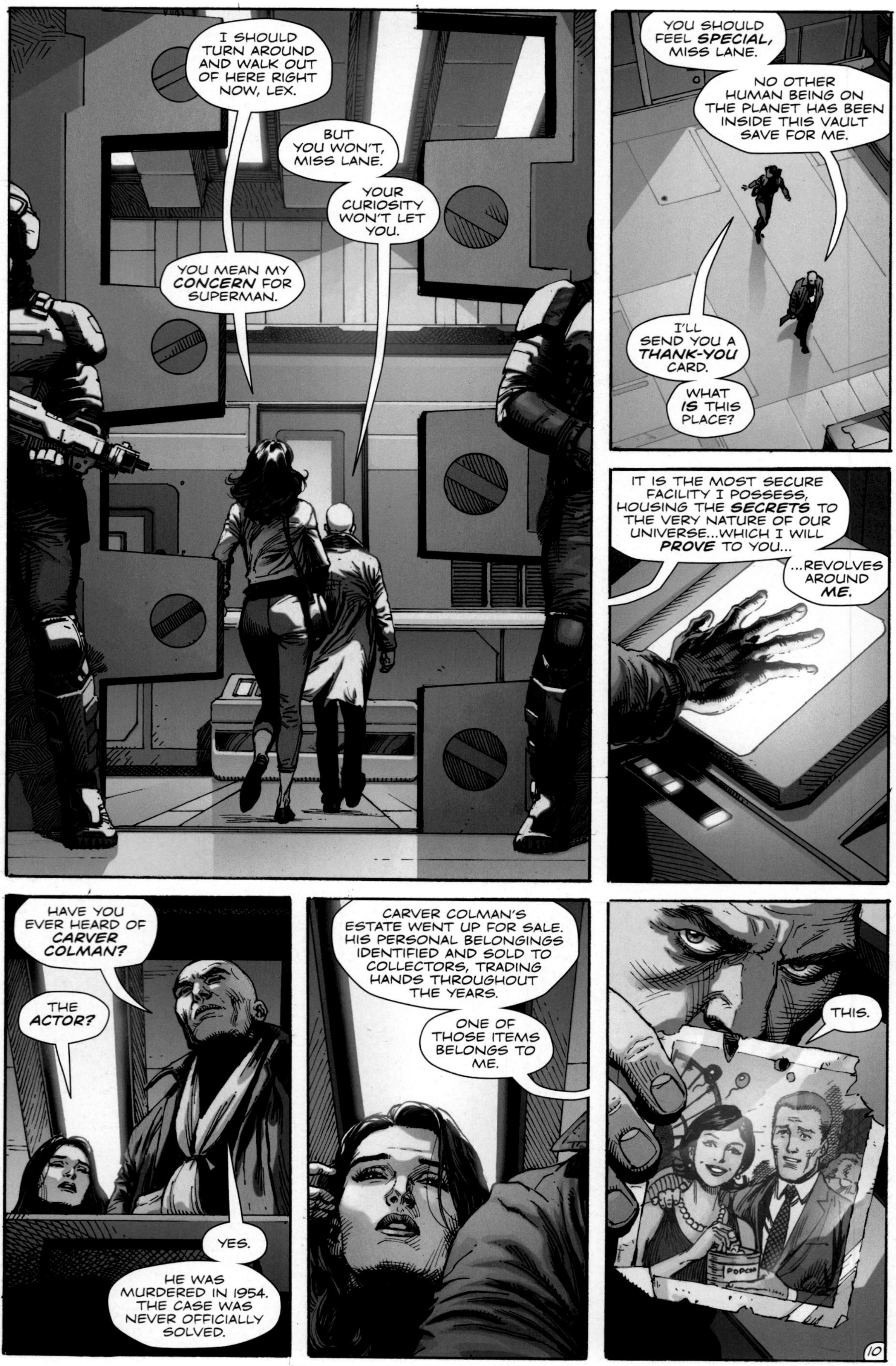
I SHOULD TURN AROUND AND WALK OUT OF HERE RIGHT NOW, LEX.
BUT YOU WON'T, MISS LANE.
YOUR CURIOSITY WON'T LET YOU.
YOU MEAN MY CONCERN FOR SUPERMAN.
YOU SHOULD FEEL SPECIAL, MISS LANE.
NO OTHER HUMAN BEING ON THE PLANET HAS BEEN INSIDE THIS VAULT SAVE FOR ME.
I'LL SEND YOU A THANK-YOU CARD.
WHAT IS THIS PLACE?
IT IS THE MOST SECURE FACILITY I POSSESS, HOUSING THE SECRETS TO THE VERY NATURE OF OUR UNIVERSE...WHICH I WILL PROVE TO YOU...
...REVOLVES AROUND ME.
HAVE YOU EVER HEARD OF CARVER COLMAN?
THE ACTOR?
YES.
HE WAS MURDERED IN 1954. THE CASE WAS NEVER OFFICIALLY SOLVED.
CARVER COLMAN'S ESTATE WENT UP FOR SALE. HIS PERSONAL BELONGINGS IDENTIFIED AND SOLD TO COLLECTORS, TRADING HANDS THROUGHOUT THE YEARS.
ONE OF THOSE ITEMS BELONGS TO ME.
THIS.

ACCORDING TO THE INSCRIPTION ON THE BACK, I BELIEVE THE MAN'S NAME IS *JON* AND THE PICTURE WAS FOUND ON APRIL 18TH, 1938.

WHO ARE THEY?

AND WHAT'S SO SPECIAL ABOUT IT?

I'VE BEEN TRACKING STRANGE ANOMALIES SINCE I WAS A BOY.

I PROVED MANY THINGS OVER THE YEARS: THE EXISTENCE OF *ALIENS*, AS YOU KNOW, THE THREAT OF *NIBIRU*, WHICH ULTIMATELY SAVED THE WORLD FROM DESTRUCTION.

BUT THE *STORY* BEHIND THIS PICTURE HAS ELUDED ME.

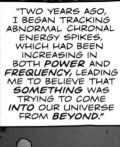
"TWO YEARS AGO, I BEGAN TRACKING ABNORMAL CHRONAL ENERGY SPIKES, WHICH HAD BEEN INCREASING IN BOTH *POWER* AND *FREQUENCY*, LEADING ME TO BELIEVE THAT *SOMETHING* WAS TRYING TO COME *INTO* OUR UNIVERSE FROM *BEYOND*."

EVERY SECOND WAS A GIFT.

"I HEARD A *WARNING*, ABOUT SOMEONE WHO HAD *ALTERED REALITY*."

HOW COULD I *EVER* FORGET YOU?

"BUT THE *FLASHES* WERE NOT THE SOURCE OF THE ANOMALY I WAS TRACKING.

"LYING THERE, IN THE GRASS...

"...WAS A PHOTOGRAPH."

THIS PICTURE IS CONNECTED TO THE *REBIRTH* OF KID FLASH?

IN A WAY, IT IS.

I FOUND *"CHRONAL DEBRIS"* IN THE AREA, INCLUDING THE *FILM* I SENT YOU, ALONG WITH OTHER *PERSONAL ITEMS* CONNECTED TO *WALLY WEST*.

EVIDENCE THAT OUR *REALITY* HAD BEEN *ALTERED*.

BUT IT WAS *THIS PHOTOGRAPH* THAT WAS THE *TRUE ANOMALY*.

OH MY GOD.

11

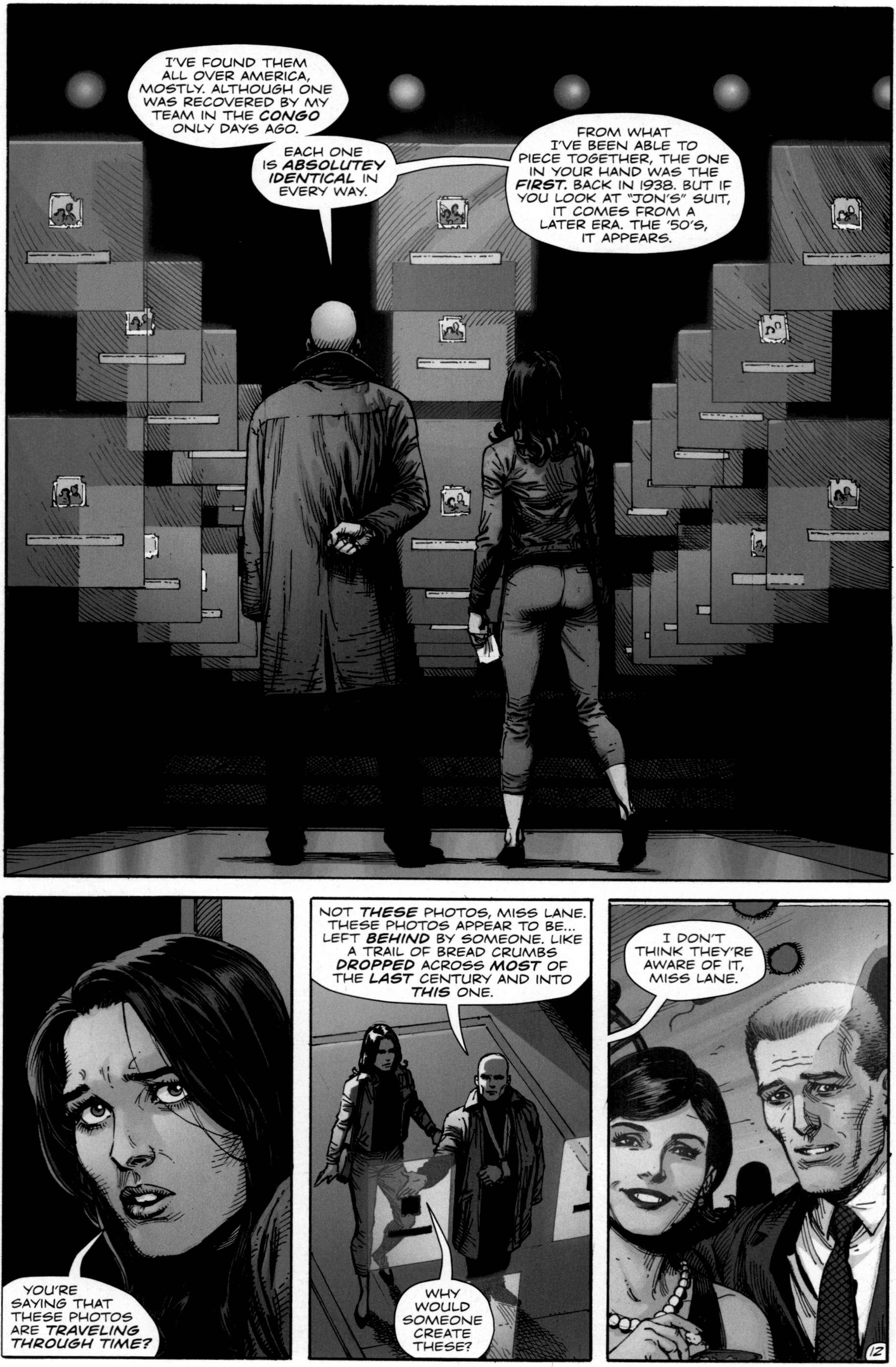
I'VE FOUND THEM ALL OVER AMERICA, MOSTLY. ALTHOUGH ONE WAS RECOVERED BY MY TEAM IN THE CONGO ONLY DAYS AGO.
EACH ONE IS ABSOLUTEY IDENTICAL IN EVERY WAY.
FROM WHAT I'VE BEEN ABLE TO PIECE TOGETHER, THE ONE IN YOUR HAND WAS THE FIRST. BACK IN 1938. BUT IF YOU LOOK AT "JON'S" SUIT, IT COMES FROM A LATER ERA. THE '50'S, IT APPEARS.
YOU'RE SAYING THAT THESE PHOTOS ARE TRAVELING THROUGH TIME?
NOT THESE PHOTOS, MISS LANE. THESE PHOTOS APPEAR TO BE... LEFT BEHIND BY SOMEONE. LIKE A TRAIL OF BREAD CRUMBS DROPPED ACROSS MOST OF THE LAST CENTURY AND INTO THIS ONE.
WHY WOULD SOMEONE CREATE THESE?
I DON'T THINK THEY'RE AWARE OF IT, MISS LANE.
12

"BUT **WHOEVER** THEY ARE, THEY'RE MORE **POWERFUL** THAN ANY OTHER BEING I'VE ENCOUNTERED."

AS THE END APPROACHES, THINGS COME INTO FOCUS.

IT'S MARCH 30TH, 1981 ON THIS WORLD. A DRIFTER NAMED JOHN HINCKLEY JR. ATTEMPTS TO ASSASSINATE RONALD REAGAN.

THE PRESIDENT'S BLOOD SPILLS ONTO THE SIDEWALK AS HIS LUNG COLLAPSES.

FOUR HOURS AND SEVENTEEN MINUTES FROM NOW, THIS STREET WILL BE RUBBLE.

AND I WILL SPEAK WITH SUPERMAN FOR THE FIRST TIME.

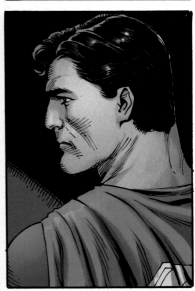

HANDS IN THE AIR!

BY ORDER OF THE PRESIDENT OF THE UNITED STATES, I'M ASKING YOU TO COME QUIETLY.

I DON'T WANT ANY TROUBLE.

LOWER YOUR WEAPONS.

PLEASE.

"SUPERMAN WILL STOP YOU."

13

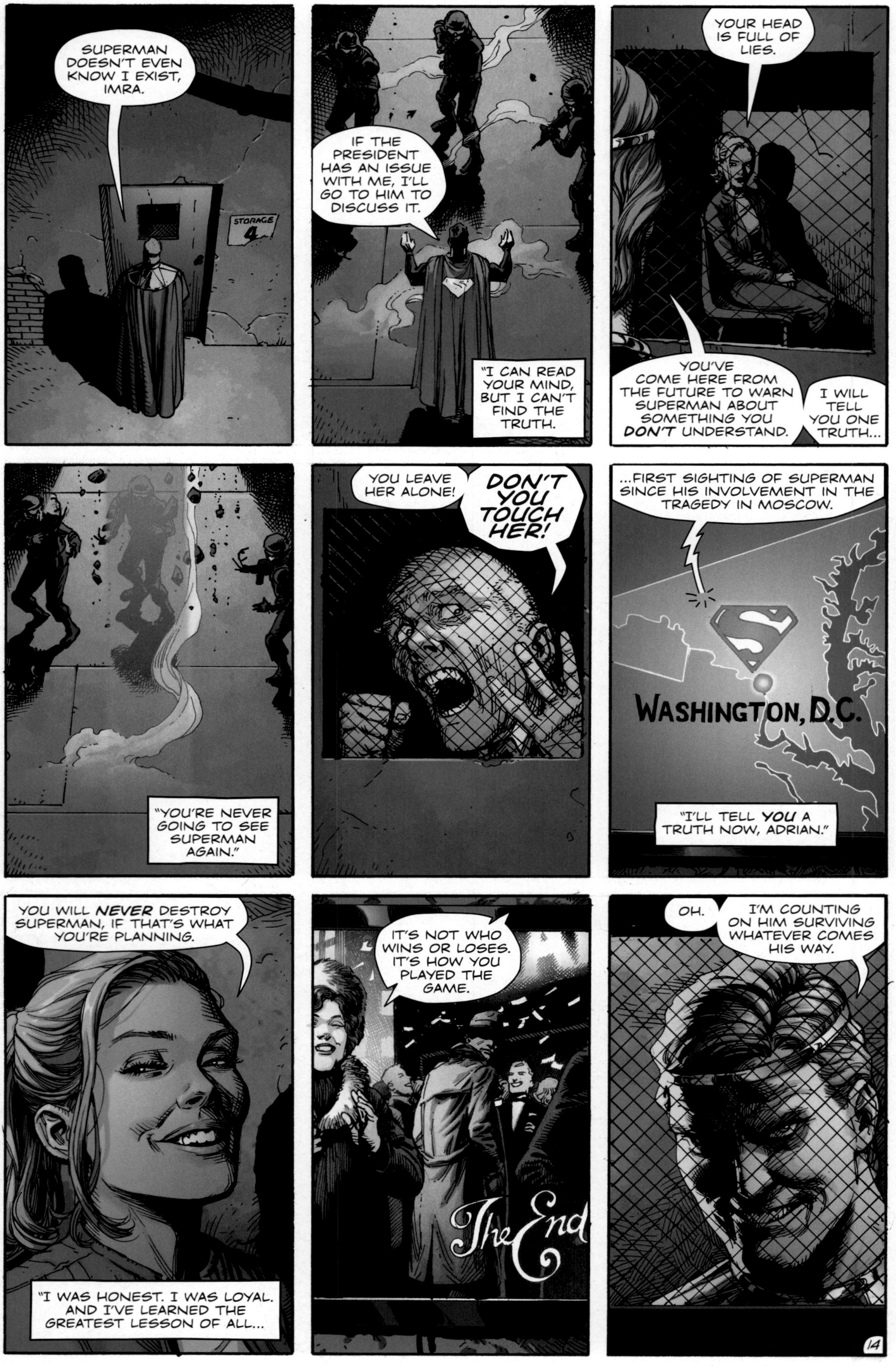
SUPERMAN DOESN'T EVEN KNOW I EXIST, IMRA.
STORAGE 4
IF THE PRESIDENT HAS AN ISSUE WITH ME, I'LL GO TO HIM TO DISCUSS IT.
"I CAN READ YOUR MIND, BUT I CAN'T FIND THE TRUTH.
YOUR HEAD IS FULL OF LIES.
YOU'VE COME HERE FROM THE FUTURE TO WARN SUPERMAN ABOUT SOMETHING YOU **DON'T** UNDERSTAND.
I WILL TELL YOU ONE TRUTH...
"YOU'RE NEVER GOING TO SEE SUPERMAN AGAIN."
YOU LEAVE HER ALONE!
DON'T YOU TOUCH HER!
...FIRST SIGHTING OF SUPERMAN SINCE HIS INVOLVEMENT IN THE TRAGEDY IN MOSCOW.
WASHINGTON, D.C.
"I'LL TELL **YOU** A TRUTH NOW, ADRIAN."
YOU WILL **NEVER** DESTROY SUPERMAN, IF THAT'S WHAT YOU'RE PLANNING.
"I WAS HONEST. I WAS LOYAL. AND I'VE LEARNED THE GREATEST LESSON OF ALL...
IT'S NOT WHO WINS OR LOSES. IT'S HOW YOU PLAYED THE GAME.
The End
OH.
I'M COUNTING ON HIM SURVIVING WHATEVER COMES HIS WAY.

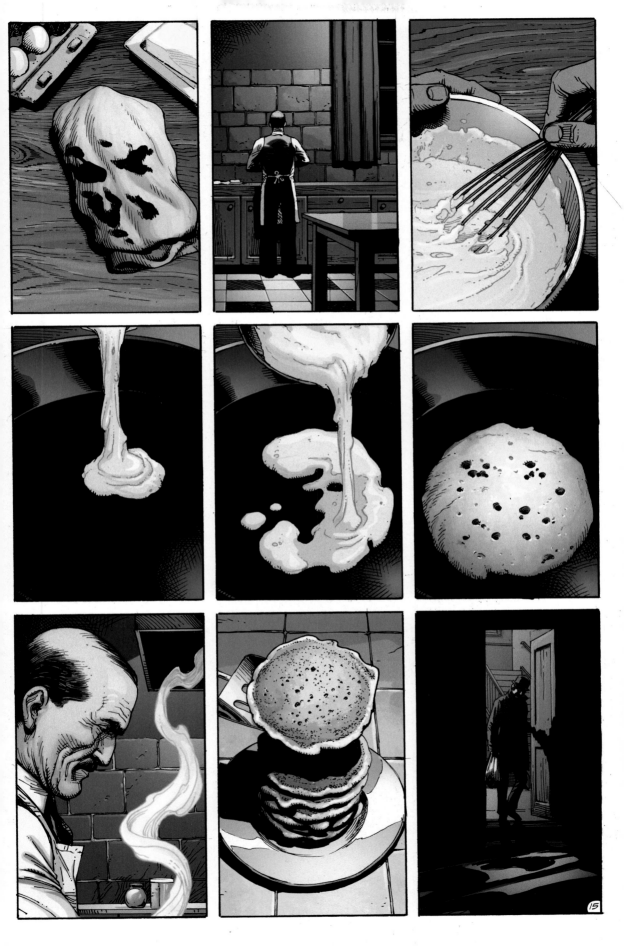

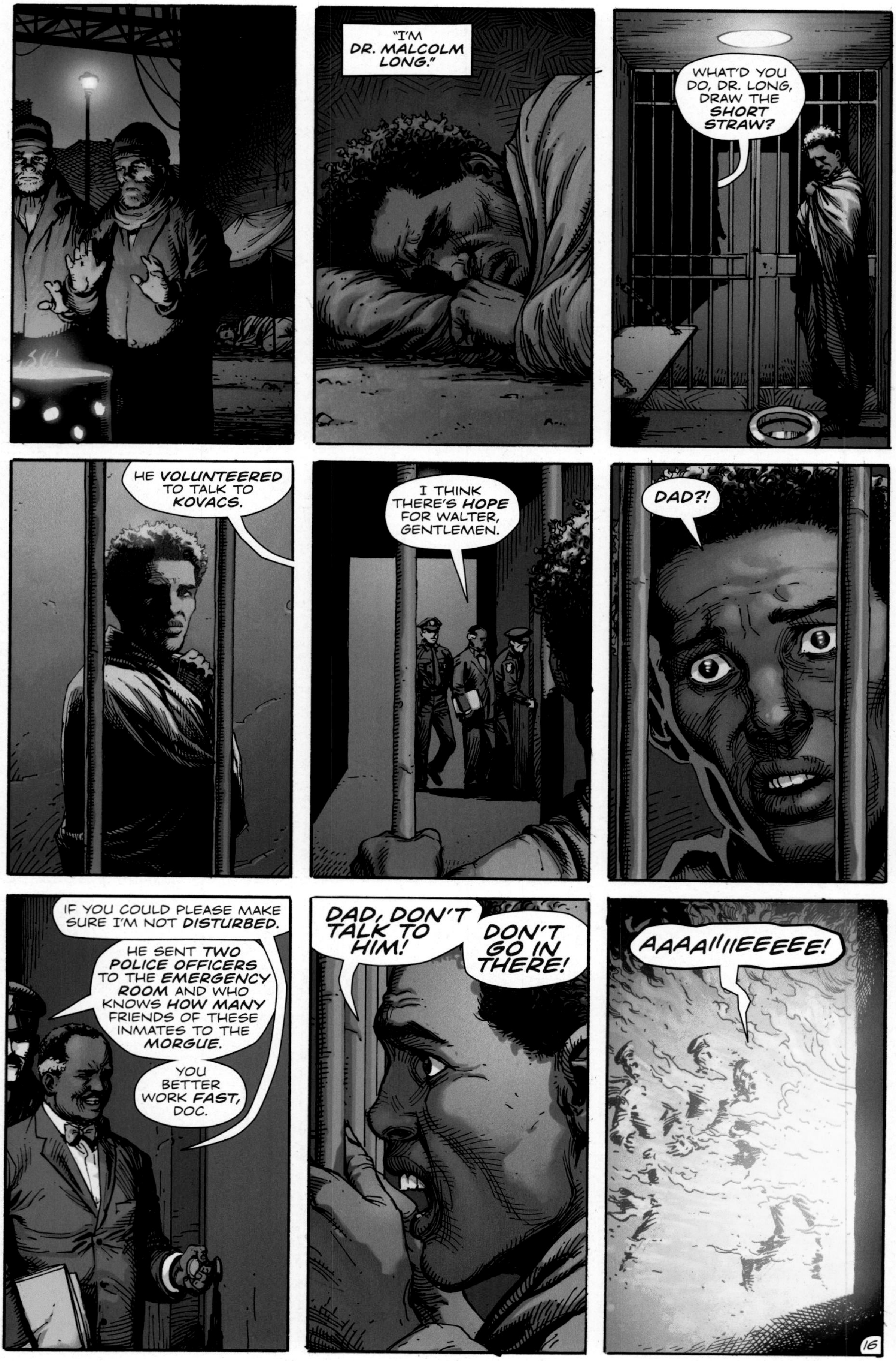
"I'M DR. MALCOLM LONG."
WHAT'D YOU DO, DR. LONG, DRAW THE SHORT STRAW?
HE VOLUNTEERED TO TALK TO KOVACS.
I THINK THERE'S HOPE FOR WALTER, GENTLEMEN.
DAD?!
IF YOU COULD PLEASE MAKE SURE I'M NOT DISTURBED.
HE SENT TWO POLICE OFFICERS TO THE EMERGENCY ROOM AND WHO KNOWS HOW MANY FRIENDS OF THESE INMATES TO THE MORGUE.
YOU BETTER WORK FAST, DOC.
DAD, DON'T TALK TO HIM!
DON'T GO IN THERE!
AAAAIIIIEEEEEE!
16

DAD!

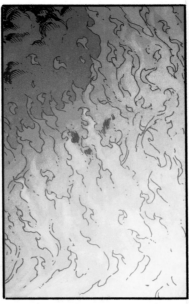

REGGIE?

RORSCHACH?

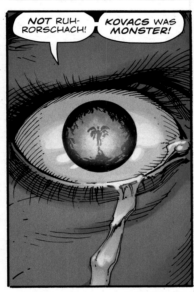

NOT RUH-RORSCHACH! KOVACS WAS MONSTER!

SEE WHAT YOU WANT TO SEE.

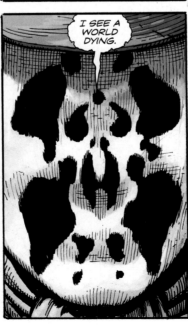

I SEE A WORLD DYING.

‹KK›

LUH-LET G-GO.

17

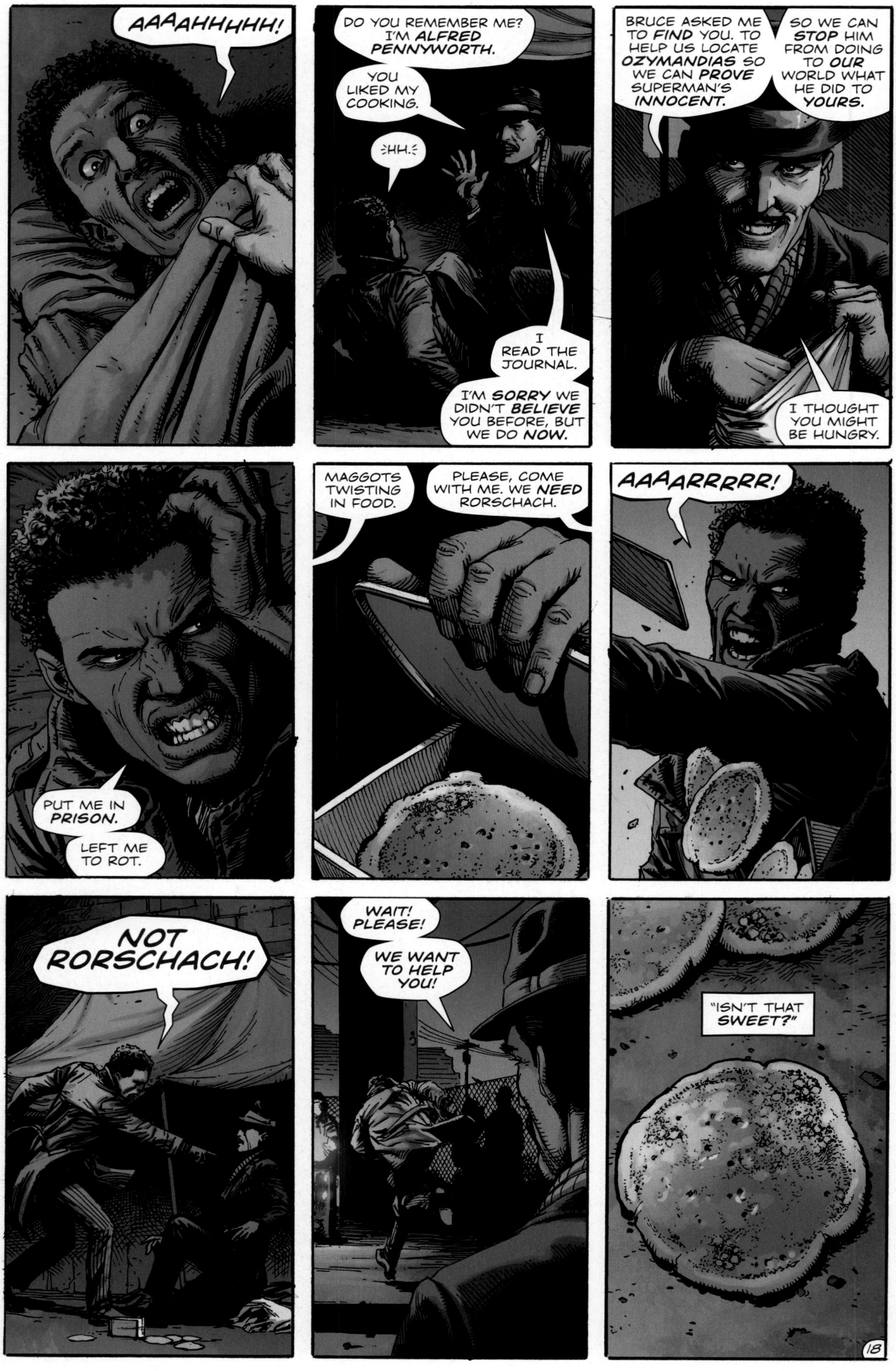
AAAAHHHHH!
DO YOU REMEMBER ME? I'M ALFRED PENNYWORTH.
YOU LIKED MY COOKING.
HH.
I READ THE JOURNAL.
I'M SORRY WE DIDN'T BELIEVE YOU BEFORE, BUT WE DO NOW.
BRUCE ASKED ME TO FIND YOU. TO HELP US LOCATE OZYMANDIAS SO WE CAN PROVE SUPERMAN'S INNOCENT.
SO WE CAN STOP HIM FROM DOING TO OUR WORLD WHAT HE DID TO YOURS.
I THOUGHT YOU MIGHT BE HUNGRY.
PUT ME IN PRISON.
LEFT ME TO ROT.
MAGGOTS TWISTING IN FOOD.
PLEASE, COME WITH ME. WE NEED RORSCHACH.
AAAARRRRR!
NOT RORSCHACH!
WAIT! PLEASE!
WE WANT TO HELP YOU!
"ISN'T THAT SWEET?"
18

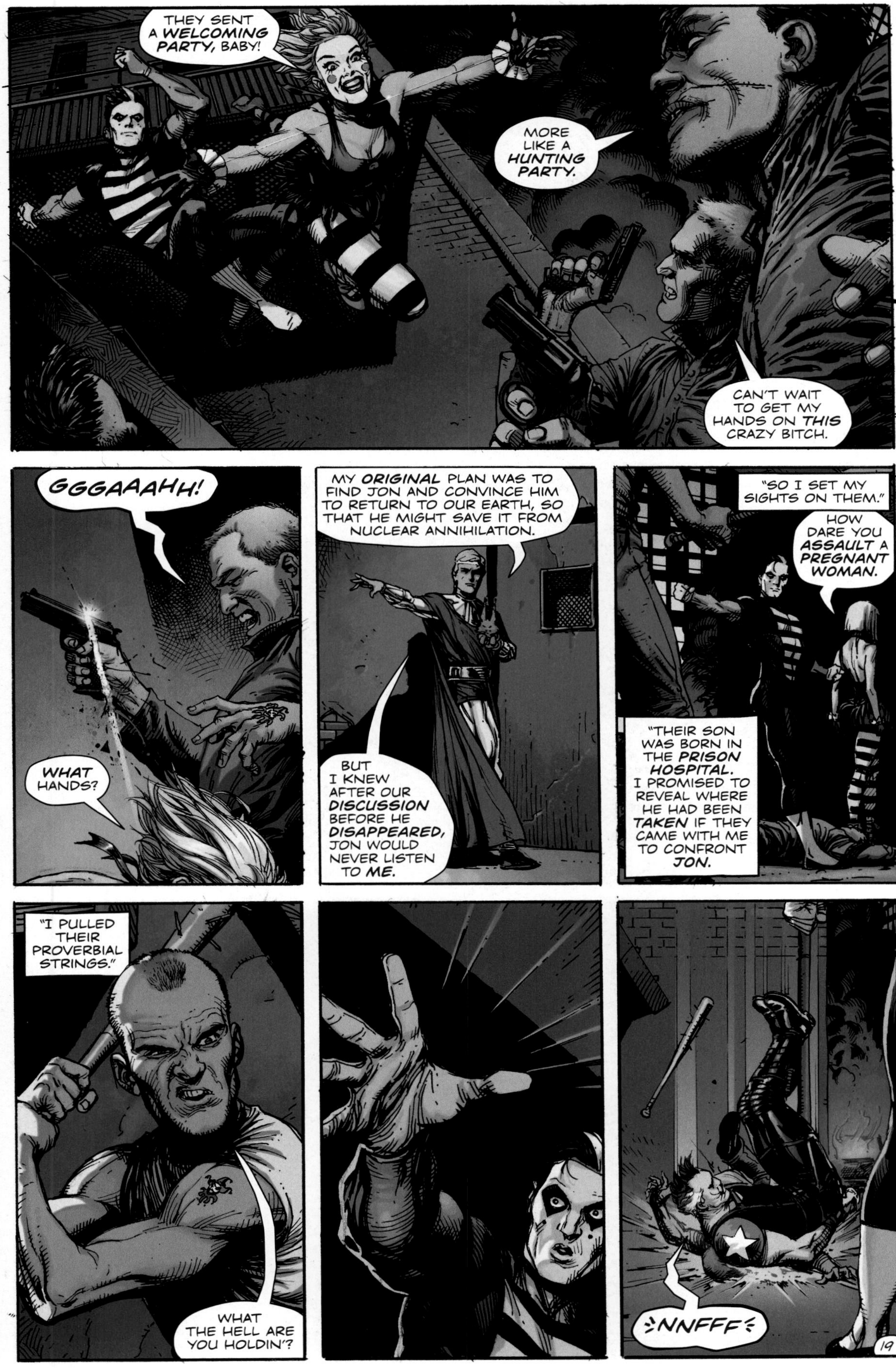

THEY SENT A **WELCOMING PARTY,** BABY!
MORE LIKE A **HUNTING PARTY.**
CAN'T WAIT TO GET MY HANDS ON **THIS** CRAZY BITCH.
GGGAAAHH!
WHAT HANDS?
MY **ORIGINAL** PLAN WAS TO FIND JON AND CONVINCE HIM TO RETURN TO OUR EARTH, SO THAT HE MIGHT SAVE IT FROM NUCLEAR ANNIHILATION.
BUT I KNEW AFTER OUR **DISCUSSION** BEFORE HE **DISAPPEARED,** JON WOULD NEVER LISTEN TO **ME.**
"SO I SET MY SIGHTS ON THEM."
HOW DARE YOU **ASSAULT** A **PREGNANT WOMAN.**
"THEIR SON WAS BORN IN THE **PRISON HOSPITAL.** I PROMISED TO REVEAL WHERE HE HAD BEEN **TAKEN** IF THEY CAME WITH ME TO CONFRONT **JON.**
"I PULLED THEIR PROVERBIAL STRINGS."
WHAT THE HELL ARE YOU HOLDIN'?
NNFFF

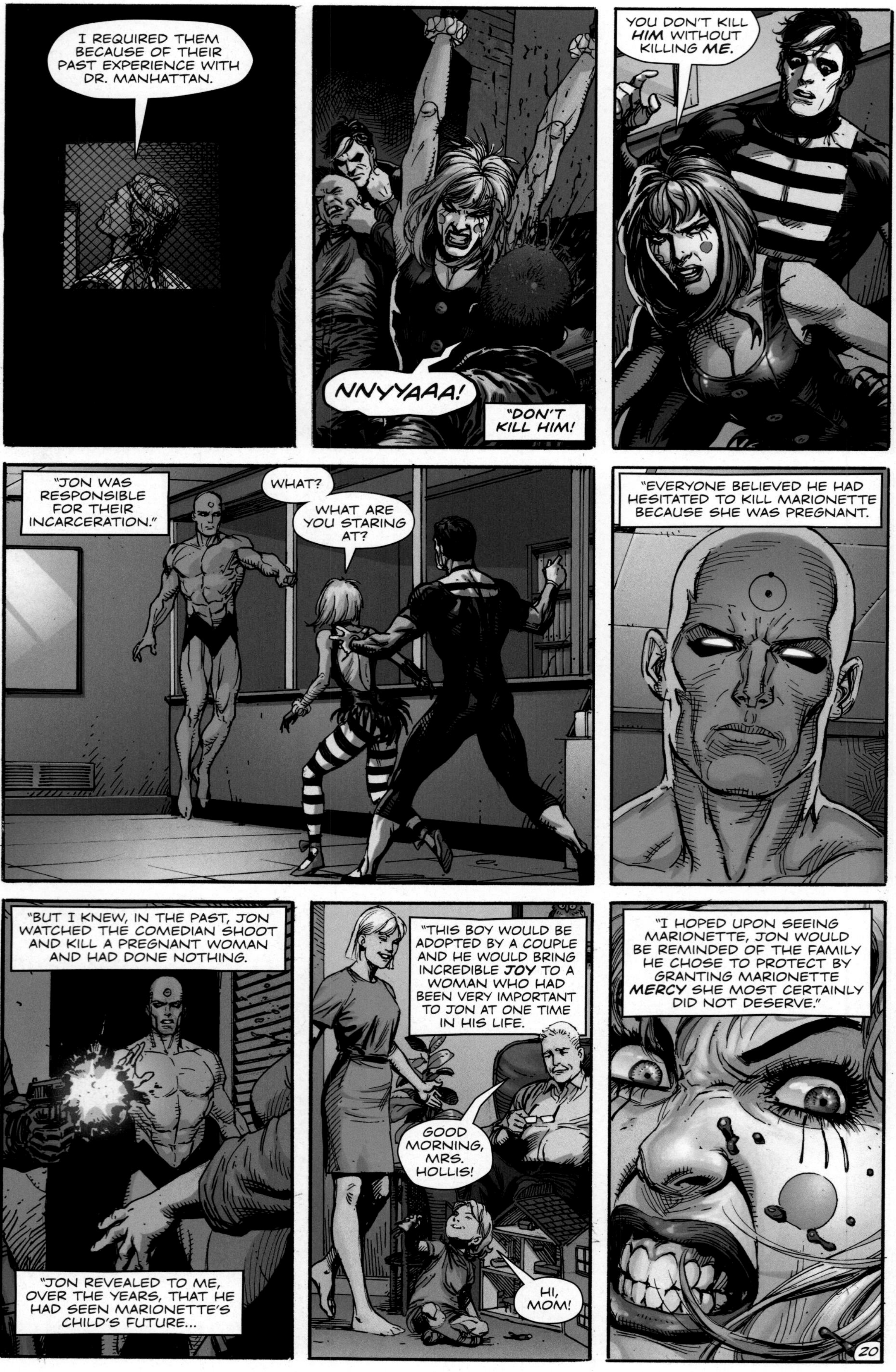

I REQUIRED THEM BECAUSE OF THEIR PAST EXPERIENCE WITH DR. MANHATTAN.
NNYYAAA!
"DON'T KILL HIM!
YOU DON'T KILL HIM WITHOUT KILLING ME.
"JON WAS RESPONSIBLE FOR THEIR INCARCERATION."
WHAT?
WHAT ARE YOU STARING AT?
"EVERYONE BELIEVED HE HAD HESITATED TO KILL MARIONETTE BECAUSE SHE WAS PREGNANT.
"BUT I KNEW, IN THE PAST, JON WATCHED THE COMEDIAN SHOOT AND KILL A PREGNANT WOMAN AND HAD DONE NOTHING.
"JON REVEALED TO ME, OVER THE YEARS, THAT HE HAD SEEN MARIONETTE'S CHILD'S FUTURE...
"THIS BOY WOULD BE ADOPTED BY A COUPLE AND HE WOULD BRING INCREDIBLE JOY TO A WOMAN WHO HAD BEEN VERY IMPORTANT TO JON AT ONE TIME IN HIS LIFE.
GOOD MORNING, MRS. HOLLIS!
HI, MOM!
"I HOPED UPON SEEING MARIONETTE, JON WOULD BE REMINDED OF THE FAMILY HE CHOSE TO PROTECT BY GRANTING MARIONETTE MERCY SHE MOST CERTAINLY DID NOT DESERVE."

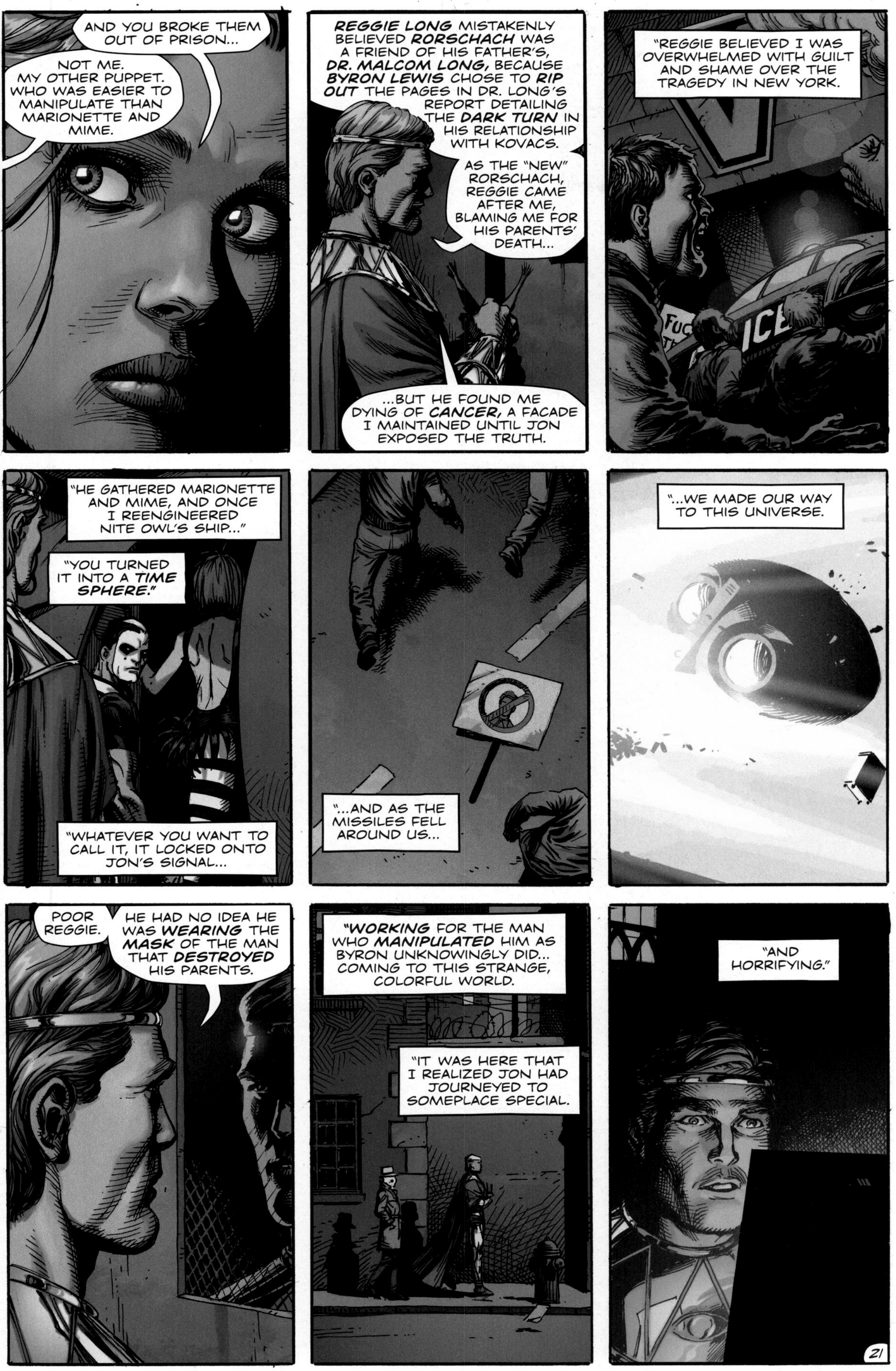
AND YOU BROKE THEM OUT OF PRISON...
NOT ME. MY OTHER PUPPET. WHO WAS EASIER TO MANIPULATE THAN MARIONETTE AND MIME.
REGGIE LONG MISTAKENLY BELIEVED RORSCHACH WAS A FRIEND OF HIS FATHER'S, DR. MALCOM LONG, BECAUSE BYRON LEWIS CHOSE TO RIP OUT THE PAGES IN DR. LONG'S REPORT DETAILING THE DARK TURN IN HIS RELATIONSHIP WITH KOVACS.
AS THE "NEW" RORSCHACH, REGGIE CAME AFTER ME, BLAMING ME FOR HIS PARENTS' DEATH...
...BUT HE FOUND ME DYING OF CANCER, A FACADE I MAINTAINED UNTIL JON EXPOSED THE TRUTH.
"REGGIE BELIEVED I WAS OVERWHELMED WITH GUILT AND SHAME OVER THE TRAGEDY IN NEW YORK.
"HE GATHERED MARIONETTE AND MIME, AND ONCE I REENGINEERED NITE OWL'S SHIP..."
"YOU TURNED IT INTO A TIME SPHERE."
"WHATEVER YOU WANT TO CALL IT, IT LOCKED ONTO JON'S SIGNAL...
"...AND AS THE MISSILES FELL AROUND US...
"...WE MADE OUR WAY TO THIS UNIVERSE.
POOR REGGIE.
HE HAD NO IDEA HE WAS WEARING THE MASK OF THE MAN THAT DESTROYED HIS PARENTS.
"WORKING FOR THE MAN WHO MANIPULATED HIM AS BYRON UNKNOWINGLY DID... COMING TO THIS STRANGE, COLORFUL WORLD.
"IT WAS HERE THAT I REALIZED JON HAD JOURNEYED TO SOMEPLACE SPECIAL.
"AND HORRIFYING."

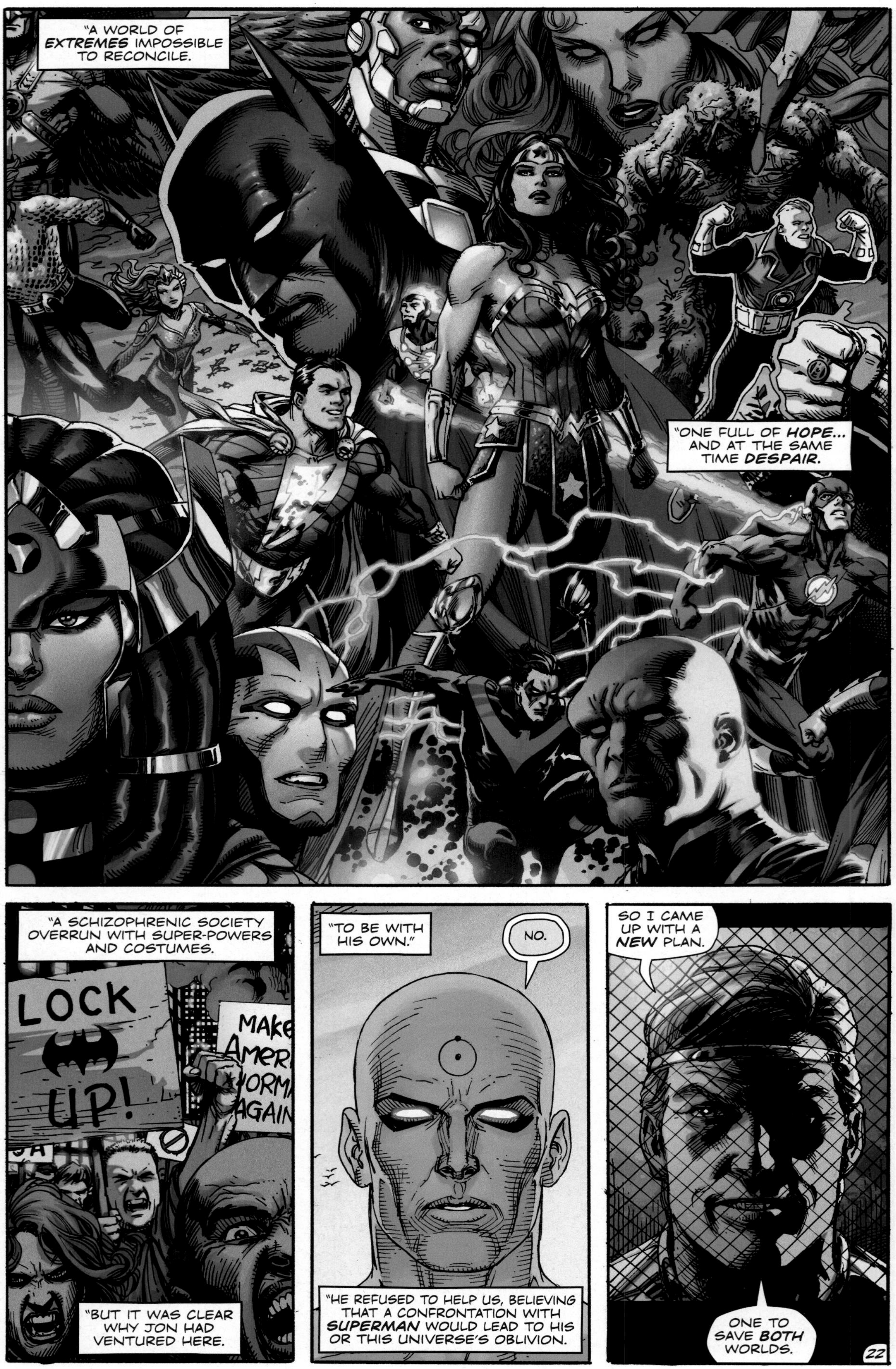
"A WORLD OF EXTREMES IMPOSSIBLE TO RECONCILE.
"ONE FULL OF HOPE... AND AT THE SAME TIME DESPAIR.
"A SCHIZOPHRENIC SOCIETY OVERRUN WITH SUPER-POWERS AND COSTUMES.
LOCK UP!
"BUT IT WAS CLEAR WHY JON HAD VENTURED HERE.
"TO BE WITH HIS OWN."
NO.
"HE REFUSED TO HELP US, BELIEVING THAT A CONFRONTATION WITH SUPERMAN WOULD LEAD TO HIS OR THIS UNIVERSE'S OBLIVION.
SO I CAME UP WITH A NEW PLAN.
ONE TO SAVE BOTH WORLDS.
22

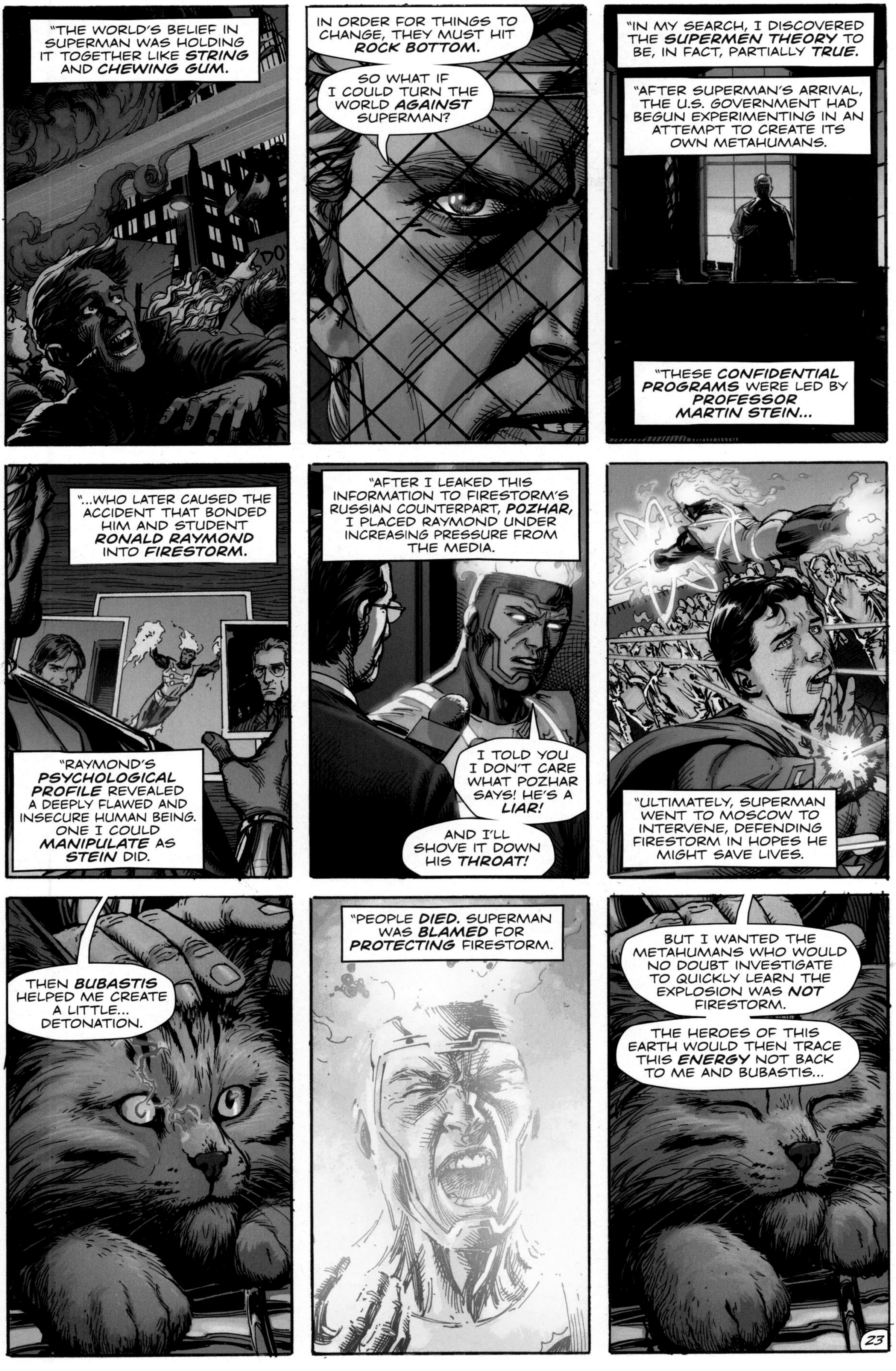
"THE WORLD'S BELIEF IN SUPERMAN WAS HOLDING IT TOGETHER LIKE STRING AND CHEWING GUM.
IN ORDER FOR THINGS TO CHANGE, THEY MUST HIT ROCK BOTTOM.
SO WHAT IF I COULD TURN THE WORLD AGAINST SUPERMAN?
"IN MY SEARCH, I DISCOVERED THE SUPERMEN THEORY TO BE, IN FACT, PARTIALLY TRUE.
"AFTER SUPERMAN'S ARRIVAL, THE U.S. GOVERNMENT HAD BEGUN EXPERIMENTING IN AN ATTEMPT TO CREATE ITS OWN METAHUMANS.
"THESE CONFIDENTIAL PROGRAMS WERE LED BY PROFESSOR MARTIN STEIN...
"...WHO LATER CAUSED THE ACCIDENT THAT BONDED HIM AND STUDENT RONALD RAYMOND INTO FIRESTORM.
"RAYMOND'S PSYCHOLOGICAL PROFILE REVEALED A DEEPLY FLAWED AND INSECURE HUMAN BEING. ONE I COULD MANIPULATE AS STEIN DID.
"AFTER I LEAKED THIS INFORMATION TO FIRESTORM'S RUSSIAN COUNTERPART, POZHAR, I PLACED RAYMOND UNDER INCREASING PRESSURE FROM THE MEDIA.
I TOLD YOU I DON'T CARE WHAT POZHAR SAYS! HE'S A LIAR!
AND I'LL SHOVE IT DOWN HIS THROAT!
"ULTIMATELY, SUPERMAN WENT TO MOSCOW TO INTERVENE, DEFENDING FIRESTORM IN HOPES HE MIGHT SAVE LIVES.
THEN BUBASTIS HELPED ME CREATE A LITTLE... DETONATION.
"PEOPLE DIED. SUPERMAN WAS BLAMED FOR PROTECTING FIRESTORM.
BUT I WANTED THE METAHUMANS WHO WOULD NO DOUBT INVESTIGATE TO QUICKLY LEARN THE EXPLOSION WAS NOT FIRESTORM.
THE HEROES OF THIS EARTH WOULD THEN TRACE THIS ENERGY NOT BACK TO ME AND BUBASTIS...

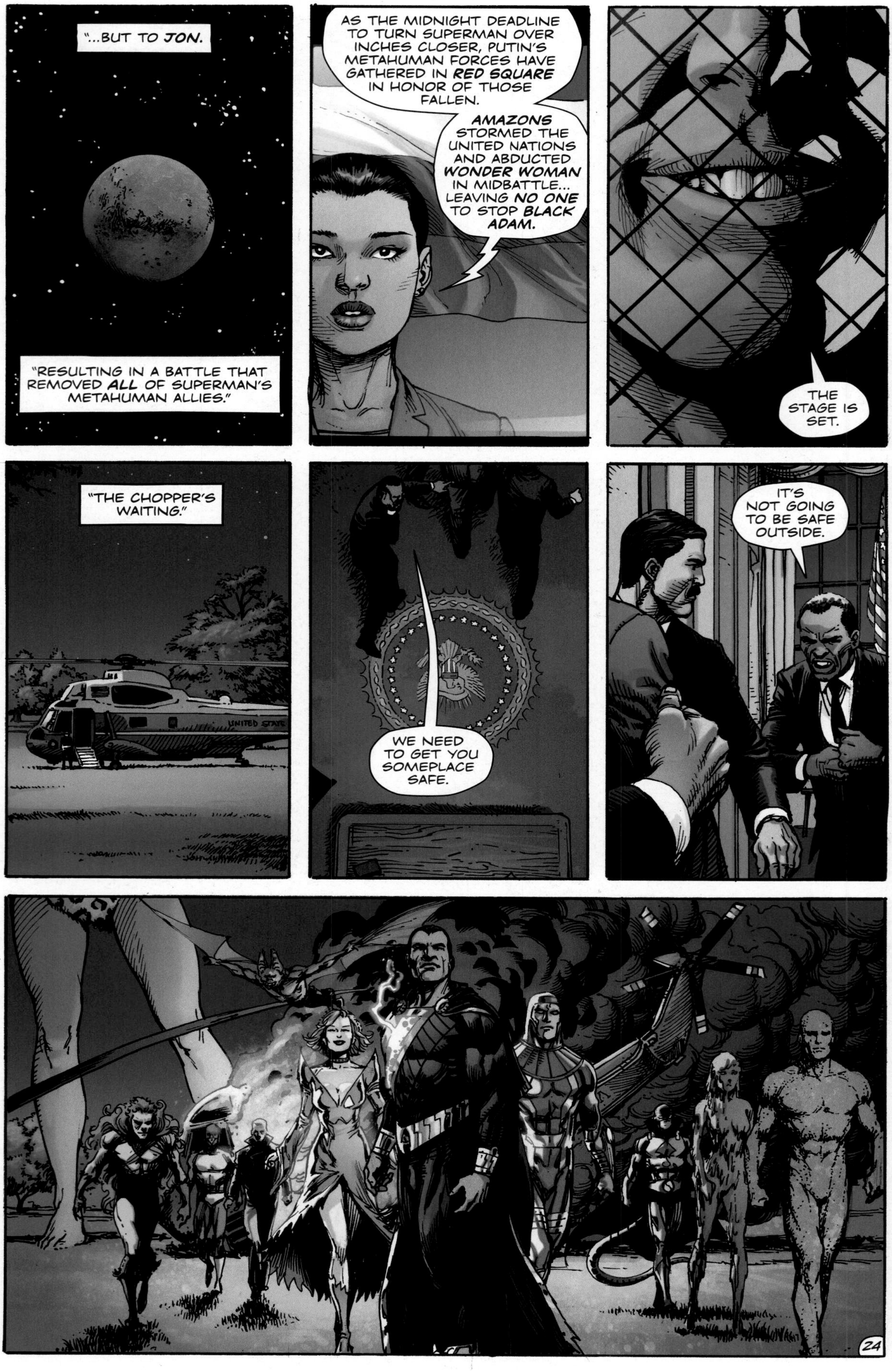
"...BUT TO JON.
"RESULTING IN A BATTLE THAT REMOVED ALL OF SUPERMAN'S METAHUMAN ALLIES."
AS THE MIDNIGHT DEADLINE TO TURN SUPERMAN OVER INCHES CLOSER, PUTIN'S METAHUMAN FORCES HAVE GATHERED IN RED SQUARE IN HONOR OF THOSE FALLEN.
AMAZONS STORMED THE UNITED NATIONS AND ABDUCTED WONDER WOMAN IN MIDBATTLE... LEAVING NO ONE TO STOP BLACK ADAM.
THE STAGE IS SET.
"THE CHOPPER'S WAITING."
UNITED STATE
WE NEED TO GET YOU SOMEPLACE SAFE.
IT'S NOT GOING TO BE SAFE OUTSIDE.

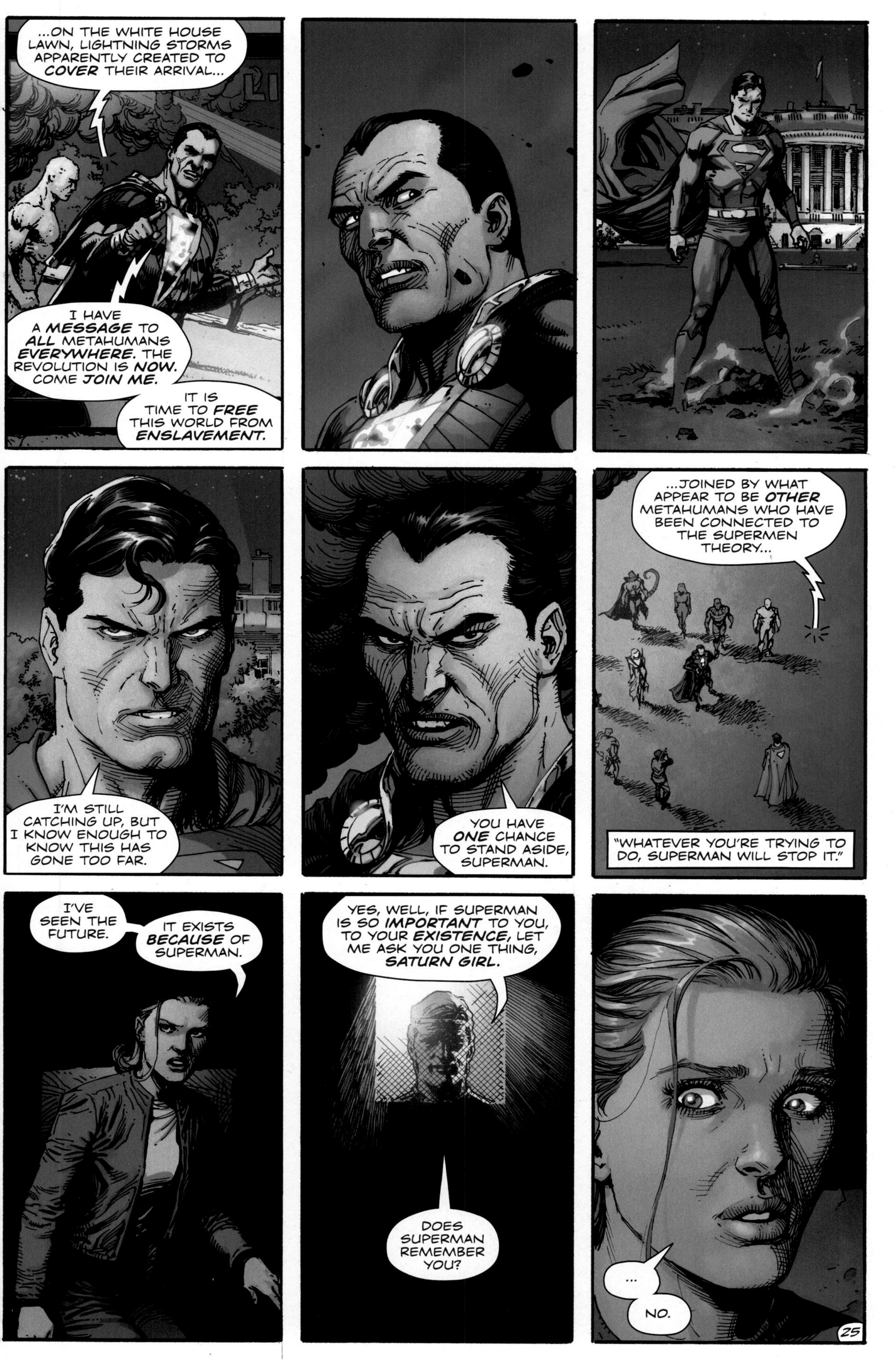
...ON THE WHITE HOUSE LAWN, LIGHTNING STORMS APPARENTLY CREATED TO COVER THEIR ARRIVAL...
I HAVE A MESSAGE TO ALL METAHUMANS EVERYWHERE. THE REVOLUTION IS NOW. COME JOIN ME.
IT IS TIME TO FREE THIS WORLD FROM ENSLAVEMENT.
I'M STILL CATCHING UP, BUT I KNOW ENOUGH TO KNOW THIS HAS GONE TOO FAR.
YOU HAVE ONE CHANCE TO STAND ASIDE, SUPERMAN.
...JOINED BY WHAT APPEAR TO BE OTHER METAHUMANS WHO HAVE BEEN CONNECTED TO THE SUPERMEN THEORY...
"WHATEVER YOU'RE TRYING TO DO, SUPERMAN WILL STOP IT."
I'VE SEEN THE FUTURE.
IT EXISTS BECAUSE OF SUPERMAN.
YES, WELL, IF SUPERMAN IS SO IMPORTANT TO YOU, TO YOUR EXISTENCE, LET ME ASK YOU ONE THING, SATURN GIRL.
DOES SUPERMAN REMEMBER YOU?
...
NO.

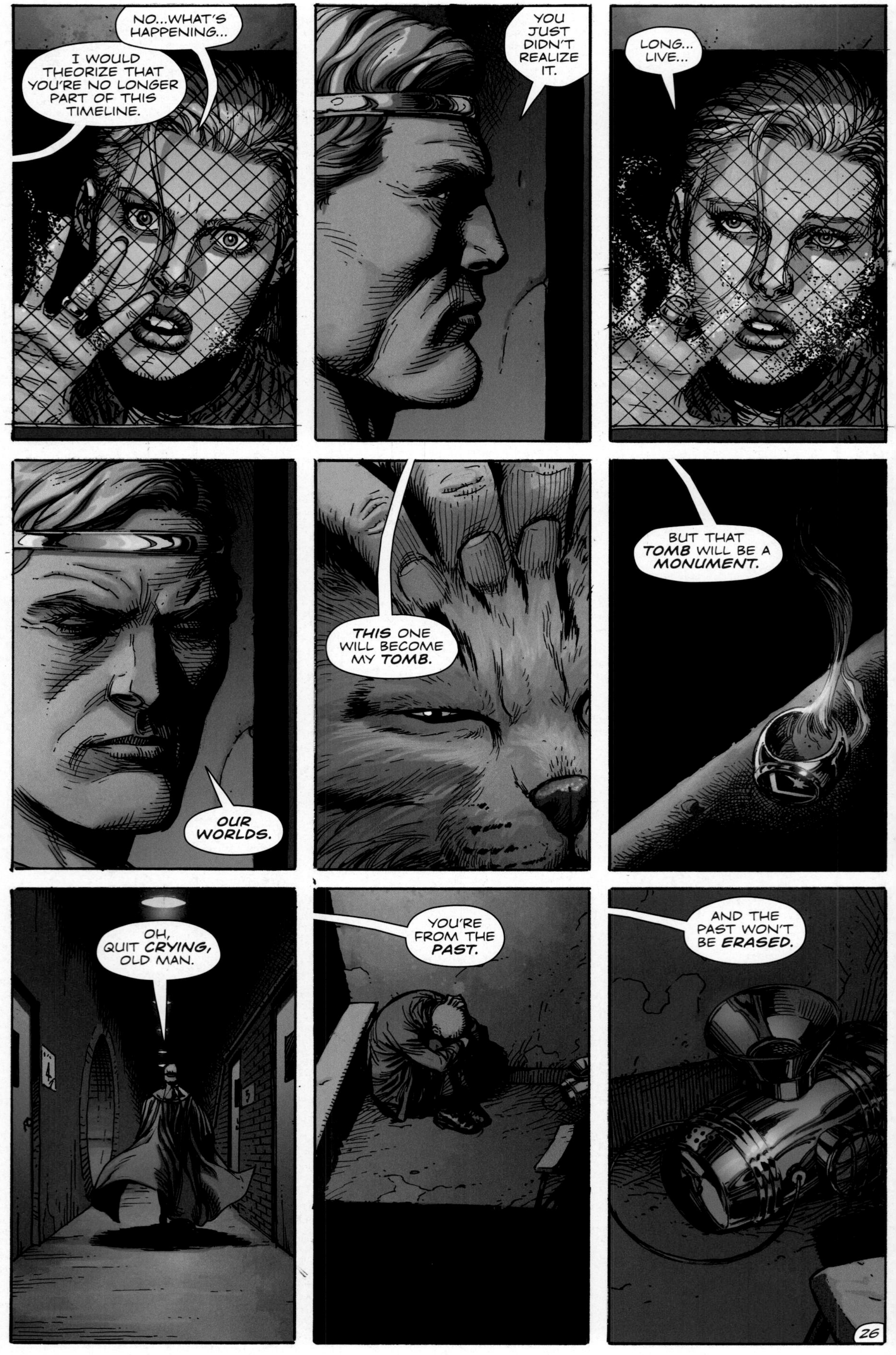
I WOULD THEORIZE THAT YOU'RE NO LONGER PART OF THIS TIMELINE.
NO...WHAT'S HAPPENING...
YOU JUST DIDN'T REALIZE IT.
LONG... LIVE...
OUR WORLDS.
THIS ONE WILL BECOME MY TOMB.
BUT THAT TOMB WILL BE A MONUMENT.
OH, QUIT CRYING, OLD MAN.
4
5
YOU'RE FROM THE PAST.
AND THE PAST WON'T BE ERASED.

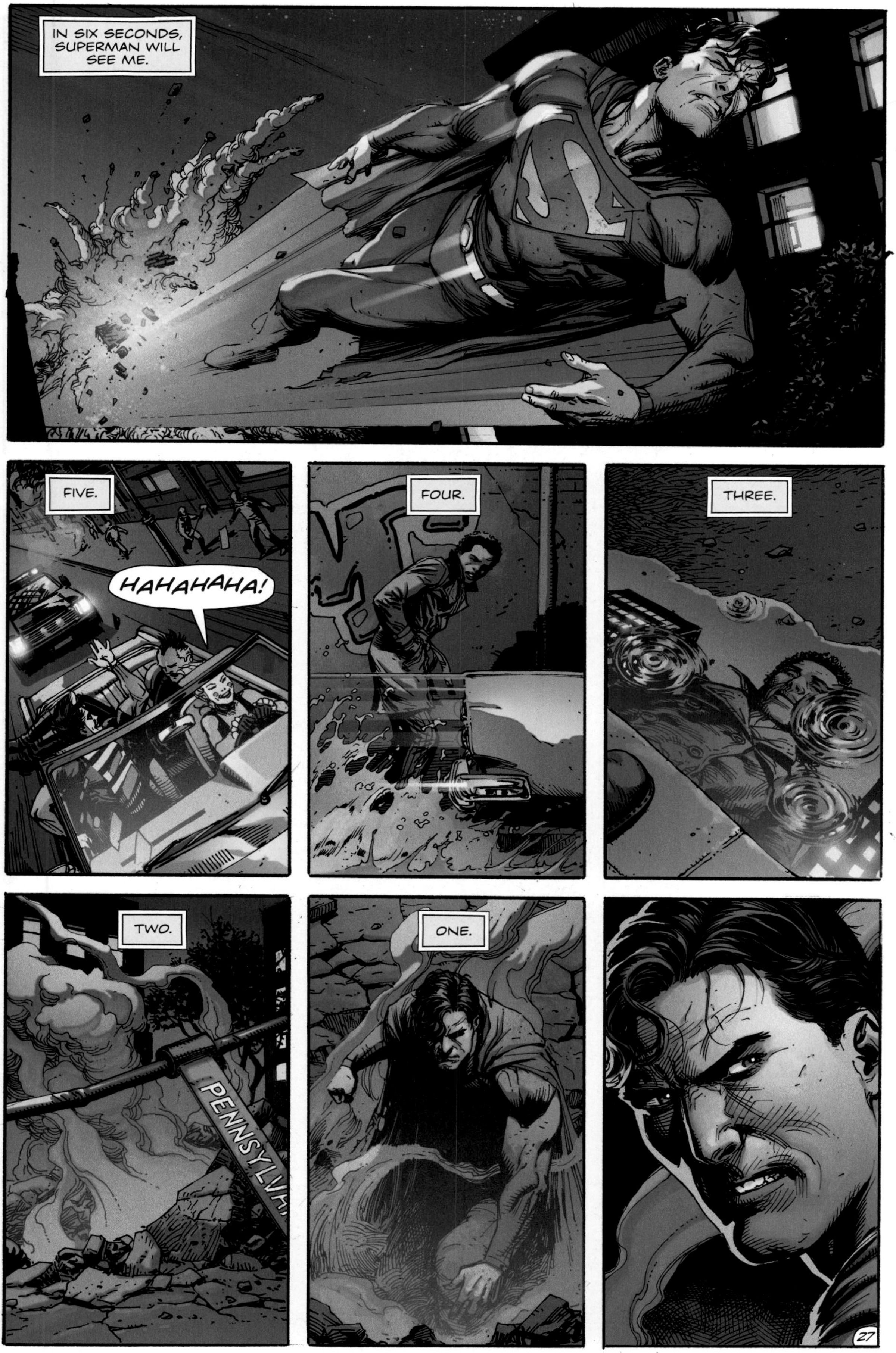
IN SIX SECONDS, SUPERMAN WILL SEE ME.
FIVE.
HAHAHAHA!
FOUR.
THREE.
TWO.
PENNSYLVA
ONE.
27

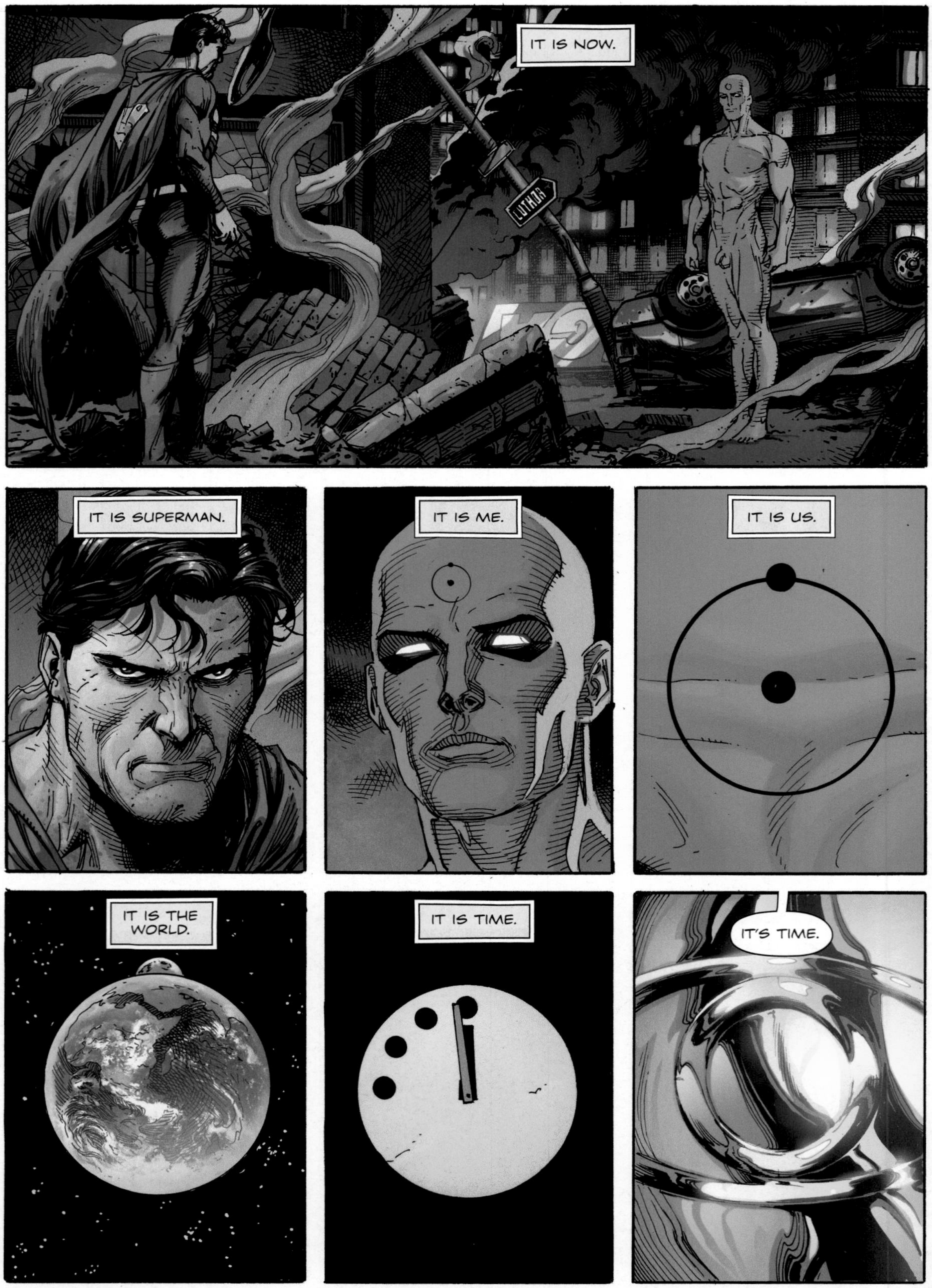
IT IS NOW.
LUTHOR
IT IS SUPERMAN.
IT IS ME.
IT IS US.
IT IS THE WORLD.
IT IS TIME.
IT'S TIME.

I am not afraid to make a mistake, even a great mistake, a lifelong mistake and perhaps as long as eternity too.

—James Joyce
A Portrait of the Artist as a Young Man

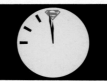

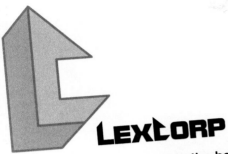

LEXCORP

ITEM #1 Originally found in the home of Carver Colman, believed to have been in his possession since April 18th, 1938. The man in the photo is known simply as "Jon."

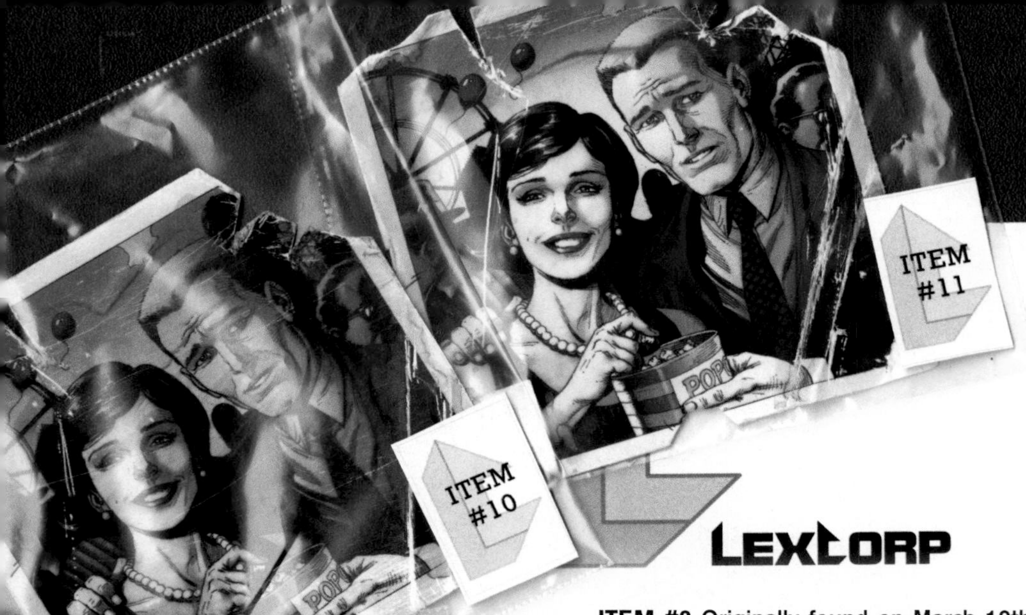
ITEM #11
ITEM #10

LEXCORP

ITEM #2 Originally found on March 19th, 1952, at the RKO Pantages Theater in Hollywood, California. The photograph was found in Carver Colman's dressing room following the 25th Academy Awards. Believing it to be a collector's item, a custodian sold it to a Hollywood collectibles shop where it remained until it was located by Lexcorp.

ITEM #3 Originally found in a train wreck in July of 1940 outside of Gotham. It was left unclaimed with other personal items, eventually finding its way to a second-hand store, where it was lost between the pages of a used copy of *Walden Two* by B.F. Skinner until it was located by Lexcorp.

ITEM #4 Originally found in a booth on April 18th, 1955, in Arnold's Diner in Hollywood, California. The photograph was put up on the wall, where it hung alongside other patron photos until it was located by Lexcorp.

ITEM #5 Originally found in November of 1940 in a brownstone in Battery Park, Manhattan. The photograph was given to the brownstone's former owner, Wesley Dodds. Dodds is said to have studied the photograph with great interest, noting that its fashions appeared "out of time." He claimed to dream about the man in it, calling him "Dr. Manhattan." He kept it until his death in 1986. It was located in an antique shop by Lexcorp, hidden inside one of Dodds's old trunks.

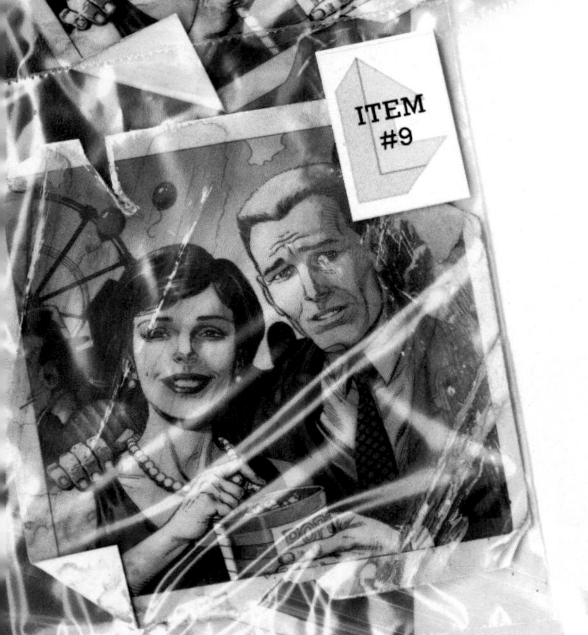
ITEM #9

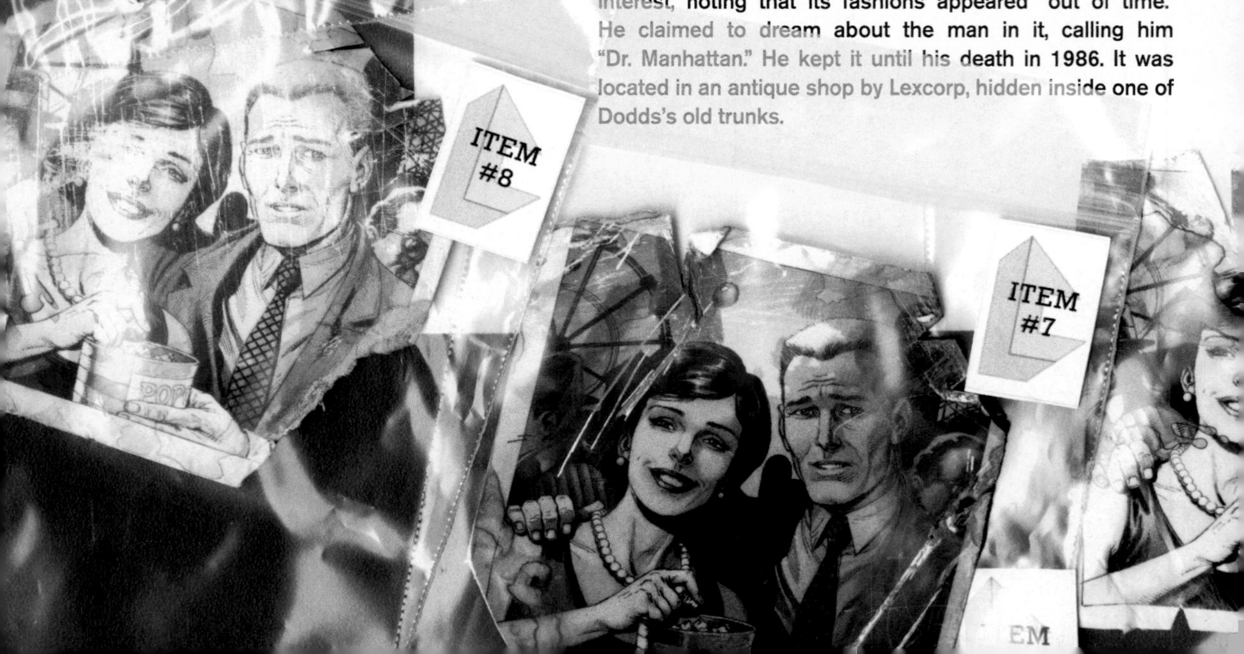
ITEM #8
ITEM #7

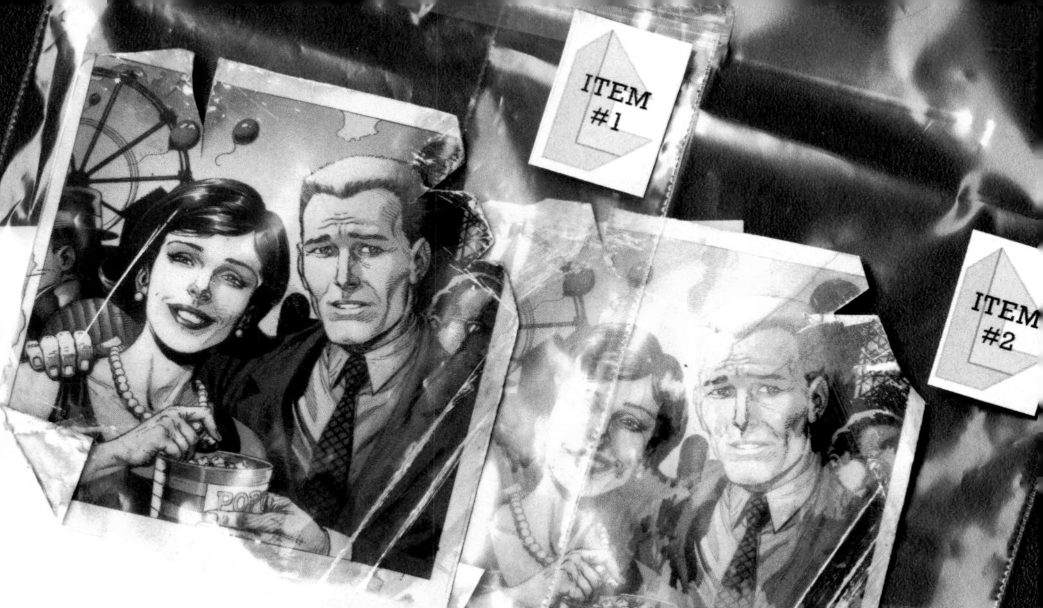
ITEM
#1
ITEM
#2

ITEM #6 Originally found in a cemetery in Smallville, Kansas, in 1956, it was brought to the local library in hopes that its owner may recover it. It remained there until it was located by Lexcorp.

ITEM #7 Originally found in a field in Smallville, Kansas, in 1986, most likely by a farmhand, it was apparently mistakenly put into a photo album belonging to the Hubbards, where it remained until it was located by Lexcorp.

ITEM #8 Recently found by Lexcorp in Arkham Asylum following a riot and subsequent mass breakout in the cell of an unknown prisoner known only as John Doe, 5'8", African-American. Brought in by Batman.

ITEM #9 Tracked down and located by Lexcorp last week. Found in the Congo Basin. Believe this to be a recent creation as the energy signature was only registered two weeks ago.

ITEM #10 Discovered in the New Beverly Cinema during a Nathaniel Dusk movie marathon, which starred Carver Colman. Evidence points to the obvious: the being had some kind of relationship or infatuation with the actor, romantic or otherwise.

ITEM #11 Additional energy readings point to dozens of new photographs, their appearance increasing at an alarming speed. The latest to be discovered was in one of the Joker's safe houses, a former warehouse on the East Side.

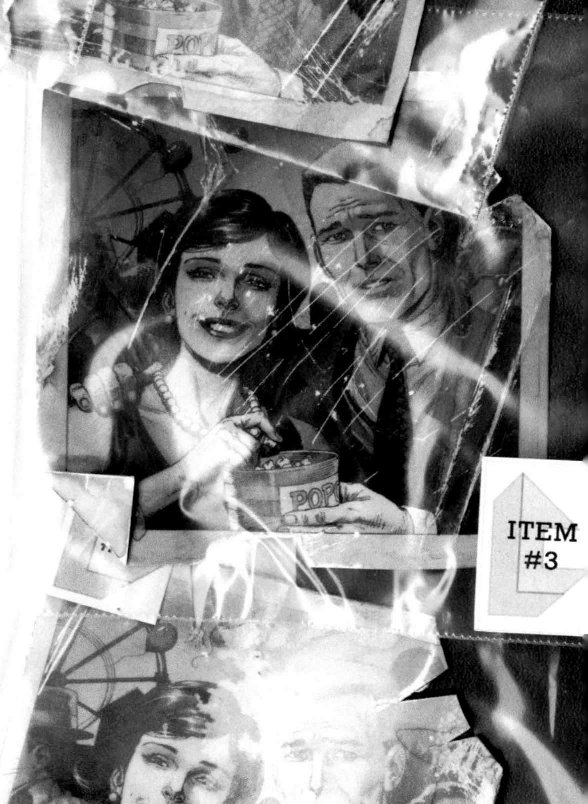
ITEM
#3

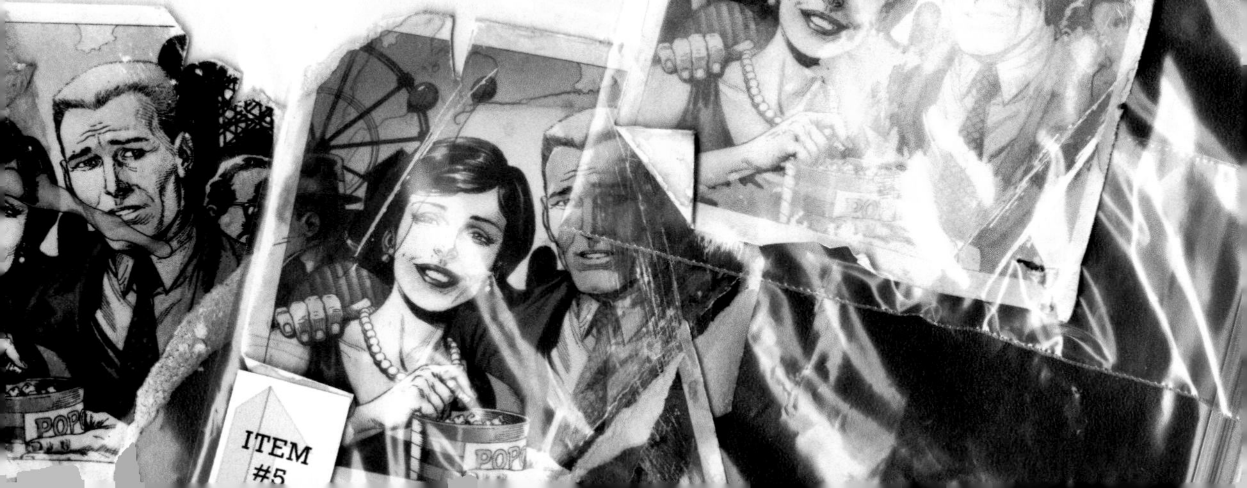
ITEM
#5

ITEM #12

LEXCORP

ITEM #12 Found among several other items in Central City at the site of the first discovery of "Jon's" photograph, this image is of the Flash and a second Flash, visually the same as the one found in the film reel of the Justice Society of America, recovered the same day at the same time. I believe it to be chronal debris from past lives or alternate histories of our world that no longer exist. In conclusion, the being I am tracking—this "Jon"—I believe him to be the cause of our revisionist reality, or at least to have knowledge of that cause.

I believe our universe is ever-evolving, that I have lived past lives—alongside Superman—and am locked in an endless battle with him that I might never win, nor will he. My goal is simple: find "Jon" and learn what I can about this endless loop between Superman and myself, and close it.

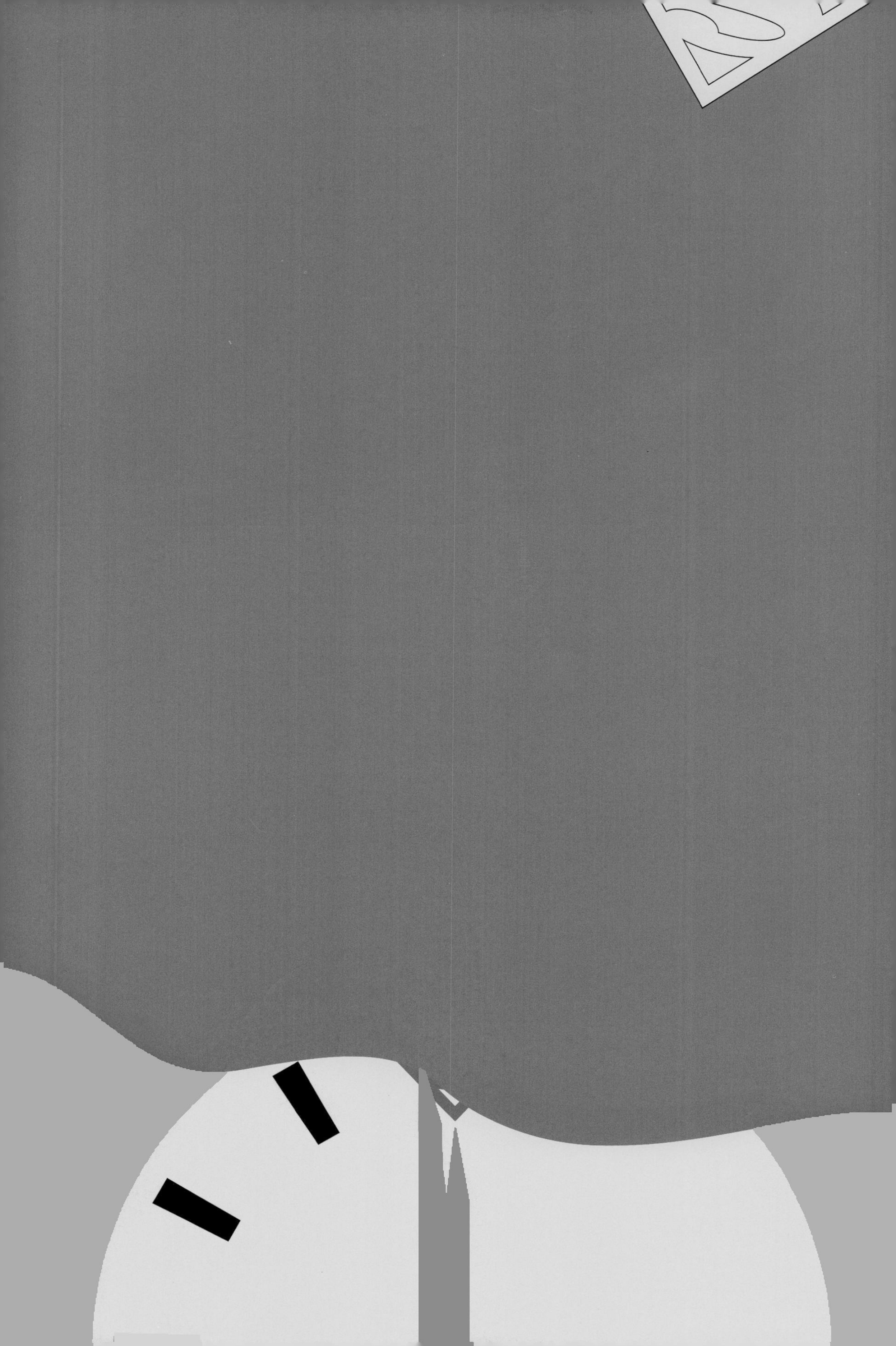

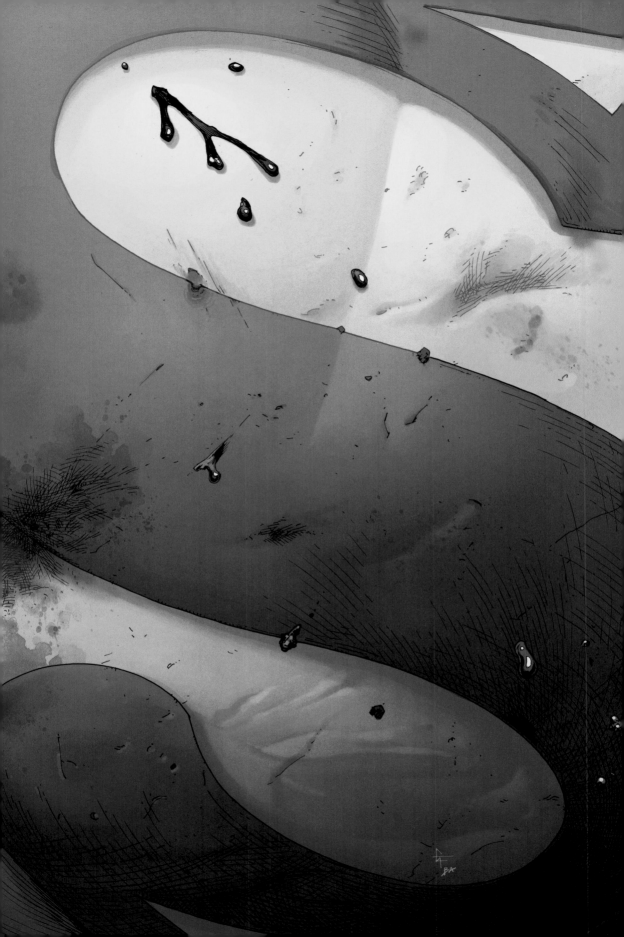

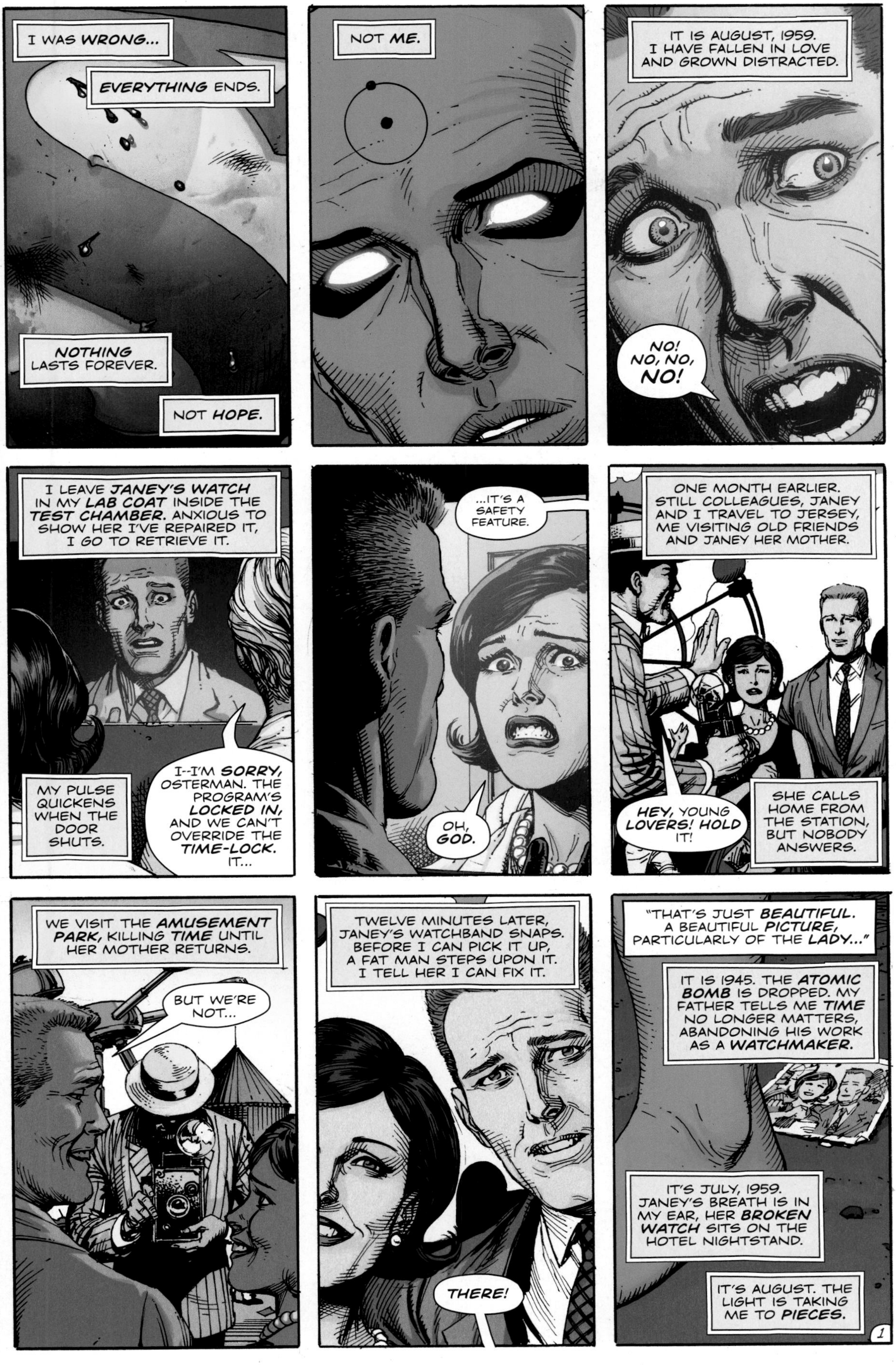
I WAS WRONG...
EVERYTHING ENDS.
NOTHING LASTS FOREVER.
NOT HOPE.
NOT ME.
IT IS AUGUST, 1959. I HAVE FALLEN IN LOVE AND GROWN DISTRACTED.
NO! NO, NO, NO!
I LEAVE JANEY'S WATCH IN MY LAB COAT INSIDE THE TEST CHAMBER. ANXIOUS TO SHOW HER I'VE REPAIRED IT, I GO TO RETRIEVE IT.
MY PULSE QUICKENS WHEN THE DOOR SHUTS.
I--I'M SORRY, OSTERMAN. THE PROGRAM'S LOCKED IN, AND WE CAN'T OVERRIDE THE TIME-LOCK. IT...
...IT'S A SAFETY FEATURE.
OH, GOD.
ONE MONTH EARLIER. STILL COLLEAGUES, JANEY AND I TRAVEL TO JERSEY, ME VISITING OLD FRIENDS AND JANEY HER MOTHER.
HEY, YOUNG LOVERS! HOLD IT!
SHE CALLS HOME FROM THE STATION, BUT NOBODY ANSWERS.
WE VISIT THE AMUSEMENT PARK, KILLING TIME UNTIL HER MOTHER RETURNS.
BUT WE'RE NOT...
TWELVE MINUTES LATER, JANEY'S WATCHBAND SNAPS. BEFORE I CAN PICK IT UP, A FAT MAN STEPS UPON IT. I TELL HER I CAN FIX IT.
THERE!
"THAT'S JUST BEAUTIFUL. A BEAUTIFUL PICTURE, PARTICULARLY OF THE LADY..."
IT IS 1945. THE ATOMIC BOMB IS DROPPED. MY FATHER TELLS ME TIME NO LONGER MATTERS, ABANDONING HIS WORK AS A WATCHMAKER.
IT'S JULY, 1959. JANEY'S BREATH IS IN MY EAR, HER BROKEN WATCH SITS ON THE HOTEL NIGHTSTAND.
IT'S AUGUST. THE LIGHT IS TAKING ME TO PIECES.
1

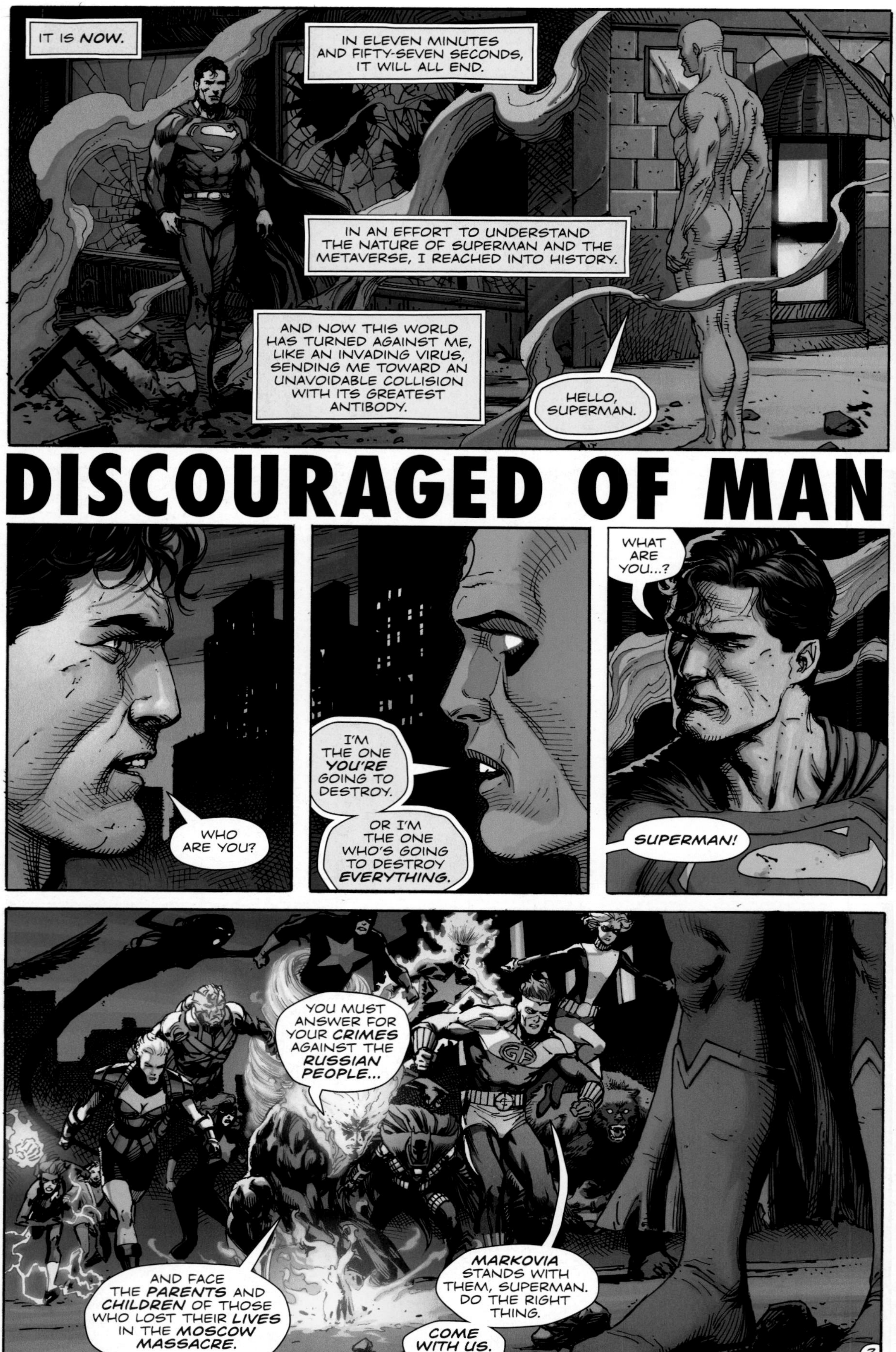
IT IS NOW.
IN ELEVEN MINUTES AND FIFTY-SEVEN SECONDS, IT WILL ALL END.
IN AN EFFORT TO UNDERSTAND THE NATURE OF SUPERMAN AND THE METAVERSE, I REACHED INTO HISTORY.
AND NOW THIS WORLD HAS TURNED AGAINST ME, LIKE AN INVADING VIRUS, SENDING ME TOWARD AN UNAVOIDABLE COLLISION WITH ITS GREATEST ANTIBODY.
HELLO, SUPERMAN.
DISCOURAGED OF MAN
WHO ARE YOU?
I'M THE ONE YOU'RE GOING TO DESTROY.
OR I'M THE ONE WHO'S GOING TO DESTROY EVERYTHING.
WHAT ARE YOU...?
SUPERMAN!
YOU MUST ANSWER FOR YOUR CRIMES AGAINST THE RUSSIAN PEOPLE...
AND FACE THE PARENTS AND CHILDREN OF THOSE WHO LOST THEIR LIVES IN THE MOSCOW MASSACRE.
MARKOVIA STANDS WITH THEM, SUPERMAN. DO THE RIGHT THING.
COME WITH US.

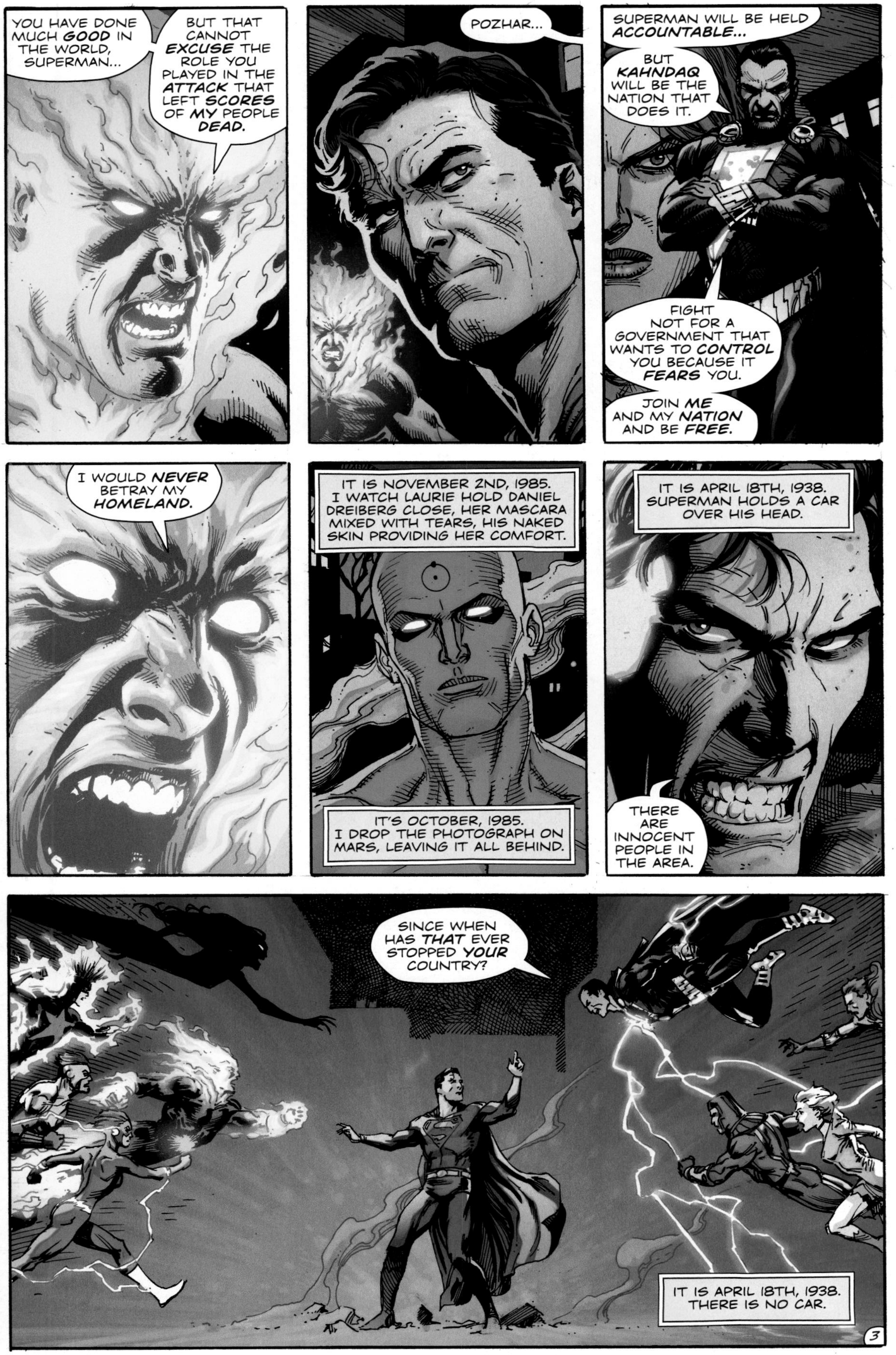
YOU HAVE DONE MUCH GOOD IN THE WORLD, SUPERMAN...
BUT THAT CANNOT EXCUSE THE ROLE YOU PLAYED IN THE ATTACK THAT LEFT SCORES OF MY PEOPLE DEAD.
POZHAR...
SUPERMAN WILL BE HELD ACCOUNTABLE...
BUT KAHNDAQ WILL BE THE NATION THAT DOES IT.
FIGHT NOT FOR A GOVERNMENT THAT WANTS TO CONTROL YOU BECAUSE IT FEARS YOU.
JOIN ME AND MY NATION AND BE FREE.
I WOULD NEVER BETRAY MY HOMELAND.
IT IS NOVEMBER 2ND, 1985. I WATCH LAURIE HOLD DANIEL DREIBERG CLOSE, HER MASCARA MIXED WITH TEARS, HIS NAKED SKIN PROVIDING HER COMFORT.
IT'S OCTOBER, 1985. I DROP THE PHOTOGRAPH ON MARS, LEAVING IT ALL BEHIND.
IT IS APRIL 18TH, 1938. SUPERMAN HOLDS A CAR OVER HIS HEAD.
THERE ARE INNOCENT PEOPLE IN THE AREA.
SINCE WHEN HAS THAT EVER STOPPED YOUR COUNTRY?
IT IS APRIL 18TH, 1938. THERE IS NO CAR.
3

...WITH THE JUSTICE LEAGUE STILL ON *MARS* FIGHTING THE BEING WHO THEY CLAIM IS *TRULY RESPONSIBLE* FOR THE EXPLOSION IN MOSCOW, THE PRIME MINISTER HAS ORDERED THE *KNIGHTS* TO PROTECT AMERICA'S INTERESTS.

WHAT THOSE INTERESTS EXACTLY *ARE* REMAINS *UNCLEAR.*

IT IS NOW.

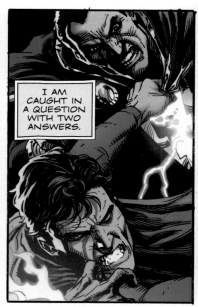

I AM CAUGHT IN A QUESTION WITH TWO ANSWERS.

AUSTRALIA ANNOUNCED THEIR INTENTIONS TO PROVIDE ADDITIONAL METAHUMAN RESOURCES TO THE U.S.

DESPITE PROTESTS THROUGHOUT SYDNEY AFTER PAST TWEETS BY *DARK RANGER* REVEALED HIS SUPPORT OF THE AUSTRALIAN PROTECTIONIST PARTY, HE REMAINS A MEMBER OF THE *SLEEPING SOLDIERS.*

I CANNOT SEE THROUGH THIS BARRIER OF BLACKNESS.

PRIME MINISTER NETANYAHU HAS COMMITTED ISRAEL TO FORCING *BLACK ADAM* BACK TO KAHNDAQ.

ISRAEL'S METAHUMAN PROGRAM, *HAYOTH*, GAINED NOTORIETY LAST WEEK AFTER A VIDEO APPEARED TO SHOW ITS LEADER, *SERAPH,* EXECUTING *UNARMED* TERRORISTS, SOMETHING WHICH HE *DENIES.*

I ONLY SEE SUPERMAN.

4

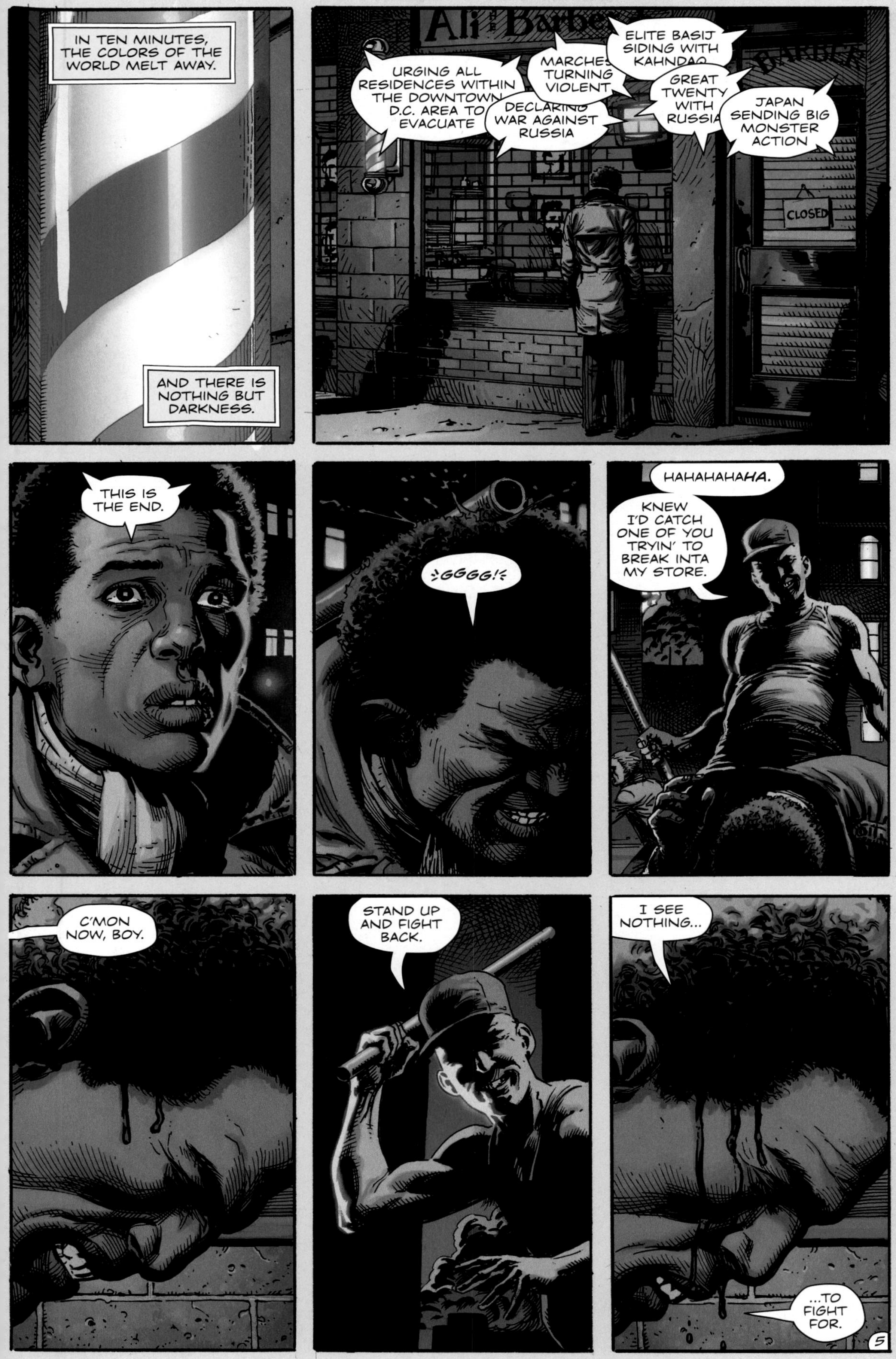
IN TEN MINUTES, THE COLORS OF THE WORLD MELT AWAY.
AND THERE IS NOTHING BUT DARKNESS.
URGING ALL RESIDENCES WITHIN THE DOWNTOWN D.C. AREA TO EVACUATE
MARCHES TURNING VIOLENT
ELITE BASIJ SIDING WITH KAHNDAQ
DECLARING WAR AGAINST RUSSIA
GREAT TWENTY WITH RUSSIA
JAPAN SENDING BIG MONSTER ACTION
CLOSED
THIS IS THE END.
GGGG!
HAHAHAHAHA.
KNEW I'D CATCH ONE OF YOU TRYIN' TO BREAK INTA MY STORE.
C'MON NOW, BOY.
STAND UP AND FIGHT BACK.
I SEE NOTHING...
...TO FIGHT FOR.

EXCUSE ME, SIR.

HUH?

YOU'VE GOT BLOOD ON YOUR HAT.

I GOT WHAT?

TOLD YOU.

LEAVE ME ALONE.

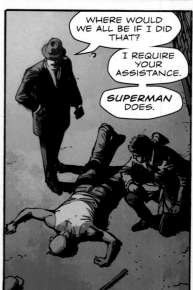
WHERE WOULD WE ALL BE IF I DID THAT?

I REQUIRE YOUR ASSISTANCE.

SUPERMAN DOES.

YOU'RE THE ONLY ONE WHO CAN HELP US FIND OZYMANDIAS BEFORE IT'S TOO LATE.

YOU DUH-DON'T KNOW...

YOU DON'T KNOW WHOSE FACE THAT IS.

YES, I DO. I'VE READ HIS JOURNAL. HIS NAME WAS...

DON'T SAY HIS NAME!

6

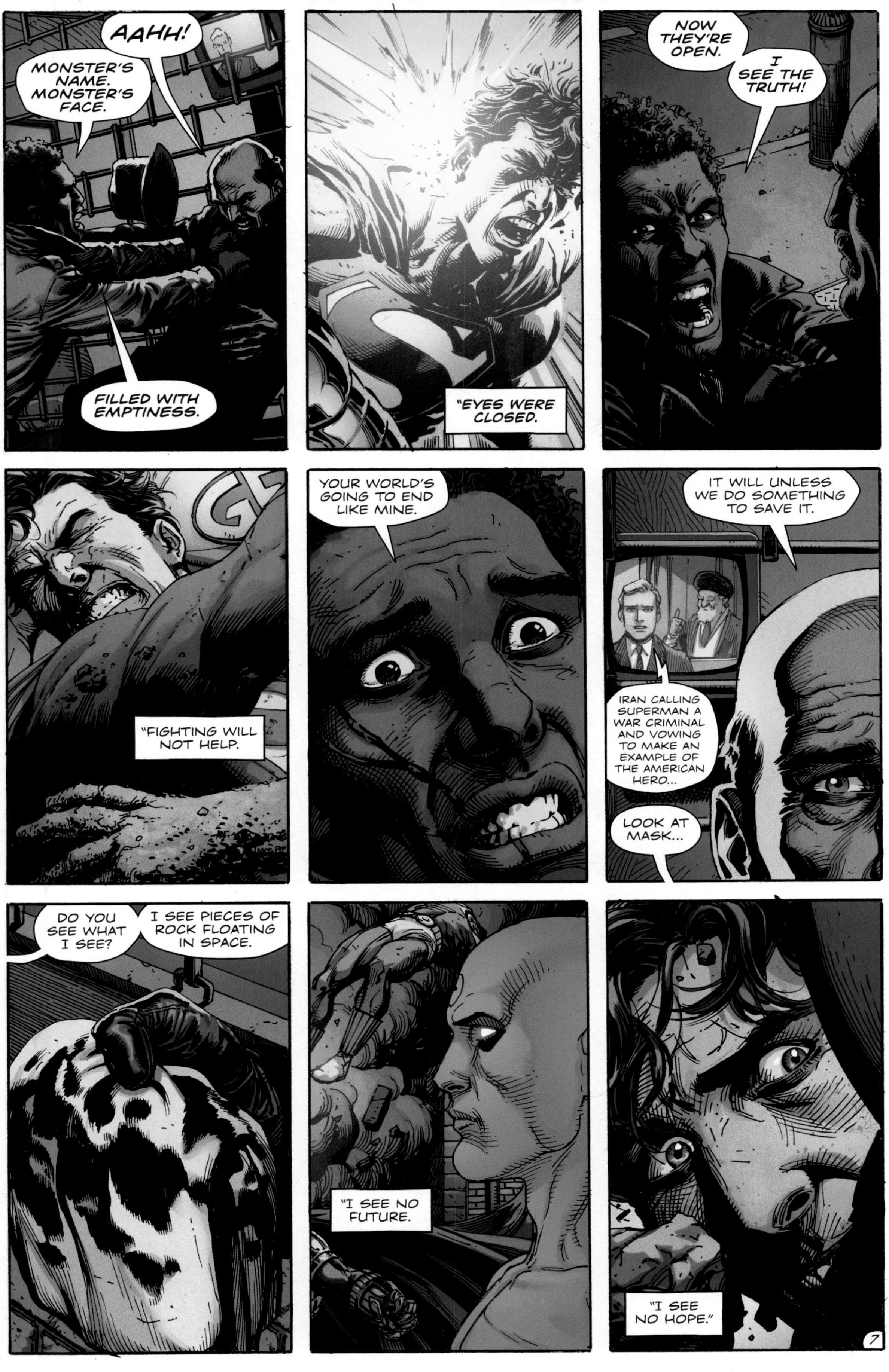
AAHH!
MONSTER'S NAME. MONSTER'S FACE.
FILLED WITH EMPTINESS.
"EYES WERE CLOSED.
NOW THEY'RE OPEN.
I SEE THE TRUTH!
"FIGHTING WILL NOT HELP.
YOUR WORLD'S GOING TO END LIKE MINE.
IT WILL UNLESS WE DO SOMETHING TO SAVE IT.
IRAN CALLING SUPERMAN A WAR CRIMINAL AND VOWING TO MAKE AN EXAMPLE OF THE AMERICAN HERO...
LOOK AT MASK...
DO YOU SEE WHAT I SEE?
I SEE PIECES OF ROCK FLOATING IN SPACE.
"I SEE NO FUTURE.
"I SEE NO HOPE."

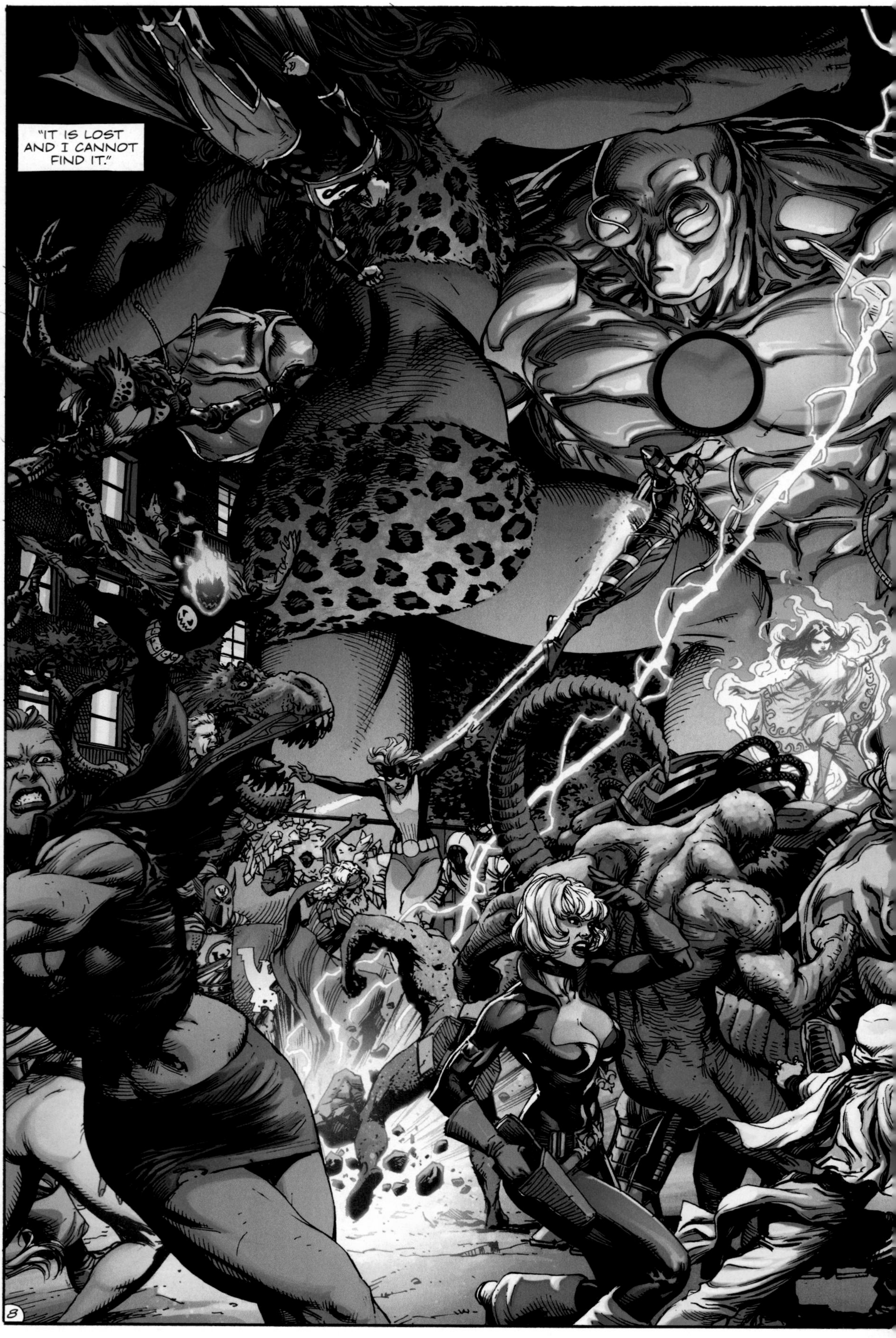
"IT IS LOST AND I CANNOT FIND IT."

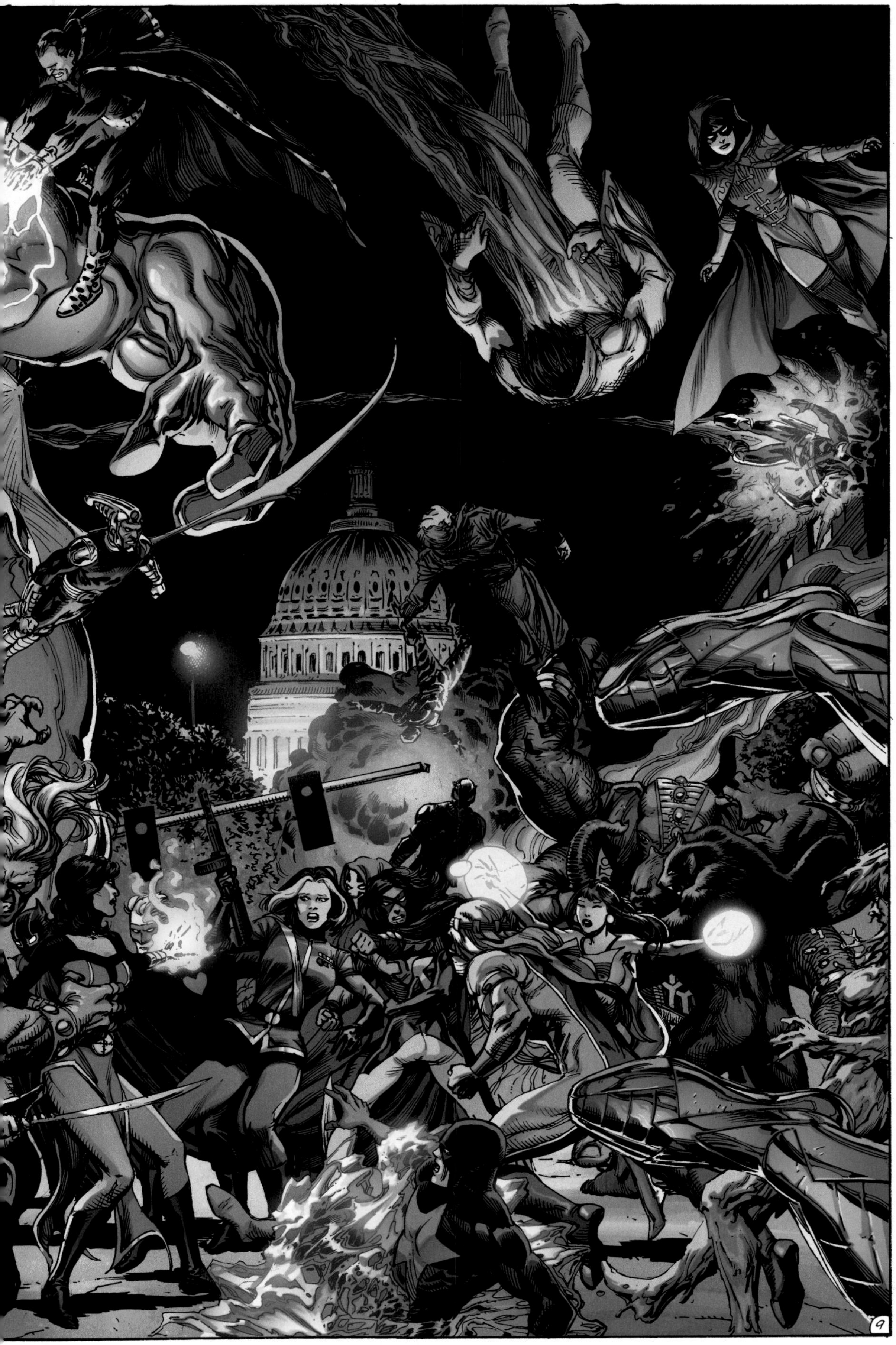

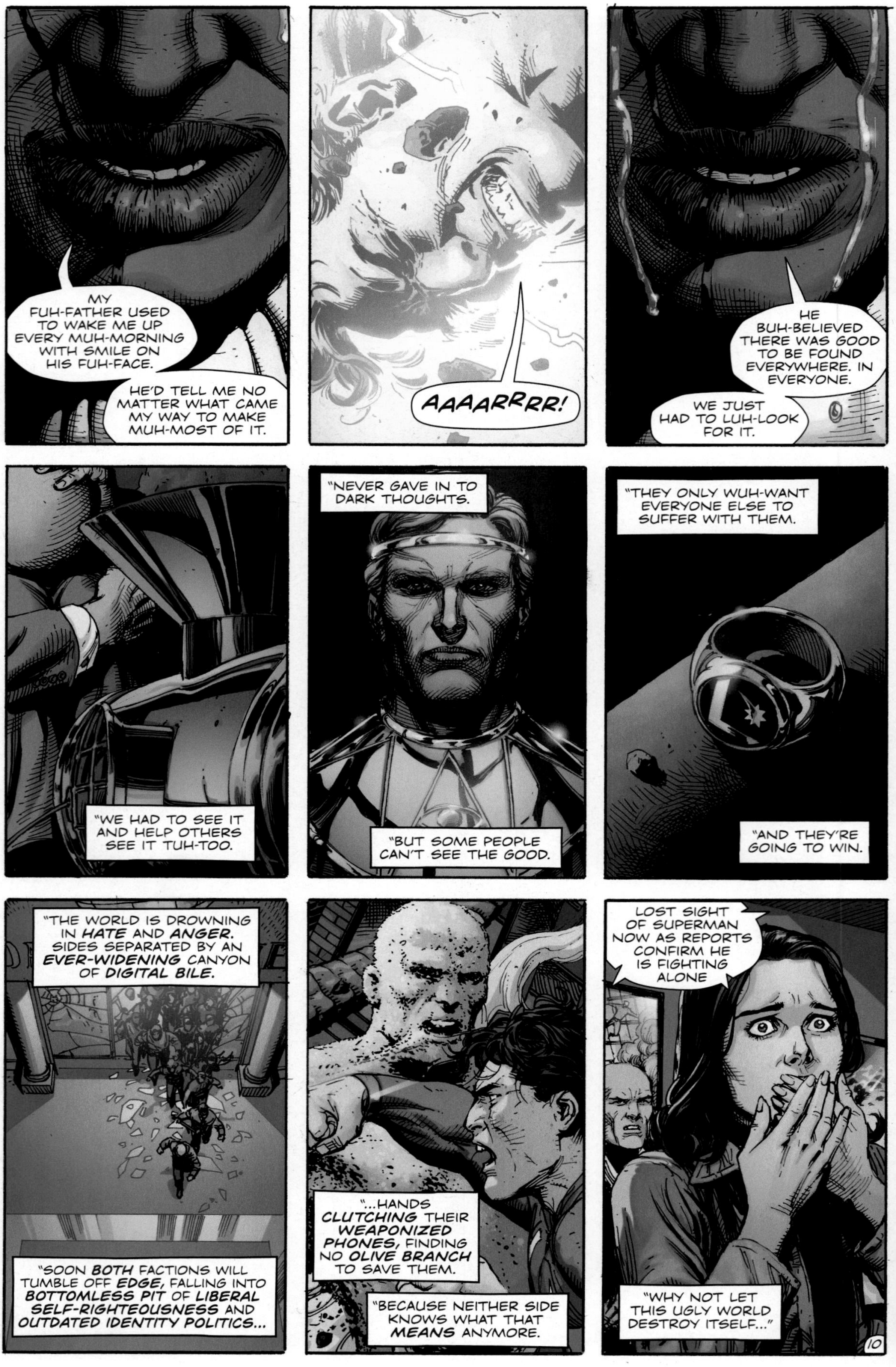
MY FUH-FATHER USED TO WAKE ME UP EVERY MUH-MORNING WITH SMILE ON HIS FUH-FACE.
HE'D TELL ME NO MATTER WHAT CAME MY WAY TO MAKE MUH-MOST OF IT.
AAAARRRR!
HE BUH-BELIEVED THERE WAS GOOD TO BE FOUND EVERYWHERE. IN EVERYONE.
WE JUST HAD TO LUH-LOOK FOR IT.
"WE HAD TO SEE IT AND HELP OTHERS SEE IT TUH-TOO.
"NEVER GAVE IN TO DARK THOUGHTS.
"BUT SOME PEOPLE CAN'T SEE THE GOOD.
"THEY ONLY WUH-WANT EVERYONE ELSE TO SUFFER WITH THEM.
"AND THEY'RE GOING TO WIN.
"THE WORLD IS DROWNING IN HATE AND ANGER. SIDES SEPARATED BY AN EVER-WIDENING CANYON OF DIGITAL BILE.
"SOON BOTH FACTIONS WILL TUMBLE OFF EDGE, FALLING INTO BOTTOMLESS PIT OF LIBERAL SELF-RIGHTEOUSNESS AND OUTDATED IDENTITY POLITICS...
"...HANDS CLUTCHING THEIR WEAPONIZED PHONES, FINDING NO OLIVE BRANCH TO SAVE THEM.
"BECAUSE NEITHER SIDE KNOWS WHAT THAT MEANS ANYMORE.
LOST SIGHT OF SUPERMAN NOW AS REPORTS CONFIRM HE IS FIGHTING ALONE
"WHY NOT LET THIS UGLY WORLD DESTROY ITSELF..."

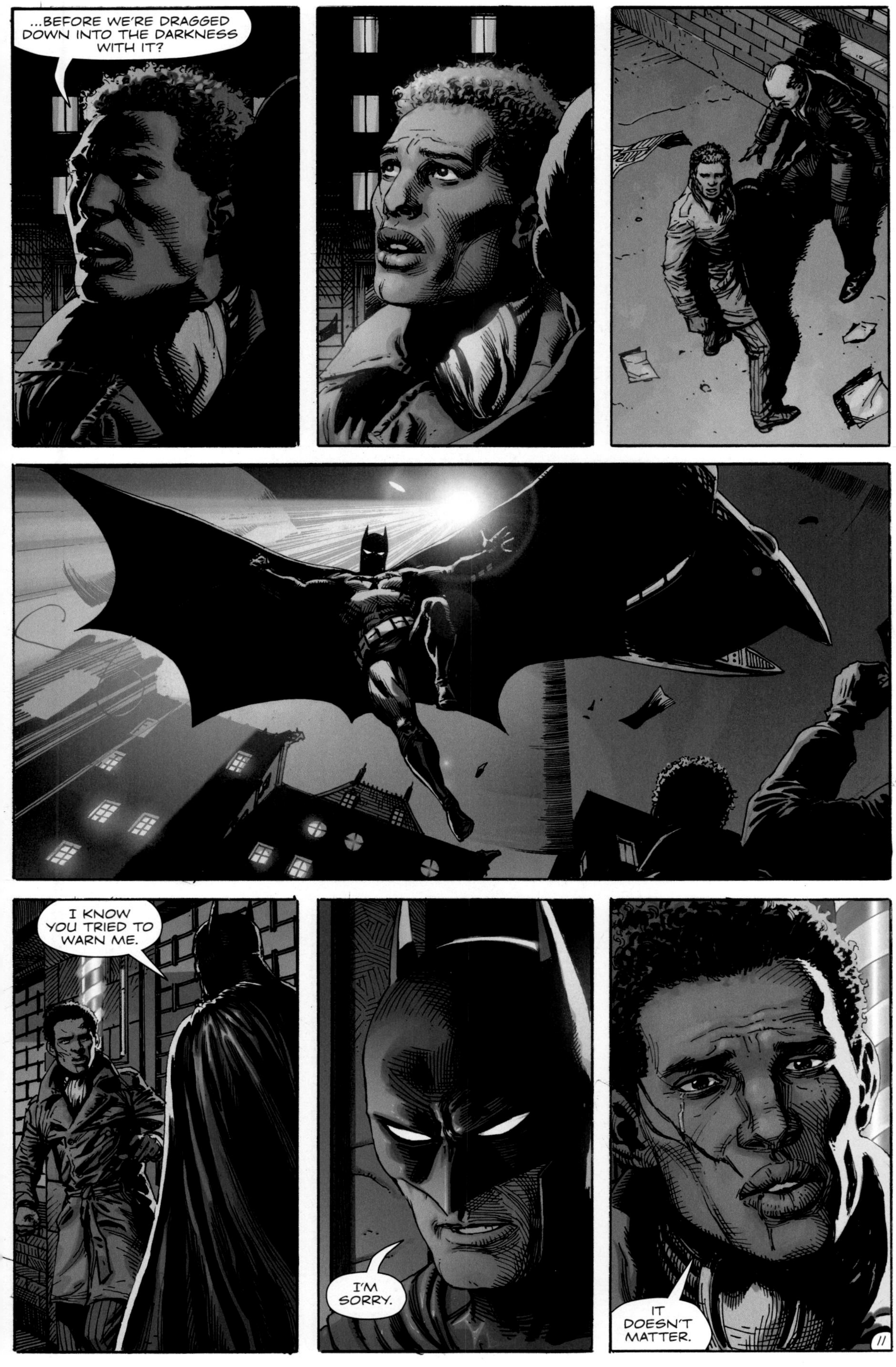

...BEFORE WE'RE DRAGGED DOWN INTO THE DARKNESS WITH IT?
I KNOW YOU TRIED TO WARN ME.
I'M SORRY.
IT DOESN'T MATTER.

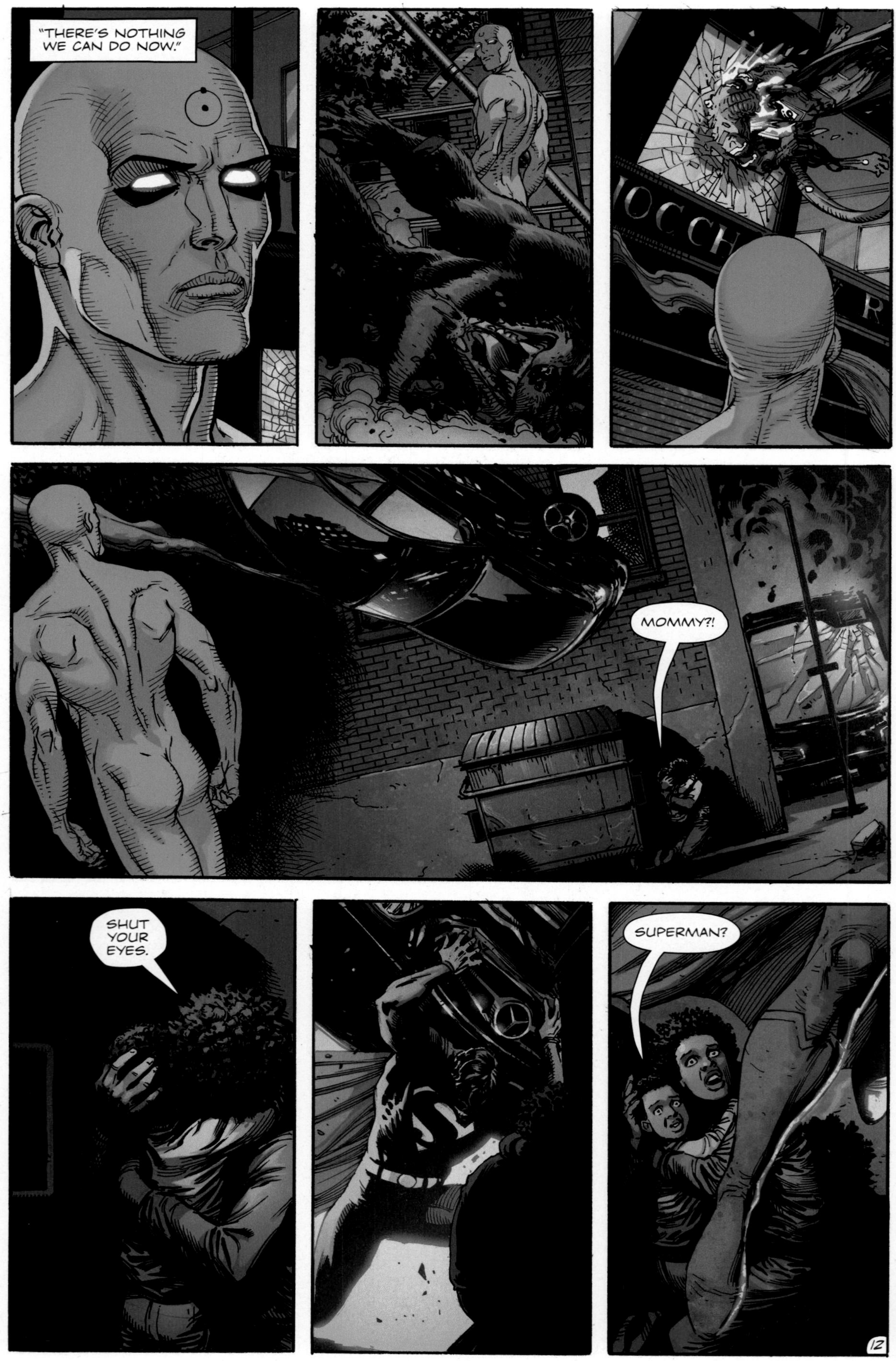
"THERE'S NOTHING WE CAN DO NOW."
MOMMY?!
SHUT YOUR EYES.
SUPERMAN?
12

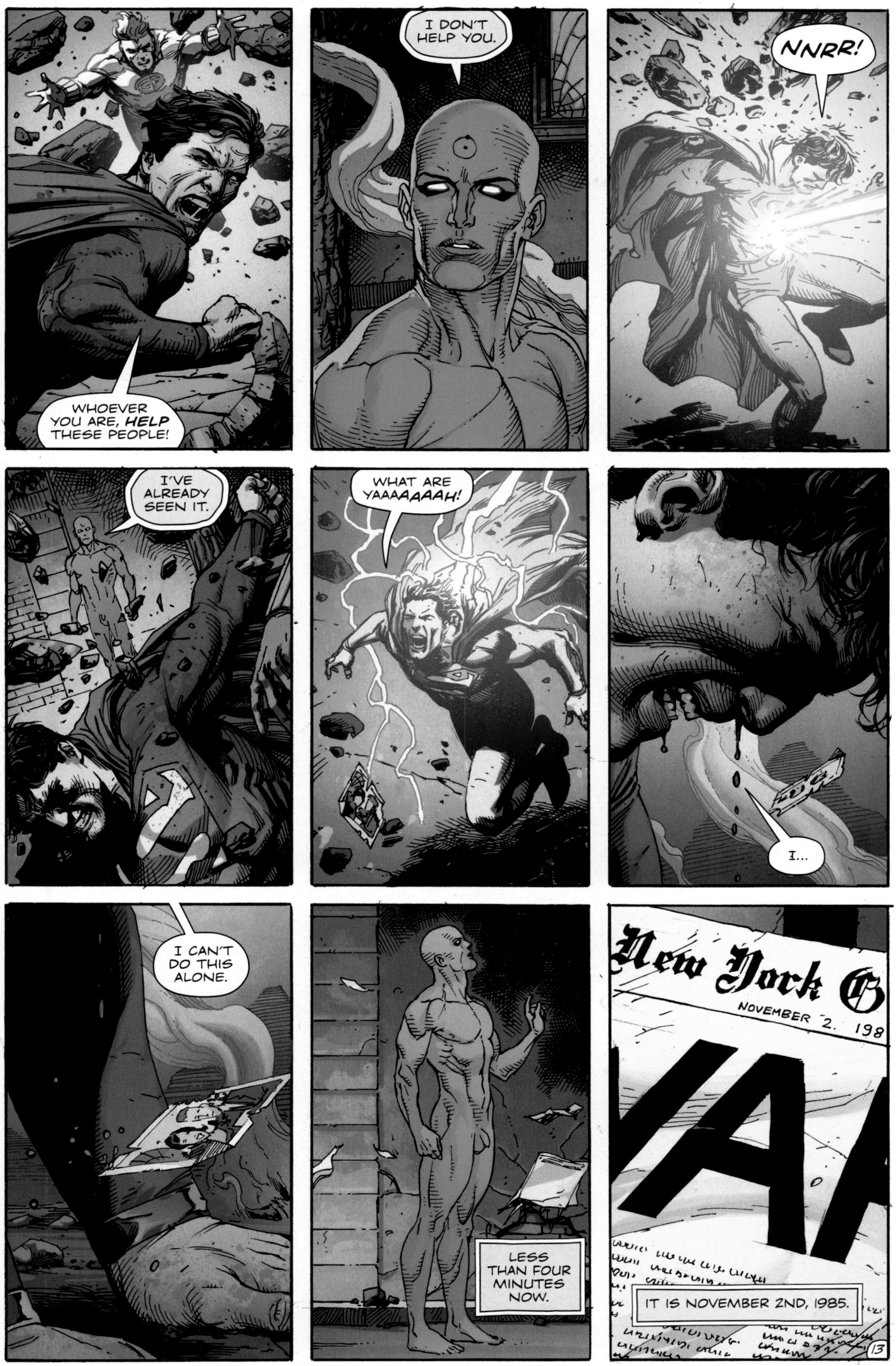
WHOEVER YOU ARE, HELP THESE PEOPLE!
I DON'T HELP YOU.
NNRR!
I'VE ALREADY SEEN IT.
WHAT ARE YAAAAAAAH!
I...
I CAN'T DO THIS ALONE.
LESS THAN FOUR MINUTES NOW.
New York G
NOVEMBER 2. 198
IT IS NOVEMBER 2ND, 1985.
13

I REMEMBER THIS FEELING.
MILLIONS WILL DIE. A COMPLICATED PROSPECT OF PEACE BROUGHT TO AN UNHINGED WORLD.
KILLING WALTER KOVACS, I BECOME PART OF THE LIE.
TUTE FOR SPATIAL STUDIES
WAR?
NOT YET REALIZING THE ILLUSION WOULD ONE DAY END.
YOU KNOW THE WAY OUT.
AND WHAT DO YOU EXPECT ME TO DO?
WRITE YOUR ARTICLE. INFORM THE WORLD. TELL THEM OUR VERY **HISTORY** HAS BEEN ALTERED BY A FORCE **BEYOND** OUR UNIVERSE.
TO ACCOMPLISH WHAT? PANICKING PEOPLE?
TO TELL PEOPLE ***I*** WAS THE ONE WHO ***UNCOVERED*** IT.
I WANT THE ***CREDIT*** FOR MY ***WORK.***
NOW IF YOU'LL EXCUSE ME, LOIS...
VIBRATIONAL EMITTER

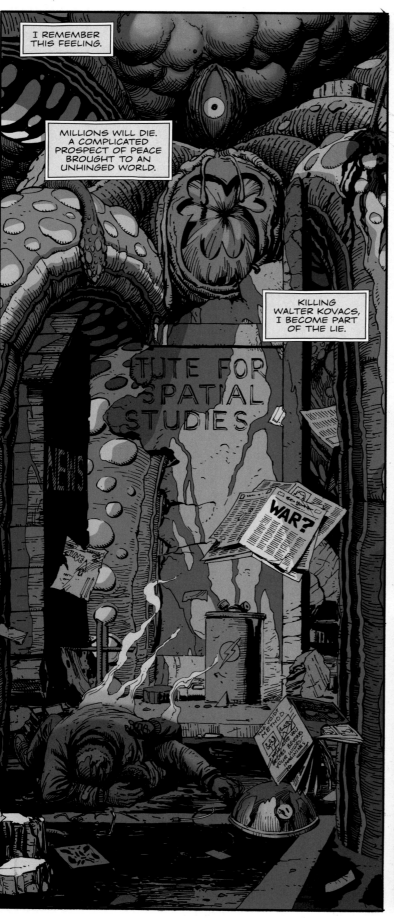

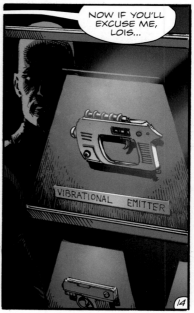

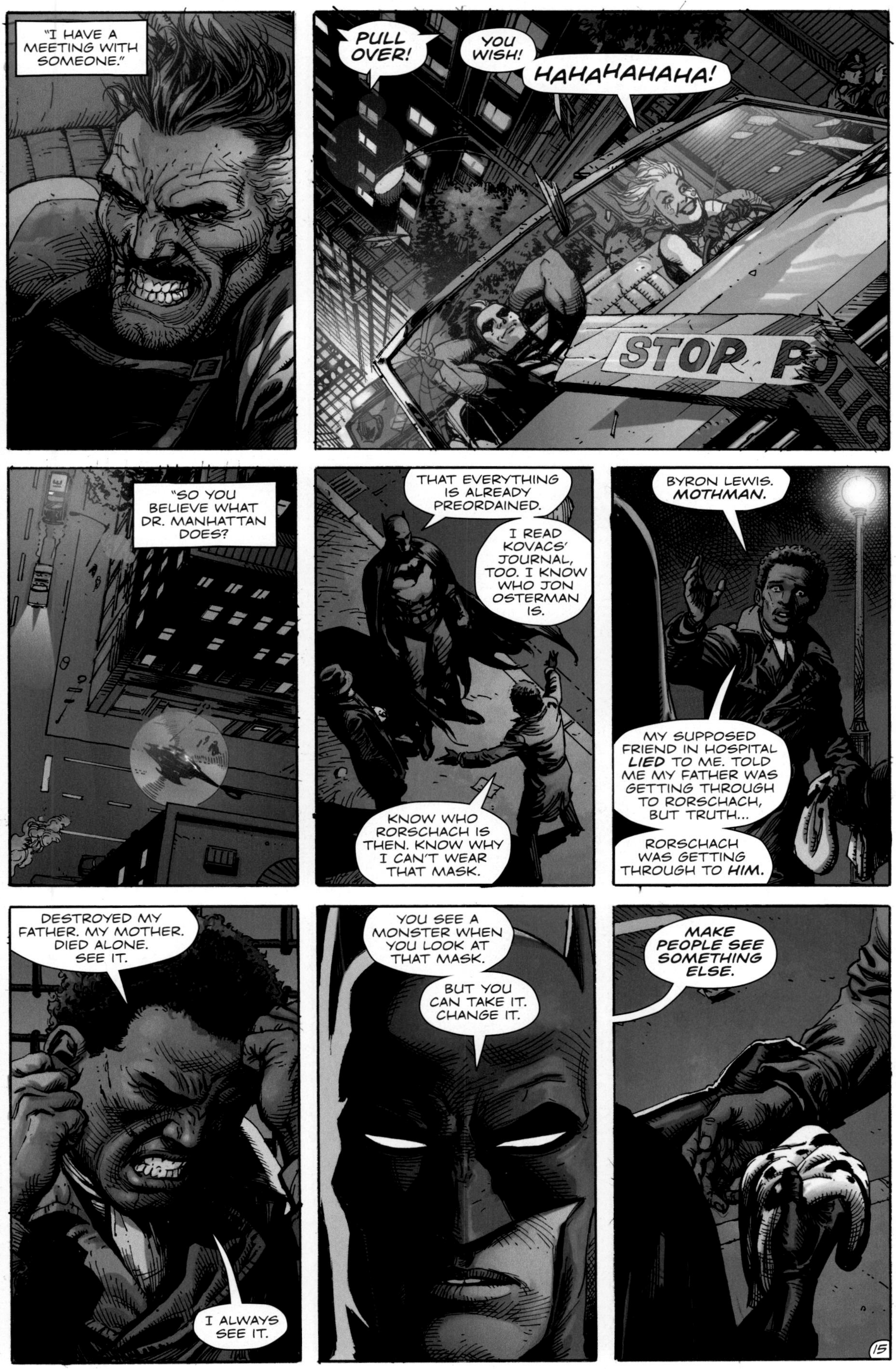
"I HAVE A MEETING WITH SOMEONE."
PULL OVER!
YOU WISH!
HAHAHAHAHA!
STOP
"SO YOU BELIEVE WHAT DR. MANHATTAN DOES?
THAT EVERYTHING IS ALREADY PREORDAINED.
I READ KOVACS' JOURNAL, TOO. I KNOW WHO JON OSTERMAN IS.
KNOW WHO RORSCHACH IS THEN. KNOW WHY I CAN'T WEAR THAT MASK.
BYRON LEWIS. MOTHMAN.
MY SUPPOSED FRIEND IN HOSPITAL LIED TO ME. TOLD ME MY FATHER WAS GETTING THROUGH TO RORSCHACH, BUT TRUTH...
RORSCHACH WAS GETTING THROUGH TO HIM.
DESTROYED MY FATHER. MY MOTHER. DIED ALONE. SEE IT.
I ALWAYS SEE IT.
YOU SEE A MONSTER WHEN YOU LOOK AT THAT MASK.
BUT YOU CAN TAKE IT. CHANGE IT.
MAKE PEOPLE SEE SOMETHING ELSE.

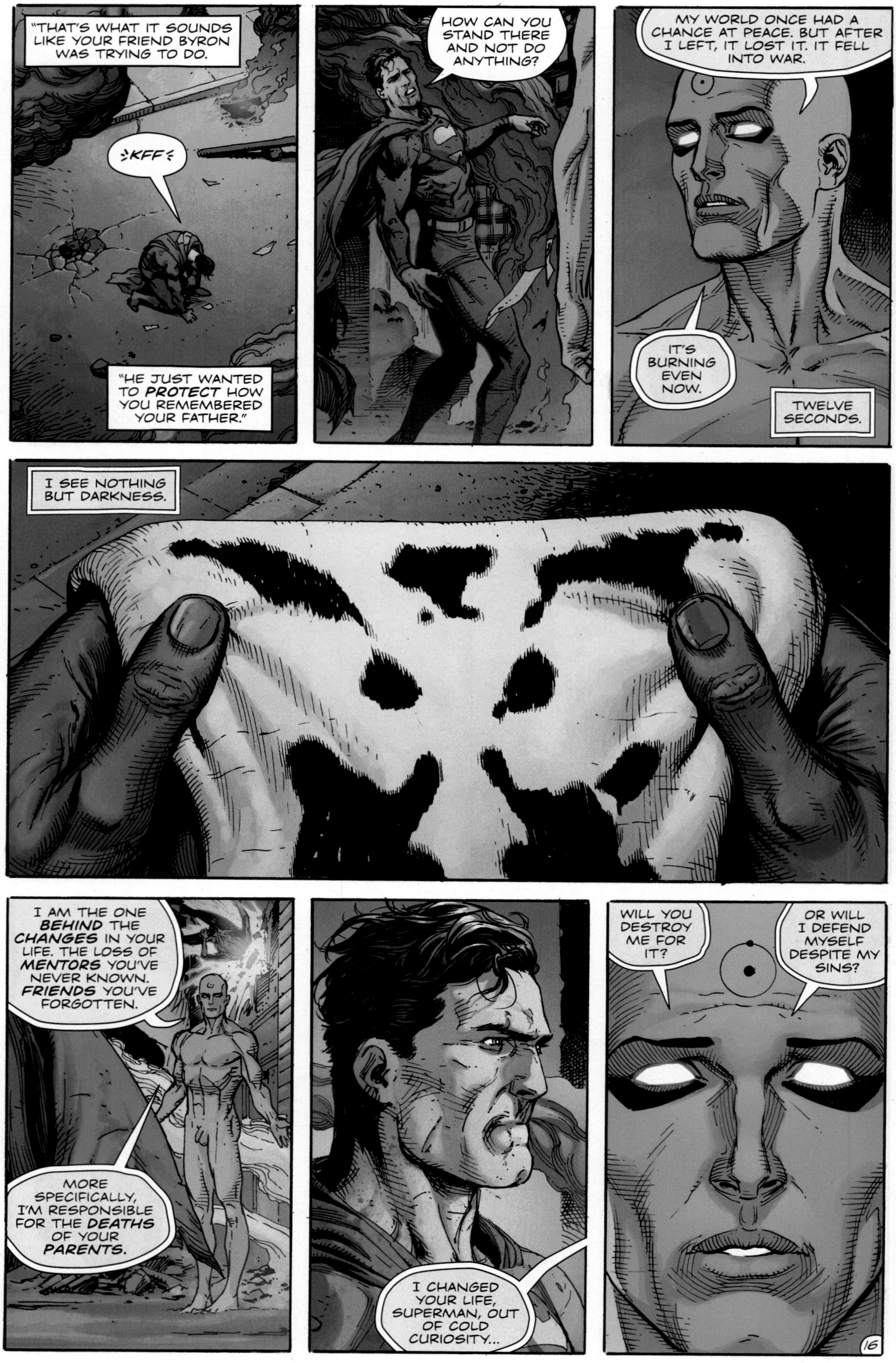
"THAT'S WHAT IT SOUNDS LIKE YOUR FRIEND BYRON WAS TRYING TO DO.
KFF
"HE JUST WANTED TO PROTECT HOW YOU REMEMBERED YOUR FATHER."
HOW CAN YOU STAND THERE AND NOT DO ANYTHING?
MY WORLD ONCE HAD A CHANCE AT PEACE. BUT AFTER I LEFT, IT LOST IT. IT FELL INTO WAR.
IT'S BURNING EVEN NOW.
TWELVE SECONDS.
I SEE NOTHING BUT DARKNESS.
I AM THE ONE BEHIND THE CHANGES IN YOUR LIFE. THE LOSS OF MENTORS YOU'VE NEVER KNOWN. FRIENDS YOU'VE FORGOTTEN.
MORE SPECIFICALLY, I'M RESPONSIBLE FOR THE DEATHS OF YOUR PARENTS.
I CHANGED YOUR LIFE, SUPERMAN, OUT OF COLD CURIOSITY...
WILL YOU DESTROY ME FOR IT?
OR WILL I DEFEND MYSELF DESPITE MY SINS?
16

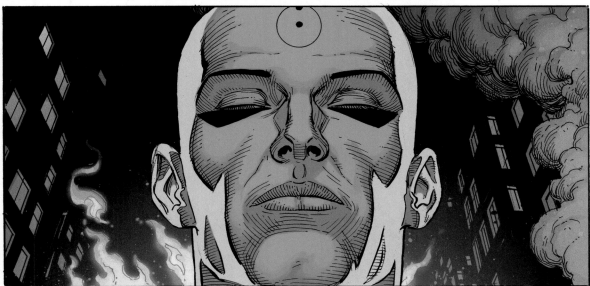

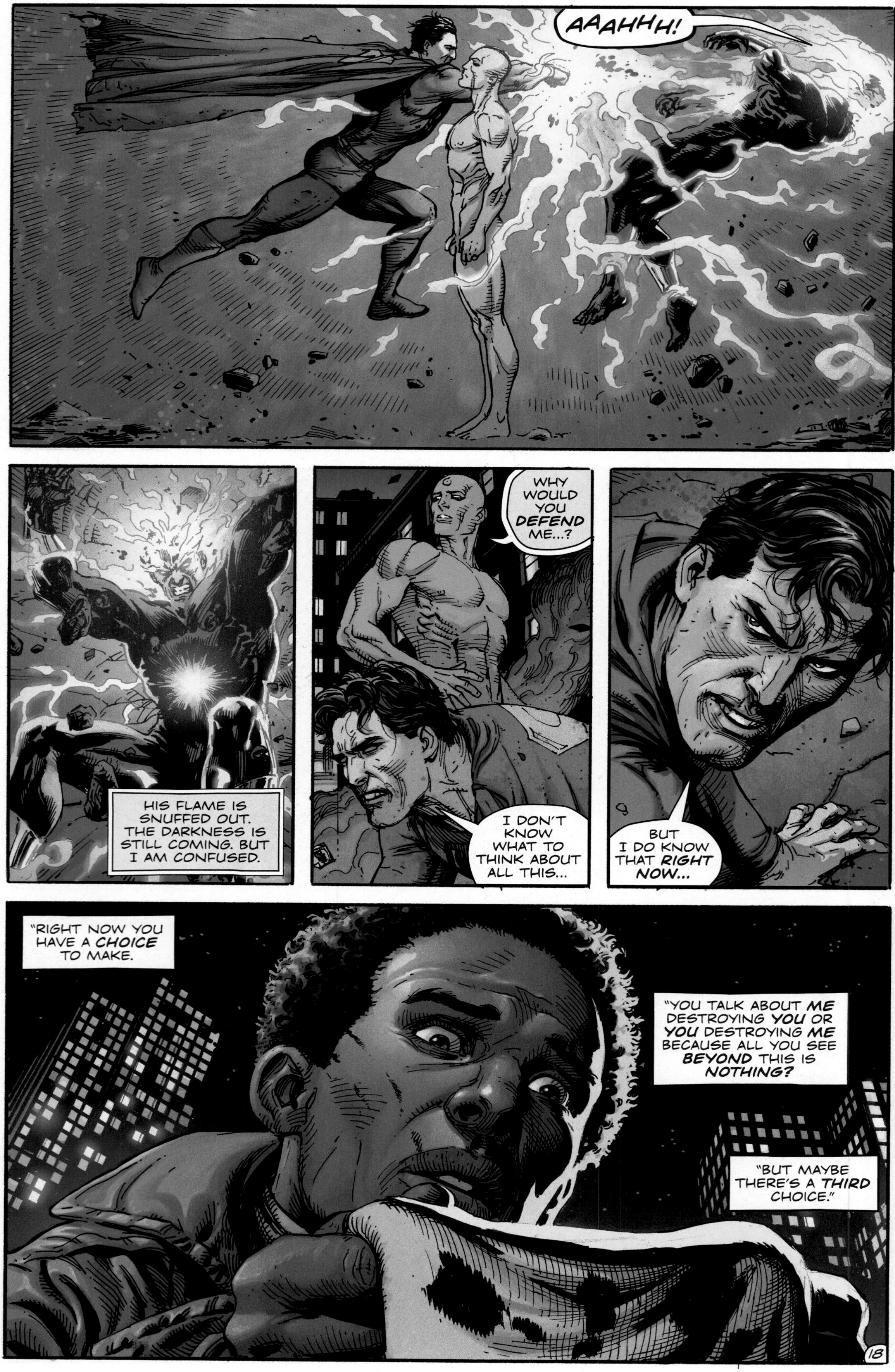
AAAHHH!
HIS FLAME IS SNUFFED OUT. THE DARKNESS IS STILL COMING. BUT I AM CONFUSED.
WHY WOULD YOU DEFEND ME...?
I DON'T KNOW WHAT TO THINK ABOUT ALL THIS...
BUT I DO KNOW THAT RIGHT NOW...
"RIGHT NOW YOU HAVE A CHOICE TO MAKE.
"YOU TALK ABOUT ME DESTROYING YOU OR YOU DESTROYING ME BECAUSE ALL YOU SEE BEYOND THIS IS NOTHING?
"BUT MAYBE THERE'S A THIRD CHOICE."
18

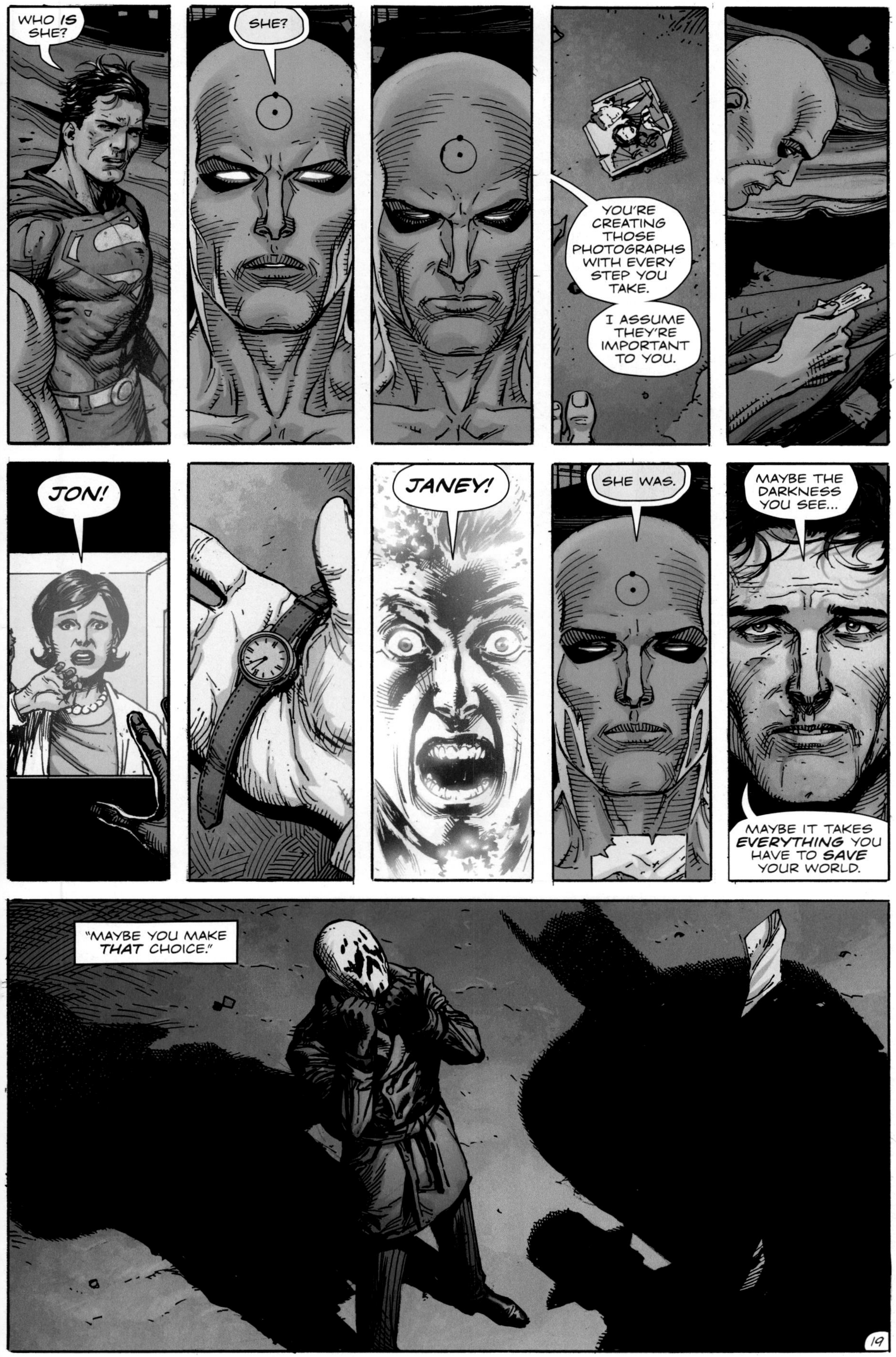
WHO IS SHE?
SHE?
YOU'RE CREATING THOSE PHOTOGRAPHS WITH EVERY STEP YOU TAKE.
I ASSUME THEY'RE IMPORTANT TO YOU.
JON!
JANEY!
SHE WAS.
MAYBE THE DARKNESS YOU SEE...
MAYBE IT TAKES EVERYTHING YOU HAVE TO SAVE YOUR WORLD.
"MAYBE YOU MAKE THAT CHOICE."
19

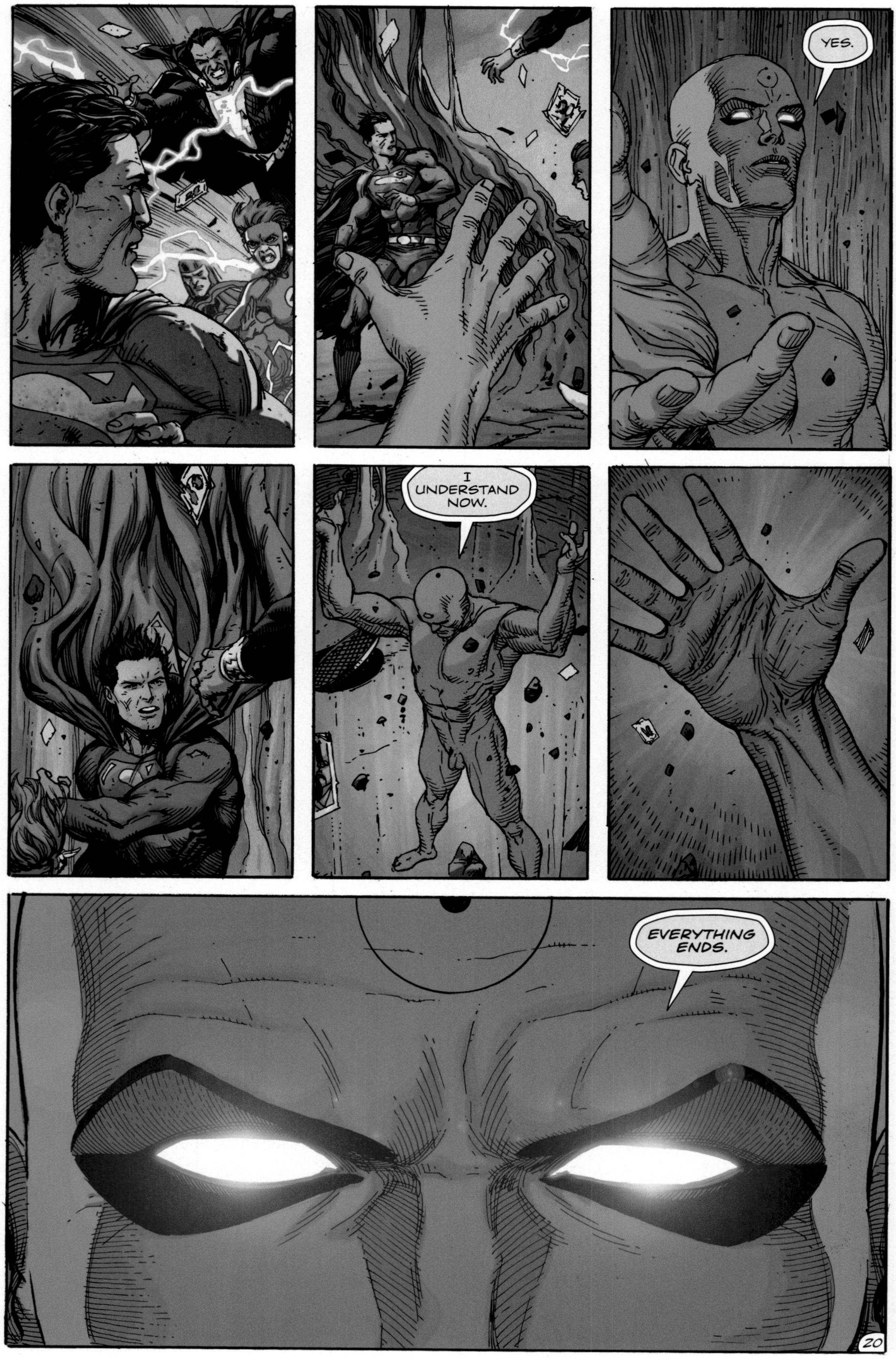
YES.
I UNDERSTAND NOW.
EVERYTHING ENDS.

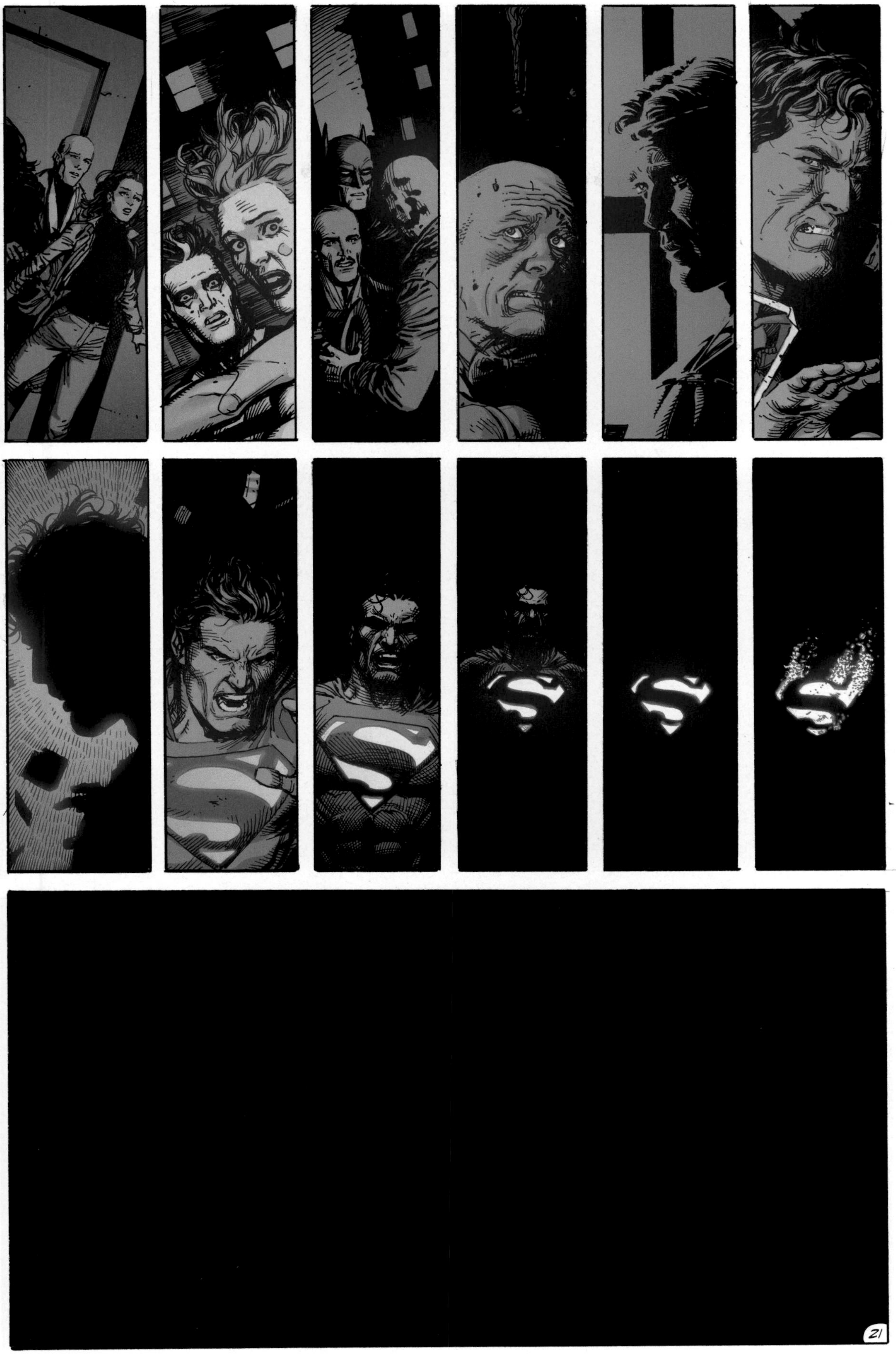

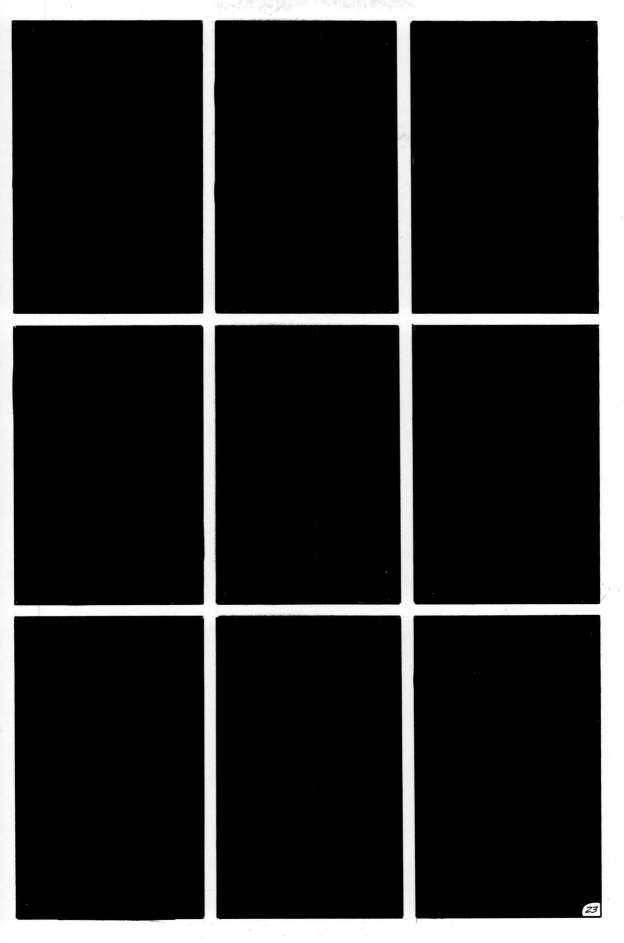

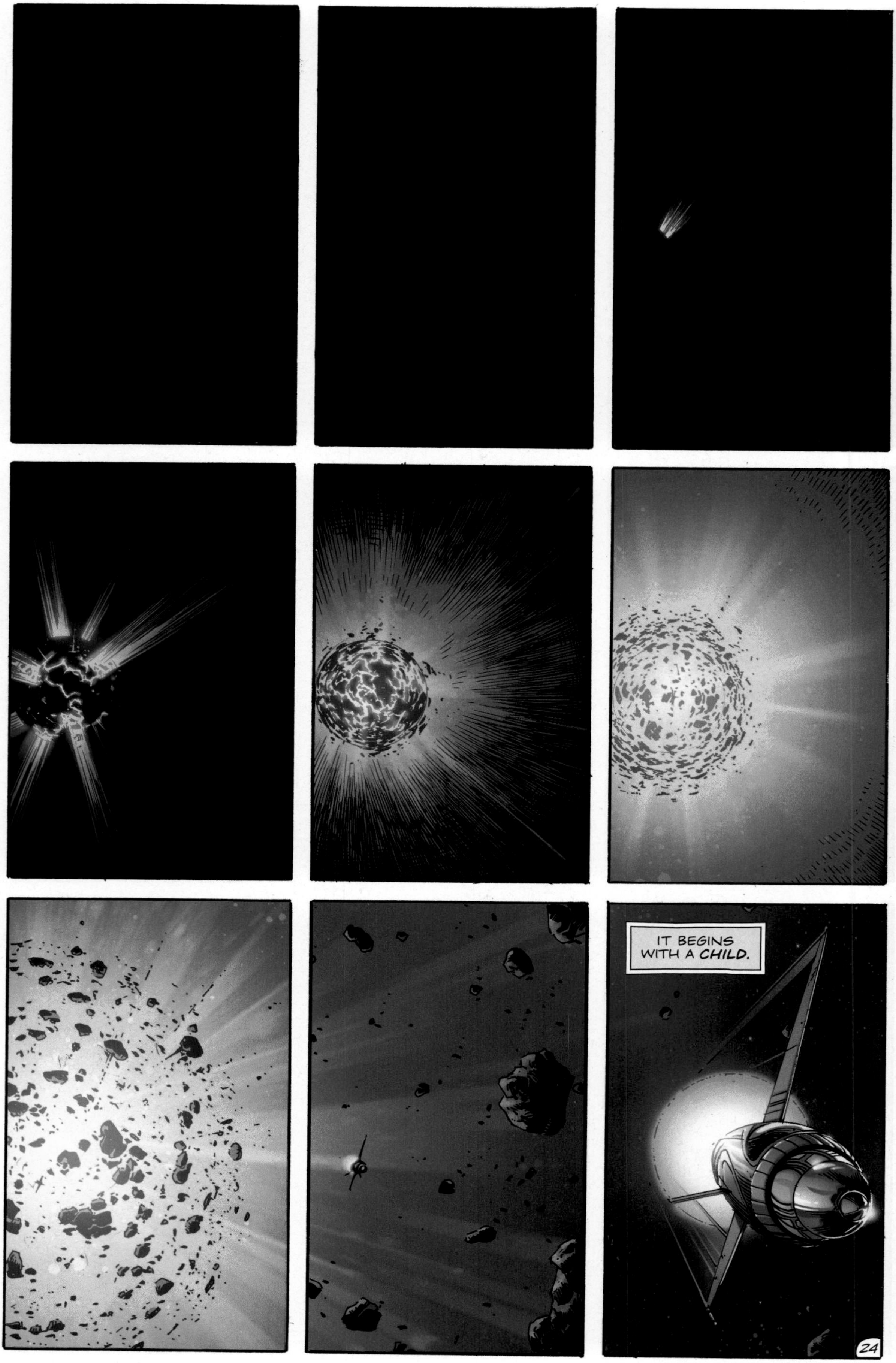
IT BEGINS WITH A CHILD.

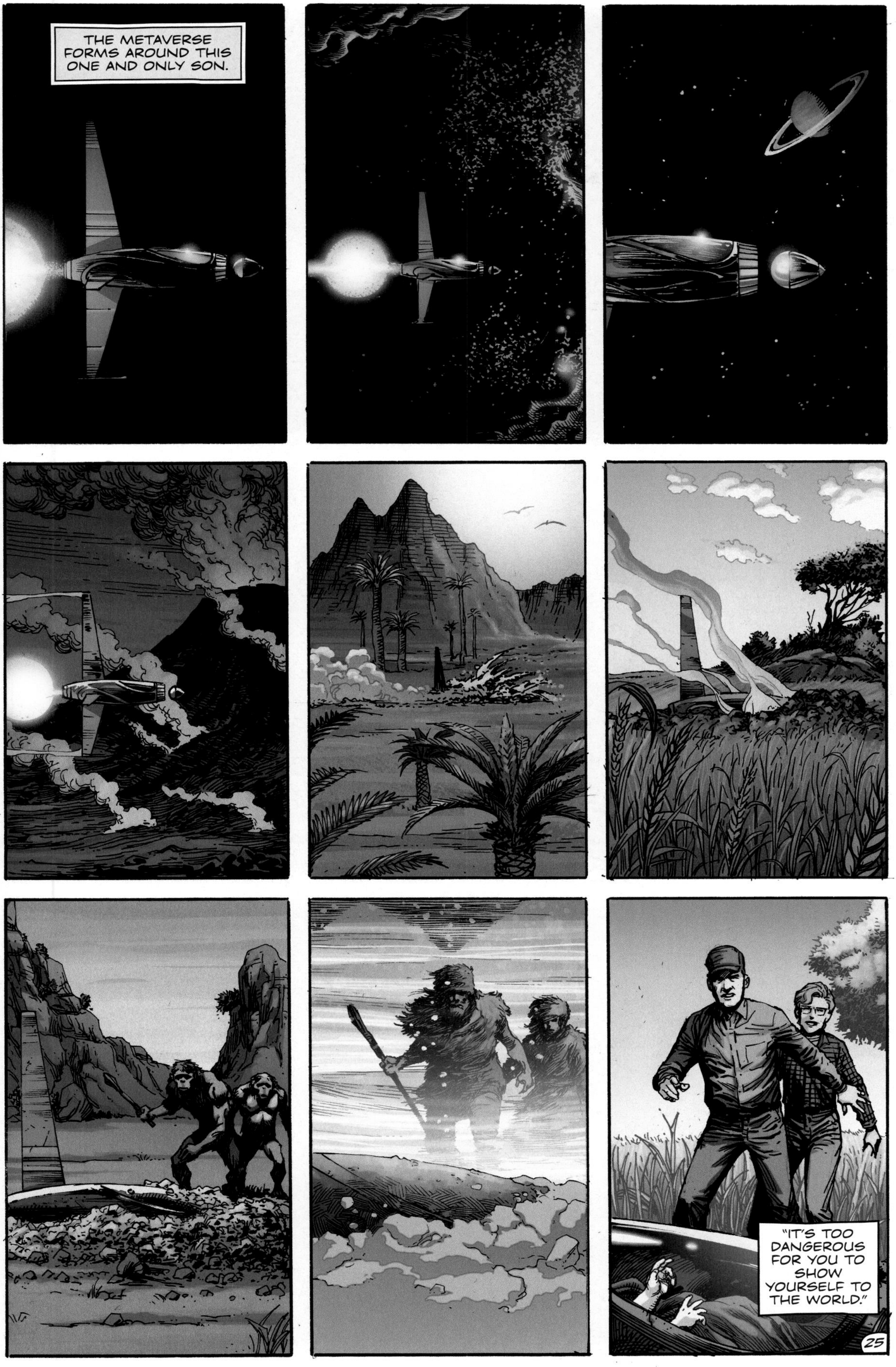
THE METAVERSE FORMS AROUND THIS ONE AND ONLY SON.
"IT'S TOO DANGEROUS FOR YOU TO SHOW YOURSELF TO THE WORLD."
25

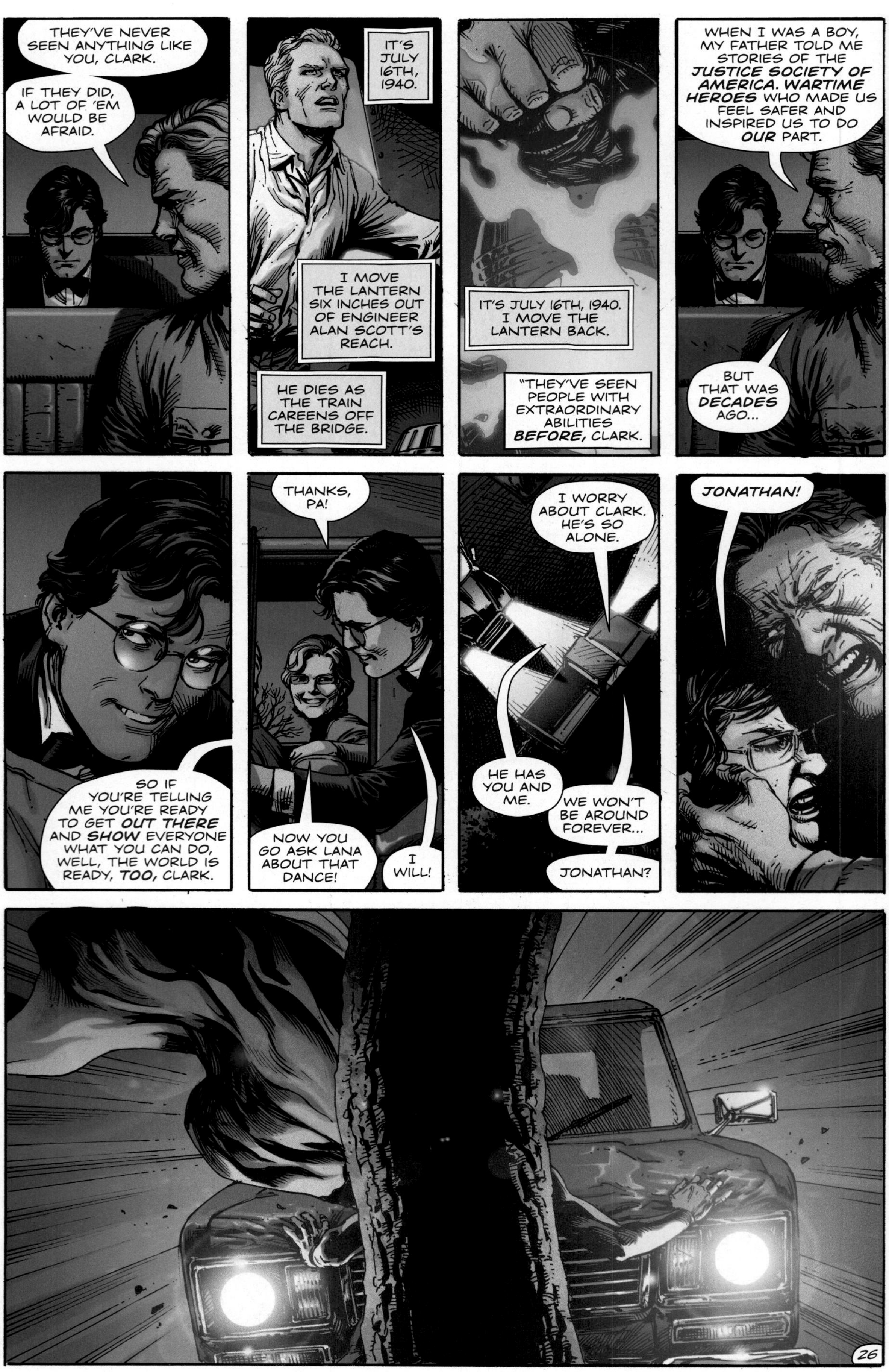

THEY'VE NEVER SEEN ANYTHING LIKE YOU, CLARK.
IF THEY DID, A LOT OF 'EM WOULD BE AFRAID.
IT'S JULY 16TH, 1940.
I MOVE THE LANTERN SIX INCHES OUT OF ENGINEER ALAN SCOTT'S REACH.
HE DIES AS THE TRAIN CAREENS OFF THE BRIDGE.
IT'S JULY 16TH, 1940. I MOVE THE LANTERN BACK.
"THEY'VE SEEN PEOPLE WITH EXTRAORDINARY ABILITIES BEFORE, CLARK.
WHEN I WAS A BOY, MY FATHER TOLD ME STORIES OF THE JUSTICE SOCIETY OF AMERICA. WARTIME HEROES WHO MADE US FEEL SAFER AND INSPIRED US TO DO OUR PART.
BUT THAT WAS DECADES AGO...
SO IF YOU'RE TELLING ME YOU'RE READY TO GET OUT THERE AND SHOW EVERYONE WHAT YOU CAN DO, WELL, THE WORLD IS READY, TOO, CLARK.
THANKS, PA!
NOW YOU GO ASK LANA ABOUT THAT DANCE!
I WILL!
I WORRY ABOUT CLARK. HE'S SO ALONE.
HE HAS YOU AND ME.
WE WON'T BE AROUND FOREVER...
JONATHAN?
JONATHAN!
26

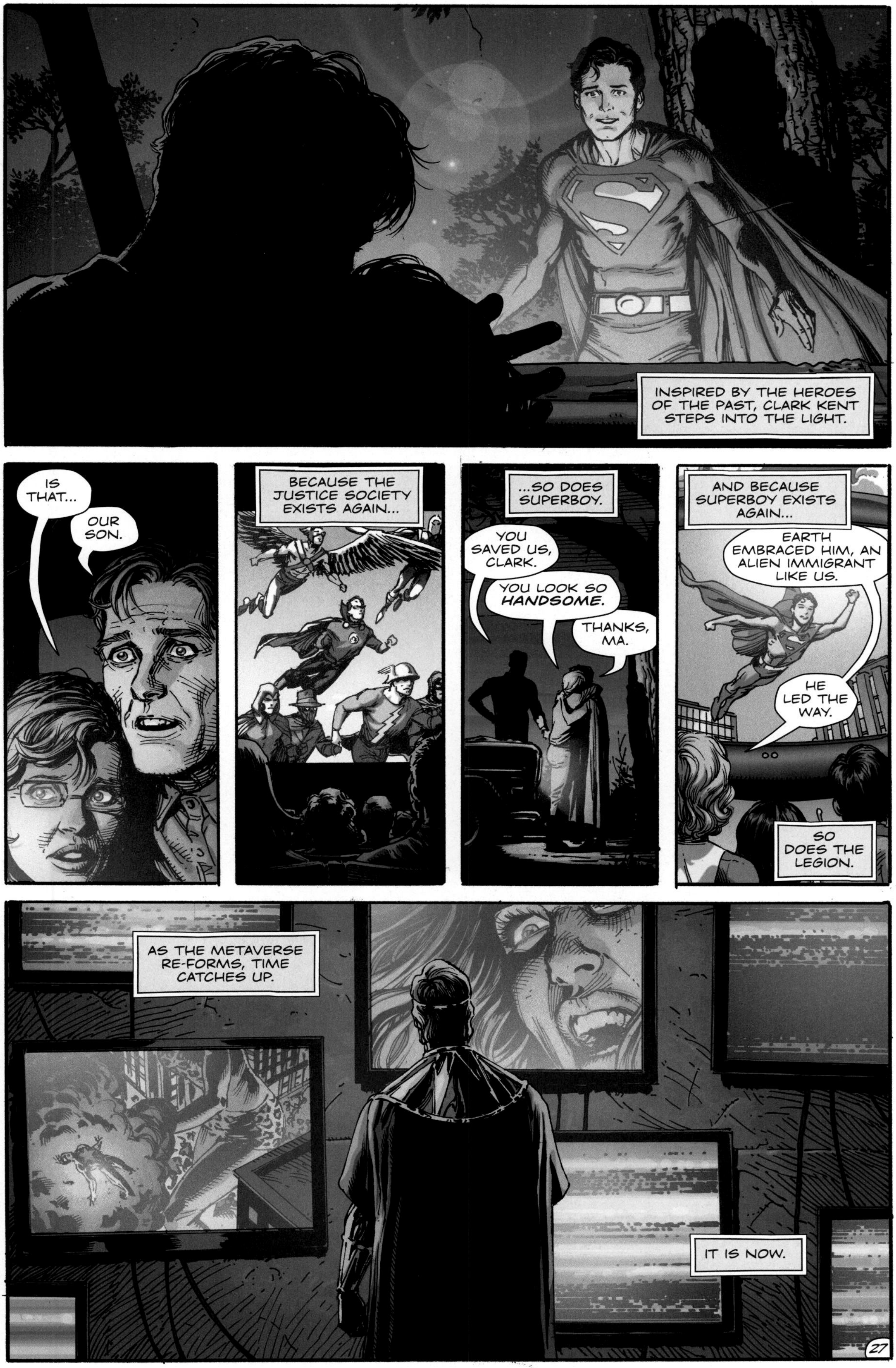
INSPIRED BY THE HEROES OF THE PAST, CLARK KENT STEPS INTO THE LIGHT.
IS THAT...
OUR SON.
BECAUSE THE JUSTICE SOCIETY EXISTS AGAIN...
...SO DOES SUPERBOY.
YOU SAVED US, CLARK.
YOU LOOK SO **HANDSOME.**
THANKS, MA.
AND BECAUSE SUPERBOY EXISTS AGAIN...
EARTH EMBRACED HIM, AN ALIEN IMMIGRANT LIKE US.
HE LED THE WAY.
SO DOES THE LEGION.
AS THE METAVERSE RE-FORMS, TIME CATCHES UP.
IT IS NOW.
27

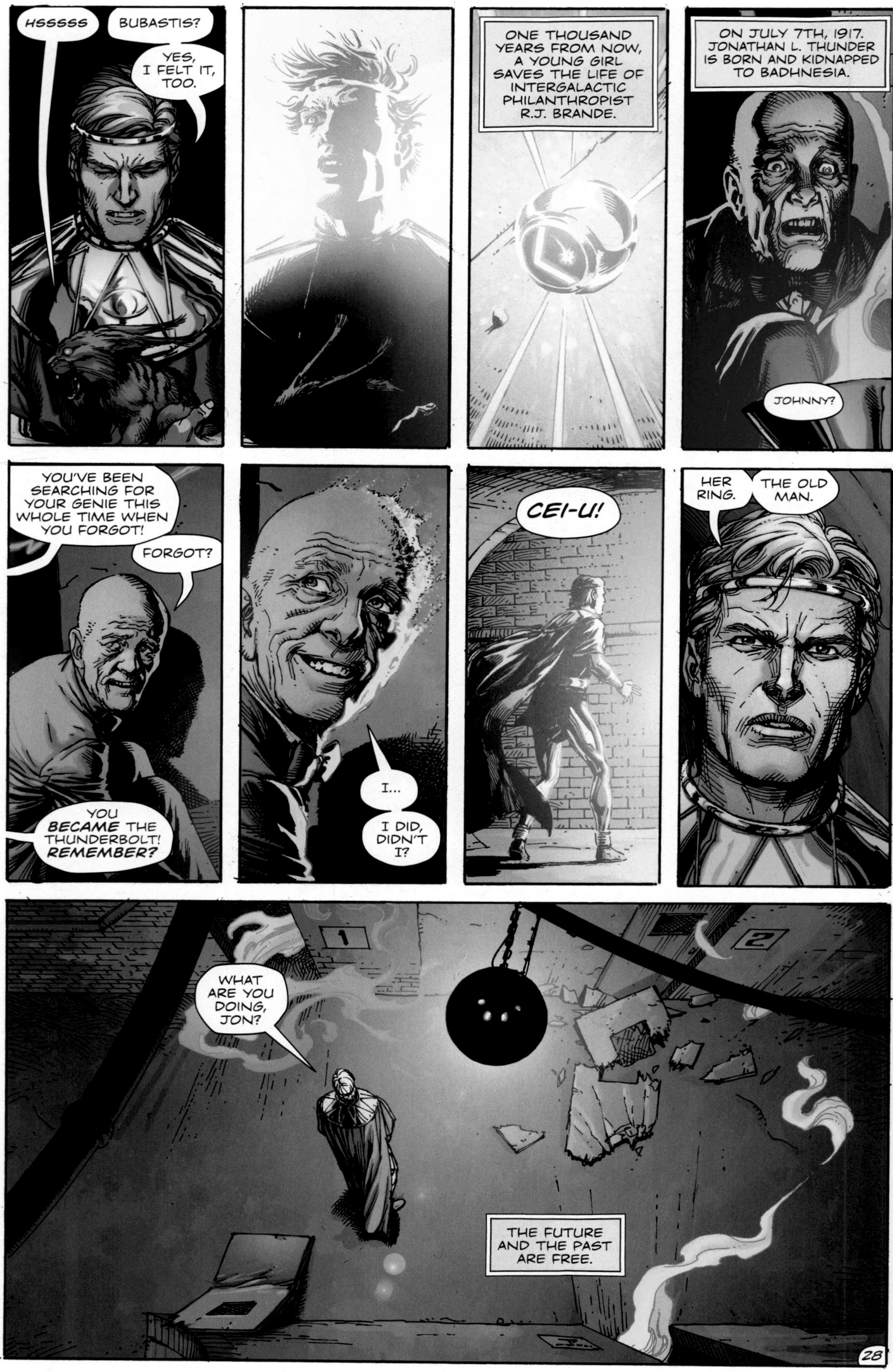
HSSSSS
BUBASTIS?
YES, I FELT IT, TOO.
ONE THOUSAND YEARS FROM NOW, A YOUNG GIRL SAVES THE LIFE OF INTERGALACTIC PHILANTHROPIST R.J. BRANDE.
ON JULY 7TH, 1917. JONATHAN L. THUNDER IS BORN AND KIDNAPPED TO BADHNESIA.
JOHNNY?
YOU'VE BEEN SEARCHING FOR YOUR GENIE THIS WHOLE TIME WHEN YOU FORGOT!
FORGOT?
YOU ***BECAME*** THE THUNDERBOLT! ***REMEMBER?***
I...
I DID, DIDN'T I?
CEI-U!
HER RING.
THE OLD MAN.
1
2
WHAT ARE YOU DOING, JON?
THE FUTURE AND THE PAST ARE FREE.

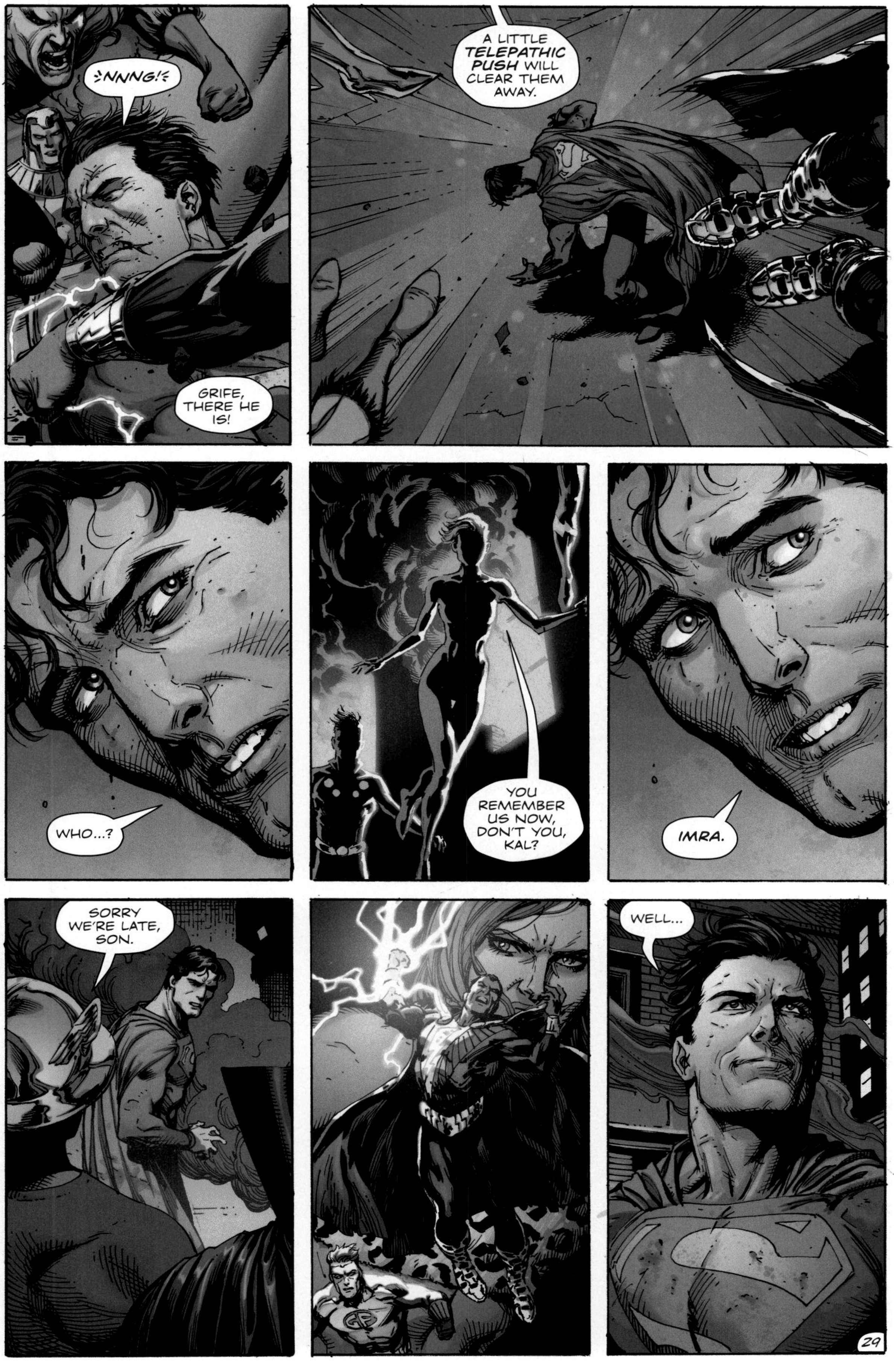

NNNG!
GRIFE, THERE HE IS!
A LITTLE TELEPATHIC PUSH WILL CLEAR THEM AWAY.
WHO...?
YOU REMEMBER US NOW, DON'T YOU, KAL?
IMRA.
SORRY WE'RE LATE, SON.
WELL...

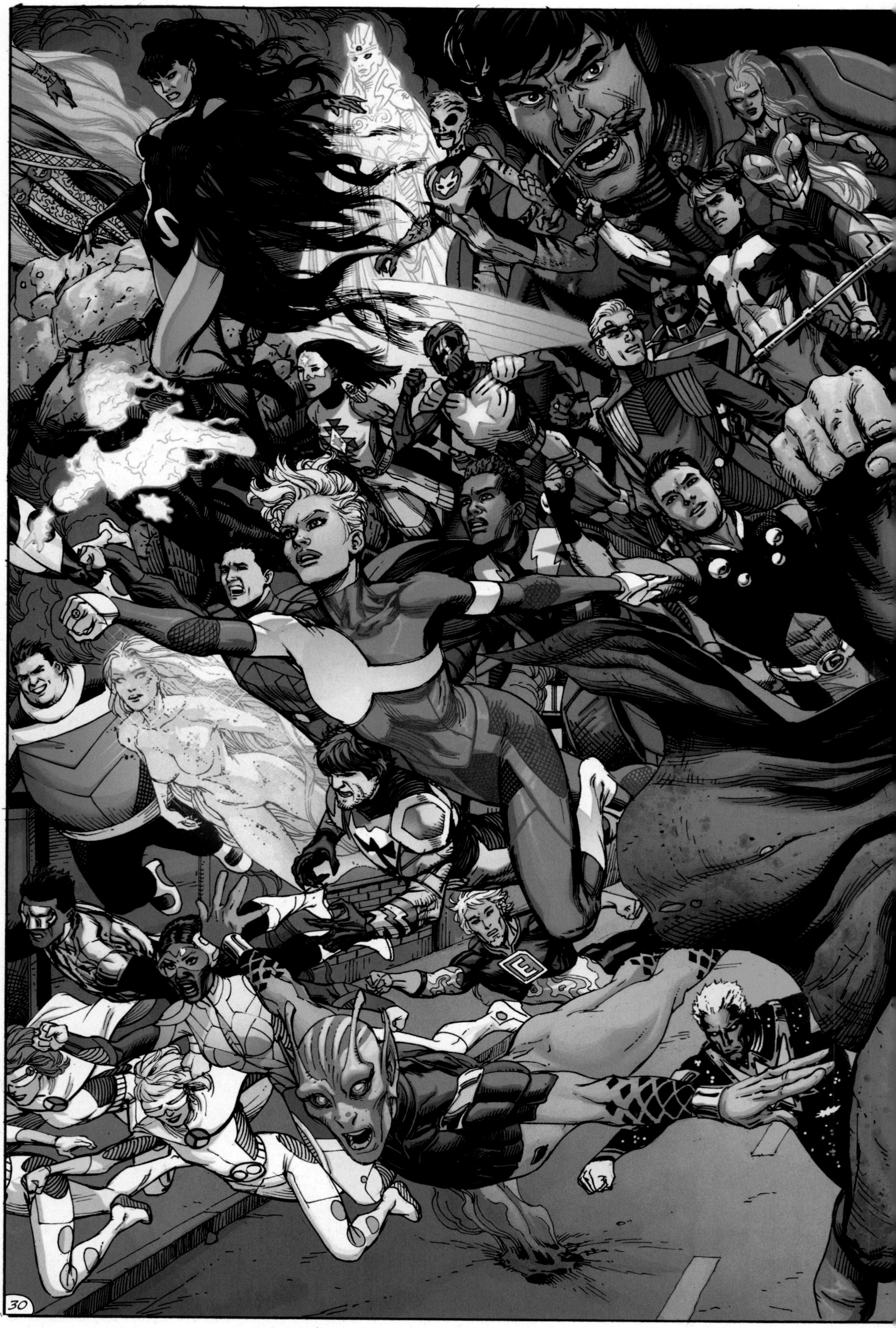

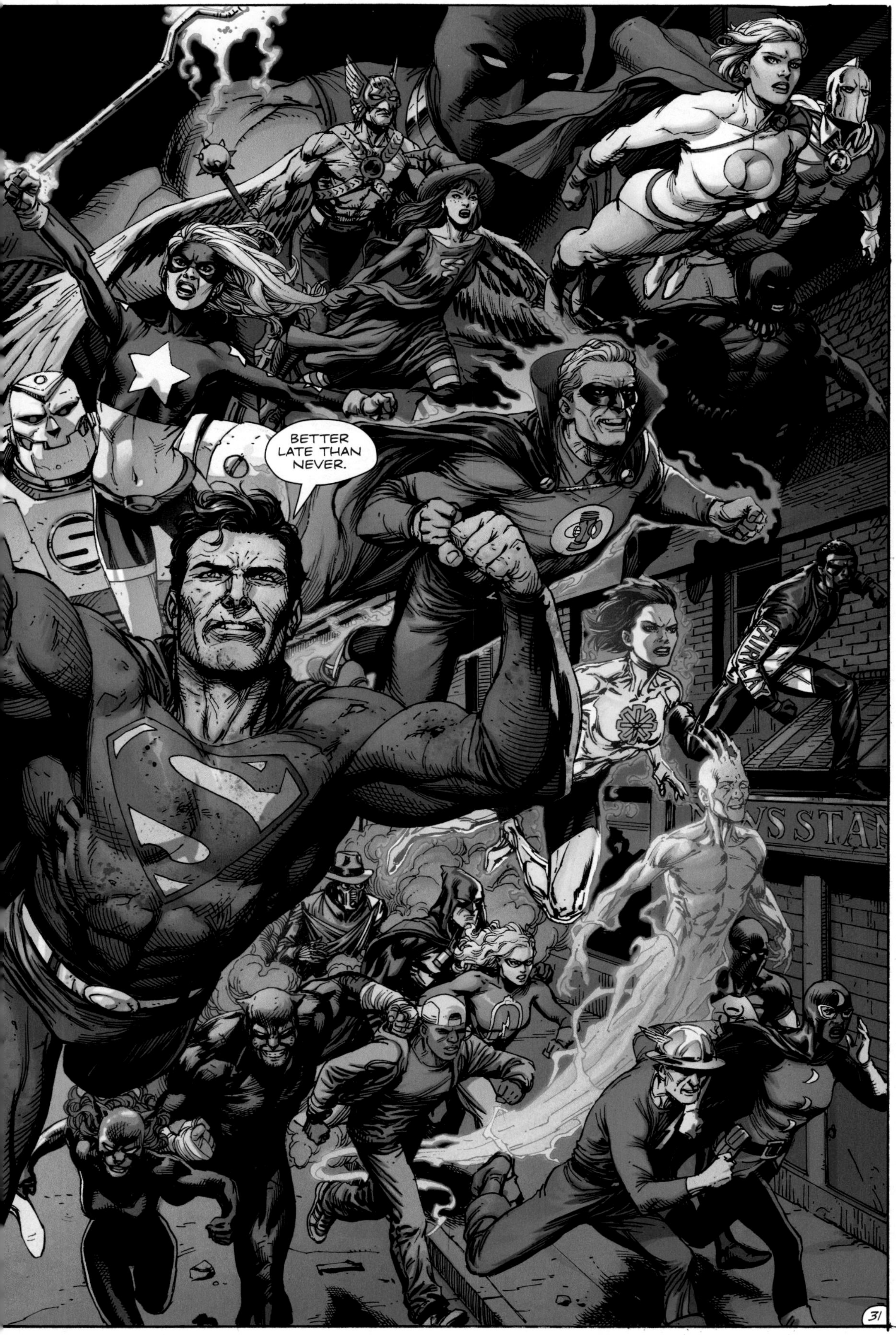
BETTER LATE THAN NEVER.
FAIRPLAY
NEWS STAN

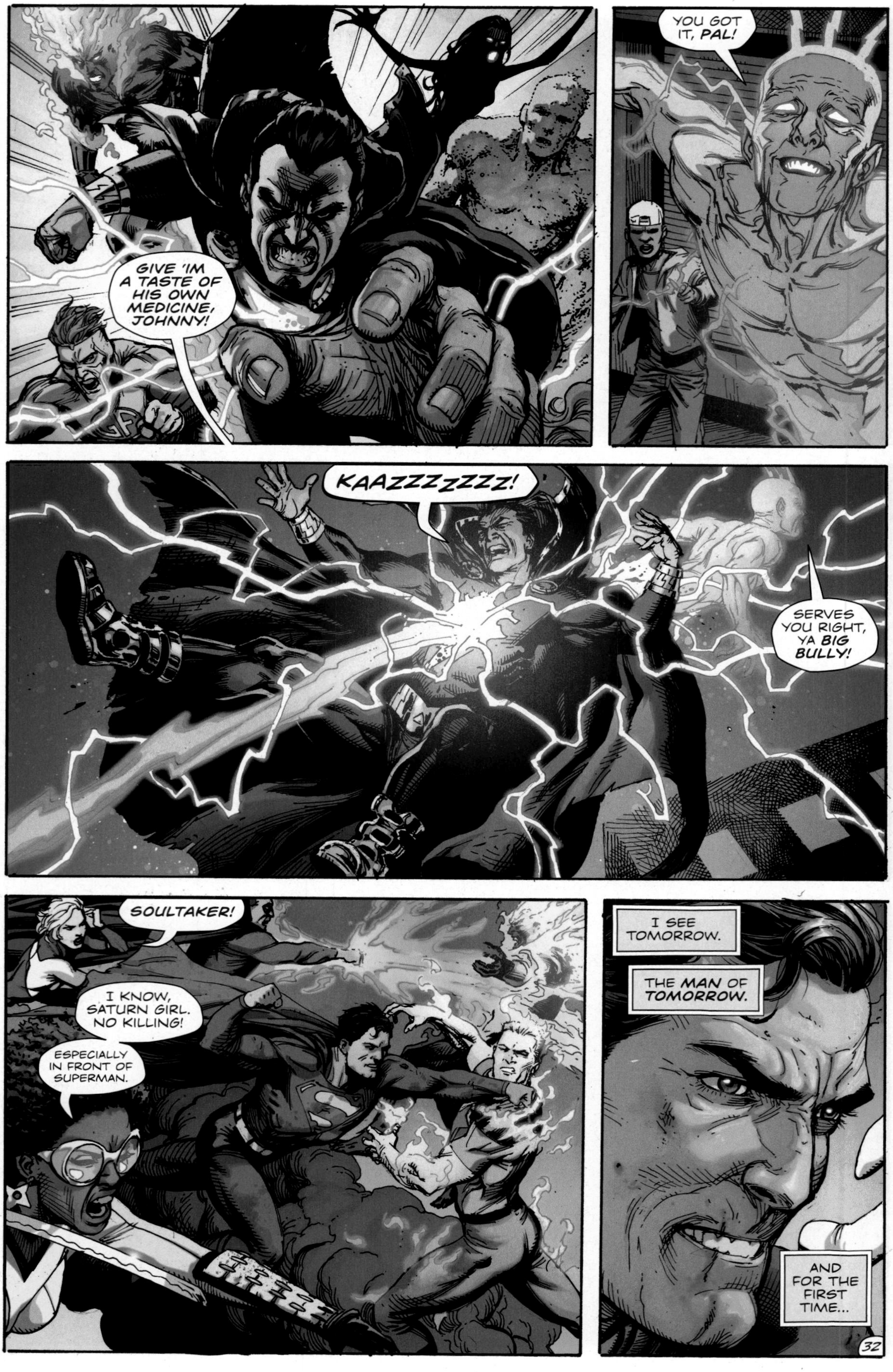
GIVE 'IM A TASTE OF HIS OWN MEDICINE, JOHNNY!
YOU GOT IT, PAL!
KAAZZZZZZZ!
SERVES YOU RIGHT, YA BIG BULLY!
SOULTAKER!
I KNOW, SATURN GIRL. NO KILLING!
ESPECIALLY IN FRONT OF SUPERMAN.
I SEE TOMORROW.
THE MAN OF TOMORROW.
AND FOR THE FIRST TIME...

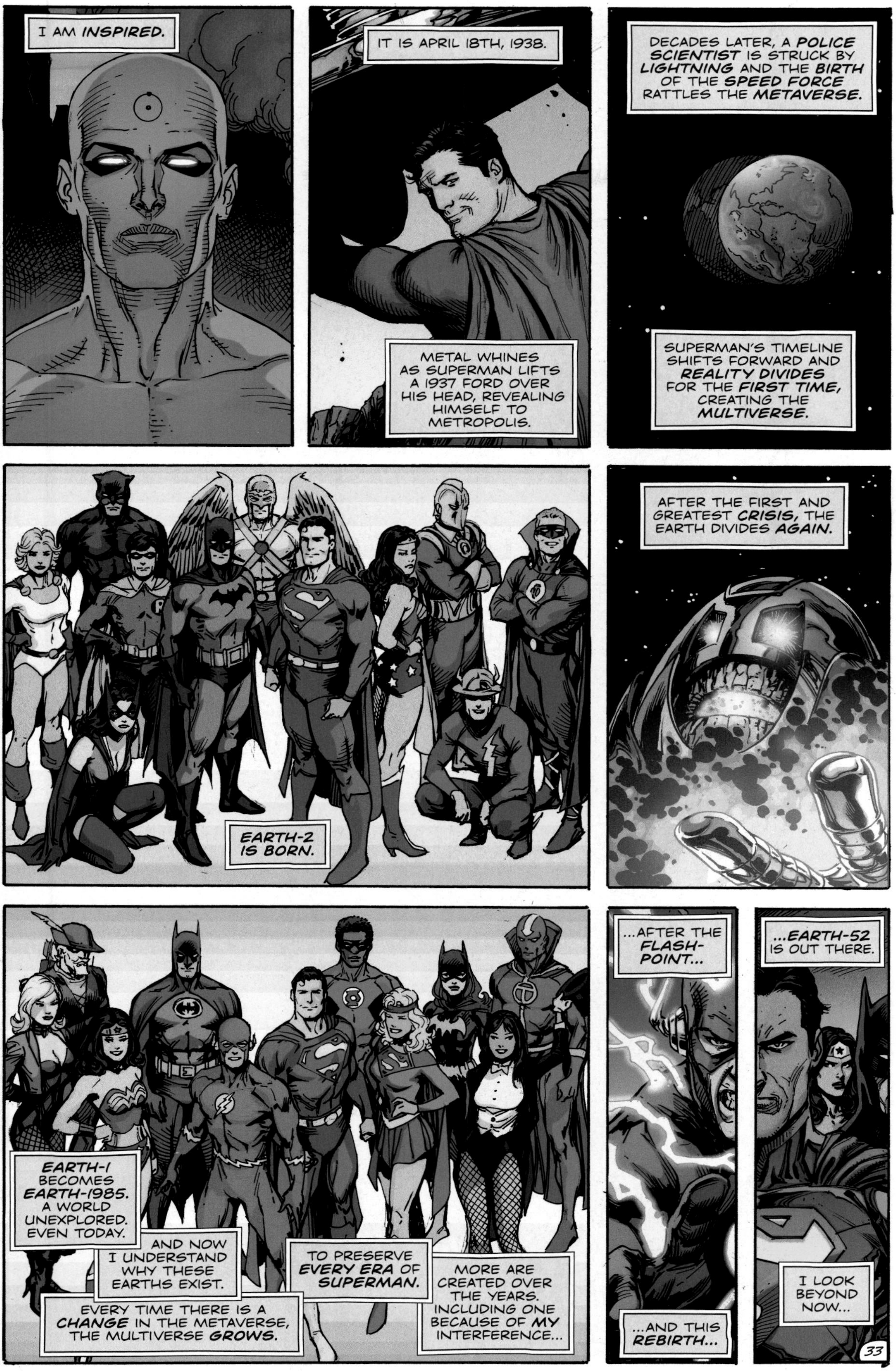

I AM INSPIRED.
IT IS APRIL 18TH, 1938.
METAL WHINES AS SUPERMAN LIFTS A 1937 FORD OVER HIS HEAD, REVEALING HIMSELF TO METROPOLIS.
DECADES LATER, A POLICE SCIENTIST IS STRUCK BY LIGHTNING AND THE BIRTH OF THE SPEED FORCE RATTLES THE METAVERSE.
SUPERMAN'S TIMELINE SHIFTS FORWARD AND REALITY DIVIDES FOR THE FIRST TIME, CREATING THE MULTIVERSE.
EARTH-2 IS BORN.
AFTER THE FIRST AND GREATEST CRISIS, THE EARTH DIVIDES AGAIN.
EARTH-1 BECOMES EARTH-1985. A WORLD UNEXPLORED. EVEN TODAY.
AND NOW I UNDERSTAND WHY THESE EARTHS EXIST.
EVERY TIME THERE IS A CHANGE IN THE METAVERSE, THE MULTIVERSE GROWS.
TO PRESERVE EVERY ERA OF SUPERMAN.
MORE ARE CREATED OVER THE YEARS. INCLUDING ONE BECAUSE OF MY INTERFERENCE...
...AFTER THE FLASH-POINT...
...AND THIS REBIRTH...
...EARTH-52 IS OUT THERE.
I LOOK BEYOND NOW...

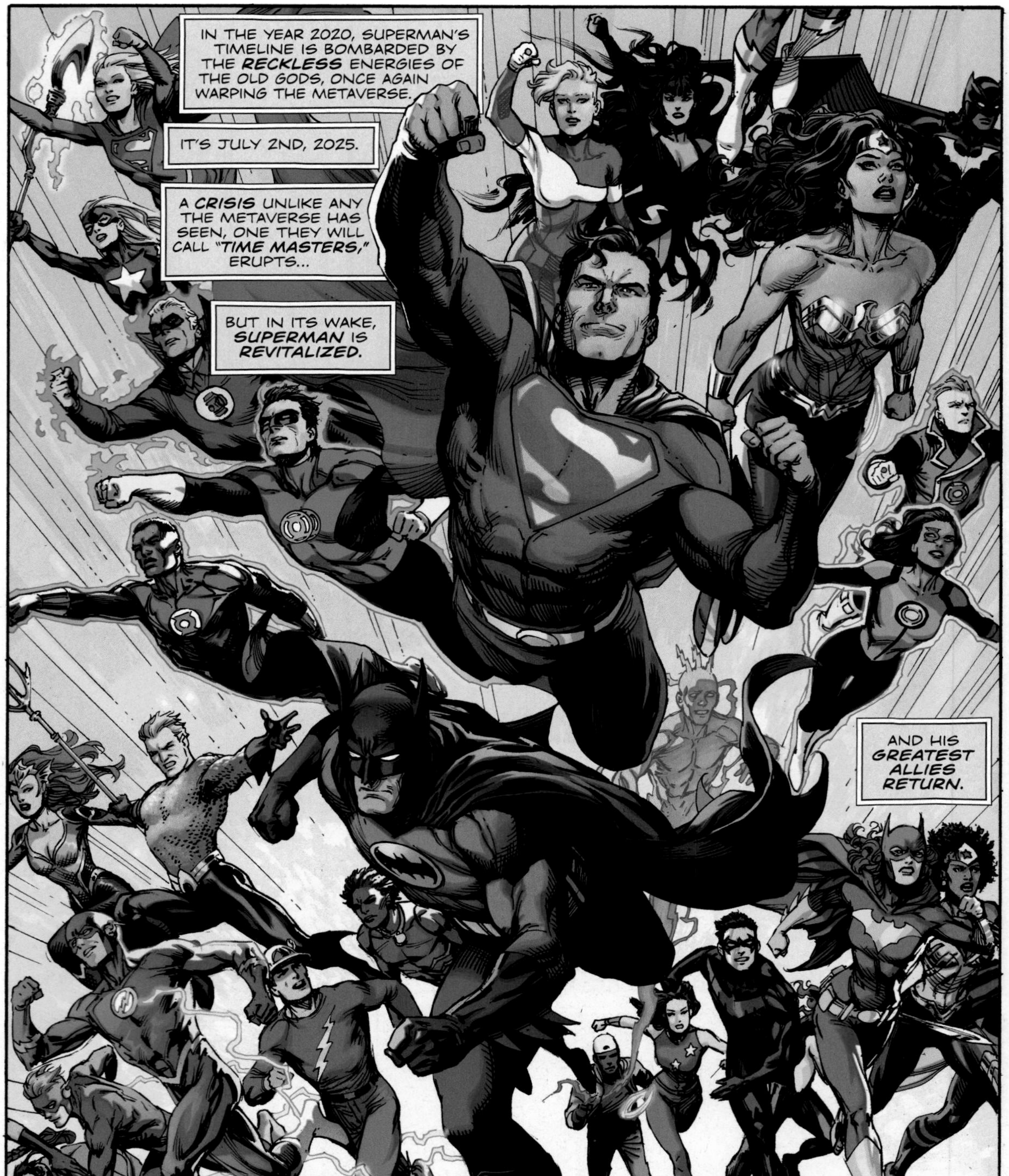
IN THE YEAR 2020, SUPERMAN'S TIMELINE IS BOMBARDED BY THE RECKLESS ENERGIES OF THE OLD GODS, ONCE AGAIN WARPING THE METAVERSE.
IT'S JULY 2ND, 2025.
A CRISIS UNLIKE ANY THE METAVERSE HAS SEEN, ONE THEY WILL CALL "TIME MASTERS," ERUPTS...
BUT IN ITS WAKE, SUPERMAN IS REVITALIZED.
AND HIS GREATEST ALLIES RETURN.
NO MATTER HOW MANY TIMES SUPERMAN'S EXISTENCE IS ATTACKED, HE WILL SURVIVE.
EVEN IF CHANGE IS A CONSTANT.
BECAUSE HOPE IS THE NORTH STAR OF THE METAVERSE.

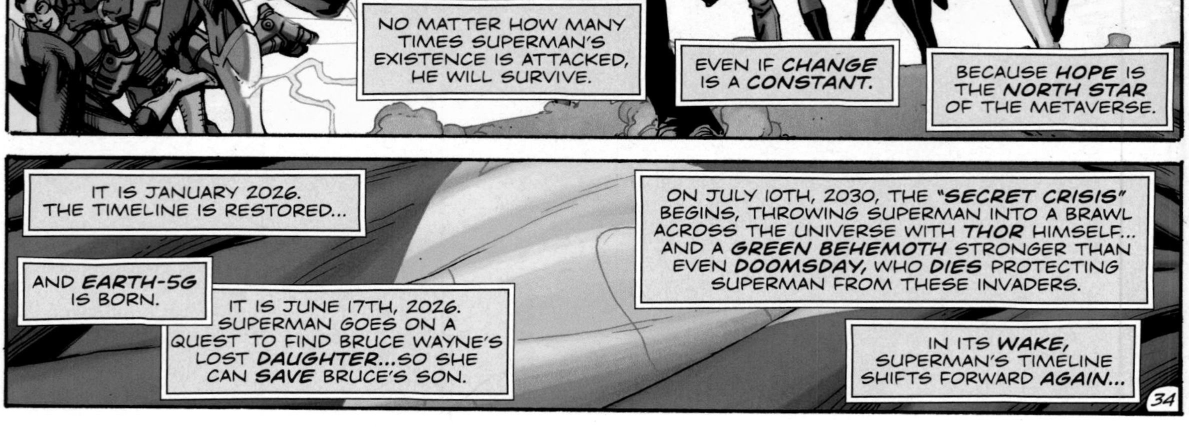
IT IS JANUARY 2026. THE TIMELINE IS RESTORED...
AND EARTH-5G IS BORN.
IT IS JUNE 17TH, 2026. SUPERMAN GOES ON A QUEST TO FIND BRUCE WAYNE'S LOST DAUGHTER...SO SHE CAN SAVE BRUCE'S SON.
ON JULY 10TH, 2030, THE "SECRET CRISIS" BEGINS, THROWING SUPERMAN INTO A BRAWL ACROSS THE UNIVERSE WITH THOR HIMSELF... AND A GREEN BEHEMOTH STRONGER THAN EVEN DOOMSDAY, WHO DIES PROTECTING SUPERMAN FROM THESE INVADERS.
IN ITS WAKE, SUPERMAN'S TIMELINE SHIFTS FORWARD AGAIN...

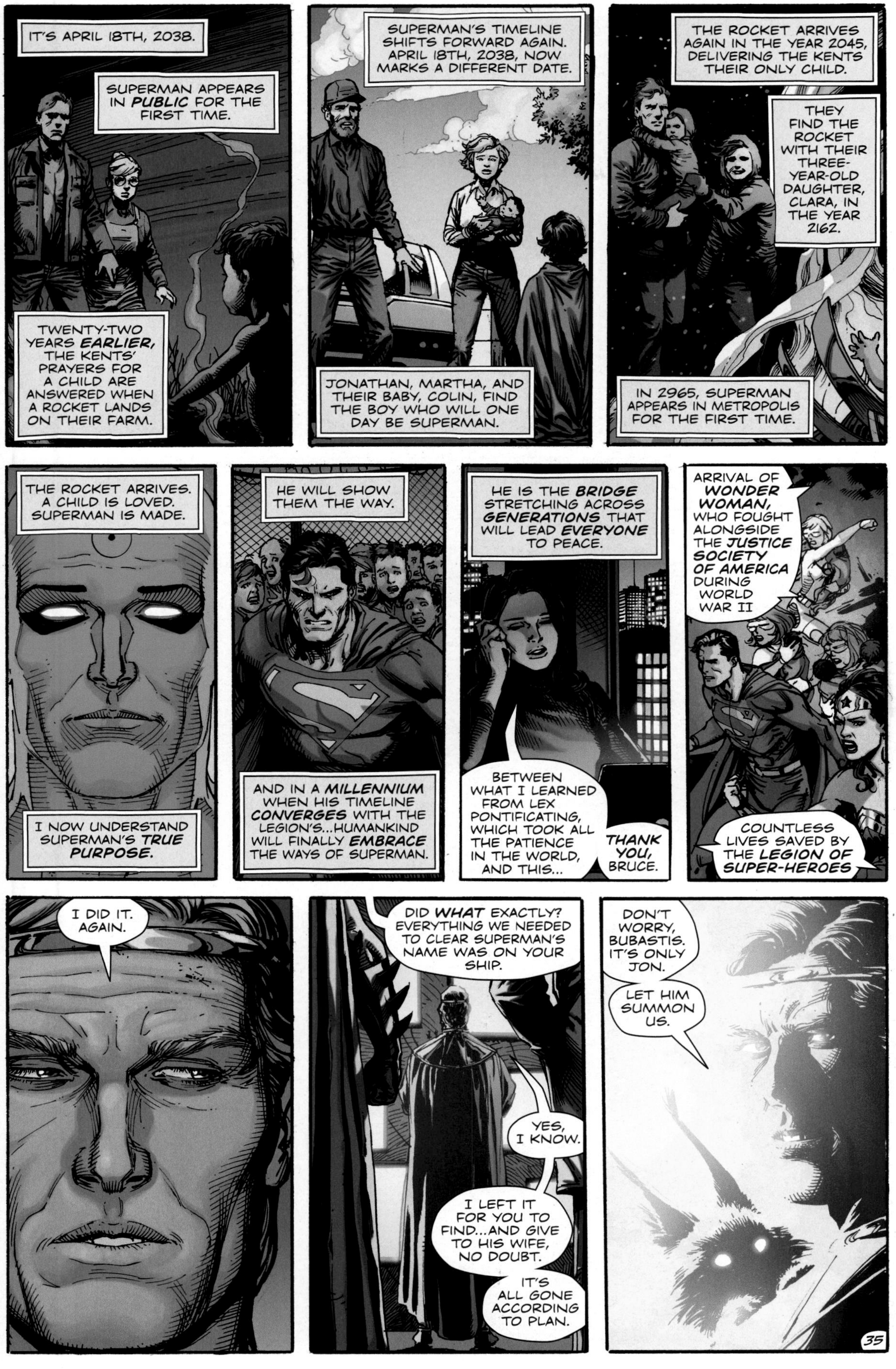
IT'S APRIL 18TH, 2038.
SUPERMAN APPEARS IN *PUBLIC* FOR THE FIRST TIME.
TWENTY-TWO YEARS *EARLIER,* THE KENTS' PRAYERS FOR A CHILD ARE ANSWERED WHEN A ROCKET LANDS ON THEIR FARM.
SUPERMAN'S TIMELINE SHIFTS FORWARD AGAIN. APRIL 18TH, 2038, NOW MARKS A DIFFERENT DATE.
JONATHAN, MARTHA, AND THEIR BABY, COLIN, FIND THE BOY WHO WILL ONE DAY BE SUPERMAN.
THE ROCKET ARRIVES AGAIN IN THE YEAR 2045, DELIVERING THE KENTS THEIR ONLY CHILD.
THEY FIND THE ROCKET WITH THEIR THREE-YEAR-OLD DAUGHTER, CLARA, IN THE YEAR 2162.
IN 2965, SUPERMAN APPEARS IN METROPOLIS FOR THE FIRST TIME.
THE ROCKET ARRIVES. A CHILD IS LOVED. SUPERMAN IS MADE.
I NOW UNDERSTAND SUPERMAN'S *TRUE PURPOSE.*
HE WILL SHOW THEM THE WAY.
AND IN A *MILLENNIUM* WHEN HIS TIMELINE *CONVERGES* WITH THE LEGION'S...HUMANKIND WILL FINALLY *EMBRACE* THE WAYS OF SUPERMAN.
HE IS THE *BRIDGE* STRETCHING ACROSS *GENERATIONS* THAT WILL LEAD *EVERYONE* TO PEACE.
BETWEEN WHAT I LEARNED FROM LEX PONTIFICATING, WHICH TOOK ALL THE PATIENCE IN THE WORLD, AND THIS...
THANK YOU, BRUCE.
ARRIVAL OF *WONDER WOMAN,* WHO FOUGHT ALONGSIDE THE *JUSTICE SOCIETY OF AMERICA* DURING WORLD WAR II
COUNTLESS LIVES SAVED BY THE *LEGION OF SUPER-HEROES*
I DID IT. AGAIN.
DID *WHAT* EXACTLY? EVERYTHING WE NEEDED TO CLEAR SUPERMAN'S NAME WAS ON YOUR SHIP.
YES, I KNOW.
I LEFT IT FOR YOU TO FIND...AND GIVE TO HIS WIFE, NO DOUBT.
IT'S ALL GONE ACCORDING TO PLAN.
DON'T WORRY, BUBASTIS. IT'S ONLY JON.
LET HIM SUMMON US.
35

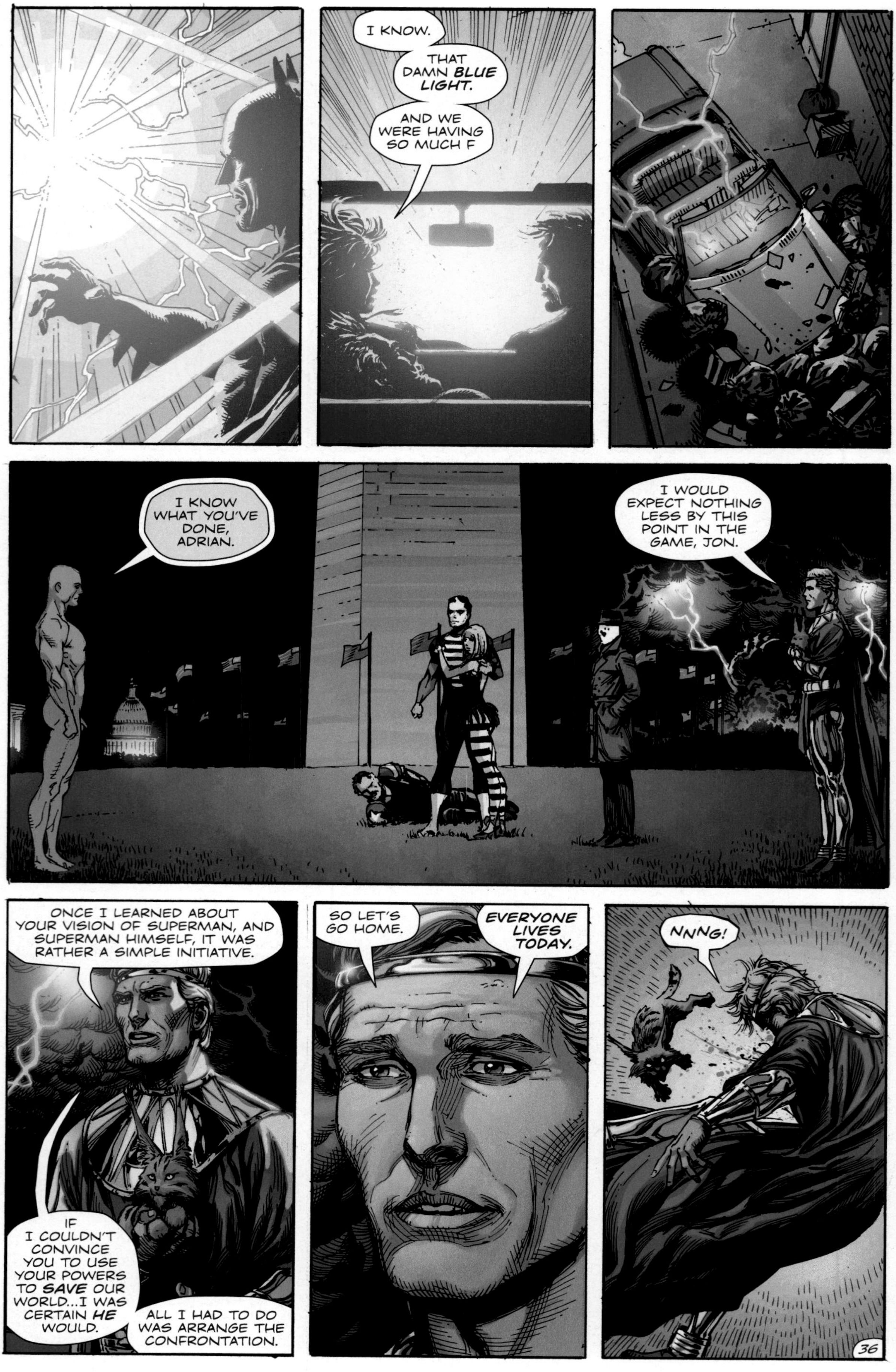
I KNOW.
THAT DAMN BLUE LIGHT.
AND WE WERE HAVING SO MUCH F
I KNOW WHAT YOU'VE DONE, ADRIAN.
I WOULD EXPECT NOTHING LESS BY THIS POINT IN THE GAME, JON.
ONCE I LEARNED ABOUT YOUR VISION OF SUPERMAN, AND SUPERMAN HIMSELF, IT WAS RATHER A SIMPLE INITIATIVE.
IF I COULDN'T CONVINCE YOU TO USE YOUR POWERS TO SAVE OUR WORLD...I WAS CERTAIN HE WOULD.
ALL I HAD TO DO WAS ARRANGE THE CONFRONTATION.
SO LET'S GO HOME.
EVERYONE LIVES TODAY.
NNNG!

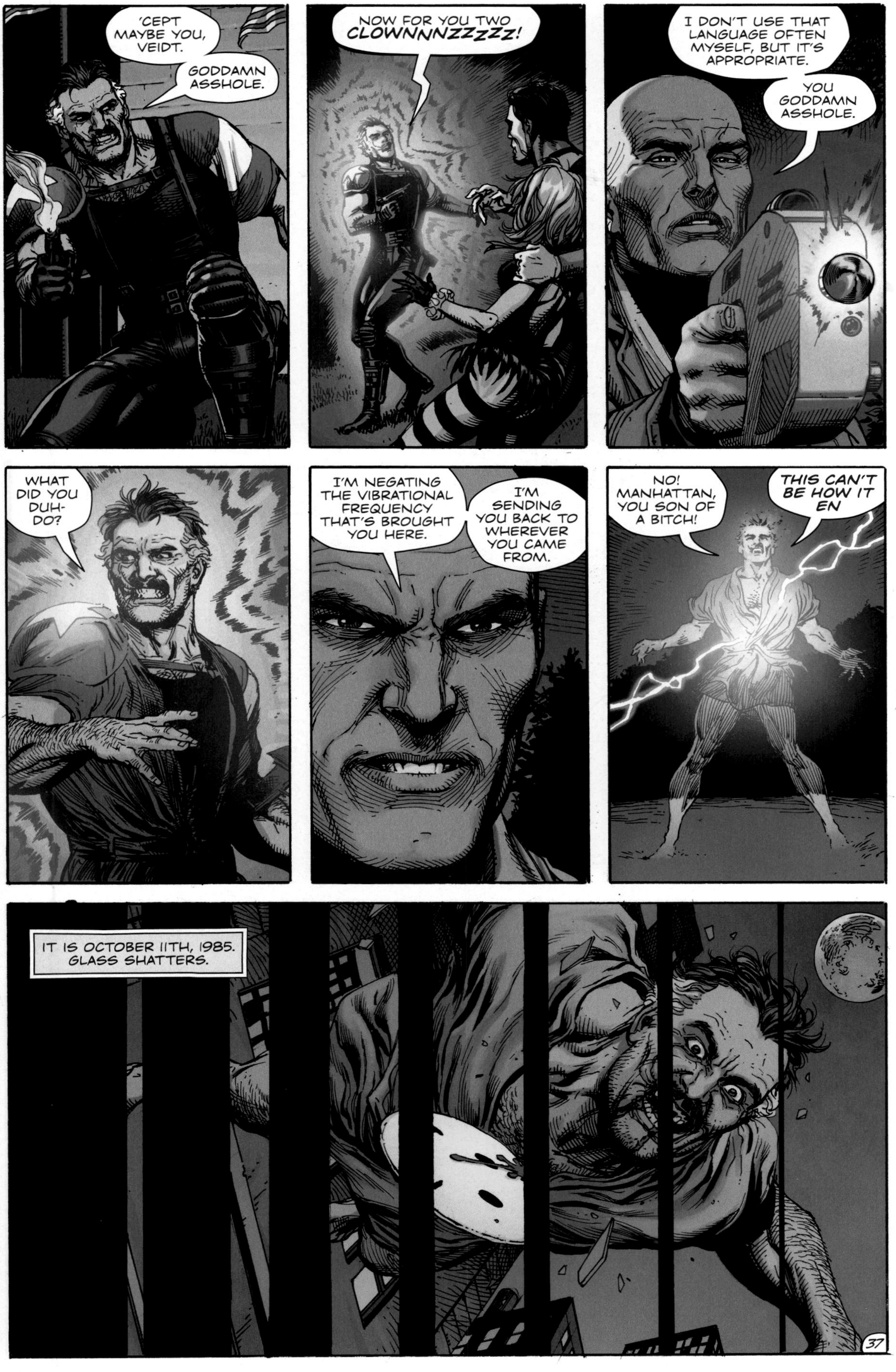
'CEPT MAYBE YOU, VEIDT.
GODDAMN ASSHOLE.
NOW FOR YOU TWO CLOWNNNZZZZZ!
I DON'T USE THAT LANGUAGE OFTEN MYSELF, BUT IT'S APPROPRIATE.
YOU GODDAMN ASSHOLE.
WHAT DID YOU DUH-DO?
I'M NEGATING THE VIBRATIONAL FREQUENCY THAT'S BROUGHT YOU HERE.
I'M SENDING YOU BACK TO WHEREVER YOU CAME FROM.
NO! MANHATTAN, YOU SON OF A BITCH!
THIS CAN'T BE HOW IT EN
IT IS OCTOBER 11TH, 1985. GLASS SHATTERS.

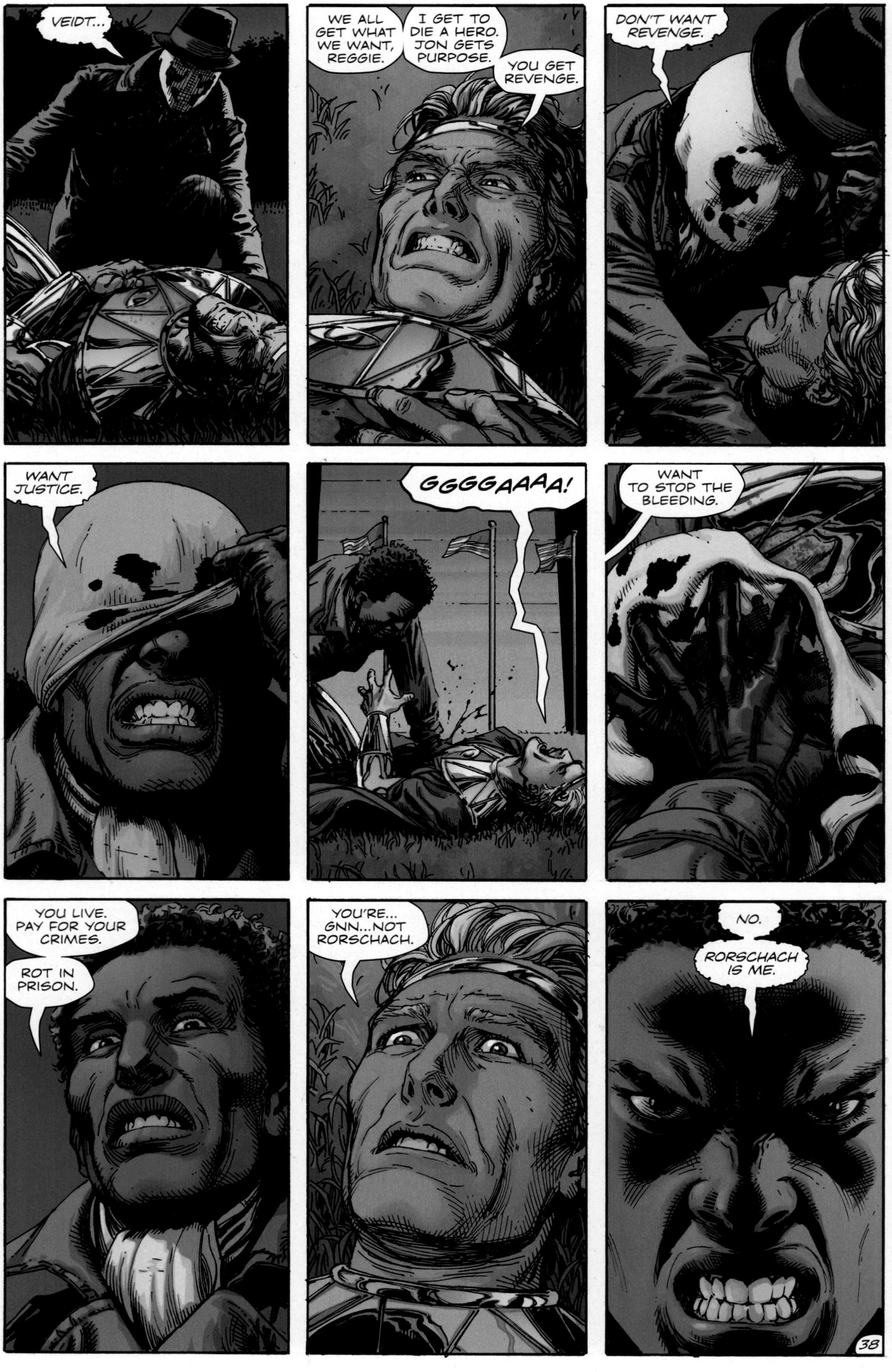
VEIDT...
WE ALL GET WHAT WE WANT, REGGIE.
I GET TO DIE A HERO. JON GETS PURPOSE.
YOU GET REVENGE.
DON'T WANT REVENGE.
WANT JUSTICE.
GGGGAAAA!
WANT TO STOP THE BLEEDING.
YOU LIVE. PAY FOR YOUR CRIMES.
ROT IN PRISON.
YOU'RE... GNN...NOT RORSCHACH.
NO.
RORSCHACH IS ME.

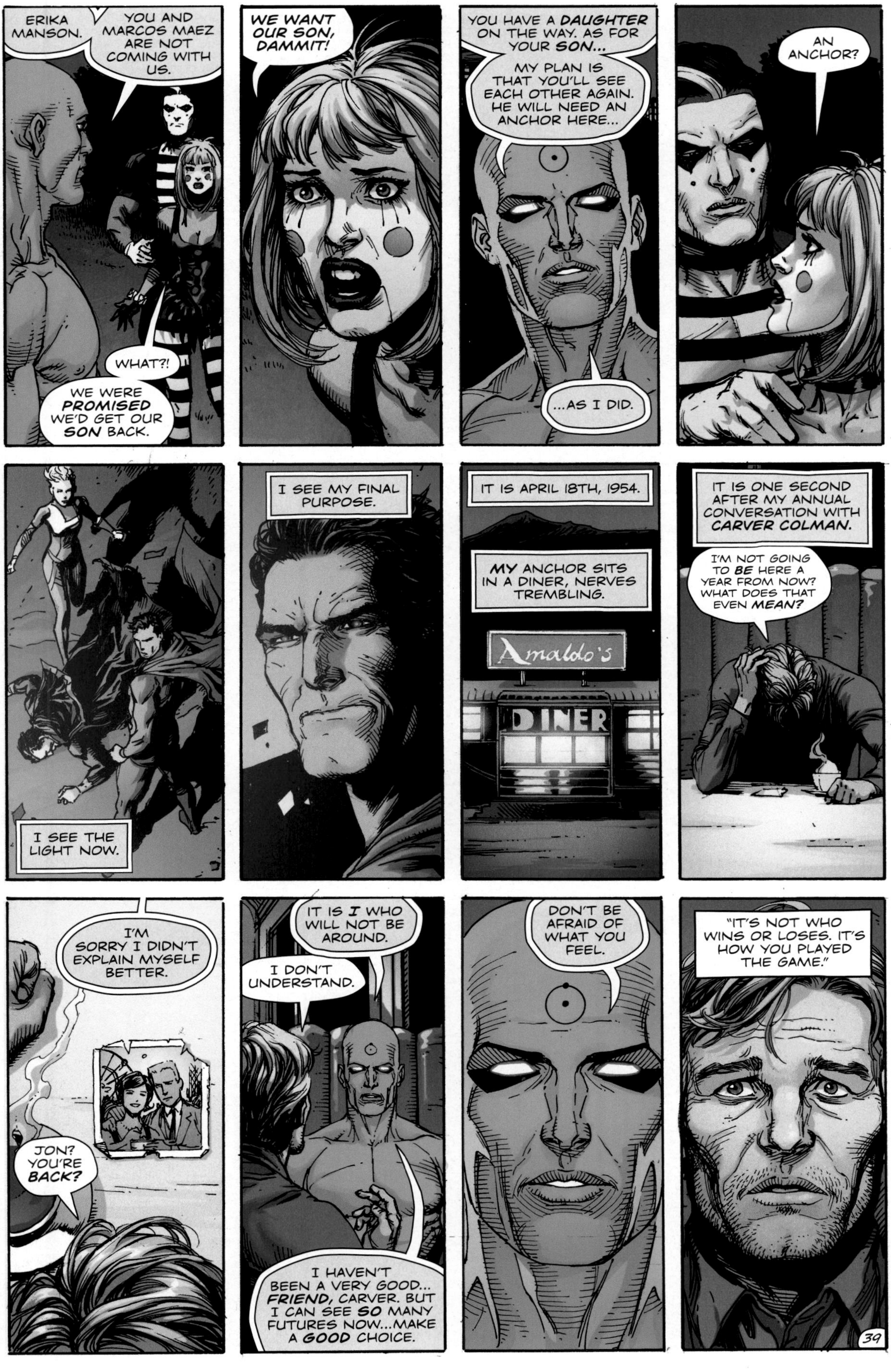
ERIKA MANSON.
YOU AND MARCOS MAEZ ARE NOT COMING WITH US.
WHAT?!
WE WERE PROMISED WE'D GET OUR SON BACK.
WE WANT OUR SON, DAMMIT!
YOU HAVE A DAUGHTER ON THE WAY. AS FOR YOUR SON...
MY PLAN IS THAT YOU'LL SEE EACH OTHER AGAIN. HE WILL NEED AN ANCHOR HERE...
...AS I DID.
AN ANCHOR?
I SEE THE LIGHT NOW.
I SEE MY FINAL PURPOSE.
IT IS APRIL 18TH, 1954.
MY ANCHOR SITS IN A DINER, NERVES TREMBLING.
Arnaldo's
DINER
IT IS ONE SECOND AFTER MY ANNUAL CONVERSATION WITH CARVER COLMAN.
I'M NOT GOING TO BE HERE A YEAR FROM NOW? WHAT DOES THAT EVEN MEAN?
I'M SORRY I DIDN'T EXPLAIN MYSELF BETTER.
JON? YOU'RE BACK?
IT IS I WHO WILL NOT BE AROUND.
I DON'T UNDERSTAND.
I HAVEN'T BEEN A VERY GOOD... FRIEND, CARVER. BUT I CAN SEE SO MANY FUTURES NOW...MAKE A GOOD CHOICE.
DON'T BE AFRAID OF WHAT YOU FEEL.
"IT'S NOT WHO WINS OR LOSES. IT'S HOW YOU PLAYED THE GAME."
39

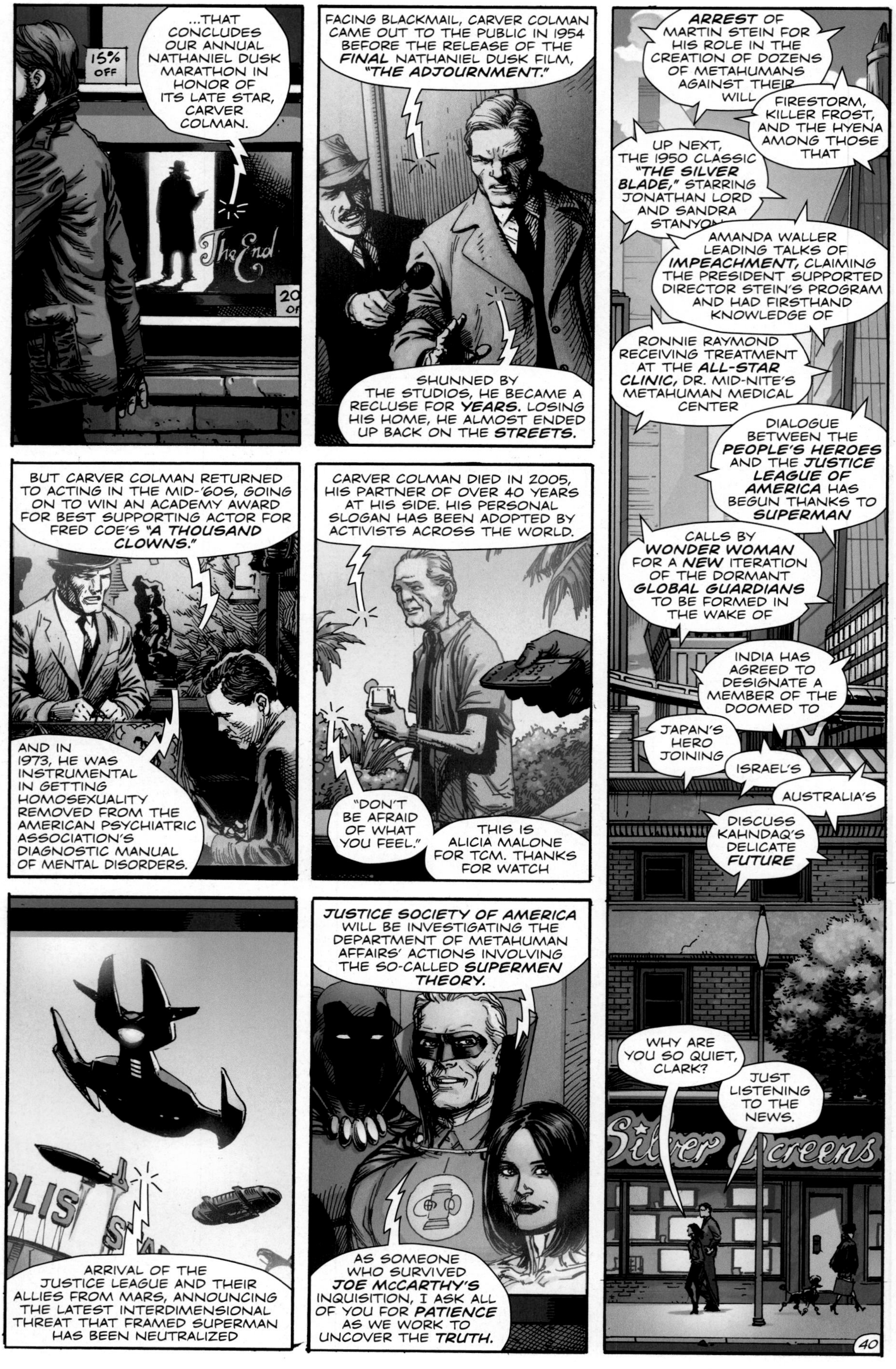
15% OFF
...THAT CONCLUDES OUR ANNUAL NATHANIEL DUSK MARATHON IN HONOR OF ITS LATE STAR, CARVER COLMAN.
The End
FACING BLACKMAIL, CARVER COLMAN CAME OUT TO THE PUBLIC IN 1954 BEFORE THE RELEASE OF THE FINAL NATHANIEL DUSK FILM, "THE ADJOURNMENT."
SHUNNED BY THE STUDIOS, HE BECAME A RECLUSE FOR YEARS. LOSING HIS HOME, HE ALMOST ENDED UP BACK ON THE STREETS.
BUT CARVER COLMAN RETURNED TO ACTING IN THE MID-'60S, GOING ON TO WIN AN ACADEMY AWARD FOR BEST SUPPORTING ACTOR FOR FRED COE'S "A THOUSAND CLOWNS."
AND IN 1973, HE WAS INSTRUMENTAL IN GETTING HOMOSEXUALITY REMOVED FROM THE AMERICAN PSYCHIATRIC ASSOCIATION'S DIAGNOSTIC MANUAL OF MENTAL DISORDERS.
CARVER COLMAN DIED IN 2005, HIS PARTNER OF OVER 40 YEARS AT HIS SIDE. HIS PERSONAL SLOGAN HAS BEEN ADOPTED BY ACTIVISTS ACROSS THE WORLD.
"DON'T BE AFRAID OF WHAT YOU FEEL."
THIS IS ALICIA MALONE FOR TCM. THANKS FOR WATCH
ARREST OF MARTIN STEIN FOR HIS ROLE IN THE CREATION OF DOZENS OF METAHUMANS AGAINST THEIR WILL
FIRESTORM, KILLER FROST, AND THE HYENA AMONG THOSE THAT
UP NEXT, THE 1950 CLASSIC "THE SILVER BLADE," STARRING JONATHAN LORD AND SANDRA STANYON
AMANDA WALLER LEADING TALKS OF IMPEACHMENT, CLAIMING THE PRESIDENT SUPPORTED DIRECTOR STEIN'S PROGRAM AND HAD FIRSTHAND KNOWLEDGE OF
RONNIE RAYMOND RECEIVING TREATMENT AT THE ALL-STAR CLINIC, DR. MID-NITE'S METAHUMAN MEDICAL CENTER
DIALOGUE BETWEEN THE PEOPLE'S HEROES AND THE JUSTICE LEAGUE OF AMERICA HAS BEGUN THANKS TO SUPERMAN
CALLS BY WONDER WOMAN FOR A NEW ITERATION OF THE DORMANT GLOBAL GUARDIANS TO BE FORMED IN THE WAKE OF
INDIA HAS AGREED TO DESIGNATE A MEMBER OF THE DOOMED TO
JAPAN'S HERO JOINING
ISRAEL'S
AUSTRALIA'S
DISCUSS KAHNDAQ'S DELICATE FUTURE
ARRIVAL OF THE JUSTICE LEAGUE AND THEIR ALLIES FROM MARS, ANNOUNCING THE LATEST INTERDIMENSIONAL THREAT THAT FRAMED SUPERMAN HAS BEEN NEUTRALIZED
JUSTICE SOCIETY OF AMERICA WILL BE INVESTIGATING THE DEPARTMENT OF METAHUMAN AFFAIRS' ACTIONS INVOLVING THE SO-CALLED SUPERMEN THEORY.
AS SOMEONE WHO SURVIVED JOE McCARTHY'S INQUISITION, I ASK ALL OF YOU FOR PATIENCE AS WE WORK TO UNCOVER THE TRUTH.
WHY ARE YOU SO QUIET, CLARK?
JUST LISTENING TO THE NEWS.
Silver Screens
40

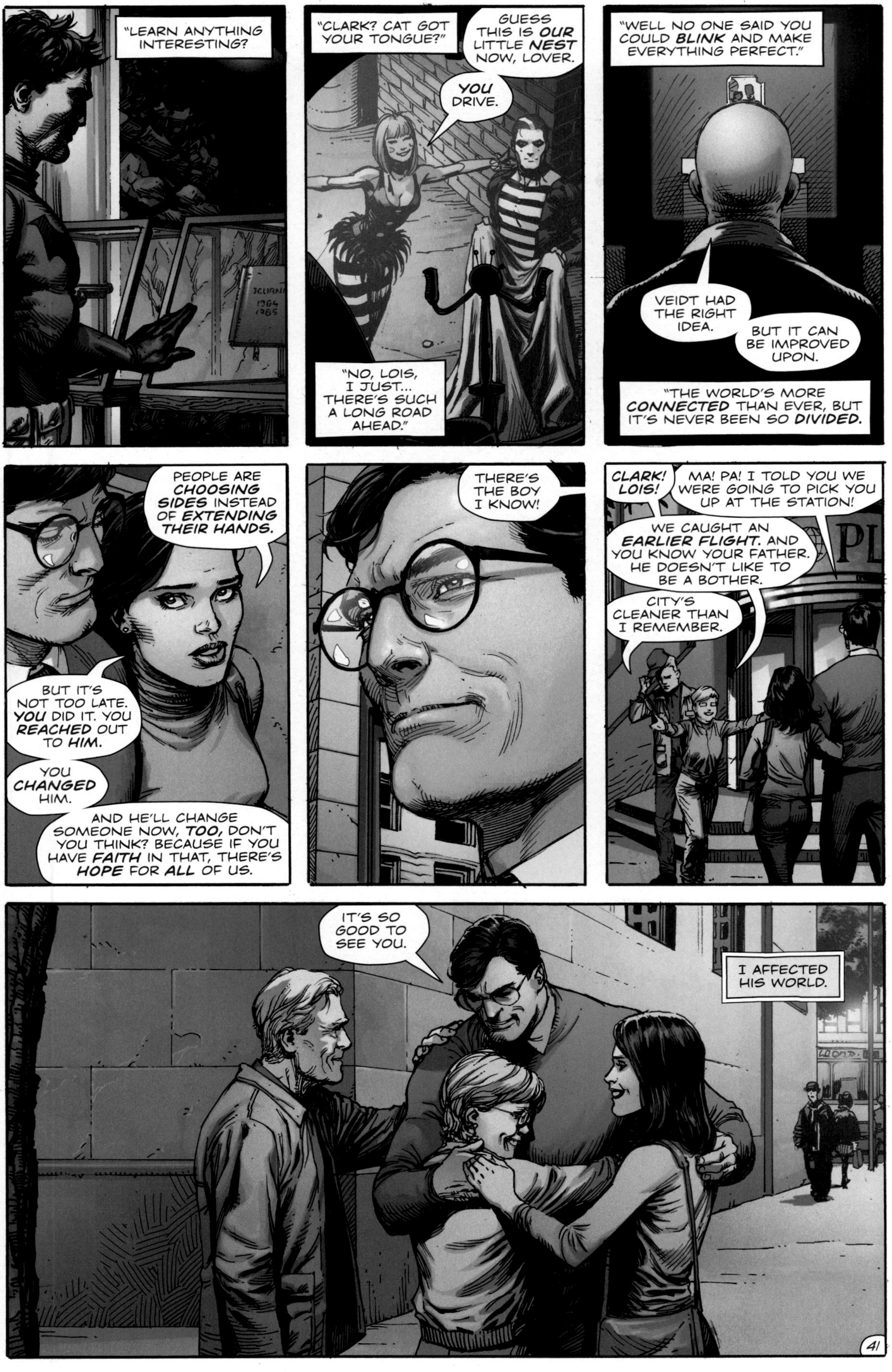
"LEARN ANYTHING INTERESTING?
JOURNAL 1964 1985
"CLARK? CAT GOT YOUR TONGUE?"
GUESS THIS IS OUR LITTLE NEST NOW, LOVER.
YOU DRIVE.
"NO, LOIS, I JUST... THERE'S SUCH A LONG ROAD AHEAD."
"WELL NO ONE SAID YOU COULD BLINK AND MAKE EVERYTHING PERFECT."
VEIDT HAD THE RIGHT IDEA.
BUT IT CAN BE IMPROVED UPON.
"THE WORLD'S MORE CONNECTED THAN EVER, BUT IT'S NEVER BEEN SO DIVIDED.
PEOPLE ARE CHOOSING SIDES INSTEAD OF EXTENDING THEIR HANDS.
BUT IT'S NOT TOO LATE. YOU DID IT. YOU REACHED OUT TO HIM.
YOU CHANGED HIM.
AND HE'LL CHANGE SOMEONE NOW, TOO, DON'T YOU THINK? BECAUSE IF YOU HAVE FAITH IN THAT, THERE'S HOPE FOR ALL OF US.
THERE'S THE BOY I KNOW!
CLARK! LOIS!
MA! PA! I TOLD YOU WE WERE GOING TO PICK YOU UP AT THE STATION!
WE CAUGHT AN EARLIER FLIGHT. AND YOU KNOW YOUR FATHER. HE DOESN'T LIKE TO BE A BOTHER.
CITY'S CLEANER THAN I REMEMBER.
IT'S SO GOOD TO SEE YOU.
I AFFECTED HIS WORLD.

AND NOW HE WILL AFFECT MINE.

IT IS NOVEMBER 22ND, 1992. VEIDT'S PLAN HAS BLOWN UP IN THE WORLD'S FACE.

THE ASH IS STILL WARM UNDER MY FEET.

THE TACHYONS FROM THE OWL SHIP DEPARTING ARE STILL DISSIPATING.

IT IS 1945. THE COGS FLY INTO THE AIR.

IT IS 1959. I FIX JANEY'S WATCH.

IT IS 1992. I SEE A LIGHT.

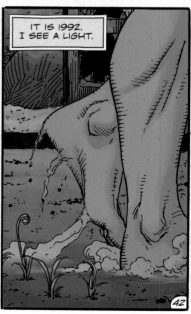

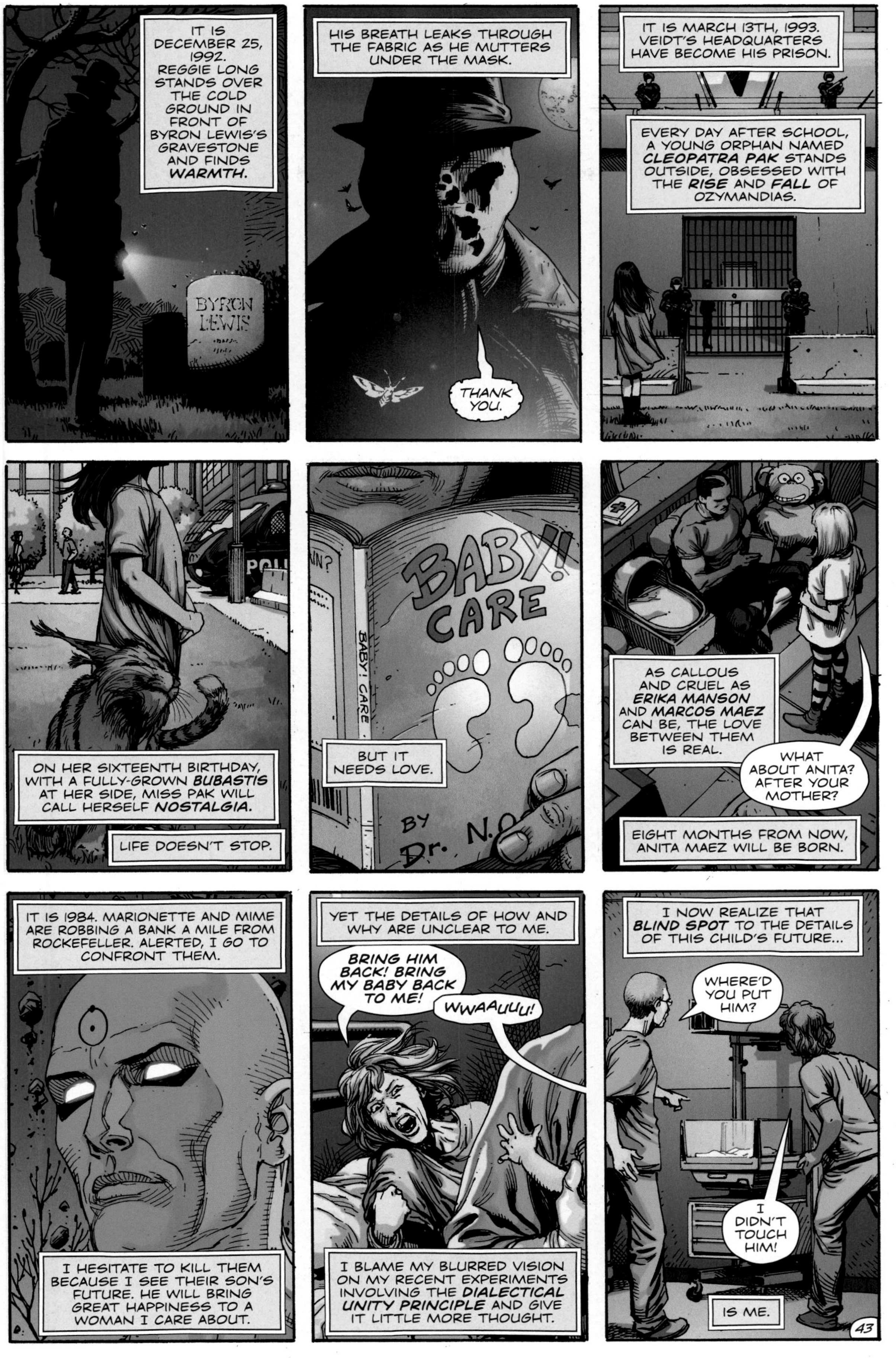
IT IS DECEMBER 25, 1992. REGGIE LONG STANDS OVER THE COLD GROUND IN FRONT OF BYRON LEWIS'S GRAVESTONE AND FINDS **WARMTH.**
BYRON LEWIS
HIS BREATH LEAKS THROUGH THE FABRIC AS HE MUTTERS UNDER THE MASK.
THANK YOU.
IT IS MARCH 13TH, 1993. VEIDT'S HEADQUARTERS HAVE BECOME HIS PRISON.
EVERY DAY AFTER SCHOOL, A YOUNG ORPHAN NAMED ***CLEOPATRA PAK*** STANDS OUTSIDE, OBSESSED WITH THE ***RISE*** AND ***FALL*** OF OZYMANDIAS.
ON HER SIXTEENTH BIRTHDAY, WITH A FULLY-GROWN ***BUBASTIS*** AT HER SIDE, MISS PAK WILL CALL HERSELF ***NOSTALGIA.***
LIFE DOESN'T STOP.
BABY! CARE
BABY! CARE
BY Dr. N.
BUT IT NEEDS LOVE.
AS CALLOUS AND CRUEL AS ***ERIKA MANSON*** AND ***MARCOS MAEZ*** CAN BE, THE LOVE BETWEEN THEM IS REAL.
WHAT ABOUT ANITA? AFTER YOUR MOTHER?
EIGHT MONTHS FROM NOW, ANITA MAEZ WILL BE BORN.
IT IS 1984. MARIONETTE AND MIME ARE ROBBING A BANK A MILE FROM ROCKEFELLER. ALERTED, I GO TO CONFRONT THEM.
I HESITATE TO KILL THEM BECAUSE I SEE THEIR SON'S FUTURE. HE WILL BRING GREAT HAPPINESS TO A WOMAN I CARE ABOUT.
YET THE DETAILS OF HOW AND WHY ARE UNCLEAR TO ME.
BRING HIM BACK! BRING MY BABY BACK TO ME!
WWAAUUU!
I BLAME MY BLURRED VISION ON MY RECENT EXPERIMENTS INVOLVING THE ***DIALECTICAL UNITY PRINCIPLE*** AND GIVE IT LITTLE MORE THOUGHT.
I NOW REALIZE THAT ***BLIND SPOT*** TO THE DETAILS OF THIS CHILD'S FUTURE...
WHERE'D YOU PUT HIM?
I DIDN'T TOUCH HIM!
IS ME.

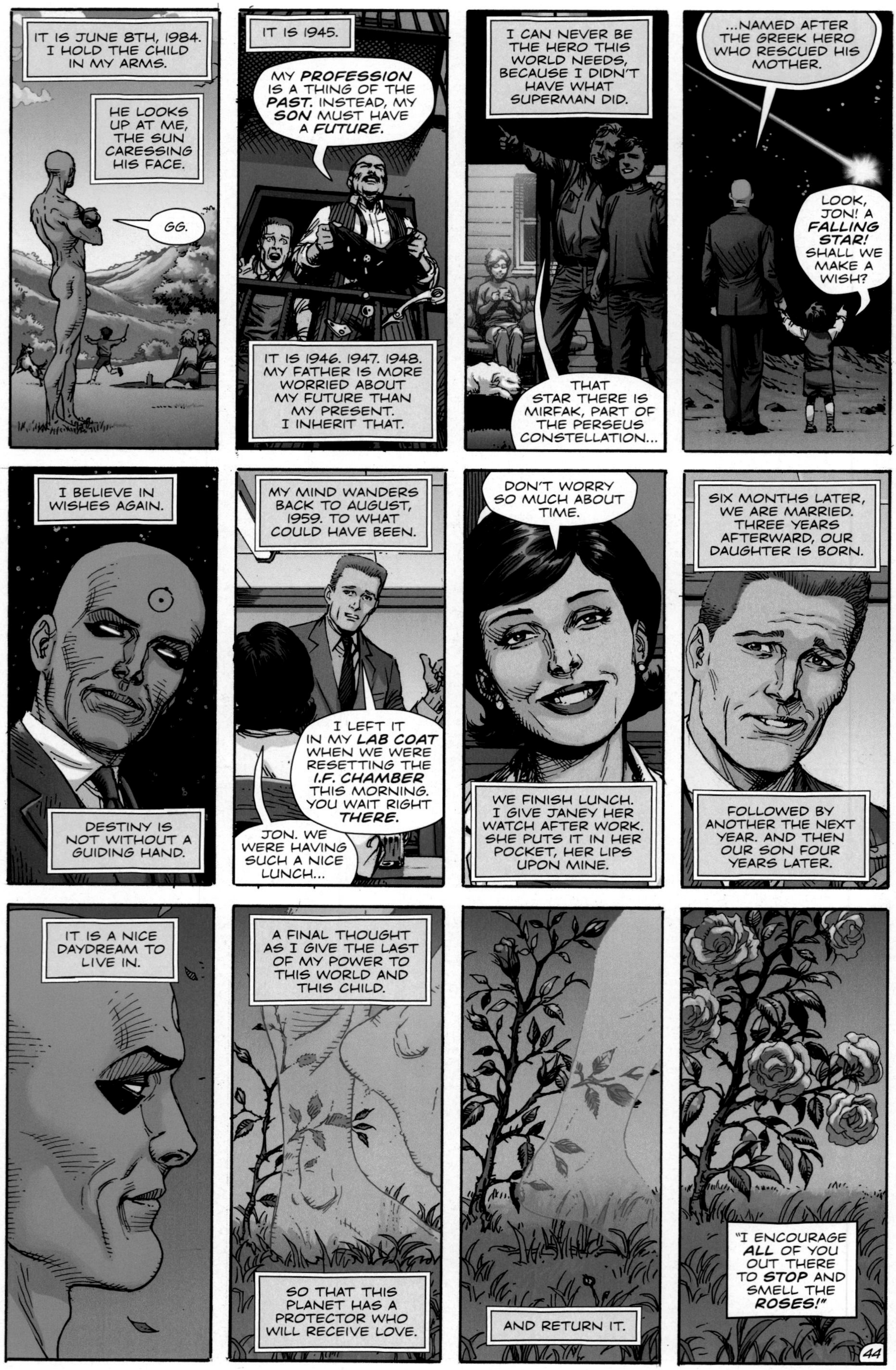
IT IS JUNE 8TH, 1984. I HOLD THE CHILD IN MY ARMS.
HE LOOKS UP AT ME, THE SUN CARESSING HIS FACE.
GG.
IT IS 1945.
MY **PROFESSION** IS A THING OF THE **PAST.** INSTEAD, MY **SON** MUST HAVE A **FUTURE.**
IT IS 1946. 1947. 1948. MY FATHER IS MORE WORRIED ABOUT MY FUTURE THAN MY PRESENT. I INHERIT THAT.
I CAN NEVER BE THE HERO THIS WORLD NEEDS, BECAUSE I DIDN'T HAVE WHAT SUPERMAN DID.
THAT STAR THERE IS MIRFAK, PART OF THE PERSEUS CONSTELLATION...
...NAMED AFTER THE GREEK HERO WHO RESCUED HIS MOTHER.
LOOK, JON! A ***FALLING STAR!*** SHALL WE MAKE A WISH?
I BELIEVE IN WISHES AGAIN.
DESTINY IS NOT WITHOUT A GUIDING HAND.
MY MIND WANDERS BACK TO AUGUST, 1959. TO WHAT COULD HAVE BEEN.
I LEFT IT IN MY ***LAB COAT*** WHEN WE WERE RESETTING THE ***I.F. CHAMBER*** THIS MORNING. YOU WAIT RIGHT ***THERE.***
JON. WE WERE HAVING SUCH A NICE LUNCH...
DON'T WORRY SO MUCH ABOUT TIME.
WE FINISH LUNCH. I GIVE JANEY HER WATCH AFTER WORK. SHE PUTS IT IN HER POCKET, HER LIPS UPON MINE.
SIX MONTHS LATER, WE ARE MARRIED. THREE YEARS AFTERWARD, OUR DAUGHTER IS BORN.
FOLLOWED BY ANOTHER THE NEXT YEAR. AND THEN OUR SON FOUR YEARS LATER.
IT IS A NICE DAYDREAM TO LIVE IN.
A FINAL THOUGHT AS I GIVE THE LAST OF MY POWER TO THIS WORLD AND THIS CHILD.
SO THAT THIS PLANET HAS A PROTECTOR WHO WILL RECEIVE LOVE.
AND RETURN IT.
"I ENCOURAGE ***ALL*** OF YOU OUT THERE TO ***STOP*** AND SMELL THE ***ROSES!***"
44

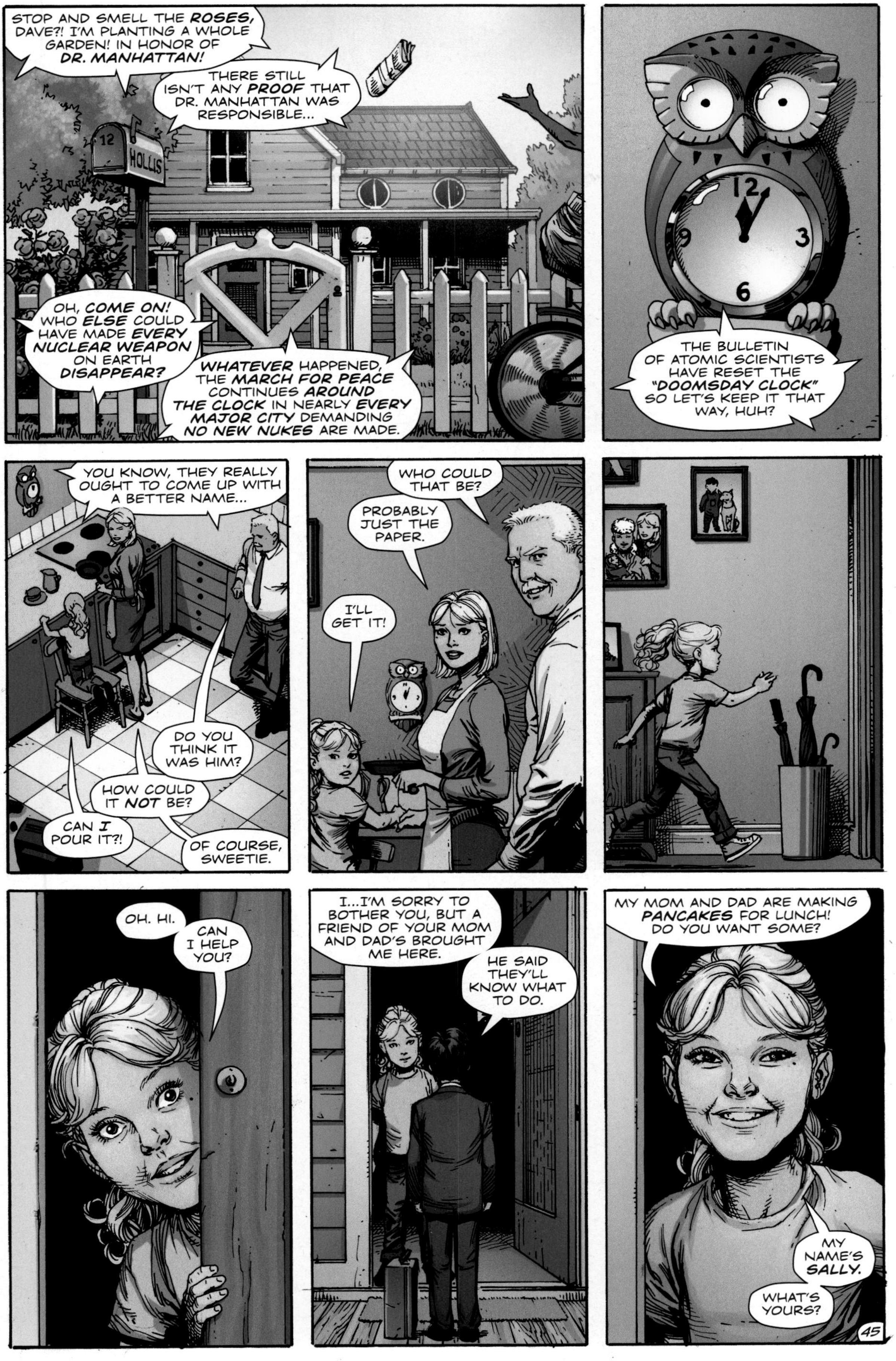
STOP AND SMELL THE ROSES, DAVE?! I'M PLANTING A WHOLE GARDEN! IN HONOR OF DR. MANHATTAN!
THERE STILL ISN'T ANY PROOF THAT DR. MANHATTAN WAS RESPONSIBLE...
12
HOLLIS
OH, COME ON! WHO ELSE COULD HAVE MADE EVERY NUCLEAR WEAPON ON EARTH DISAPPEAR?
WHATEVER HAPPENED, THE MARCH FOR PEACE CONTINUES AROUND THE CLOCK IN NEARLY EVERY MAJOR CITY DEMANDING NO NEW NUKES ARE MADE.
12
9
3
6
THE BULLETIN OF ATOMIC SCIENTISTS HAVE RESET THE "DOOMSDAY CLOCK" SO LET'S KEEP IT THAT WAY, HUH?
YOU KNOW, THEY REALLY OUGHT TO COME UP WITH A BETTER NAME...
DO YOU THINK IT WAS HIM?
HOW COULD IT NOT BE?
CAN I POUR IT?!
OF COURSE, SWEETIE.
WHO COULD THAT BE?
PROBABLY JUST THE PAPER.
I'LL GET IT!
OH. HI.
CAN I HELP YOU?
I...I'M SORRY TO BOTHER YOU, BUT A FRIEND OF YOUR MOM AND DAD'S BROUGHT ME HERE.
HE SAID THEY'LL KNOW WHAT TO DO.
MY MOM AND DAD ARE MAKING PANCAKES FOR LUNCH! DO YOU WANT SOME?
MY NAME'S SALLY.
WHAT'S YOURS?

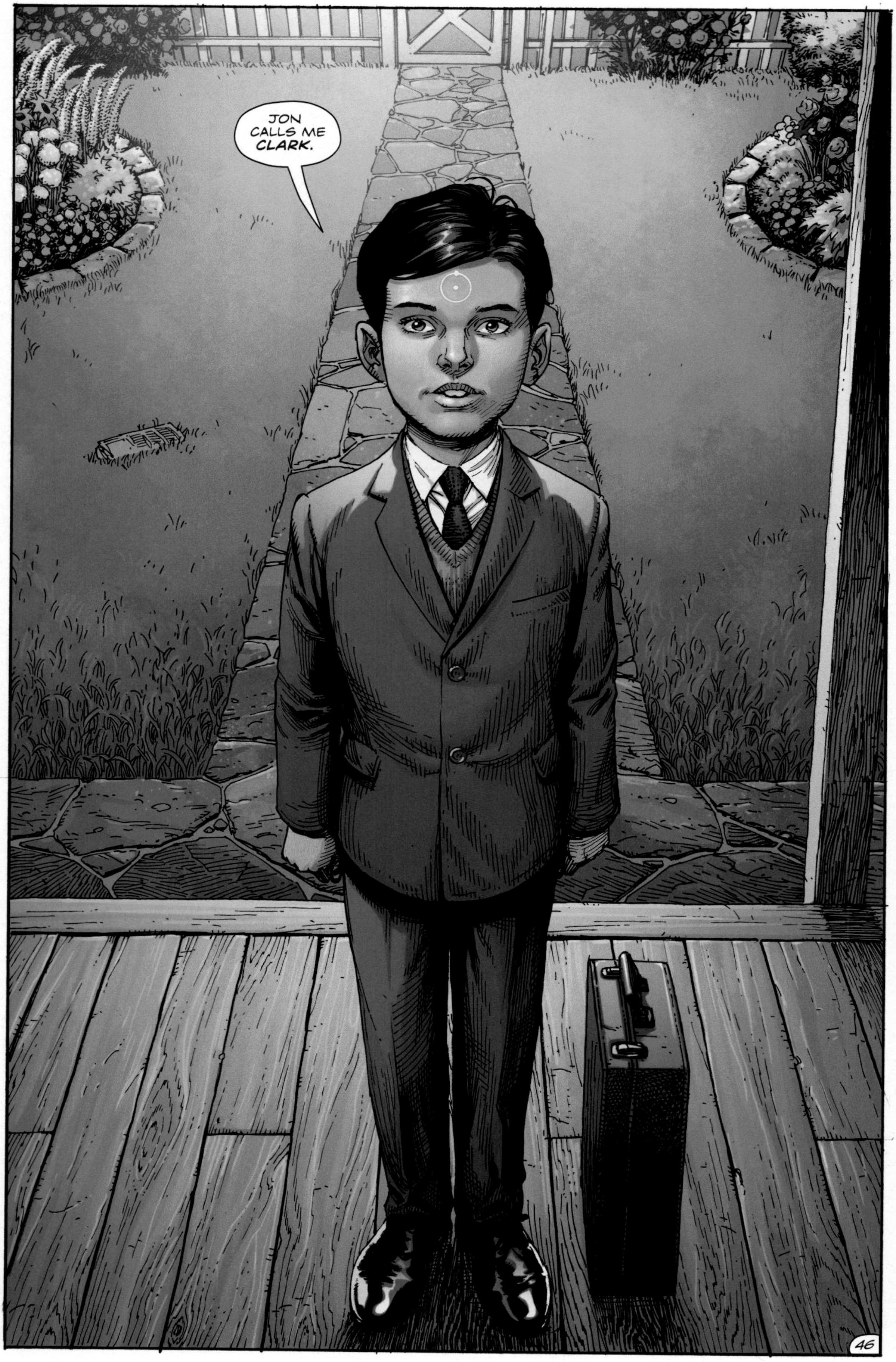
JON CALLS ME CLARK.

Every child comes with the message that
God is not yet discouraged of man.

—Rabindranath Tagore

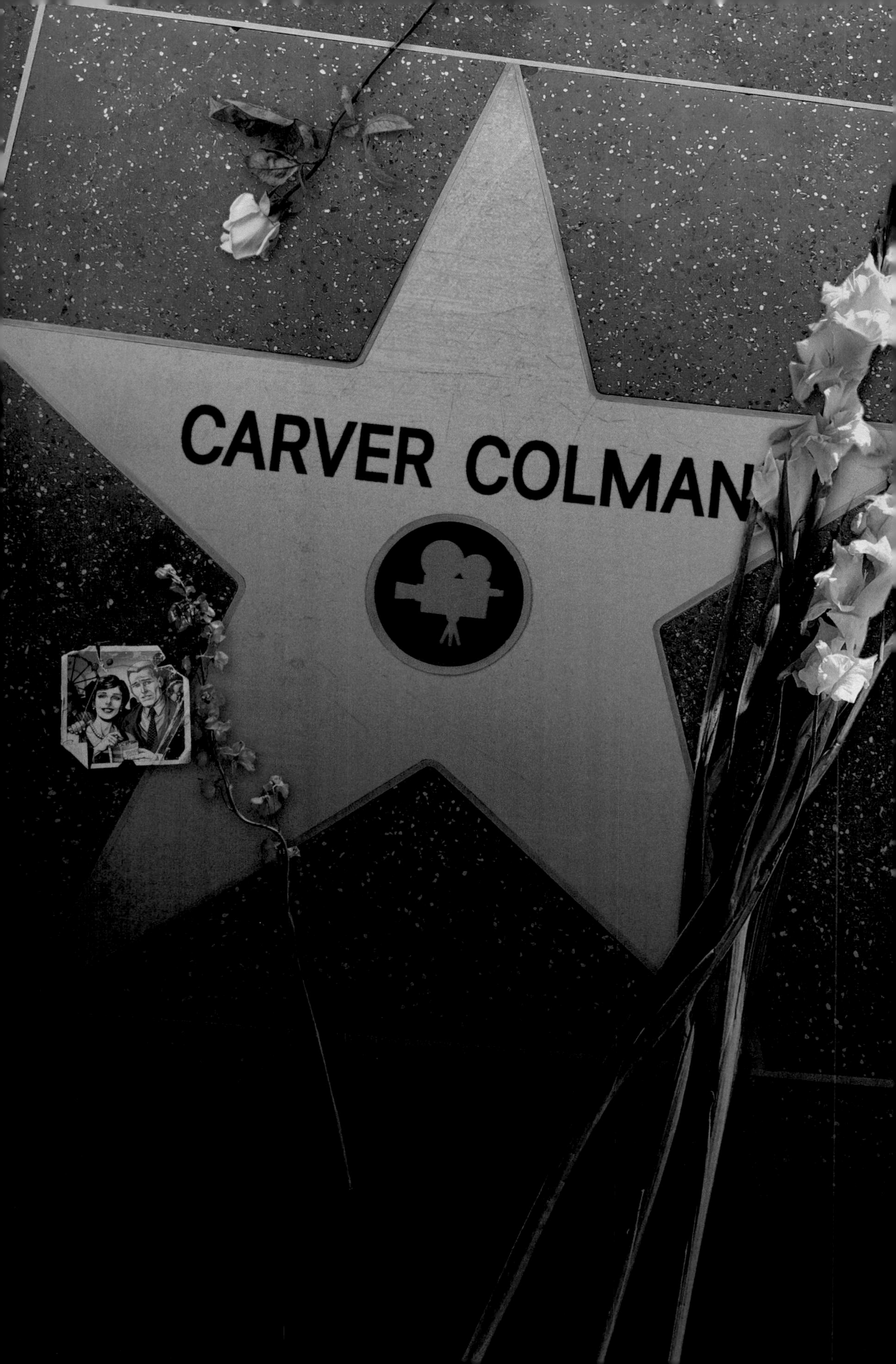
CARVER COLMAN

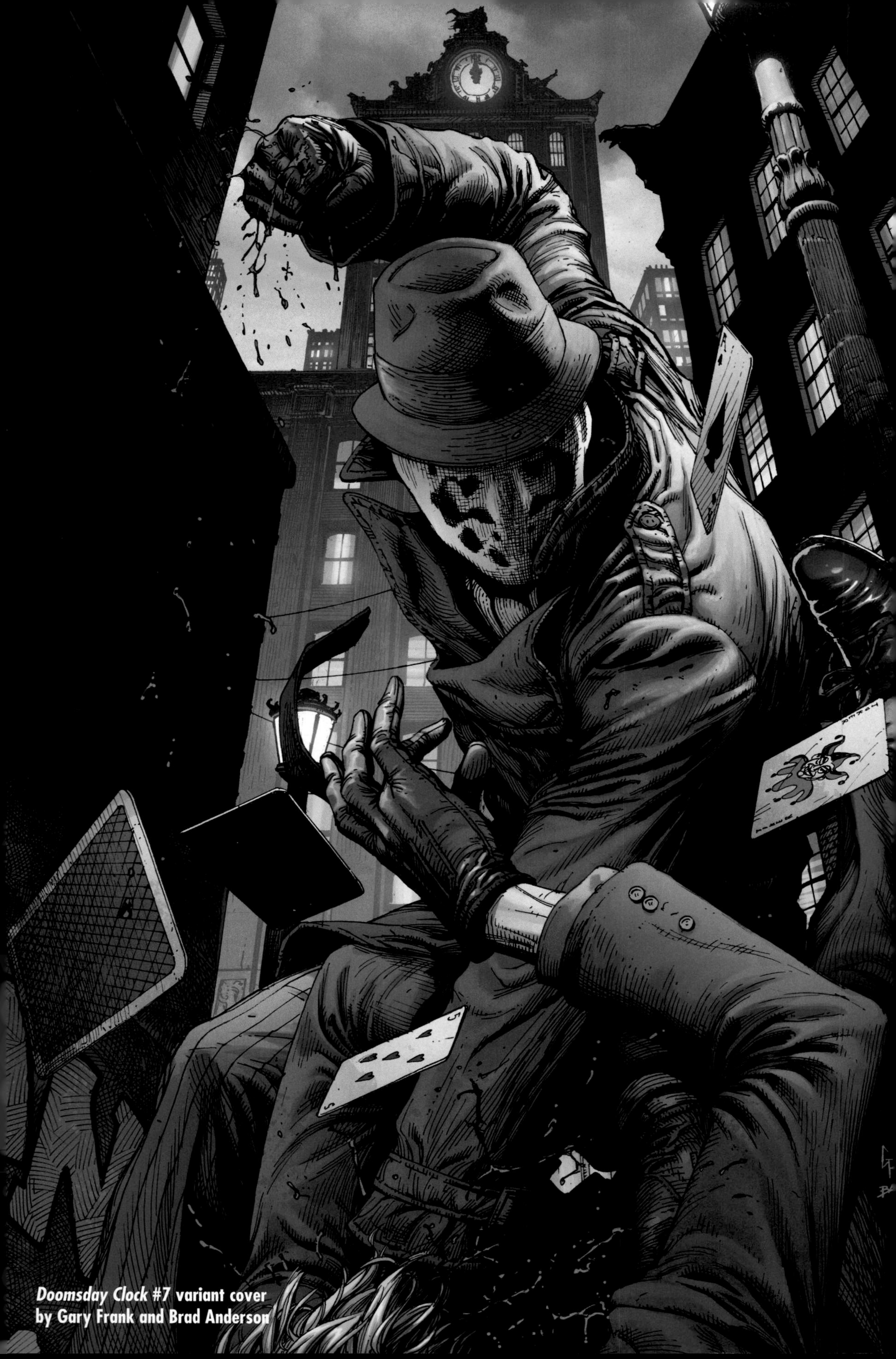

Doomsday Clock #7 variant cover
by Gary Frank and Brad Anderson

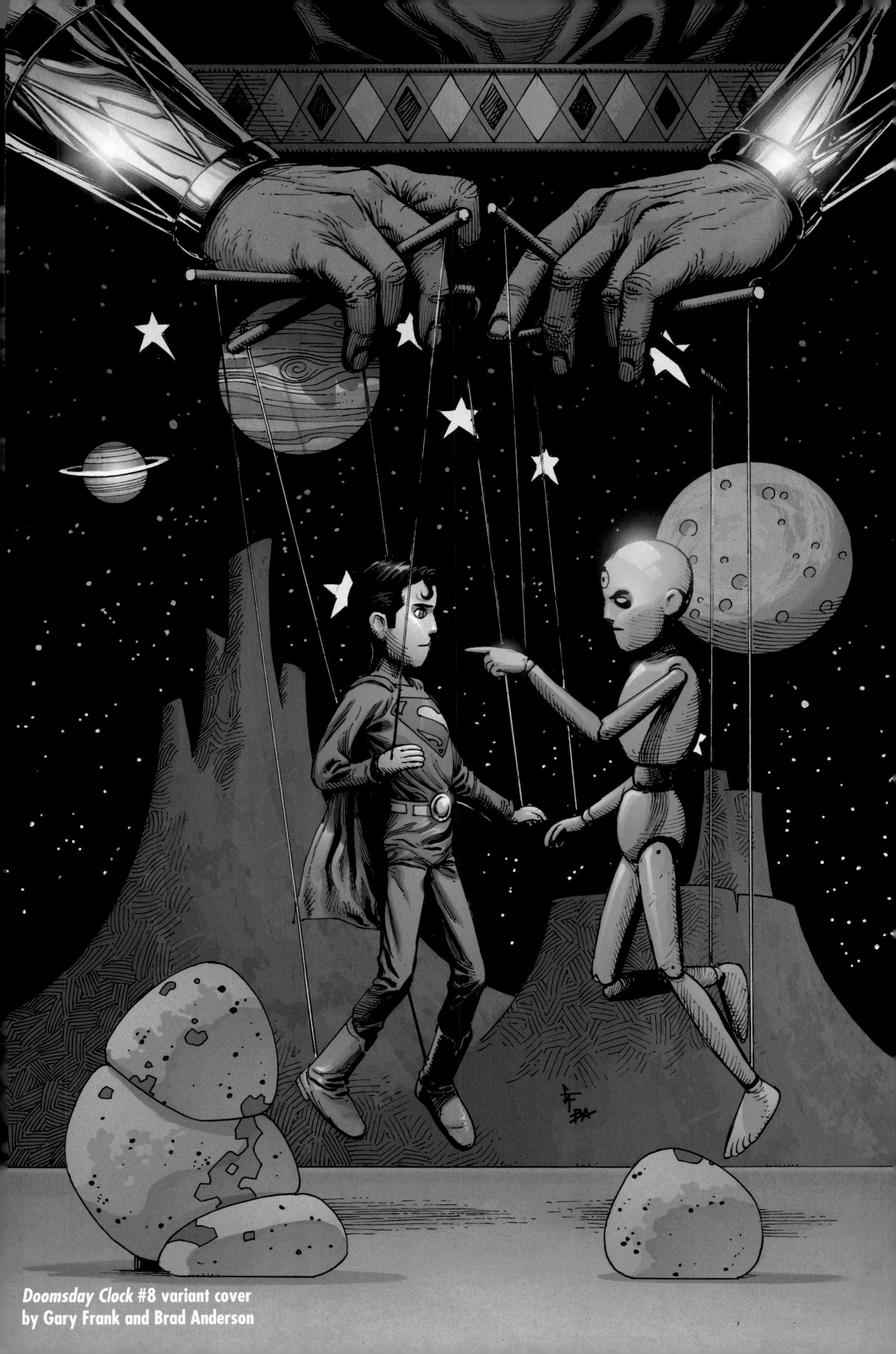

***Doomsday Clock* #8 variant cover**
by Gary Frank and Brad Anderson

Doomsday Clock #9 variant cover
by Gary Frank and Brad Anderson

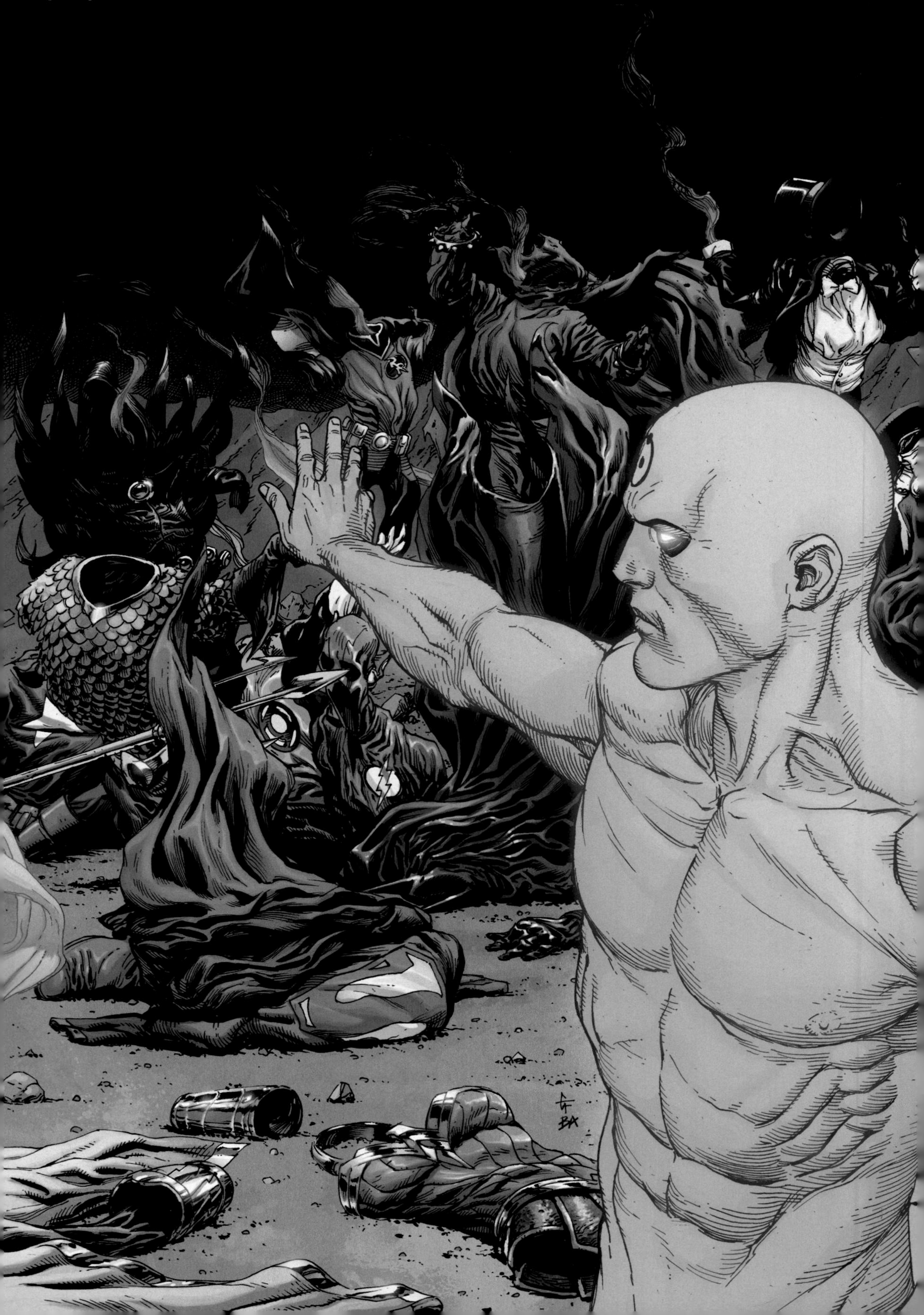

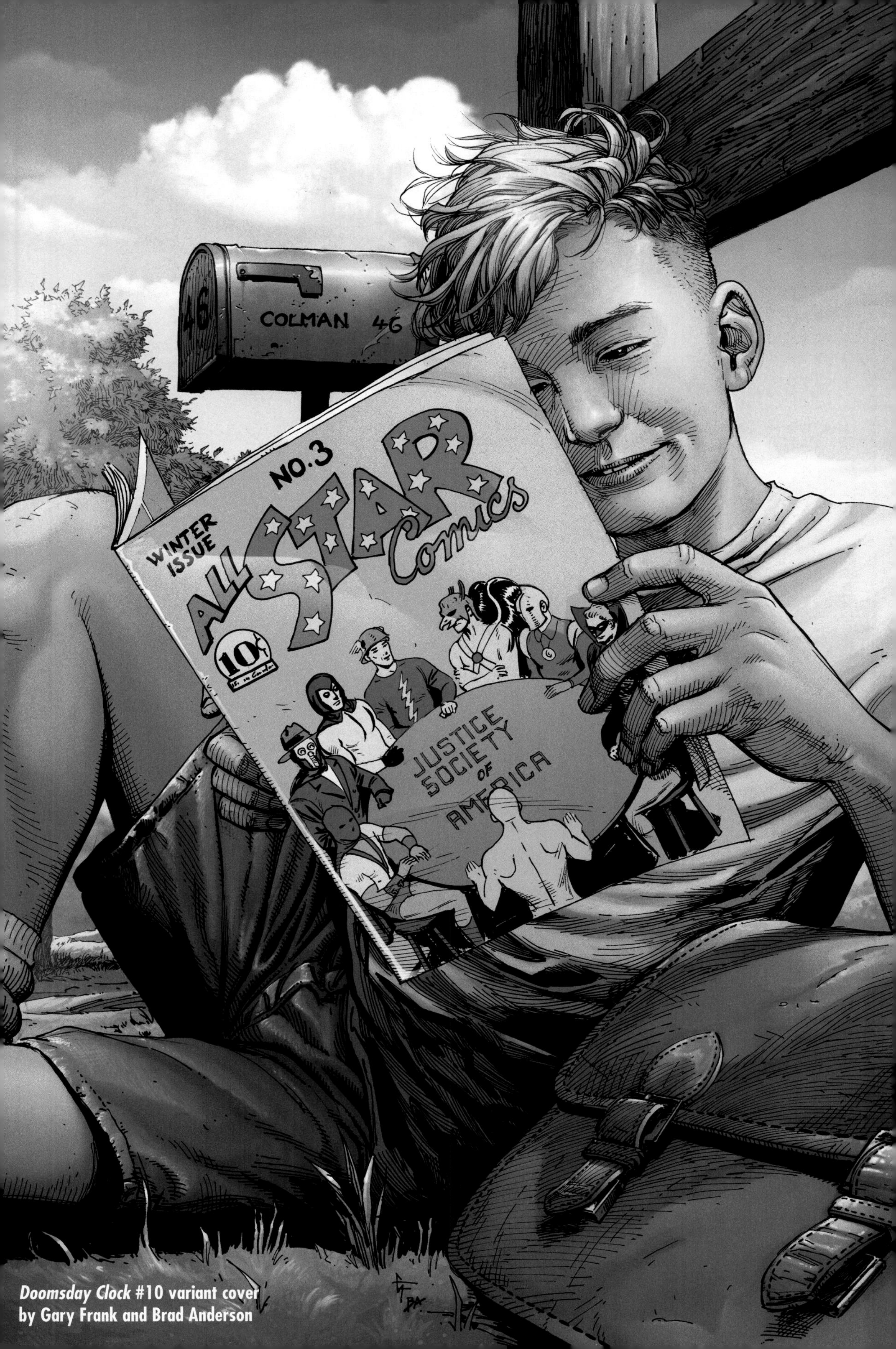
46
COLMAN 46
NO.3
WINTER ISSUE
ALL STAR Comics
10¢
JUSTICE SOCIETY OF AMERICA

Doomsday Clock #10 variant cover
by Gary Frank and Brad Anderson

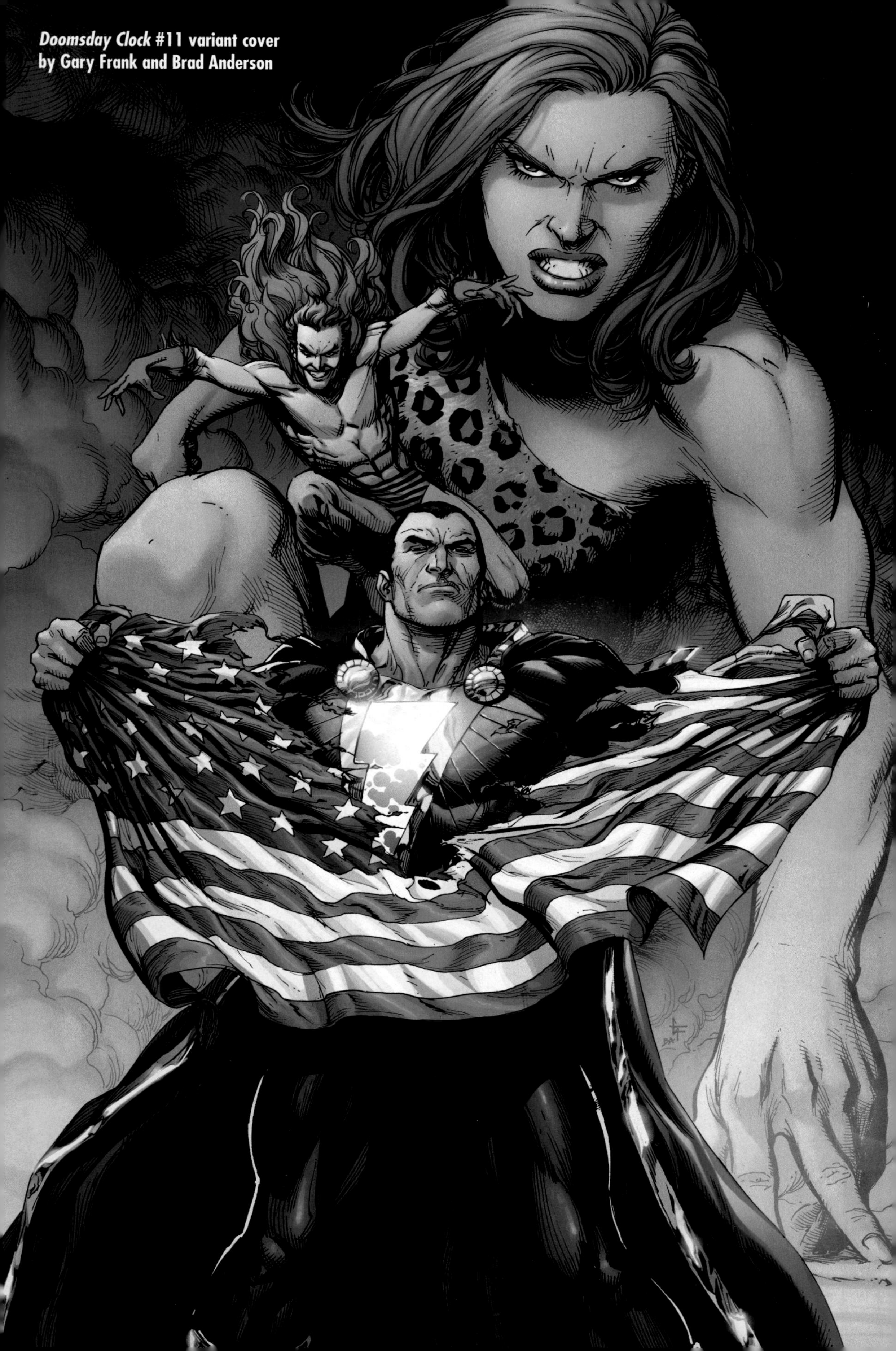

Doomsday Clock #11 variant cover
by Gary Frank and Brad Anderson

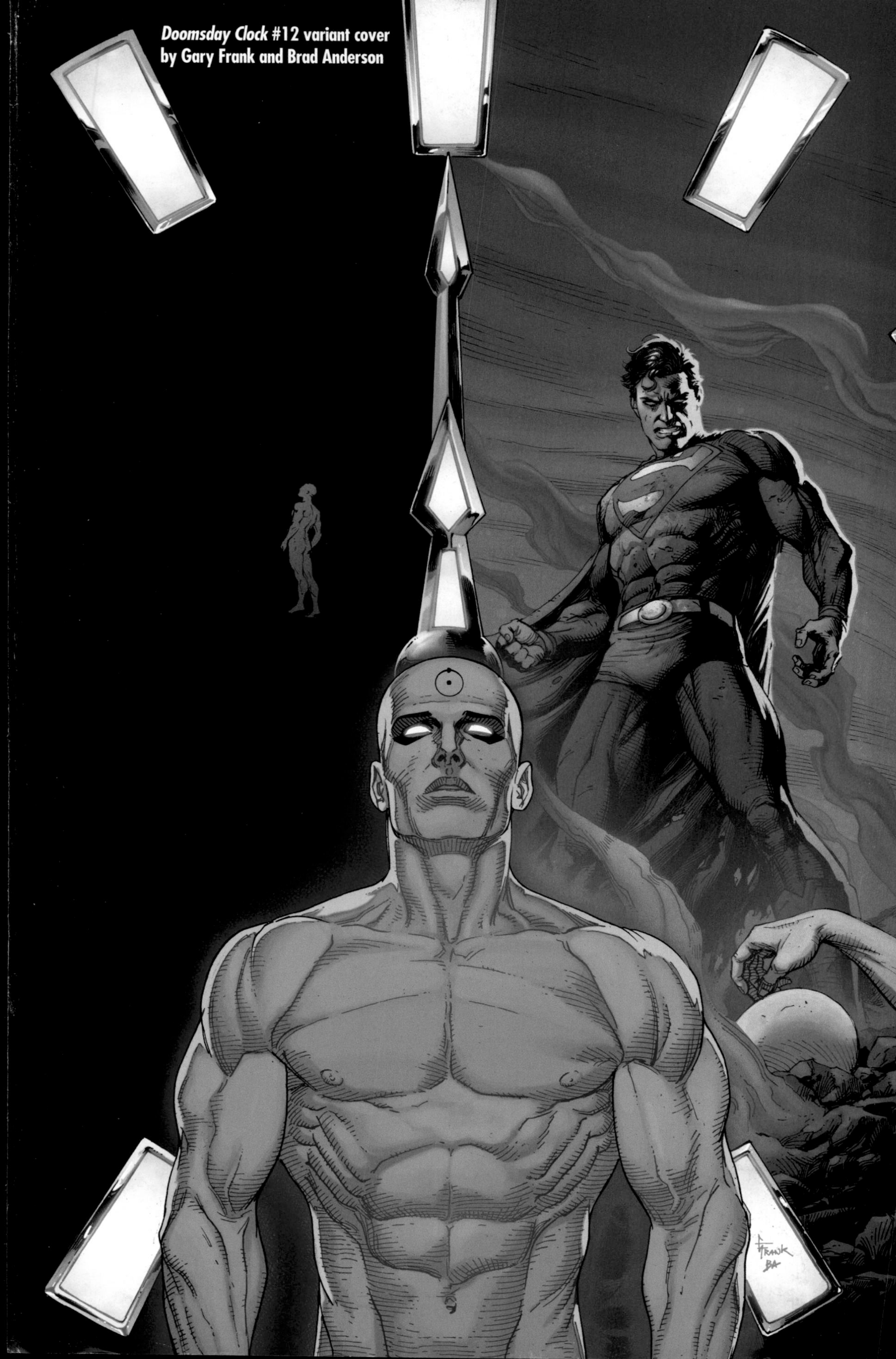

Doomsday Clock #12 variant cover
by Gary Frank and Brad Anderson

GEOFF JOHNS is an award-winning screenwriter and producer and one of the most successful comic book writers of his time. He has written dozens of *New York Times* bestselling graphic novels, including some of the most recognized and highly acclaimed stories featuring Superman and the Justice League. He has also reinvented lesser-known characters with great commercial and critical success.

Under his Mad Ghost Productions banner, Johns is currently in various stages of production on an extensive list of projects in television and film. Among his upcoming projects, he is writing and producing *Stargirl* for the DC Universe streaming service and writing the anticipated *Green Lantern Corps* feature; he is also producing the second installment of the Wonder Woman film franchise, *Wonder Woman 1984*, which he co-wrote with director Patty Jenkins. On the comic book side, he developed the commercial and critical hit *Doomsday Clock*.

GARY FRANK, a native of Bristol, England, began his comics career working on various titles for Marvel UK before entering the American comics scene as the penciller on Marvel's *Incredible Hulk*. Frank then came to DC Comics, where he was the original artist on *Birds of Prey* and pencilled the adventures of Supergirl. He has also worked on WildStorm's *Gen 13* as well as his creator-owned series *Kin*. Frank, along with writer Geoff Johns, has worked on the bestselling titles *Superman: Brainiac, Superman and the Legion of Super-Heroes, Shazam,* and the *New York Times* #1 bestseller *Batman: Earth One*, as well as the landmark issue *DC Universe: Rebirth* #1.